The Soviet Prefects

The Soviet Prefects: The Local Party Organs in Industrial Decision-making

JERRY F. HOUGH

Harvard University Press
Cambridge, Massachusetts
1969

Distributed in Great Britain by Oxford University Press, London

The Russian Research Center of Harvard University
is supported by grants from the Ford Foundation.
The Center carries out interdisciplinary study of
Russian institutions and behavior and related subjects.

This volume was prepared in part under a grant from the Carnegie
Corporation of New York. That Corporation is not, however,
the author, owner, publisher, or proprietor of this publication
and is not to be understood as approving by virtue of its grant any
of the statements made or views expressed therein.

Library of Congress Catalog Card Number 69–18033
Printed in the United States of America

TO MY PARENTS, IN PROFOUND GRATITUDE

Acknowledgments

This book grew out of a doctoral dissertation begun a decade ago, and many persons have been kind enough to comment upon various drafts of different chapters. So many persons have contributed to this book that the desire to make acknowledgment of debt is tempered by the fear that many will inadvertently be left out.

There is one man to whom I hardly need express gratitude. Any reader familiar with Soviet studies will know from the most cursory examination of this book that its author wrote his dissertation under the direction of Professor Merle Fainsod. The man from whom I took my first course on the Soviet Union, the only man to have given guidance from the first stages of the study until the final drafts — Professor Fainsod not only offered invaluable specific advice on the manuscript, but also shaped in the most fundamental way its basic assumptions about the structure of power in the Soviet Union and about the most fruitful approach to the study of that country.

I also owe a major intellectual debt to Professor Barrington Moore, Jr. In a seminar on the Soviet system and a course on the sociological aspects of political power — as well as in his *Terror and Progress, USSR* — he raised questions about the relationship of industrialization and political development well before this subject became fashionable in political science. His impact was great indeed. In addition, Professor Moore read several drafts of the concluding chapters and offered a number of very helpful suggestions. Together with David Granick, he was responsible for the expansion of the conclusion beyond the analysis found in Chapter XIV, and whatever clarity is found in the argument in these chapters is the result of the rewriting required by his incisive comments.

I am also grateful to a number of other men for their willingness to examine the manuscript at some stage of its development and to make suggestions for improvement. Professors David Granick and Victor

Thompson reviewed the entire manuscript in one of its last drafts, while Professors Robert Scott and George Fischer reviewed large sections of this draft. I am particularly obliged to Professors Granick and Fischer for their impact on Chapter 3; without them the tables would not have existed, and the data would have been much less complete. At earlier stages of the study, the following men read part or all of the manuscript and contributed greatly to it: John Armstrong, Jeremy Azrael, Abram Bergson, Joseph Berliner, Paul Cocks, Nicholas De-Witt, Murray Edelman, Robert Hey, Grey Hodnett, Herbert Levine, Robert Miller, Philip Monypenny, Leon Smolinski, Adam Ulam, and Peter Wiles.

It is customary for an author to attribute all virtues of his book to those who helped him and to take upon himself the blame for all its faults. In this case, such an assertion is particularly necessary because most of those to whom acknowledgments are made have not even had the opportunity to protest against the final version of the manuscript. However, there are two men — Professor Herbert Levine of the University of Pennsylvania and Professor Philip Monypenny of the University of Illinois — who deserve special mention because of the countless stimulating hours of conversation that I have had with them. I have stolen so many ideas from them (more, no doubt, than I recall) that they may warrant not only credit for any of the book's virtues, but also some small share of the blame for its defects.

Besides scholarly advice, I received a great deal of other assistance from a variety of sources. The late Taras Butoff of the Russian Research Center provided many insights into the Soviet Union and the Russian language.

I am, of course, also particularly grateful to the dozens of Soviet officials who were kind enough to grant me interviews and who contributed much to my understanding of the Soviet system. Many employees of that much-maligned institution, Intourist, were extremely helpful in arranging these interviews.

To my wife, Barbara, and to Janice, Susan, and Bobby go immeasurable thanks not only for inspiration but also for patience and forbearance over a very long period indeed.

Finally, in an age of organizations one cannot forget the assistance rendered by a number of institutions. The Russian Research Center (and indirectly the Carnegie Corporation) provided financial support both for the latter part of the period in which the dissertation was written and for a year of post-graduate work. The Center for Russian Language and Area Studies of the University of Illinois financed two trips to the Soviet Union, while the Comparative Administration Group of the American Society for Public Administration (and indirectly the Ford Foundation) made possible a most valuable summer seminar on the spatial aspects of development administration, a seminar held at the University of Pittsburgh in 1965 under the chairmanship of Professor James Heaphey. But institutions are ultimately people, and my greatest good fortune has been the great and diverse intellectual stimulation provided by colleagues at the CAG seminar, the Russian Research Center, and the Department of Political Science at the University of Illinois.

Much of the material of Chapters IV and V appeared in my article in *Slavic Review,* 24 (June 1965), 215–240. I would like to thank the journal for permission to use it in this book.

Contents

Tables

I. Introduction

For many years those concerned with the course of development in Soviet society have been fascinated with the relationship of the political elite to the increasing number of industrial managers and technical personnel. Many theories of social and political development have emphasized the crucial role of the economic "substructure" in shaping the political system, and it is clear that the Soviet substructure has undergone substantial change in the last four decades. Whether one speaks of the key political role of the group controlling the means of production, of the force of industrialization in developing rationalized structures, procedures, and authority systems, or simply of the effect of education on dogmatic belief systems, one looks almost inevitably for signs of change in the Party-manager relationship. Or, if one is curious whether industrialization does indeed have the impact attributed to it, one is drawn to a study of this relationship as a nearly perfect test of the hypotheses advanced on this question.

Originally this study was set almost exclusively within the framework of such a set of interests. Western studies of the role of the Party in industrial management had — directly or indirectly — been based in large part on sources dating from the 1930's, and it seemed worth while to reexamine the relationship of the Party apparatus to the industrial managers using the materials of the postwar period and particularly those of the post-Stalin period. In this way, it was hoped, it would be possible to ascertain whether several decades of a major industrialization drive had produced significant changes in this key relationship, changes that might illuminate the course of development of Soviet society.

These general economic and political questions remain a central concern of this book, but in many ways the focus has shifted somewhat with the passage of time. First, the scope has been considerably narrowed. Despite the frequent tendency for Westerners to speak of "the" Party and of "its" functions and "its" relation to the state, the

1

different levels of the Party hierarchy actually have strikingly different functions and relationships to the state apparatus, and cannot be discussed most fruitfully as a unit. Focus on one type of Party organ provides a much more coherent understanding of its responsibilities and its relationship with state officials. One is then on much solider ground in evaluating the many broad generalizations made about the Party apparatus and in advancing meaningful new hypotheses.

The Party organs that have been chosen for study are those on the middle levels of the Party hierarchy — those the Soviet leaders call "the local Party organs" (*mestnye partiinye organy*).[1] They are the *raikom* (the district or borough committee), the *gorkom* (the city committee), the *obkom* (the regional committee), and most of the republican central committees. (Except in a few special instances the Russian and Ukrainian republican Party organs are excluded from consideration because of the size and importance of these republics.) By focusing on these Party organs, one may not only examine that section of the Party apparatus most affected by the industrial reorganizations of the Khrushchev era, but may also obtain at least a limited insight into the work of the higher Party organs and of the primary Party organizations as the local Party organs come into contact with them.

A second change in focus is in the nature of the questions asked. Even under Lenin the local Party organs were essentially administrative organs, and subsequent events served only to confirm them in this role. Inevitably, therefore, a study of the local Party organs became more an administrative study than a political one. Many of the questions that arose related more to the theory of field administration than to that of totalitarianism.

Because the participation of the local Party organs in industrial decision-making has not only introduced a political party into the administrative process but has also greatly complicated the administrative lines of authority, the question thrust forward with particular, almost irresistible, force is one that has been raised most directly by Joseph LaPalombara. How has it been possible for the Soviet industrialization program to have been basically successful and for the Soviet Union to have made great strides in public health, education, and defense technology when it has "a chaotic and archaic public administration" by Anglo-American standards, a system featuring "what appears to the Westerner as rampart particularism and irrationality"? As LaPalombara recognizes, the conclusion must be drawn that somehow "public administration can be managed — even managed well in terms of measurable outputs — without the existence of every ideal element of a classical bureaucracy." [2] As in most discussions of the Soviet administrative system, however, the reasons that such an apparently chaotic system has been able to function fairly well remain rather obscure.

The central thesis of this book is that, in fact, the paradox is only apparent. One of the most important reasons that public administration in the Soviet Union has been "even managed well in terms of measurable outputs" is precisely that it does not contain "every ideal element of a classical bureaucracy," that it does feature what appears to be "rampart particularism and irrationality." The involvement of the local Party organs in the administrative process has, indeed, prevented a precise definition of the authority and responsibilities of every official and the establishment of clear lines of authority, but this has been, in large part, a positive, a necessary development rather than a harmful one.

The best clue for understanding the role of the local Party organs in the Soviet administrative system comes from an examination of the system of field administration in nearly all countries except those in the Anglo-Saxon world. Such an examination reminds us that many countries (all of those in continental Europe, for example) have consciously violated the principles of "a classical bureaucracy" by establishing at the provincial level an authoritative figure who cuts across the departmental lines of command. Although the title of this official varies from country to country (governor, civil governor, commissioner of the Queen, provincial governor [3]), the most usual generic designation is "prefect," the term derived from the French administrative system that served as the model for the rest of the continent.

The original French prefects, established by Napoleon, had responsibility for all officials in the field, and in the classic prefectoral model all communications between the field administrators and the center passed through the prefect's office. Originally, the prefect's primary function was to maintain law and order. Like the district officer in colonial India (essentially a prefectoral official), he was "responsible for taking the urgent measures to meet any emergency that might arise whatever the source." [4] In such cases he had the duty to "govern in Napoleon's name . . . interpret by his own sense of the nation's interests, what Napoleon would wish in the circumstances." [5]

As time has passed, the role of the prefect in France (and in the rest of the world) has changed considerably. On the one hand, the extent of his authority over the local administrators has been substantially undermined. Some of the specialized administrators have been removed from his direct supervision, and elected local officials have acquired influence on local decisions. The specialized local administrators that have remained within his jurisdiction are no longer under his exclusive control; instead, direct lines of communication and authority have been established between these administrators and their respective ministries. In essence, the specialized administrators have been placed under what Arthur Macmahon has called "dual supervision." [6]

The growing differentiation and complexity of the network of governmental agencies has not only weakened the exclusive authority of the prefect in the field, it has also created an important additional function for him to perform: the providing of regional coordination, particularly in those countries where the government has an active economic development program. As Brian Chapman contends, this coordinating role may well have become the most important which the prefect performs:

> Coordination at a provincial level of the growing services of central ministries is one of the major justifications for the prefect-governor system at the present day. There are clearly many matters which require close and frequent contact between different departments of government, and the formation of a common policy. The general feeling on the continent is that unless there is a single state authority on the spot with a general responsibility and a recognized superiority over other state officials, this cooperation must either consist in informal arrangements between the local heads of service, or be imposed by decisions taken at

the centre by ministries. The first alternative is unlikely to result in effective cooperation, while the second is contrary to the principle of divesting central administration of as much detailed administration as possible.[7]

The role of the local Party organs — and the primary explanation for that role — is best understood by recognizing that the local Party organs have been serving as the prefects of the Soviet system. If the original French prefects were to serve as the direct representative — almost the direct embodiment — of Napoleon in the provinces, so the local Party organs have been the representative and embodiment of the Party at each territorial level.

Like other prefects, the local Party organs originally had as their principal responsibility the maintenance of political stability. (Of course, since it was to be a political stability based on a new social-economic order, the Party organs always have had much broader responsibilities for political socialization than those normally associated with a prefect.) The local Party organs have not been relieved of responsibility for political stability or for socialization, but they, like other modern prefects, have come to fill a much broader role. As the threat of political instability dwindled, they could concentrate on the "coordination at a provincial level of the growing services of central ministries." [8] They could become, in T. H. Rigby's phrase, primarily the local offices of a "Ministry of Coordination." [9]

Indeed, the evolution of the Soviet prefect from a law-and-order prefect into what we will call a "developmental prefect" took place more rapidly in the Soviet Union than in other countries because of the scale of governmental control over the economy there and particularly because of the nature and intensity of the industrialization drive. In the minds of the Soviet leaders, rapid industrialization became the precondition not only for material abundance needed for the establishment of full communism, but also for maintenance and extension of the leadership's political power. Industrialization was seen as the panacea that would protect Russia (and the Communist regime) from outside attack and that would create the proletariat necessary to end the anomaly of a workers' government in a peasant country. Whether it was recognized at first or not, the rapid expansion of industry also would by itself serve to furnish legitimacy for the Party leadership and thereby to strengthen its political support. For these reasons it is not surprising that the local Party organs soon were given responsibility for the economic development program, and that the performance of the Party officials came to be judged primarily by success or lack of it in this field.

If the local Party organs are seen as a prefectoral institution responsible for the orderly fulfillment of the economic development program in their respective areas (and, of course, also for political stability), it becomes easier to understand why their presence in the administrative system has helped it function more effectively instead of interfering with its operation. Coordination at the provincial level has been needed. In fact, the need has been much greater in the Soviet Union than in a non-Communist system, for the government apparatus has supervised a far wider range of activities and there has been no effective market mechanism to coordinate the efforts of economic organizations. Although it was not necessary from an administrative point of view that the local Party organs be given the coordinating functions of a prefect, any other solution (for example, the executive committees of the soviets being given responsibility for all aspects of the economy) would have entailed a governmental restructuring that would have equally complicated the organization chart.

Although this book will concentrate primarily on an analysis of the role of the local Party organs in Soviet industrial decision-making, the concluding chapters will explore some implications of this role both for administrative theory and for the theory of "political modernization" and "political development." For those without experience of prefectoral institutions, there is a conscious or unconscious predisposition to think of bureaucracies as institutions that can and should function in relative isolation from each other. The conventional American image of the ideal organization embodies what Victor Thompson calls "the monistic concept" [10] — the belief that duties can and should be defined so precisely that the bureaucrat can function independently, subject only to clearly defined directives and rules that reach him through a clear line of authority.

Although administrative theorists of the last two decades have increasingly rejected the monistic model of administration, the model has had a major impact on recent theory in comparative government, particularly of political modernization and political development. Directly or indirectly, these theories have been greatly influenced by the work of the great German sociologist, Max Weber — a man who, like early American administrative theorists, was highly impressed by the administrative principles of the Prussian army [11] and whose discussion of rational-legal authority and the bureaucratic ideal-type contained many of the features and much of the spirit of the conventional American images. Because of this influence (and perhaps also because the relative decline of public administration as a field within political science has created a generation of scholars little exposed to contemporary administrative theory), much of the discussion of "modern" society is based on assumptions about administration and administrative decision-making that are quite unrealistic.

If the Soviet experience casts doubts on many of the conventional American assumptions about administrative structure and practice, if the monistic model makes the Soviet administrative system seem more chaotic and irrational than it really is, then a study of that administrative system is appropriate for exploring changes that should be introduced both into the monistic model of administration and into the models of "modern society" that incorporate it. Because these assumptions about administration and political development are found in one of the most famous models of Soviet studies — Barrington Moore's model of rational-technical society — the discussion in the last three chapters will be focused primarily on it.

However, before one generalizes on the basis of Soviet experience, the nature of that experience must be defined. The major task of this book is to explain how it is that in the Soviet Union "public administration can be managed — even managed well in terms of measurable outputs — without the existence of every ideal element of a classical bureaucracy."

II. The Organization of the Local Party Organs

An indispensable precondition to understanding the relationship of the local Party organs and the industrial administrators is a familiarity with the inner structure of those parts of the Party apparatus that deal with industrial questions. Only by recognizing the differences in function and authority of the various officials and units of the Party organs can one move beyond a simplified notion of "the" Party-state relationship and come to an appreciation of the subtleties involved in it.

Because this book is concerned primarily with the postwar period, no attempt will be made to treat all the various organizational experiments of the last four decades.[1] Significant variations within the postwar period will be mentioned, but focus will be on the Party structure existing in the summer of 1967. Such an approach might seem foolhardy in light of the frequent reorganizations of the Party apparatus, but actually the basic structure of the middle Party apparatus has remained more unchanged than appears on the surface. The major 1948 reorganization of the All-Union Central Committee departments from a functional to a branch basis had much less impact on the local Party organs, for (except for a brief period in 1939 to 1940) branch line officials had already been in existence at the local level.[2] Even the 1962 division of the Party apparatus into urban and rural components still left a surprising number of relationships unchanged, for each half of the bifurcated Party was organized along lines very similar to those that prevailed earlier in the unified Party and were restored in 1964.[3]

Introductory Summary

For administrative purposes the Soviet Union has been subdivided into a large number of territorial units, each of which has a local Party organ. The major units (in descending order) are the republic, the

8

oblast (usually translated "region"), the city, the rural *raion* (usually translated "district"), and the urban *raion* (also translated "district" or occasionally "borough"). Two other important territorial units are the autonomous republic and the *krai* (usually translated "territory"). These latter two units are similar to the oblast, the difference in terminology being associated with the desire to give recognition to various nationality groups.

In constitutional terms the republic is the highest provincial territorial unit. However, nearly all the oblasti are located in the republics of the RSFSR, the Ukraine, Kazakhstan, and Belorussia, and the ten republics on which this book concentrates are so small that they approximate the oblast in importance. In practice, the small union republic, the krai, the oblast, and the autonomous republic all correspond roughly to the American state, and they will be treated as a unit. Like the American states they vary widely in size. In European Russia they normally range from the size of New Hampshire to that of Indiana, but in Siberia they are usually much larger (the Yakutsk Autonomous Republic, the largest, is twice the size of Alaska). In certain of the areas inhabited by non-Russians they may be nearly as small as Rhode Island.

Within the oblast and the oblast-less republics there are two independent territorial subdivisions. The rural areas are divided into raiony, which are roughly equivalent to the American county. (In 1965 the European raion averaged approximately 1,000 to 1,500 square miles; in the 1950's it was little more than half that size.) The institutions of the raion have jurisdiction only over the countryside and the small towns and villages within it.

The larger towns and cities are administered independently of the rural raion, being directly subordinate to the oblast or the oblast-less republic.[4] If the city is large enough (a population of over 150,000 to 300,000),[5] it in turn is subdivided into boroughs (which, unfortunately, are also called raiony).

The point at which a town becomes large enough to warrant independence from the rural raion has varied greatly over time. A town of 15,000 may have soviet institutions of its own, but normally only a larger town warrants an independent city Party committee. In the past, cities with as many as 50,000 to 100,000 people might still be supervised by the rural Party committee, but one legacy of the 1962 reorganization seems to be a policy of forming separate city Party committees in smaller cities.[6]

Whatever the situation with respect to the medium-sized city, each area defined as a territorial unit has both a set of governmental and Party institutions. At the republican level the official governmental legislature is the republican supreme soviet, and the governmental executive consists of the republican council of ministers and the ministries, committees, and councils under it. At lower levels the legislature is termed simply "krai soviet," "oblast soviet," "city soviet," or "raion soviet." The basic executive body at these levels is "the executive committee of the soviet" (abbreviated *"ispolkom"* in Russian) and the administrative offices it heads. It should definitely be noted that large-scale industry, transportation, and construction have been administered by agencies independent from the local ispolkomy. Most of the time the agencies administering these branches of the economy have not had offices below the republican level (and not always even there), but from 1957 to 1962 industry and much of construction were administered directly by an oblast-level institution, the regional economic council or *sovnarkhoz.*

Each of the territorial subdivisions also has a set of Party institutions that head the Party members located within it. One may speak simply of the republican, oblast (or krai), city, or raion Party organization, but it is far more usual to refer to the institutions of the organization by the abbreviation of the main Party committee at each level. These are the republican TsK (the abbreviation for *tsentralnyi komitet* or central committee); the *kraikom* (*kraevoi komitet* or krai committee); the *obkom* (*oblastnoi komitet* or oblast committee); the *gorkom* (*gorodskoi komitet* or city committee); and the raikom (*raionnyi komitet* or raion committee).[7] (Incidentally, similar abbreviations are used for the local governmental organs: the raion executive committee of the Soviet is the *raiispolkom,* the city executive committee is the *gorispolkom,* the oblast executive committee is the *oblispolkom,* and the krai executive committee is the *kraiispolkom.*)

Like the central Party organization, the local Party organs have a fairly well differentiated set of institutions. Indeed, if changes in nomenclature and size are taken into consideration, these institutions are basically similar to those of the central Party organs, and one unfamiliar with the local Party institutions may find it easier to keep them in mind if he thinks of the different central institutions: the Party Congress that meets with great fanfare every few years, the Central Committee that usually meets several times a year to discuss important policy questions, the Politburo (called the Presidium from 1952 to 1966) of a dozen or so men who are recognized as the top officials in the Soviet Union, and the Secretariat of full-time Party officials that was the seat of power of both Stalin and Khrushchev. The local Party organs, too, have their Congress (called a conference below the republican level), their committee, their bureau, their secretariat, and their first secretary. The most important for this discussion are the bureau and the secretariat.

The Party Organization in the Republic and the Oblast

Despite all the Party reorganizations there is one aspect of Party structure that has remained quite stable throughout the years — the congress in the republic or the conference in the oblast. Convened once every two years in the oblast and once every four years in the republic,[8] the congress and the conference have long been designated as the highest Party authority in the republic and the oblast respectively. Because higher policy is the province of the central organs, Party theory has not emphasized the policy-making functions of the congress and the conference, but instead it has defined them primarily as institutions that review the performance of the old republican or oblast committee and select the membership of the new one.[9] But whatever the Party Rules may say, the real function of these bodies seems indistinguishable from that of the All-Union Party Congress — that is, to serve as "a rally of the faithful, chiefly significant as a convenient platform from which the leadership proclaims new policies and goals." [10]

At the conclusion of each conference and congress (except for the extraordinary ones of 1958–59 to discuss the new seven-year plan), there is announced the "election" of a committee empowered to act as the supreme Party organ in the region until the next congress. In the republics these organs are termed "central committees," following

11

the nomenclature at the All-Union level, but in the oblasti they are merely called "oblast committees" — abbreviated *obkom*. (As indicated earlier, the word "obkom" is used to describe not only the committee, but also its full-time officials. In fact, when the word "obkom" appears in a Soviet source, it almost always refers to these officials unless there is a special reference to a plenary session or *plenum* of the obkom.)

In 1958 the republican and oblast committees were said to average 120 to 125 full and candidate members,[11] but they have grown considerably in recent years. A central committee of an oblast-less republic usually contained between 75 and 90 full members in 1956, between 95 and 105 full members in 1961, and between 110 and 125 in 1966.[12] In Krasnodar, Rostov, Ulianovsk, Volgograd, and Yaroslavl the oblast committees elected in 1966 ranged in size from 99 to 145 full members and from 29 to 71 candidate members.[13]

Although approximately 10 percent of the full members of the 1966 republican central committee were rank-and-file workers and farmers (a much higher percentage than in 1956), the committee basically constituted a cross-section of the area's elite.[14] In a typical 1966 central committee in an oblast-less republic, 10 to 15 percent of the members were republican Party officials (secretaries and heads of departments), 20 to 25 percent were lower Party officials (almost exclusively gorkom and raikom first secretaries), 30 percent were republican state officials (the high officials of the republican council of ministers and most of the ministers), and 5 to 10 percent were enterprise directors (including kolkhoz chairmen). In addition, the committee contained a scattering of military officials, chairmen of local soviets, newspaper editors, writers, scientists, and leaders of "public" organizations. The membership of a typical oblast committee was very similar, but it included fewer oblast-level state officials and more lower Party officials and enterprise directors.[15]

Although the republican and oblast committees contain a great number of important people, their plenary sessions appear to be little more than forums for announcing decisions and discussing important decrees emanating from the All-Union Party Central Committee. Obligated to be held at least three times a year,[16] the sessions very often deal with the subject matter of the preceding session of the All-Union Central Committee. The speakers bring up the problems discussed in Moscow and unanimously endorse the policies just adopted. The speeches contain a variety of specific investment proposals, but the policy differences among the speakers manifest themselves only in subtle nuances.

Although the plenary sessions of the committees may not be particularly important, the preparation for these sessions does have some significance. The drafting of the decision to be approved by the session gives the important Party officials in the area the opportunity to make a comprehensive survey of one aspect of the area's life and to focus their attention on its problems. The gathering together of the area's elite may also provide the occasion for useful informal interaction between the formal sessions.

According to the Party Rules, one of the prime duties of the Party committee is to select an executive organ — the bureau — which is to provide leadership between sessions of the committee itself. (Between 1962 and 1964 there were three executive bodies in the republic: a bureau for industry and construction, a bureau for agriculture, and a presidium to coordinate the activities of the two bureaus.[17]) Prior to 1966 the bureau of a republican central committee usually contained eleven full members and several candidate members and that of the obkom usually contained nine full members. In 1966, however, the republican bureau (then called the presidium) was limited normally to nine voting members, and the obkom bureaus on whom information is available had eleven voting members.

Although the bureau is not actually the creature of the local Party committee, official Party theory concerning the bureau does bear some resemblance to reality within the Soviet Union. The bureau does meet at least once every two weeks, and its discussions apparently do have real significance. The scope of its activities is described quite accurately in an official Soviet summary: "The bureau is the executive organ of the Party committee. . . . In the period between plenary sessions of the committee, it leads all the activity of the Party organizations; it secures the execution of the directives of the higher-standing Party organs; it gives instructions on the most important economic, cultural, and Party questions; it selects and confirms a de-

13

fined circle of officials; and it examines and decides cases concerning the personal behavior of Communists." [18]

Throughout the postwar period the bureaus have contained the area's top governmental officials, but they have clearly been dominated by full-time Party officials. For example, in the 1966 nine-man bureaus of the republican central committees, five of the members were invariably republican Party secretaries; in the two eleven-man bureaus these five men were joined by an obkom first secretary. A typical nine-man bureau contained five secretaries, the chairman of the republican council of ministers, the chairman of the presidium of the supreme soviet, the chairman of the peoples' control committee, and the first deputy chairman of the council of ministers.[19] In 1961 a military or police official usually held the seat later occupied by the chairman of the peoples' control committee, with the sovnarkhoz chairman and the first secretary of the capital gorkom added to bring the total membership to eleven.[20]

In the past, the Party representation on the obkom bureaus was usually larger than in the republics, but in 1966 the pattern of membership on the obkom bureaus was quite similar to that found in the republics. In the seven oblasti on which information is available, the full members of the bureau normally included the five obkom secretaries, the chairman of the oblispolkom, the first secretary of the capital gorkom, and four other officials — usually chosen from among the oblast trade union chairman, the first deputy chairman of the oblispolkom, the chairman of the oblast peoples' control committee, the newspaper editor, the chairman of the oblast KGB, and the secretary of an outlying gorkom.[21]

In theory, the bureau is a collective organ in which all members are equal, but in practice it is probably best visualized as a device to ensure that the first secretary's top lieutenants have an opportunity to keep informed on major oblast problems and to express to him their point of view on them. At times the bureau may be not only dominated by the first secretary, but may be also by-passed by the secretariat as a group. At the Nineteenth Party Congress in 1952 Khrushchev announced the reduction of the number of secretaries in each local Party organ from five to three, explaining that this was necessary "in order to prevent the secretariats from supplanting the bureaus." [22] Apparently Khrushchev was announcing a policy change with which he did not agree, for the number of secretaries was once again increased to five after he became First Secretary. As leader of the Party apparatus, Khrushchev either had little concern whether the bureaus were dominated by the secretariats or perhaps he felt that the post-Stalin emphasis on consultation and persuasion would be sufficient to induce the first secretary to consult beyond the secretariat.

Although the secretaries may meet together as a collective secretariat,[23] they do not constitute an undifferentiated group. Instead, each secretary has been assigned responsibility for a definite sphere of activity.[24] Two of them are singled out and given the titles "first secretary" and "second secretary" respectively. The others are termed simply "secretary," although they may be identified by reference to their special responsibility — that is "the secretary in charge of industry."

Among the secretaries the first secretary is without doubt more than first among equals. He is the most powerful individual in the region — "the head" (*nachalstvo*), he is called in a Soviet novel [25] — and he exercises general supervision over all aspects of life within it. In a very real sense he is *the* prefect at the oblast level, the direct representative of the center with the authority normally associated with that role. In addition to his general supervisory duties, the first secretary may also have more detailed responsibility for particular sections of work.[26]

The stature of the republican and obkom first secretary within the region is strengthened by the fact that he is usually a figure of national importance, almost invariably being either a member or candidate member of the All-Union Party Central Committee. At the Twenty-third Party Congress in 1966, for example, all of the republican first secretaries were elected full members of the Central Committee, and 90 percent of the obkom first secretaries in the RSFSR were named full or candidate members (50 percent of them, full members). Another twenty-one secretaries from non-Russian obkomy were also included.

The other secretaries serve as assistants to the first secretary, and each concentrates on specified sections of life within the region. Because the first secretary has some discretion in distributing the work load within the secretariat, the nature of the division of labor is not the same in all cases, but there are certain patterns that are more or less regular.

One of the lower secretaries has normally been assigned responsibility for political-organizational work (including supervision of socialist competition, the police, the Komsomol, and personnel selection for lower Party and Soviet organs); another secretary has been concerned with industry, construction, trade, and transportation (he is called simply "the secretary handling industry" [*sekretar vedaiushchii promyshlennostiu*] and in the republics between 1962 and 1964 he was chairman of the bureau for industry and construction); a third secretary has handled agricultural questions (and from 1962 to 1964 was chairman of the agricultural bureau in the republic); a fourth bears the title "secretary for ideological questions," a phrase that connotes supervision not only of agitation-propaganda work, but also of the political and nonpolitical aspects of education, science, culture, publishing, and so forth. Between 1962 and 1965 a fifth lower secretary served as chairman of the Party-State Control Committee and supervised rather wide-ranging investigations of wrongdoing and mismanagement.

In most republics the second secretary has been in charge of political-organizational work, but this is not an unbending rule. In Belorussia, for example, the second secretary was in charge of agriculture in early 1962, but in Estonia and Armenia he dealt with ideological questions. Here political-organizational work was handled by one of the unnumbered secretaries. For years the first secretary in Georgia seems to have assumed almost all responsibility for political-organizational work, leaving one of the lower secretaries free to concentrate most of her time on trade questions.[27]

There is too little information available to justify categorical statements about the normal responsibilities of the second secretary of the obkom. In 1959, about two-thirds of these officials in the RSFSR and the Ukraine seemed to be handling organizational questions, 15 percent of them seemed to supervise agricultural matters, and another 15 percent industrial questions.[28] In obkom secretariats examined in 1967, however, nearly all second secretaries were in charge of organizational work.

In addition to the secretaries, the republican and oblast secretariats include a number of departments (*otdely*) that act as "the service apparatus" of the Party committee.[29] In a medium-sized oblast the minimum pattern formerly consisted of six departments: (1) organizational-party work (earlier called the Party organs department), (2) agriculture, (3) propaganda and agitation (called "the ideological department" from 1962 through 1964), (4) industry-transportation, (5) science, colleges, and schools, and (6) administrative, trade, and financial organs. In recent years it has also become normal for a medium-sized obkom to have a construction department and a light industry and food industry department to supplement the industrial-transportation department.[30]

In the more populated areas the work of the Party organization has been too voluminous to be handled by six or seven departments, and consequently, several of the basic departments have frequently been split. The industrial-transportation department, for example, has often been divided into several separate departments, each handling a different branch of the oblast's or republic's industry. Thus, in the summer of 1962 the Leningrad obkom had five departments in the industrial realm: (1) the "industrial department," which supervises heavy industry, (2) defense industry, (3) light industry and food industry, (4) construction and building materials, and (5) transportation-communications.[31]

In oblasty where one industry is of exceptional importance, there is usually a special obkom department concerned solely with it. The obkomy in both the Donbass and the Kuznetsk areas have a department for the coal industry; the Arkhangel obkom has a timber industry department; the Kharkov obkom, a machinebuilding department; the Ivanovo obkom, a textile industry department; the Kuibyshev obkom, a department for the oil and chemical industry; and so forth.[32]

The basic structure of the secretariats emerges quite clearly from Soviet sources, but these sources provide far less information about the responsibilities of the individual secretaries and the branch departments and about the relationships between the secretaries and the departments. The Party Rules state only that the secretariat has the duty of "examination of current questions and verification of fulfillment,"[33] and the secretaries are described as executive officers who carry out the policies decided by the collegial Party organs. The secretaries, it is explained, should manifest independence and initiative in carrying out their executive functions, but they should not display improper independence from bureau guidance — a combination which Party spokesmen have not succeeded in defining with precision.[34]

As for the department, Party theorists assert that as the "service apparatus," it does not have the rights of the Party committee as a whole. In particular, it "does not have the power to take decisions or to give guiding instructions in its own name." If, for example, the officials of an obkom department believe that a decision of a raikom is incorrect, they cannot annul that decision themselves, but instead can only suggest such an action to the obkom bureau.[35]

In practice, the role both of the secretaries and the departments is more complex and more important than Party theory would indicate. The scope of work of the industrial secretary was perhaps best indicated in the explanation given for the removal of a secretary for industry in Moldavia in 1961. This man energetically fulfilled his responsibilities of deciding "current questions," but the list of duties he performed poorly was a revealing one: "know the condition of things," "study personnel . . . [and] evaluate their work," and "manifest initiative in raising and deciding the most important problems of the development of industrial production." [36]

In an interview a Party official stated that the heads (zaveduiushchie) of the departments in the industrial sphere report directly to the secretary in charge of industry and that, in effect, they occupy a position like a deputy secretary. The secretary and the department head work together as a team. (Indeed, this position was formalized in the republics from 1962 to 1964 as the department head was often named deputy chairman of the bureau for industry and construction.[37])

The staff of the departments (termed "instructors") are supposed to spend most of their time helping lower officials, but in reality their main function (as well as that of the department head) is to assist the secretary. In particular, they help to keep him informed on conditions in the plants and on the course of plan fulfillment, they carry out investigations, and, on the basis of these investigations, they prepare the reports to be discussed at sessions of the bureaus. In the words of an obkom first secretary, "The officials [of the departments], while at the enterprises, construction sites, and state farms, are chiefly interested in such questions: are there enough raw materials, how is the plan being fulfilled. Moreover, as a rule, they conduct their conversation on all these questions with the economic leaders alone." [38]

In reporting to the bureau and the first secretary and in making suggestions to them, the industrial secretaries and the departments under them often may be the actual initiators of policies approved by the bureau. One reads, for example, that the bureau of the Ivanovo obkom ordered the machinebuilding department of the obkom "to investigate within a week's time the condition of the service facilities for young workers at the Ivanovo Textile Machinebuilding Plant and to present their recommendations." [39] In such cases the recommendations are likely to be of considerable importance.

The industrial secretary and the departments also make a number of minor economic decisions on their own. As will be discussed later, many officials bring supply problems and departmental disputes to the secretariat for solution. If these are of truly major importance, they will be handled by the first secretary or the bureau. On many such matters, however, the industrial secretary or even the head of the department serves as a court of first instance, and his decision is frequently accepted as final.

The Party Organization in the City and the Raion

Below the level of the oblasty, the organization chart of the Party is relatively simple and corresponds to the territorial subdivisions within the country.[40] Each territorial subdivision has its own set of Party institutions, and these institutions are organized in much the same way as at the higher levels. Like the oblast Party organization, the city and raion Party organizations have a Party conference, a Party committee, a bureau, and a secretariat (or at least secretaries), though each of these institutions is usually smaller in size than in the oblasty.

Although the oblast committee of a decade ago included 120 to 125 members, the city committee was said to have 50 to 70 members and the raion committee only 40 to 50.[41] The only information available about the composition of these committees involves several very large cities where the committee membership is larger than normal but does represent a cross-section of elite fairly similar to that found in the republic and the oblast. If one looks at the 1957 Baku city committee, with 90 percent of full members identified, one finds ten Azerbaidzhan Party and governmental officials, eight gorkom officials, twelve officials of the gorispolkom, thirteen raikom secretaries, three raiispolkom chairmen, ten plant-level industrial and construction managers, seven personnel from the scientific-educational-cultural sphere, six army officers, four workers, and six miscellaneous officials. An examination of the 1966 Ulianovsk gorkom (over 75 percent identified) reveals a similar pattern in membership, the lesser number of raikom secretaries in the smaller city being compensated for by a larger number of secretaries of primary Party organizations.[42]

During the last decade the percentage of nonofficials on the Party committees has been much higher than it was in Baku. In Leningrad, for example, workers comprised 5.5 percent of the members of the Leningrad gorkom in 1954 but 18.5 percent of the members in 1957. In the raion committees in Leningrad 9.3 percent of the members were workers in 1954 compared with 21.5 percent in 1957.[43] Particularly after 1959, this growth in the representation of rank-and-file Communists seems to have become standard practice throughout the Soviet Union (including Ulianovsk in 1966).

The bureaus and secretariats of the gorkomy and raikomy have usually been organized along lines similar to those in the obkom, but, again, their size may be somewhat smaller. Prior to 1962, the bureau at this level contained seven to nine members, compared with a maximum of eleven at the higher level. The typical size of the bureau no doubt remains at seven to nine, but the bureaus in some of the larger cities have recently been increased to eleven members and one even to thirteen members.[44] The gorkomy in all cities but Moscow, Leningrad, and Kiev have been limited to three secretaries except in extraordinary circumstances. (For example, after the Tashkent earthquake, a fourth secretary was added to the gorkom, probably on a temporary basis.[45]) The secretariats of the urban raikomy usually have also contained three men.

The smaller number of secretaries at the lower levels has not lessened their dominant position in the bureaus. Indeed, the percentage of Party officials on the gorkom bureau normally seems higher than at the republican and oblast level. No case has been observed in which less than five of nine gorkom bureau members were Party officials. (A typical example with this percentage is the 1966 Tbilisi gorkom bureau: the three gorkom secretaries, the head of a gorkom department, a raikom secretary, the chairman and first deputy chairman of the gorispolkom, a plant director, and an army officer — himself a political worker.[46])

Prior to 1966 it was more usual for the Party officials to occupy six or seven of the positions on a nine-man bureau or five positions on a seven-man bureau.[47] In these cases the first deputy chairman of the gorispolkom and/or the military officer has usually been replaced by one or two additional raikom secretaries or by a secretary of a primary Party organization. In 1966, however, the inclusion of the chairman of the peoples' control committee in the bureaus of many of the gorkomy has often narrowed the majority of the Party officials in those bureaus.[48] The Party majority may also be reduced in those occasional cases in which a rank-and-file worker has been named to the bureau.[49]

The somewhat reduced scale of the raion and city Party organizations has also not affected the key role of the first secretary within the organization. Particularly revealing is one passage in Vsevolod Kochetov's *Bratia Ershovy* (*The Brothers Ershov*), a Soviet novel considered to be the official answer to Dudintsev's *Not By Bread Alone*. In this passage a non-Party engineer, talking with the first secretary of the local gorkom, refers to the Party official as "the highest authority in the city." The first secretary objects that he is only an official of the gorkom, but the engineer retorts sharply: "Well, all the big shots (*bolshie liudi*) say that it is so. You are objecting because of modesty or coyness. You are the authority, and don't be ashamed of it. Will you help me?" The secretary did not attempt to correct the engineer again.[50] The raikom first secretary clearly occupies a similar position within the raion. For example, in one interview a Soviet plant official spontaneously used the phrase "boss (*khoziain*) of the raion" in referring to the first secretary. Likewise, an article in the Soviet press described in a matter-of-fact manner a particular raikom secretary as "the head (*glava*) of the raion."[51] Such informal descriptive terms are found throughout the world in countries with a strong prefectoral system.

As at the oblast level, the other gorkom and raikom secretaries are not general assistants of the first secretary, but are each given a special area of responsibility. Indeed, the first secretary himself also has a set of specialized duties in addition to his general responsibility for the entire area. Usually the work of the Party organ in the city or urban raion is divided into three segments: (1) organizational-political work, (2) industrial and construction questions, and (3) ideological matters (including education and culture). In the gorkomy and raikomy each of these sectors is assigned to one of the secretaries, but there has been no rigid rule as to which should be the responsibility of the first and second secretaries respectively.

Most frequently the first secretary seems to assume responsibility for organizational-political work (as well as for overall leadership of the area), and the second secretary for industrial problems. However, when an industrial administrator has been named to the secretariat, he often has been named first secretary, and, of course, has handled industrial questions. It is not altogether clear why industrial administrators have often been named first secretaries of the gorkom or the raikom rather than second secretaries, but it has probably been necessary to give these men the status and the pay of a first secretary in order to attract them to Party work.[52]

The staff assistance given the gorkom and raikom secretaries varies greatly depending on the population of the area and the degree of its industrial development. In the biggest cities there is a network of departments as complicated as that in the obkom, but in some of the small cities and raiony the departments have been abolished (the instructors then reporting directly to the secretaries) or have been turned into part-time operations staffed by volunteer help.

Normally the instructors are grouped into three departments: the industrial-transportation department, the organizational department, and the agitation-propaganda department (called the ideological department from 1962 to 1964). Each department is supervised directly by a head (*zaveduiushchii*) but is ultimately under the leadership of the relevant secretary. The department heads who report to the second and third secretaries serve essentially as deputy secretaries, although the

22

department head reporting to the first secretary probably has a more substantial role because of the pressure of other duties on his superior.

The size of the departments depends on the peculiarities of the particular city or raion. Each gorkom is placed into one of six groups and each urban raikom into one of four groups, and it is permitted the staff established for that group.[53] In a city with a population of several hundred thousand, the gorkom typically may have a staff of approximately twenty-five, but in a city as large as Leningrad, the industrial departments alone may employ that many full-time officials.[54] A raikom in an important raion such as Smolnii in Leningrad has a staff probably comparable to that of the gorkom in most large cities — eleven officials in the organizational department, ten in the propaganda-agitation department, and six in the industrial-transportation department.[55] The maximum size of the industrial-transportation department of the raikom is probably not much more than the seven found in the Lenin raikom in Leningrad, and even in a raion in industrialized Ivanovo the department may have as few as two officials.[56]

The responsibilities of the departments, and particularly of the instructors, are extremely wide and demanding. The role of the instructor emphasized most frequently in Party literature is that implied in their title. As an official of the Party organ immediately superior to the primary Party organization, the gorkom or raikom instructor is supposed to have quite intimate contact with those engaged in production. He is depicted as the "comrade who has definite experience and is capable of understanding complicated questions and rendering practical assistance." [57]

Yet at the same time the instructors have also been assigned a series of "typical" staff functions. They spend much of their time (70 to 80 percent, according to one study [58]) not at the enterprises but in their own office. When they do go into the field, it often is to perform investigatory functions. They are told to check on complaints of supply bottlenecks, to ascertain when the offending plant manager will deliver a needed order, and often to indicate the importance of a particular order.[59] They are asked to write the reports and memoranda that serve as the bases for discussions in the bureau, and they must be sure to include enough "negative" or "sharp" (ostrye) facts to permit the secretaries to ask searching questions.[60] In carrying out these duties, the instructor is not the friendly "comrade," but the potentially dangerous representative of the superior, the man who operates according to the principle, "I came, I saw, . . . I reported." [61]

The instructors have found it very difficult to fulfill all the responsibilities given them, particularly those of an "instructing" nature. Their numerous duties have placed a severe strain on their time, and it is hardly surprising that the various assignments and requests of the secretaries receive their promptest attention. The instructors' performance of their "instructing" responsibilities has also been hampered by the division of the instructors among three departments. Not only has this practice meant that no one instructor concentrates on all aspects of Party and economic work within an enterprise, but it has also tripled the number of enterprises that an instructor must cover. In practice, each instructor may be responsible for thirty to fifty enterprises, and, as a gorkom secretary once stated, "it is, of course, impossible to embrace such a number of organizations with one's personal influence . . . [or even] to visit each of them frequently." [62]

The Party leaders have realized that the abolition of the departments might make it much easier for the instructors to render assistance to the enterprises, and such a reorganization was actually attempted in many of the raiony and small to medium-sized cities in the late 1950's. The enterprises and institutions of the area were divided by branch of the economy, and one instructor was assigned to each of the groups and handled all of the Party work for the enterprises in it. [63] In this way the instructor could concentrate his attention on a fewer number of enterprises with a narrower range of technical problems, and he could better coordinate ideological and organizational work in an enterprise with the requirements of its technological development.

Yet, for all its advantages, the abolition of the departments did not prove to be a successful experiment. It increased the span of control of each secretary very substantially and complicated his work. The reorganization also made the preparation of reports and the drafting of bureau decisions more difficult. After several years the departments were reestablished in those committees where they had been abolished. Although Party theory may speak fondly of the instructor as a comrade always giving aid to the enterprise, the failure of the department-less form of organization clearly demonstrates the importance of his other functions.

In recent years another attempt to increase the amount of assistance provided by the local Party organs to the enterprises has been the encouragement of "public" participation in the work of the Party committees. Volunteer (*neshtatnyi*) instructors have been recruited for a great many departments at the city and raion level. In all, there were 50,000 such officials in 1962 and 95,000 in mid-1965.[64] In addition, many raikomy have established volunteer commissions and councils, some of which concern themselves with questions in the industrial sphere (for example, the spread of technical innovations). The Kuibyshev raikom in Moscow, for instance, has a commission on socialist competition and spread of progressive experience with fifty-one members; a commission for checking the speed and quality of construction with fifteen members; and a technical-economic council with eleven sections of thirty to thirty-five men each.[65]

Often entire subdepartments or even departments have been formed on a volunteer basis with the head of the department or subdepartment as well as all the instructors performing their duties in their off-hours. In Leningrad, for example, there were fifty-five volunteer units in the city's raikomy in 1965.[66] Normally these departments and subdepartments have not replaced the regular industrial-transportation departments, but instead have supplemented them. Thus, in Ashkhabad, Turkmenia, the Lenin raikom created a volunteer department for construction and municipal services to aid its industrial-transportation department, and in 1963 the volunteer department prepared five questions for consideration by the raikom bureau.[67]

The use of volunteer Party workers has been officially justified on the grounds that it furthers the democratization of the Soviet political system. As men who work in industry (or elsewhere) on a regular basis and engage in supervisory political work in their spare time, they symbolize the nonprofessionalized political and administrative system of which Lenin wrote in *State and Revolution*. A skeptic might note the amount of investigatory work they are asked to do and might conclude that they are also a convenient device to keep the secretaries better informed while avoiding an expansion of the payroll.[68]

The Interrelationships among the Different Levels
of the Local Party Organs

In the Soviet Union there are two, three, or four local Party organs that stand above the primary Party organization of every plant. Each of these Party organs has the duty of supervising industry, and each is held responsible for plan fulfillment. The question therefore arises: How do the republican central committee, obkom, gorkom, and rai-kom effect a division of labor and responsibility among themselves as they all supervise a given plant?

To a certain extent, at least, the answer to this question is short and unequivocal: Party theory makes it clear that the lower Party committees are unquestionably subordinate to those above them. Democratic centralism, the official foundation of Party structure, includes as one of its four principles, "the unconditionally binding nature of the decisions of the higher organs for the lower." [69] Frol Kozlov's report on the Party Rules at the Twenty-second Congress was unwavering in its insistence on this principle: "It is necessary to say that the KPSS is not a federation of parties or of Party committees. It is a centralized organization. . . . The strict subordination of the individual organizations of the Party to the center, of the lower organizations to the higher is an indispensable condition of the successful fulfillment by the Party of its historical tasks." [70]

The subordination of the lower organs to the higher is strengthened by the practice of naming Party secretaries from above rather than electing them from below as stipulated in the Party Rules. To be sure, the proprieties are observed and a change of secretaries is formally accompanied by an election in the Party committee, but the results of the elections are predetermined by a "recommendation" of the higher Party organ.

The first secretaries in the republics, in the RSFSR oblasty, and probably even in the non-Russian oblasty would seem invariably to be "recommended" for their post by the central Party organs. Indeed, a 1954 Soviet novel indicates that at that time even the lower secretaries of the obkomy were essentially appointed from the center. At the beginning of this novel a secretary of a Siberian gorkom is summoned to the office of a secretary of the Central Committee. Anxious because he had received no hint of the purpose of the meeting and did not know whether it meant good news or bad, the gorkom secretary's worries prove to be unfounded, for he is told of his promotion: "We want to recommend you as second secretary of the Volga obkom." The Central Committee secretary clearly takes it for granted that this recommendation will be unquestionably accepted by the Volga obkom. Later passages in the novel make it obvious that the lower obkom secretaries are selected in a similar manner. The secretary in charge of industry, for example, has been "sent" to the obkom by the Central Committee. The obkom first secretary even feels compelled to call the Central Committee for permission to make a change in the membership of the obkom bureau.[71]

Recent information on the process of selecting lower obkom secretaries is not available, but Khrushchev's speeches confirmed that at least the first secretaries continued to be selected and removed by the central authorities in the post-Stalin period. In his first year as Central Committee first secretary, Khrushchev reported, "Recently we heard the report of the [first] secretary of the Novgorod obkom, comrade Fedorov, and we were required to free him from the post he occupies." [72] Five years later he severely criticized the first secretary of the Saratov obkom for providing insufficient leadership in the industrial sphere. He ended his remarks with these words: "We in the Central Committee will think over the solution of this question, for it is impossible to leave it as it is." [73] In less than six weeks Saratov had a new obkom first secretary.[74]

The principle of "recommendation" from above is also followed in the selection of the secretaries of the gorkomy and the raikomy. According to the Party Rules, all gorkom and raikom secretaries are confirmed by the obkomy or by the republican central committees,[75] and in general this probably does reflect the fact that their selection is centered in these organs. The Turkmenian republican newspaper, for example, reports that the "plenum [of the Mary obkom] approved the decision of the bureau of the obkom to remove A. Babaev from the post of gorkom first secretary." [76] However, it would be surprising if the Central Committee did not concern itself with the selection of gorkom first secretaries in the most important cities.

Whichever higher Party organ has the initiative in selecting lower

Party secretaries, there is little doubt about the meaning of the "confirmation." Consider the following statement by a gorkom first secretary in Latvia: "In February 1952 the Latvian Central Committee discussed the work of the Elgav gorkom and took a decision concerning it. This decision revealed with full directness the degree of negligence in a number of sectors of the city's economy, and it indicated that there were serious defects in the activity of the Party gorkom. The Central Committee mapped out measures for improving the work of the Elgav Party organization. The gorkom was given help by sending new personnel to it. In particular, I was directed to work in Elgav, and there I was elected first secretary of the Party gorkom." [77]

We may turn once more to Panferov's *Volga-Matushka Reka* for illumination about the impact of these practices on the thinking of the lower secretaries themselves. In one passage the leading character, the obkom second secretary, explains to a raikom secretary and the chairman of a raion soviet executive committee the disastrous consequences of a poor decision by the obkom: "A report of the result is sent to the Central Committee. After that [the obkom first secretary] is called to the Central Committee, and he is told: 'You are losing the confidence of the Central Committee.' " The obkom second secretary asks, "Do you know what it means to lose the confidence of the Central Committee?" The raiispolkom chairman answers quickly, "The same as if we lose the confidence of the obkom." The second secretary of the obkom agrees that this is so. [78]

But to say that lower Party officials are subordinate to the higher Party organizations and that they are accountable to higher Party officials for their performance is to give only a partial explanation of the interrelationships within the Party apparatus. There are many ways in which a superior and subordinate can divide responsibility, many ways in which lines of command and influence may flow.

Given the centralization within the Party apparatus, one traditional arrangement would be a strict line of command. In this arrangement the raikomy and small gorkomy would be concerned with the work of the industrial plants; the larger gorkomy, with the work of the urban raikomy; and the obkomy, with the work of the gorkomy and rural raikomy. The higher Party organs would respect the "proper" lines of command and channels of communication, dealing with plant management only through the lower Party organs.

Such an arrangement might seem natural, but in practice it has never been adopted in the Soviet Union. The Party leadership has encouraged the local Party organs to intervene at all levels of the chain of command beneath them. Indeed, it has instructed them to maintain direct contact with economic managers, with shop officials, and even with workers (non-Party as well as Party members). Concentration of obkom attention on the gorkomy and the raikomy alone has explicitly been criticized as "a bureaucratic method of work." [79]

The obkom officials may, in actuality, find little time for conversations with workers, but they often do "violate" the chain of command by dealing directly with individual industrial enterprises and their managers. Indeed, the very structure of the obkom departments may require such behavior. In at least one obkom in 1941 the instructors of the light industry department were each assigned not to specific raikomy and gorkomy but rather to groups of factories. [80]

The division of responsibilities among the instructors of other obkomy is not known, but it is obvious that there has always been much contact between obkom officials and the enterprises. In fact, the contact with plant officials may be quite continuous. Even during the Stalin period one finds, for example, that the head of the heavy industry department of the Kemerovo obkom called the director of the Kuznetsk Metallurgy Combine daily on the telephone. [81] These calls were not part of any special investigation, but instead involved fairly routine production and scheduling questions.

A second possible way of dividing authority among the local Party organs would have been to assign the Central Committee responsibility for the most important plants, the obkomy responsibility for plants of second-rank importance, the gorkomy responsibility for those of third-rank importance, and the raikomy responsibility for the smallest plants. Except to a very limited extent in personnel selection, however, this practice has also not been followed.

It is true that each Party organ has a list of governmental and non-governmental posts (called its *nomenklatura*) for which it has special responsibility and that the significant administrative posts are distributed among the Party organs according to the importance of the post. (The Party organ must give its approval before an official in a post on its nomenklatura is removed or his successor chosen.) The directorships of the giant plants are in the nomenklatura of the Central Committee in Moscow, and those of progressively lesser importance are in the nomenklatury of the republican central committees, obkomy, gorkomy, and raikomy respectively.

The possibility of a clear division of authority on these bases is, however, completely destroyed by the practice of including different posts within the same factory in the nomenklatury of different Party organs. In the large and medium-sized plants the directorships are placed in the nomenklatura of one Party organ (ranging from the gorkom to the All-Union Central Committee), but other key managerial posts (down to that of shop head in the largest plants) are placed within the jurisdiction of one or more lower Party organs. Moreover, as will be seen, Party organs at several levels are called upon to participate informally in decisions about posts in each other's nomenklatury.[82]

The policy with respect to the nomenklatura seems designed to ensure an overlap in the local Party responsibility for the significant plants, and such a development has occurred. The foremost Party theorist has not only acknowledged that "the gorkomy usually concentrate their attention on the leading enterprises," but has asserted that "this is, of course, correct." [83] Indeed, the Soviet press refers repeatedly to cases in which individual plants are supervised by different local Party organs simultaneously. For example, when the large Serp and Molot Agricultural Machinery Plant in Kharkov was in trouble in 1947, the leading officials of both the obkom and gorkom were said to be at the plant every day.[84] Similarly, in 1954 and early 1955 when the Stalingrad Tractor Plant was basically fulfilling its gross output plan, the bureau of the Stalingrad obkom discussed ways of improving the performance of the tractor works. At the same time the local raikom took a decision calling upon the plant director to reconstruct four electric smelting furnaces in the casting shop. It is true that (because of the obkom's intense interest) the gorkom leaders decided not to have a formal session discussing the plant, but they were severely criticized by a *Pravda* correspondent for failing to do so.[85] Even during the sovnarkhoz period the various local Party organs supervised the industrial plants not only through the sovnarkhoz but also directly. In 1959, for example, the work of the New Karaganda Machine-building Works "was repeatedly discussed in the Party obkom, at sessions of its bureau, and even at a plenary session of the Karaganda gorkom." [86]

This absence of a clear line of command and a clear division of responsibility in the Party apparatus is an aspect of Party operating procedure that is vital to keep in mind if the role of the local Party organs in industrial decision-making is to be understood correctly. Frequently the Soviet political and administrative system has been pictured as consisting essentially of two parallel and separate hierarchies — the Party and the state. In this model the Party leaders intervene in economic affairs by sending an order down the Party hierarchy to the committee at the appropriate level, and this committee then compels the governmental officials to take appropriate action. In practice, however, this is not typical behavior except for certain (but not all) types of tasks of an investigatory or verifying nature. When a local Party organ wants a government official to take a certain action, it usually contacts him directly and by-passes intermediate Party officials. Thus, the Kemerovo obkom official who telephoned the Kuznetsk director daily had not once in fourteen months called the secretary of the combine's primary Party organization. [87]

There are several crucial corollaries to this point. First, the free contact between a local Party organ and both the administrators and the Party officials within its region gives the local Party organ a very independent position vis-à-vis lower Party officials. Consequently, if there is disagreement between a factory director and the secretary of a primary Party organization, there is no particular probability that the raikom will support the Party secretary just because he has the title of "Party." Likewise, if the raikom or gorkom disagrees with the position of a ministerial (or earlier a sovnarkhoz) official, the higher Party organs may support either side, depending on their judgment of the facts of the situation. Indeed, as will be discussed later, in both cases there is greater likelihood that the industrial administrator would be supported than the Party officials.

Second, one must be extremely careful before concluding that a press report about the ineffectiveness of a plant Party secretary or even of a raikom secretary signifies little Party supervision over that particular plant. For example, Leonard Schapiro in his discussion of Party control of agriculture remarks, "In the case of agriculture, the continued absence of adequate Party organizations on the collective farms . . . inevitably threw the lion's share of administrative responsibility on the governmental officials." [88] This conclusion need not, however, follow from the premise, and the word "inevitably" is misplaced. It is just as logical — and more accurate — for John Armstrong to conclude that the low percentage of Communists in the collective farm has, in fact, "endowed the first secretary of the rural raikom with a peculiar importance in the economic field." [89]

Finally, the absence of the concept of rigid lines of command means that it is difficult to generalize about the division of labor among the various local Party organs. The local first secretaries have considerable leeway in ordering the working arrangements within their area, and, consequently, the division of responsibility within the Party apparatus varies from place to place, from time to time, and from one type of decision to another.

The interrelationships within the Party apparatus are not, of course, completely formless. Out of an administrative situation such as has been described here, certain solutions prove to be more viable, more reasonable than others, and they naturally tend to recur with some frequency. One type of informal division of responsibility among the local Party organs has flowed from an inevitable tendency in large-scale organization — the tendency for a high-level executive to be less an initiator of policies, less a director of people's actions, than a broker who resolves conflicts among the departments beneath him. To the extent that this is a key function of the local Party organs, it imposes its own logic on the division of responsibility. When a departmental dispute arises, there is a natural tendency for it to be taken to the lowest common superior who can resolve it, and this usually has been the practice in the Soviet Union. If a dispute arises between a plant and an institution within the same raion, it is handled by the raikom; if it occurs between a plant and a city institution, the gorkom is involved, and so forth. (This question will be explored at much greater length in Chapter XI.)

When the local Party organs initiate action whether of a directing or investigatory nature, there are no such firm rules as to the division of responsibility among them. Of course, the pressure of time does ensure that the obkom will be primarily concerned with oblast-wide questions and institutions and with supervising the lower Party committees. It certainly may intervene in the affairs of any plant, but is likely to do so only in the case of major enterprises (such as the Kuznetsk Metallurgy Combine or the Stalingrad Tractor Plant) or in the case of smaller plants whose slow deliveries are affecting major plants. It was not surprising, therefore, when a director of a factory in a textile combine stated in an interview that he had been to the obkom only once in six months (in contrast with his frequent discussions with gorkom officials), nor was it astonishing that an official of a spinning works in the metropolis of Kiev declared that his plant dealt primarily with the raikom and had comparatively little contact with the gorkom, let alone the obkom.

Still, the division of responsibility is not clear-cut, particularly with respect to the most significant plants. The gorkom and raikom may devote more attention to a small factory then does the obkom, but they too have responsibility for the larger plants and spend a disproportionate amount of time on them. Because lower officials are judged primarily on the basis of the economic performance of their area as a whole, their self-interest directs them toward a concern with those plants contributing most significantly to that performance.

It would probably be inaccurate, however, to conclude that these overlapping responsibilities lead to a great deal of confusion. The most notable Soviet discussion of a case in which there were "eternal arguments and misunderstandings" [90] concerned the medium-sized city of Orsk where there were only two raiony and where almost all of the important industrial enterprises were located in one of them. This degree of duplication of effort is unhealthy, and, no doubt, has usually been prevented by the solution adopted in Orsk — namely, the abolition of the raion divisions. The type of duplication likely to be more common is that raised by a complaint of the Party secretary in a large machinebuilding plant: "An official will phone from the raikom about some question, and then on the very same day someone will phone from the obkom about the very same question." [91] Yet, although such a practice is annoying to lower officials, any confusion in instructions can be easily straightened out through the use of the same telephone that brought the instructions.

The interrelationships among the local Party organs are probably more complex on paper than they are in practice. A short telephone call can keep the different Party committees informed of one another's work plan and major interests for a particular day or week, and the "expedient distribution of obligations" [92] that Party theorists demand can thus be achieved. By turning to the Party organs' relation with the industrial administrators and seeing the Party officials acting in concrete situations, the complexities that exist on paper may seem even less involved.

III. The Party Secretary and the Industrial Manager

Examination of the structure of an organization and the laws defining its mission may provide some general sense of the organization's role, but this is only the beginning of understanding. The definitive study of an organization should be based on close observation of its operating practices as well as on examination of its files, but where this is impossible, it is important at least to have some sense of the type of men who staff it. In this case, for example, if the secretaries of the local Party organs were all to be men with careers in agitation-propaganda work, then the local Party organs would surely have a different role in practice than if all the secretaries were former factory directors.

Therefore, before exploring the formal responsibilities of the local Party organs and their relationship to the industrial hierarchy, it is necessary to examine the men who have occupied the posts to be discussed. The purpose of this chapter is not to present a comprehensive study of the background of all types of Party secretaries, but instead to illuminate the Party-state relationship in the industrial sphere. It is concerned only with those Party officials who participate in industrial decision-making, and even then primarily with those characteristics most helpful in understanding their relationship with the industrial managers. Because this relationship is the focal point, the major industrial managers will also be treated in this chapter — in particular, the factory directors who work under the local Party officials and the ministerial and Gosplan officials with whom these Party officials must deal on any significant appropriation question.

Western discussions of the Party official often refer to a uniform "Party apparatchik." [1] However, the Party apparatus, rather than being strictly homogeneous, has come to be staffed by men with a great diversity of preparation and background. Perhaps the most striking variation in the career patterns of the *"apparatchiki"* is found among the lower officials of the individual local Party organ. Armstrong has noted the differences in the background of the first secretaries and the ideological secretaries in the Ukrainian obkomy,[2] and with certain exceptions his conclusions on this point are valid for all areas in the Soviet Union during the entire postwar period.

Even more striking than the variation between the "line official" and the "indoctrination specialist" discussed by Armstrong are the differences among the various specialized secretaries of the Party organs. Looking, for example, at the republican Party secretaries selected in 1966, one finds that in at least one-half of the fourteen republics (excluding the RSFSR) the industrial secretary (*sekretar vedaiushchii promyshlennostiu*) had experience in industry or construction at the level of enterprise director, head of administration or deputy chairman of a republican sovnarkhoz, or republican minister. In at least five of the other seven republics, the industrial secretary had an engineering education and years of Party work associated with industry.

In contrast, the men selected as republican secretaries for agriculture in 1966 include at least four former republican ministers of agriculture, at least two former republican deputy ministers of agriculture, and at least one chief inspector of the republican ministry. The others can be identified in the past in agricultural staff positions in the Party organs or in the post of Party secretary in a rural raion. (Of the eight agricultural secretaries whose education is known, seven are agronomists and the eighth is a graduate of the Higher Party School.)

Of the 1966 republican ideological secretaries, at least five were once Komsomol officials, one was a republican minister of education, one was a newspaper editor, and all of the others were in Party ideological work for at least five years prior to 1966. The seven ideological secretaries whose education is known include four graduates of pedagogical institutes, two university graduates (one listed as a candidate of historical science), and one graduate from the Academy of the Social Sciences.

Another type of variation that has become increasingly pronounced is among the first secretaries themselves. Of course, throughout the postwar period the background of the first secretary of the rural raikom has usually been different from that of the first secretary of the urban raikom or gorkom, but the differences among the obkom first secretaries also have become quite substantial. Thus, among the men who were obkom first secretaries in 1966, the first secretary of the Semipalatinsk obkom in the Virgin Lands was a former USSR deputy minister of agriculture who was transferred from agricultural administration to Party work for the first time at the age of forty-nine, while the first secretary of the Kemerovo obkom (the center of the Kuzbass region) had been a coal industry administrator, rising to the post of head of the Sverdlovsk Coal Combine before moving to Party work at the age of forty-five. The first secretary of the Dnepropetrovsk obkom had been a school principal and head of the Dnepropetrovsk city education department before being transferred to Party work at the age of thirty-four; the first secretary of the Mogilev obkom had sixteen years of experience in Komsomol work before becoming a Party official; the first secretary of the Kalmyk obkom had been a career army officer until the age of fifty-one. Far more typical was the first secretary of the Vologda obkom. Before assuming this post, he had successively been director of a sovkhoz, chairman of a raiispolkom, raikom secretary, head of the agricultural department of the obkom, first deputy chairman of the oblispolkom, and obkom secretary for agriculture.[3]

If the 1966 obkom first secretaries are examined statistically, striking variations appear, variations tending to correspond to differences in the problems arising in different types of oblasti. In the twenty-five most industrialized oblasti in the RSFSR and the Ukraine,[4] nineteen of the obkom first secretaries had engineering training, two had a technical secondary education, two graduated from a physics-mathematics division of a university, and one was an economist. In the twenty-five most important agricultural oblasti in the RSFSR,[5] there were only four engineers among the first secretaries (and one of them graduated from an institute for the mechanization of agriculture), while thirteen of the first secretaries were agronomists.[6]

The early work experience of the 1966 first secretaries in the most industrialized and in the important agricultural oblasti was as disparate as their education. Of the twenty-five secretaries in the agricultural oblasti, nine had held posts in governmental administration of agriculture at the level of MTS director or higher. Eighteen had once been first secretary of a rural raikom or head of the agriculture department of an obkom or both. On the other hand, none of the first secretaries in the twenty-five most industrialized oblasti had held administrative jobs in agriculture at the level of MTS director or higher. Indeed, despite the fact that eight of the twenty-five were listed as being of peasant origin (as compared with twelve of the first secretaries in the agricultural oblasti), only three of their biographies include any work experience in agriculture: two as kolkhozniki in their teens prior to entering college, one as head of a political department of a sovkhoz. Only five seem to have held the post of first secretary in a rural raikom, three of them in raiony with major industrial development.

Because of the focus of this book, the reader should not expect a definitive summary of "the Party apparatchik." The chapter describes industrial secretaries and first secretaries in the more industrialized areas, and does not attempt to account for other regions with needs for secretaries with different biographical patterns.

"The Men of 1938"

A study of the Party and administrative elite of the postwar period must begin with the Great Purge of 1936 through 1938. During this period the Red Directors (the men of proven loyalty to the Party, of considerable organizational ability, but of limited technical education) were removed wholesale from the key administrative posts in industry that they had occupied for the past decade.[7] The same fate befell the Party apparatchiki who had supported Stalin in his struggle with Trotsky and Bukharin and who had shared in the rewards of victory with him.

Replacing these officials were men with many early experiences in common — men who (particularly in the case of the industrial administrators) continued to dominate the Soviet scene for the next two decades. The author has followed Armstrong's lead in calling these beneficiaries of the Great Purge, "the Men of 1938," but the post-Purge shakedown really did not end until 1941 and our summary of characteristics will be based on the officials of that year.[8]

In examining the biographies of the most important officials in the industrial and construction hierarchy and in the local Party organs in 1941 (that is, the peoples' commissars and the obkom first secretaries), the first impression is that of the similarities in many aspects of their background (Table 1). The officials in each category de-

Table 1. Industrial commissars and obkom first secretaries, 1941.[a]

Officials	Average year of birth	Average age of entry into Party	Proportion with engineering education
Heavy industry commissars	1902	21	12 of 13
(N = 20)	(N = 15)	(N = 15)	
Light industry commissars	1899	26	1 of 6
(N = 6)	(N = 6)	(N = 6)	
Construction commissars	1896	21	2 of 2
(N = 2)	(N = 2)	(N = 2)	
Obkom first secretaries, 25 most industrialized oblasti	1904	22	8 of 14
(N = 25)	(N = 13)	(N = 13)	
Obkom first secretaries, 25 agricultural oblasti RSFSR	1900	21	1 of 8
(N = 25)	(N = 8)	(N = 8)	

[a] The commissars described in this table are all USSR Peoples' Commissars, except for three men (Kosygin, Malyshev, and Pervukhin) who had actually become Deputy Chairmen of the Council of Peoples' Commissars by June 1941. They are included because at times they later dropped back to the ministerial level. (The 1941 commissars are listed in note 10.)

The methodology for determining the 25 most industrialized and most important agricultural oblasti is described in notes 4 and 5. However, the lists of the oblasti were adjusted to reflect the 1939 census results.

viated relatively little from the average. Nearly all of them were in their late thirties or early forties; nearly all joined the Party after the Revolution — indeed, two-thirds of both the commissars and the secretaries became Party members after Lenin's death in 1924. All of them began working in their teens either in a factory, on a farm, or in lower political jobs. Even those who graduated from an engineering institute entered that institute only after a number of years in such work. Nearly all of these men enjoyed a precipitous rise during the Purge.

The major visible difference between the 1941 obkom first secretaries and the commissars supervising heavy industry and construction was in the level of their technical training and work experience. The commissars almost all had an engineering diploma from a regular institute (not an industrial academy) — in fact, usually from one of the elite institutes in their respective industries. Although their promotion was extremely rapid, the average commissar had eight years of administrative experience in industry by 1941, and this almost invariably included a stint as director of one of the most important plants in his industry.

A fairly typical example of a 1941 Peoples' Commissar is Peter F. Lomako.[9] Lomako was born in 1904 of a peasant family, and in 1927 he entered the Moscow Institute of Nonferrous Metals and Gold, graduating in 1932. He then worked at the important "Krasnyi Vyborzhets" Copper Works, rising from the post of brigadier to foreman to head of a shop to deputy chief engineer to the directorship. After a short period as head of a glavk (chief administration) of the Peoples' Commissariat of Nonferrous Metallurgy and then as deputy commissar, Lomako became Peoples' Commissar of Nonferrous Metallurgy.

Whatever the shortcomings of men with this type of background, they had survived the shakedown after the Purge, and presumably had demonstrated an excellent ability to secure plan fulfillment. They scarcely had the experience and self-confidence to pose a political challenge to Stalin, but they still had sufficient experience and technical authority to be formidable opponents if they came into conflict with the obkom first secretaries on a specialized question involving their particular branch of industry.

The obkom first secretaries of 1941 — like those of 1966 — were a fairly diverse group, but none on whom there is information could be considered technically qualified in any real sense. In the more rural oblasti very few first secretaries seem to have had an engineering education, and an equally small number had practical experience in industrial management. (Of course, a significant percentage of them had been factory workers in their teens or early twenties.)

In the twenty-five most industrialized oblasti, the proportion of first secretaries with technical education was much higher (although probably not as high as our sample of fourteen secretaries would suggest). In this case, however, the bare statistics can be very misleading, particularly if they imply a comparability between the preparation of the obkom first secretaries and that of the commissars. Frequently the secretaries had passed not through a regular industrial institute but through an industrial academy or a military mechanization academy. With only one exception, neither those with technical training nor without it had any significant administrative experience in industry. Those who did graduate from an institute or academy nearly always did so in 1936, 1937, or 1938, and became obkom first secretaries after a year or two of lower Party work.[10] Because these engineers rose so rapidly after their graduation, it seems certain that they were quite active politically while in the institute, and, consequently, there is a real question about the meaningfulness of their engineering education.[11]

Not only did the industrial commissar assume his post with greater technical authority than any of the obkom first secretaries, but the passage of time only served to strengthen his relative authority. The first secretary was responsible for all aspects of life within the oblast, and had to concentrate much of his attention on sectors of the economy in which he had a more exclusive operational responsibility than in industry (for example, in agriculture and in mobilization of men and supplies for the war effort). He was in a very poor position to increase his technical expertise in any particular branch of industry or even to keep abreast of technological improvements.

The peoples' commissar, on the other hand, was a man who continued to specialize in one branch of industry,[12] a man who supervised not only its many plants (with their diversity of experience) but also the scientific and design institutes and in many cases the machine-building plants advancing its technology. The commissar held a post that should have permitted him the opportunity to deepen his technical knowledge of an industry, and those of 1941 were certainly given ample time for such a process to occur. Nearly all of them retained their post (or a roughly comparable one) throughout the war, and half of them still remained in essentially the same position or a higher one in 1955. (Another 20 percent remained as deputy ministers in 1955; 15 percent had died in high office.) [13] By the late Stalin period their technical authority should have become very substantial indeed. In addition, they continued to be supported by a large apparatus of even more specialized officials.[14]

Although the relative technical expertise of the people's commissars and the obkom first secretaries may well have been of crucial importance in the case of a dispute having to be referred to the central Party leaders, the day-to-day interaction between the local Party organs and the industrial hierarchy usually involved men of lower rank — the plant director, the gorkom and raikom first secretaries, and the local Party secretaries for industry.

The Soviet plant director clearly is one of the key figures in industrial decision making, but there is no official in the Soviet Union about whom it is more difficult to generalize. The words "plant" or "enterprise" (*zavod* or *predpriiatie*) can refer to institutions of completely diverse nature. An "enterprise" may be a huge integrated complex such as the Magnitogorsk Metallurgy Combine, or it may be essentially a one-man operation with the "director" having a few workers as assistants. One would not expect uniformity among the directors of such differing institutions, and, in fact, one does not find it. Consequently, there is no contradiction between Andreev's assertion in 1939 that only 27.6 percent of enterprise directors had higher education,[15] and Granick's finding that by this time "it became the rule for a director in heavy industry to be a graduate engineer." [16]

Despite the variations, the post-Purge plant directors with higher education often had biographies closely resembling those of the industrial commissars. The vast majority of such directors were young men (often a few years younger than the commissars) who had joined the Party after Lenin's death and who had almost invariably entered the industrial institute only after a period of factory or political work. Some (for example, G. I. Nosov, director of the Magnitogorsk Metallurgy Combine) [17] had administrative experience fully as impressive as that of the peoples' commissars, but many had a much weaker technical preparation. Among these men one finds graduates of the lesser institutes and of the industrial academies, many with very short managerial careers. When one young engineer complained that he did not have the experience necessary to manage the giant Moscow Electric Works, his superiors replied that he should not worry. "After twenty-four hours we consider a director to be experienced." [18]

Nevertheless, the 1941 director of a large plant, like the industrial commissars, could pose a difficult problem for the local Party officials if he differed with their views about the best line of development for his plant. By the beginning of the war the directors who had survived the shakedown period had substantially more than twenty-four hours experience, and they too had demonstrated an ability to "meet a payroll." Undoubtedly many of the plants subordinate to light industry and particularly to the local soviets had directors whose technical expertise was of a very dubious nature. However, the type of plant with sufficient priority to be considered a candidate for significant capital investment and technical innovation was likely to be a plant whose director had the technical authority to play a major role in determining how this investment was to be spent.

No doubt in large part because of the technical qualifications of the director and the problems raised by these qualifications, the Party leadership soon came to follow a policy of selecting lower Party secretaries of considerably greater technical expertise than the obkom first secretaries. As has been noted, after the spring of 1940 each obkom and republican central committee had at least one secretary who specialized in industrial questions, and in February 1941, the Eighteenth Party Conference decreed a substantial expansion in the number of these officials. Although some of these men had little previous experience with industry before receiving the specialized Party assignment, a great many were engineers with pre-1937 biographies more similar to those of the peoples' commissars than to those of the obkom first secretaries.

One such Party secretary was Georgii V. Eniutin.[19] Born in 1903, Eniutin joined the Party in 1924. After being a metalworker and then a raikom Komsomol secretary, he entered the Dnepropetrovsk Metallurgy Institute. On graduating in 1932, he was sent to the giant Azov Steel Plant where he worked for seven years as a shop head and then as a deputy chief engineer. In 1939 he became a Party Organizer of the Central Committee at the Azov Plant, and in 1941 was named secretary of the Stalino obkom (presumably a secretary handling industrial questions). During the war he held the same post in Novosibirsk oblast (at that time the oblast in which the Kuznetsk Metallurgy Combine was located) and then on its formation in Kemerovo oblast (the new oblast of the Combine).

Men with industrial experience were also directed to the gorkomy and the urban raikomy. The nature of their experience could be quite varied, but some sense of its range can be obtained by examining the background of eight officials with industrial experience who were raikom secretaries in Moscow in 1939 or 1940. One of the eight (Pavliukov) had not attended an institute, but he had spent a decade in Party and trade union work at the enterprise level before becoming raikom secretary. Another (Isachenko) had worked for four years as an engineer before becoming secretary of a plant primary Party organization and then raikom secretary. Two (Abramov and Gurina) were engineers who had risen to the posts of shop head at a plant and chief engineer of a construction site respectively before being transferred to Party work. Three other raikom secretaries (Kolotyrkin, Afanasev, and Surova) had worked in important industrial research or education institutes — one in a research institute in the defense industry, one as deputy head of the Zhukovskii Aviation Institute, and the third as Director of the Institute of Steel. The eighth secretary (Sazonov) had been head of the machinery industry department of the USSR Gosplan.[20] On the average, the raikom secretaries in Moscow were, no doubt, more technically qualified than their counterparts in less important industrial centers, but the Moscow officials still probably represent a reasonably good cross-section of the type of industrial personnel entering lower Party positions during this period.

It would be most interesting to know the percentage of industrial specialists among the lower Party officials who had responsibility for industry in 1941, but this information is unavailable. In June 1938 there were but six engineers among all the raikom and gorkom secretaries in the fifty-three cities and raiony of Moscow oblast, but this figure clearly increased rapidly in the years prior to the war. In the spring of 1939 it was stated that 92 percent of the plant Party Organizers of the Central Committee had higher education, and this was one of the important groups from whom raikom and gorkom secretaries were later recruited.[21]

Although no generalization can be proved about the raikom and gorkom secretaries in the early post-Purge period, the pattern of biographical information available suggests that by mid-1941 there were few if any Party secretariats in an industrialized city or industrialized urban raion that did not include at least one official (either as first secretary or a lower secretary) with the type of industrial experience described above. During World War II the number of such officials was greatly increased, as many of the nonspecialized Party secretaries were transferred into political work in the army and as the number of industrial secretaries and deputy secretaries was expanded.[22]

By 1941 the Party apparatus obviously included many men with much the same early technical education and experience as the industrial administrators, but the question remains: were these two groups of men *really* as similar in nature as their career patterns would indicate? Until he became Party organizer of the Central Committee at the Azov Steel Plant at the age of thirty-six, Georgii Eniutin had a biography corresponding classically to the normal pattern for the Soviet industrial administrator of this period. But was he *really* the same type of person as the man who moved from the post of shop head to become a plant director and perhaps then a high official in a peoples' commissariat?

Despite the great difficulty in finding a reliable answer to this question, it can be said with some confidence that at least in 1941 the industrial administrator and the industrially trained lower Party official were not so different that a young man's early experience and behavior would make it obvious to his superiors whether he should be promoted to higher Party or higher industrial work. There are enough cases of men being promoted to a higher Party or industrial post and then later being transferred to the other hierarchy to make it clear that the Party leadership was not drawing on two completely distinct types of person for industrial Party work and higher industrial management.

In particular, the reader should be warned against the assumption that the Party officials were chosen from among the dynamic, ideologically committed, politically active engineers and that the top industrial managers came from among the more conservative elements, from among the less dynamic and the less committed. It would be a great injustice to the plant manager of 1941 (and later) to see him as the soulless "bureaucrat" (in the pejorative sense of the word), anxious to avoid responsibility and to seek a peaceful life. It is difficult to believe that such a man would be attracted to top managerial positions, particularly just after observing the fate of his predecessors. A seeker of the peaceful life would be far more likely to search out a staff job where the pressure for plan fulfillment would be less direct.

Those who remained managers of important plants after the Purge were engineers who had the daring to stand out during the Purge, who had the resourcefulness to produce results in jobs for which they did not have sufficient experience (and under conditions of extraordinary psychological strain). They were in large part undoubtedly chosen from the young engineers of the 1930's described by Solomon Schwarz: "These young engineers were a restless element, inclined toward experimentation, record-breaking, speed-up, 'storming.' They brought *elan* into the plants, a sense that people somehow become embodied in the gigantic recovery of the new revolutionary country through work in which they submerge themselves completely. Confident of advancement, but largely not conscious careerists, they saw their rise as a natural consequence of the development of the young country." [23]

Yet, whatever the similarities among engineers who entered Party work and those who worked within the industrial hierarchy, it probably was not simply a matter of chance that one supervisor like Eniutin became an obkom secretary and another became a plant director. The two jobs, both involving responsibility for plan fulfillment and participation in managerial decision-making, were sufficiently different to require men of a somewhat different type. The plant directorship meant day-by-day responsibility for one particular enterprise in one branch of industry; the Party post entailed responsibility for all branches of industry and implied a shifting focus of attention and more concern with the interrelationships among different branches of the economy. One may could easily perform both jobs, but the differences between them probably meant that on the average the more technically inclined administrative types tended to be selected for the industrial posts (and to find it congenial and remain there), whereas those who were more effective in the broker or trouble-shooter roles tended to gravitate to Party posts.

The Ministerial Period

As men in their mid-thirties and early forties, the "Men of 1938" were many years short of retirement age, and it is perhaps not surprising that these men — at least those in the industrial hierarchy — continued to occupy a predominant role for the next quarter of a century. Despite political upheavals, the very suspicious nature of Stalin, and the sometimes unreasonable demands of plan fulfillment, a considerable proportion of the men who occupied important ministerial posts in 1941 continued in high position well into the Khrushchev period and in some cases beyond it.

When men in top positions in 1941 were demoted, they continued for a long time to be replaced by other beneficiaries of the Great

Table 2. Background of industrial and construction ministers (commissars), 1941–1957.[a]

Officials	Average year of birth	Average age of entry into Party	Proportion with engineering education	Average date of college graduation
1941 commissars	1901	22	15 of 21	1931
(N = 28)	(N = 23)	(N = 23)		(N = 15)
New ministers of 1940's	1906	24	13 of 13	1933
(N = 23)	(N = 17)	(N = 13)		(N = 12)
New ministers of 1950's	1906	29	23 of 23	1932
(N = 30)	(N = 25)	(N = 24)		(N = 20)

[a] As before, this table refers only to USSR ministers. The total number of new ministers indicated in the table was found by compiling individual cases of new appointments. It is possible that a few changes of ministers were overlooked, but the size of total N indicated should be nearly accurate.

No attempt has been made to distinguish between ministers in heavy industry, light industry, and construction, for no significant differences among them were observed after 1941.

Purge, by men who in their own right should also be considered members of the "Men of 1938." Thus, the new men who became industrial ministers after 1941 had almost all risen to the level of plant engineer or (more usually) higher by 1941.

Although there are similarities in the biographies of the 1941 commissars and those who rose to this level later (the vast majority of both were drawn from the factory bench or political work into an engineering institute at the beginning of the industrialization program), the differences between the groups are even more striking. Even the practice of selecting new ministers from among the men who graduated in the early 1930's meant that with the passage of each year the new ministers came to their posts with ever larger amounts of administrative experience. Many of those becoming ministers in the 1950's had remained in more technical posts such as chief engineer or in design or research work until the age of forty.

Moreover, by the 1950's the men rising to ministerial rank increasingly came to have characteristics indicating that political factors were becoming even less of an influence on promotion within the industrial hierarchy. The significance of the later age of Party admission is self-evident, but the combination of a later date of birth and a constant date of college graduation is also quite important from this point of view. It signifies that the new ministers had spent a considerably shorter period in political or factory work before beginning their engineering training. For some, this period of work may have been little more than an expedient to gain the proletariat background necessary for college admission in the 1920's.

A similar development also took place at lower levels of the industrial hierarchy. Biographical information available on thirty-three men who became deputy ministers in the 1950's indicates that these men had much the same background as the new ministers.[24] On the average, they had been born in 1908, had graduated from an engineering institute in 1934, and had become Party members at the age of twenty-eight.

The plant directors of the ministerial period are as difficult to summarize as were those of 1941, and information about them is very scanty for reliable statistical analysis. However, examination of the biographies of the directors of 170 of the largest plants reveals evidence of the same type of growing professionalism observable in the ministries.[25] The 1941 directors of these plants tended to remain at the same administrative level well into the postwar period, but in the late 1940's and early 1950's many of them (at least many of those not in the iron and steel industry) were replaced. Thus, in January 1953 only 32 percent of the directors of the largest 170 plants had occupied their post for five years or more: 61 percent in the iron and steel industry, 25 percent in other industries.[26] In some cases the old directors were promoted into the ministries, in other cases they were moved to the directorships of lesser plants, in still other cases they have disappeared from public view.

Whatever the fate of the old directors, they often were replaced by men with a rather different life pattern. Biographies have been found of twenty-one men who became directors at the 170 plants between 1947 and 1952, and sixteen of them have similar enough biographies to be considered a type — a type we will call the "post-revolutionary professionals." [27] These sixteen men were in the age group just below that of those who had benefited most spectacularly from the Purge: none was older than thirty-three in 1938, and ten were twenty-eight or younger. All had entered the Party after the Purge (at an average age of thirty-one), and their promotion during the Purge often was not rapid. These new directors usually had little (if any) work experience prior to entering an institute, and the younger of them had received their engineering education in the mid-1930's when the curriculum had become technologically more rigorous.[28]

The "post-revolutionary professionals" were not a temporary phenomenon of the Stalin era. Biographies are available of eighteen men who first became director of one of the 170 plants in the four years between Stalin's death and the creation of the sovnarkhozy. Sixteen of these men correspond to the pattern of the "post-revolutionary professionals." Each was born between 1903 and 1917 (over two-thirds between 1908 and 1913); each entered the Party after the Purge at the average age of 32 (none before the age of 26).[29]

Unfortunately, there is not any really good evidence as to the personality structure of the new plant manager in the postwar period. However, the experiences of a man born after 1910 and joining the Party after 1938 could be quite different from those of one who, for example, was born in 1904 and joined the Party in 1926. The former was likely to have had a far smoother political socialization and might well have avoided many of the dysfunctional insecurities often associated with a transitional period.[30] It could be hypothesized that the new director probably would be able to grow up taking the political system more or less for granted, would be better able to identify with his profession and its demands, would be more concerned with technological questions, and would be a more secure administrator. Although he might be even more disturbed by the central obsession with growth at all costs than were the Red Directors and the Men of 1938, one cannot forget that he had accepted administrative work (rather than a technical position) at a time when the Stalin priorities and the imperatives of these priorities were abundantly clear.

Although a great many plant managers had a less impressive background than the newer directors of the largest plants, the rising level

Table 3. Background of obkom first secretaries, November 1952.[a]

Officials	Average year of birth	Average age of entry into Party	Proportion with engineering education
First secretaries of most industrialized oblasti, RSFSR and the Ukraine (N = 25)	1905 (N = 21)	22 (N = 20)	8 of 18
First secretaries of most important agricultural oblasti, RSFSR (N = 25)	1907 (N = 20)	24 (N = 18)	4 of 17
First secretaries of other oblasti, RSFSR and the Ukraine (Approximate N = 55)	1907 (N = 26)	22 (N = 25)	5 of 23
First secretaries of other oblasti (Approximate N = 67)	1910 (N = 28)	25 (N = 28)	1 of 26

[a] The most industrialized and most important agricultural oblasti are selected as described in notes 4 and 5. Unlike Table 1, however, this table is based upon a selection of oblasti from the 1959 census.

of professional competence among the more important managers was surely the major factor behind the simultaneous Soviet policy of increasing the levels of technical competence of local Party officials.

At first glance it might seem that the technical qualifications of the Party officials concerned with industry were not much higher in the postwar period than they had been in 1941. At the time of the Nineteenth Party Congress, for example, a chart summarizing basic background information on the obkom first secretaries looks little different from a chart dealing with the secretaries of 1941.

In the years after Stalin's death there was a fairly substantial turnover among the obkom first secretaries. The new obkom first secretaries tended to be somewhat younger, and some had a more substantial technical education than their predecessors. Yet, on the eve of the creation of the sovnarkhozy, the overall level of their formal technical training was still not impressive.

Table 4. Background of obkom first secretaries, April 1957.[a]

Officials	Average year of birth	Average age of entry into Party	Proportion with engineering education
First secretaries of most industrialized oblasti, RSFSR and the Ukraine (N = 25)	1909 (N = 22)	23 (N = 22)	12 of 22
First secretaries of most important agricultural oblasti, RSFSR (N = 25)	1909 (N = 25)	24 (N = 25)	6 of 25
First secretaries of other oblasti, RSFSR and the Ukraine (N = 57)	1908 (N = 47)	24 (N = 47)	8 of 47
First secretaries of other oblasti (N = 48)	1911 (N = 34)	25 (N = 33)	2 of 33

[a] The basic categories of this table are defined as before. The biographies of most of the 1957 obkom first secretaries can be found in *Deputaty Verkhovnogo Soveta* (1958).

As late as 1955, even the Party officials who specialized in industrial questions included a surprisingly large number of persons without technical education. As Bulganin complained in calling for an improvement in the situation at the July 1955 plenum of the Central Committee, "The industrial departments of the Party organs are frequently staffed by inexperienced officials, who do not have the necessary technical and economic knowledge and who cannot deeply analyze the work of the enterprises." [31] In Leningrad only seven of the twenty-two heads of the industrial-transportation departments of the raikomy had higher or secondary specialized education. Similarly, there were but ten engineers and ten technicians among the fifty-three officials of the industrial-transportation departments of the gorkomy and raikomy in Voroshilovgrad (later Lugansk) oblast.[32]

However, although these general statistics about the Party officials of the late ministerial period are undoubtedly accurate, it is possible to be seriously misled by them. (Any reader of the disssertation on which this book is based can testify that I am not speaking of a hypothetical possibility.) When one closely examines the Party secretariats in the more urbanized areas, the levels of industrial expertise turn out to be much more substantial than appears on the surface.

Although the data on the obkom first secretaries in the industrialized oblasti in Tables 1 and 3 show little change from 1941 to 1952, there are still significant differences among these officials in the two periods. Only five of the 1952 secretaries in the industrialized oblasti had been first secretaries in 1941, and the engineers among the new first secretaries had a rather different background than the engineering first secretaries of 1941. They normally had not entered Party work directly from the institute; rather, they came from among those engineers who had been transferred to lower Party work after a period of engineering work in industry. This work experience might have been quite short (two years as a design engineer in the case of A. P. Kirilenko), but it could be much more substantial (for example, V. K. Klimenko had spent six years in industry, rising to the directorship of a factory). In addition, the engineers — as well as most of the first secretaries in these oblasti without an engineering education — had worked for years in lower Party work in industrialized areas, work (as will be seen) entailing very great involvement with detailed industrial problems.[33]

By 1957 the leadership was making an even more systematic effort to ensure that the obkom first secretaries in the ten to fifteen most industrialized oblasti had substantial experience with industry and, in most cases, an engineering degree. If one looks at the twelve oblasti where 60 percent of the population is urban and where the urban sector totals at least one million persons,[34] one finds that in 1957 nine first secretaries had an engineering education and the other three had long experience in urban Party work. (In 1941 five of the secretaries in these twelve oblasti are known to have had engineering training, four are known not to have had it, and information is not available on three of them. In 1952 there are seven with such education, three without it, and two on whom no information is available.)

As in 1941, the lower Party secretaries of the mid-1950's often had far more managerial experience than the obkom first secretaries. The statistics on the Party secretaries in Leningrad and Voroshilovgrad certainly raise doubts about the technical qualifications of many of the lower Party officials, but the Party leadership seems to have followed the policy of ensuring that every first secretary in an industrialized oblast had at least one man in his "team" who had been a major industrial administrator.

The available biographical information is too limited to provide a definitive analysis of the background of lower Party officials dealing with industry, but the widespread use of former industrial administrators in the Party apparatus is easy to document. In early 1957, a former plant director, an industrial or construction deputy minister, or an industrial or construction minister can be identified in the secretariat of nine of fourteen republican central committees.[35] In two other republics a former republican industrial minister can be found in the secretariat of the capital gorkom or obkom. Although even less information is available about the lower obkom secretaries in the RSFSR and the Ukraine, former plant managers can be identified in the secretariats of ten of the twenty-five most industrialized oblasti and former shop heads (or roughly equivalent officials) from major plants in nearly all of the other fifteen oblasti.[36]

In many areas the number of high Party officials with technical experience was fairly high, particularly if the obkom, gorkom, and urban raikomy are considered as a collective unit (and in an oblast center they should be so considered, at least with respect to the larger plants). As one statistic has already been cited on the Leningrad situation, it is worthwhile to continue with an examination of the important Leningrad Party officials who dealt with industry at that time (the summer of 1955). The obkom first secretary (F. R. Kozlov) was an engineer with three years of low-level supervisory work in a metallurgical plant; the gorkom first secretary (I. K. Zamchevskii) had been the Party organizer of the Central Committee (*Partorg TsK*) at the Moscow Aviation Works No. 1 at the beginning of the war. The industrial secretary of the obkom (I. V. Spiridonov) had been in "leading economic work" from 1927 to 1950 with the last eleven of these years being spent as plant manager at three different enterprises. The second secretary of the gorkom (N. N. Rodionov) had for seven years been head of a sector at the Magnitogorsk Metallurgy Combine and head of a laboratory at a Leningrad research institute. The industrial secretary of the gorkom (S. P. Mitrofanov) had twelve years of managerial experience at the giant Leningrad State Optics-Mechanical Works. Few biographies of the raikom secretaries have been uncovered, but at this level, too, there could be found a former chief power specialist at a major textile plant, a former deputy chief engineer at the Izhorski Ship Works (who had been at the plant for eighteen years), and a former plant director.[37]

One of the most interesting facts about these Leningrad officials with managerial experience is the diversity of their industrial specialties. This diversity seems to represent a conscious policy of the leadership, for it was not peculiar to Leningrad. (For example, in 1955 the Stalino obkom had three secretaries with managerial experience: one came from the oblast's largest steel plant, one from its largest machine-building plant, and one from a coal mine.)[38] The intention of the leadership was apparently to ensure that a technical proposal or complaint about a plant in one of the major industries in an area could be referred to a Party official who had special competence to evaluate it and who would have the stature needed to give his evaluation and advice authority.

As long as the local Party organs had such men, the leadership (prior to 1955 at least) did not seem too concerned if the staff assistants of the secretaries did not always have technical expertise. After all, if there were many reports to be filled out, many decisions to be drafted, and many speeches to be written, there was much to recommend a policy of selecting staff assistants "on the basis of whether [they] could collect facts and compile reports . . . [in short, on the basis of] an ability to write." [39]

The levels of engineering-industrial experience found among lower Party officials at the end of the ministerial period was the end-product of a long-term trend, not the result of a crash program launched after the July 1955 plenum of the Central Committee. All the Leningrad and Stalino Party officials mentioned held their jobs prior to that plenum, and, indeed, most of them had been directed to Party work in the last three years of the Stalin period. Although managerial personnel attracted into specialized Party posts during the war continued to comprise by far the largest group among the Party's industrial specialists during the first postwar years, men continued to be transferred directly from industry into Party work throughout the postwar period. This practice became particularly pronounced after Khrushchev's appointment to the Central Committee secretariat in December 1949.

The Sovnarkhoz Period

The trends toward increased technical competence within both the industrial and the Party hierarchies were not interrupted by the industrial reorganization of 1957. To be sure, the creation of the sovnarkhozy resulted in a very considerable shake-up within the industrial sphere, for the officials of the abolished ministries were scattered throughout the country. However, it would be incorrect to accept uncritically either Western speculation about Khrushchev's desire to destroy the ministerial officials as a political force or post-Khrushchev criticism about the level of technical knowledge in the sovnarkhozy. Whatever may be the validity of these propositions from certain points of view,[40] the ministerial officials were not removed from the industrial scene, and the top-level supervisors of Gosplan and the sovnarkhozy were men with much the same experience and technical training as the ministerial officials.

Indeed, the men who came to occupy the top posts in the USSR, RSFSR, and Ukrainian gosplany and in the sovnarkhozy were to a very large extent the same men who occupied the top posts in the ministries. Nearly all of the twenty-four ministers whose ministries were abolished were given strategic industrial positions in the sovnarkhoz period.[41] Of the 105 men who can be identified as deputy ministers in these ministries in 1956 and 1957, over 85 percent were in high planning or administrative posts during the sovnarkhoz period, and this percentage might be higher if data on the other 15 percent were available.[42]

After the reorganization, the All-Union and republican gosplany came to occupy much the same role for the obkomy as had the industrial ministries earlier. The republican gosplany began to participate in industrial planning in a totally unaccustomed manner, and the USSR Gosplan was transformed from an institution that confined itself largely to coordination of the plans of the different ministries into one that formulated the plan for each branch of industry and played the key role in appropriating the funds for it. It was the officials of the various gosplany who came to represent the interests of the branch industries in 1957, and they were an especially impressive group of highly trained industrial administrators.

In proposing the creation of the sovnarkhozy, Khrushchev had stated that "in terms of their preparation and experience the leaders of the basic departments of the USSR Gosplan should be on the level of the present ministers," [43] and he had not spoken idly. A Party official (the head of the machinebuilding department of the Party Central Committee) was selected as the new chairman of the USSR Gosplan, but the deputy chairmen and the leaders of the departments included at least seven former USSR ministers and at least sixteen former USSR deputy ministers.

The republican gosplany also came to be major centers of industrial expertise. Former USSR ministers were appointed chairman and first deputy chairman of the RSFSR Gosplan, and at least fourteen former deputy USSR ministers were named to other leading posts within it. In the Ukraine, the Gosplan contained one former USSR minister, two former USSR deputy ministers, five deputy chairmen of the Ukrainian Council of Ministers, and six Ukrainian ministers.[44]

With the passage of time the central and republican industrial apparatus became much more complex. In 1960 the USSR Gosplan was split into a State Economic Council (*Gosekonsovet*) for long-range planning and a Gosplan for short-range planning, and at that time republican sovnarkhozy were created in the RSFSR, the Ukraine, and Kazakhstan. In 1962 the leadership began to create a large number of state committees to supervise technical policy in each of the branch industries, and the USSR Gosplan was transformed into the USSR sovnarkhoz. (At this time the long-range planning organ, the State Economic Council, was given the name Gosplan.) [45] In 1963 a Supreme Economic Council was formed to coordinate the work of all these organizations.[46]

The administrative system resulting from the reorganizations was a rather chaotic one, but it did involve substantial expansion in the number of highly experienced industrial administrators concentrated in the center. Many of the ministers and deputy ministers previously sent into the economic regions were recalled to the capital. Thus, by the fall of 1963 there were nineteen former USSR industrial and construction ministers who occupied administrative posts of sufficient stature to earn them a seat on the Council of Ministers.[47]

Of the eleven chairmen and deputy chairmen of the USSR Supreme Economic Council, Gosplan, and Sovnarkhoz among the 1963 Council of Ministers members, five had been ministers prior to 1957, four had been deputy ministers, and one had been a deputy chairman of Gosplan. Of twenty-six chairmen of state committees in the industrial and construction fields, eight had been USSR ministers prior to 1957, ten had been USSR deputy ministers, and another six had risen to a post above that of plant manager. The average year of birth of these 1963 Council of Ministers members was only two years later than that of the 1957 ministers (1908 versus 1906), the average age at which they joined the Party was but one year later (twenty-eight versus twenty-seven). They were drawn from all the groups of peoples' commissars and ministerial officials discussed earlier, and their early backgrounds were rather diverse (Table 5).

Table 5. Date of birth and age of Party admission of top industrial administrators, 1957 and 1963.[a]

Officials		Age of Party admission		
		26 and under	Over 26	Total
1957				
Industrial and con-	1893–1908	15	8	23
struction ministries	1909–1914	2	3	5
(based on 28 of 33				
ministries)				
	Total	17	11	28
1963				
Industrial and con-	1898–1908	16	12	28
struction members	1909–1916	1	13	14
of the Council of				
Ministers (based on				
42 of 44 officials)				
	Total	17	25	42

[a] N. A. Obolenski, the Chairman of the State Committee for Electronics, is included among the 44 officials of the Council of Ministers even though at the time of the publication of the 1963 Yearbook of the *Bolshaia sovetskaia entsiklopediia* (the source of the list of officials) his State Committee apparently did not confer membership in the Council of Ministers.

The creation of the sovnarkhozy did not greatly change the technical authority of the industrial officials with whom the local Party organs dealt in the center, but it did result in an influx of many highly experienced industrial administrators into the provinces. Consequently, the local Party organs faced a much more severe problem in maintaining their authority over the industrial establishment they were required to supervise.

Like the higher Gosplan officials, the sovnarkhoz chairmen were nearly all selected from among the most experienced officials of the industrial hierarchy. Information is available on 97 of the 105 sovnarkhoz chairmen appointed in June 1957. These men included: eight USSR ministers, thirty USSR deputy ministers, nine lower ministerial officials (usually heads of glavki), eight deputy chairmen of a republican council of ministers, sixteen republican ministers, six republican deputy ministers, fourteen directors of plants or combines (almost always men with a decade of experience at this level), and six Party officials.[48] Hence, it is not surprising that the average year of their birth (1908) and the average age at which they entered the Party (28) is almost identical with that of the ministers and deputy ministers of the 1950's.[49]

The sovnarkhoz chairmen came from nearly all major branches of industry: 26 percent from light industry; 10 to 13 percent from the coal, defense, machinery, and metallurgical industries; 4 to 7 percent from the automobile-agricultural machinery, construction, oil, timber, and transportation machinery industries. In the twenty-five most industrialized oblasti, twenty-three of the chairmen came from heavy industry, sixteen from the USSR ministries. At least sixteen of the twenty-five sovnarkhozy also had at least one former USSR deputy minister among their deputy chairmen. In almost all cases, the sovnarkhoz chairmen were assigned to economic regions in which one of the major industries (and usually the major industry) corresponded to their particular specialized background. For example, the USSR Minister of the Coal Industry headed the sovnarkhoz in Kemerovo, the RSFSR Minister of the Fish Industry became sovnarkhoz chairman in Murmansk, and deputy ministers of the USSR Ministry of Oil Industry were named sovnarkhoz chairmen in Azerbaidzhan, Bashkiria, and the Chechen-Ingush republic.

The appointment of top administrators to the post of sovnarkhoz chairmen was not a short-lived policy. Three years later over 70 percent of the 1957 sovnarkhoz chairmen in the RSFSR and the Ukraine remained in the same post, and over one half of those removed had been promoted.[50] Over one third of the newly appointed chairmen were former USSR ministers or deputy ministers, and nearly all of the others had been enterprise directors for a considerable period prior to 1957.

After the creation of the republican sovnarkhozy in the summer of 1960, an increasing number of the original sovnarkhoz chairmen were recalled to Moscow or Kiev. Their replacements were normally younger men (average date of birth — 1911) who had not progressed beyond the level of plant manager in 1957. Information is available on twenty-seven sovnarkhoz chairmen appointed in 1960 or later. While seven were men with many years in soviet and party work and two others had shorter periods of work as obkom secretaries specializing in industry, the other eighteen had the classic career-pattern of the professional industrial administrator. The latter eighteen chairmen had joined the Party at the average age of 31, the other nine at the average age of 28.[51]

At the plant level the degree of experience and technical expertise among the top managerial officials remained much the same as it had been in the mid-1950's. A number of directors were promoted into sovnarkhozy, but the turnover among the managers of the most important plants was surprisingly small considering the requirements of staffing the sovnarkhozy and the support that the top managers are sometimes thought to have given Malenkov in his struggle with Khrushchev. On January 1, 1962, 56 percent of the directors of the 170 most important plants had been in their post for five years or more (that is, since before the creation of the sovnarkhozy), and another 7 percent had held it for four and a half years (that is, since the summer of 1957). If we exclude the thirty plants in the automobile and agricultural machinery industries (at least 40 percent of which had their directors promoted into high posts in the sovnarkhozy), the proportion of directors with at least five years tenure rises to 64 percent, the proportion with at least four-and-a-half years tenure to 70 percent.

The creation of the sovnarkhozy produced relatively few changes in the patterns of technical preparation among the plant managers. There was much talk of replacing the *praktiki* (men without technical experience but often with long industrial experience) among the directors of the small plants, but no more than slow progress was made in this realm. Even in Leningrad and Moscow only one half of the plant directors had higher education as late as 1963.[52] It should be noted, however, that even in *krupnyi* (significant) industry, 66.6 percent of the plants had 100 workers or less in 1955 and an additional 13.9 percent had between 101 and 250 workers.[53] It is undoubtedly here that the vast majority of the praktiki were to be found.

In the plants where the fate of the industrialization drive was being decided, the directors seem almost always to have had an engineering education.[54] It was possible to find the biographies of fifty of the men who managed the 170 most important plants during the

Table 6. Tenure of directors at a given plant, January 1, 1962, in the 170 most important plants.[a]

Type of plant	Years as director at the plant				
	0–3	3–5	5–10	Over 10	Unknown
Iron and steel (N = 30)	6	2	10	9	3
Auto and agricultural machinery (N = 30)	14	6	5	1	4
Transportation machinery (N = 15)	4	2	5	3	1
Other machinery and machine tools (N = 30)	3	4	8	3	12
Electrotechnical (N = 20)	3	4	4	5	4
Chemistry (N = 15)	5	0	3	5	2
Miscellaneous heavy industry (N = 15)	2	0	6	3	4
Miscellaneous light industry (N = 15)	2	1	3	2	7
Total (N = 170)	39	19	44	31	37

[a] The names of the plants and the methodology for selecting them can be found in Appendix B.

The table refers to total tenure at the plant, not uninterrupted tenure. Two of the directors of the steel plants had their tenure at a plant broken by a few years of work in the sovnarkhoz.

In 15 percent of the cases it was possible to determine only that a director had been at a plant for more or less than five years. In these cases, extrapolation was used to place the director in a more precise category. If it was impossible to determine whether a director had a tenure of five years, the plant was placed in the "unknown" category.

sovnarkhoz period and all but one was an engineer. I have found forty-eight biographies of directors of other important heavy industry plants during this period (the availability of the biography is one indication that the plant is important), and they reveal that forty-six of these men were graduate engineers. The sixty-seven for whom age of Party admission is known joined the Party at the average age of 29. Of those born after 1907 88 percent were admitted into the Party at the age of 26 or later.

The directors of the largest plants in particular were overwhelmingly men in their late forties and their fifties — men with two to three decades of experience in industrial management. The year of birth is known for fifty-three of the directors of the 170 most important plants in 1958. Forty-seven percent were 50 or over, and another 42 percent were in the 45 to 49 age range. Despite Khrushchev's announced policy of appointing younger officials, an examination of the year of birth of fifty-five directors of the 170 most important plants in 1963 reveals that 75 percent were 50 and over, and that another 16 percent were between 45 and 50. In the five years the proportion of those 55 and over had risen from 13 percent to 35 percent. A small sample of unknown reliability suggests that the directors in the less important plants were on the average younger than in the most important plants, but that their average age had also risen from 1958 to 1963.

Although the creation of the sovnarkhozy changed the type of Soviet industrial administrator relatively little, it had a much more dramatic impact on the Party officials dealing with industrial questions. In the most industrialized oblasti, the proportion of the obkom first secretaries with technical training increased sharply.

Table 7. Distribution of plant managers by year of birth, 1958 and 1963.

Year of birth	170 most important plants		Other plants	
	1958 (N = 53) [a]	1963 (N = 55) [a]	1958 (N = 35)	1963 (N = 34)
Before 1904	13	9	20	9
1904–1908	34	26	20	18
1909–1913	42	40	20	18
1914–1918	9	16	26	35
1919 and later	2	9	14	20

[a] If a change of directors occurred in 1958 or 1963 and the biographies of both directors are known, both have been included. This occurred in two cases — in 1958 and in 1963.

Table 8. Background of obkom first secretaries in the twenty-five most industrialized oblasti, April 1957 and September 1962.

Officials	Average year of birth	Average age of entry into Party	Proportion with engineering education
First secretaries of most industrialized oblasti, April 1957 (N = 25)	1909 (N = 22)	23 (N = 22)	12 of 22
First secretaries of most industrialized oblasti, September 1962 (N = 25)	1914 (N = 25)	26 (N = 25)	19 of 25 [a]

[a] In addition, one of the 1962 nonengineers was a university physics and mathematics major who had worked in industrial administration until the age of 40, rising to the post of plant director. Another of the nonengineers had completed three years in an industrial academy and had a decade of experience in industrial management, rising to the level of shop head and then chief power specialist.

The most striking changes occurred in those oblasti having both a large urban and a large rural population.

Table 9. Proportion of obkom first secretaries with engineering education in oblasti with over one million urban population.[a]

Date	Percentage of oblast's urban population	
	Over 60 percent (N = 12)	50–59 percent (N = 9)
September 1952	7 of 10	0 of 6
April 1957	9 of 12	2 of 8
September 1962	8 of 12	6 of 9 [b]

[a] This chart is based on the 1959 census. The twelve oblasti in the "over 60 percent" category are Cheliabinsk, Dnepropetrovsk, Donetsk (formerly Stalino), Irkutsk, Kemerovo, Kharkov, Kuibyshev, Leningrad, Lugansk (formerly Voroshilovgrad), Moscow, Sverdlovsk, and Tula. The nine oblasti in the "50–59 percent" category are Gorki, Kiev, Krasnoiarsk, Novosibirsk, Perm (formerly Molotov), Rostov, Saratov, Tashkent, and Volgograd (formerly Stalingrad).

[b] As in Table 8, one of the nonengineers in the "50–59 category" in 1962 was a former plant manager with a physics-mathematics background.

In one such oblast (Saratov) the change of first secretary was color-fully explained by Khrushchev himself. The first secretary of the Sara-tov obkom was Georgii Denisov, a Party official with little education who had headed oblast Party organizations in rural areas for at least fifteen years,[55] and at the July 1959 plenum of the Central Committee Khrushchev criticized him directly:

> Last year the Saratov people [that is, the Party leaders] con-ducted the grain harvest wonderfully, and they fulfilled the state plan for grain with great success. But, surely, you have not prop-erly concerned yourselves with industry. You know how many calves and how many milkmaids there are in the oblast, but you do not have a good idea about the kind of machines that are produced in Saratov or the way in which they are produced. Com-rades, in saying this, I do not want to belittle the role of milk-maids. I think that you will not suspect me of this. But you can-not become absorbed in agriculture and the development of live-stock and suck milk like a calf who does not know that this re-quires metal, coal, and machines. Without these things there will be no milk.
>
> It is necessary to treat this lopsidedness, this swollen cheek. Earlier, in treating swollen cheeks, people resorted to a home remedy — hot packs made of bran. And this helped. I don't know what kind of hot packs are necessary now, but obviously they are needed even in our conditions. Think about this, com-rades. We in the Central Committee will think over the solution of this question, for it is impossible to leave it as it is.[56]

In less than six weeks the second secretary of the obkom, a man who had been a plant manager until the age of forty, was named first secretary, and Denisov was sent to Moscow to head the agriculture department of the Central Committee for the union republics.[57]

The new first secretary in Saratov was but one representative of a different type of industrial administrator who became obkom first secretary after the creation of the sovnarkhozy. Many of the engineer first secretaries in the twenty-five most industrialized oblasti had en-tered Party work before or during the war, but twelve of them had remained in the industrial hierarchy into the postwar period. Seven of them had risen to the level of enterprise director and had been transferred to Party work only in the early 1950's (or in one case, in 1961).[58]

The obkom first secretaries with a substantial managerial background had early biographies more similar to those of the new plant directors of the late 1940's than to those of the engineers who had entered Party work in the prewar or early World War II period. Those obkom first secretaries transferred from industry into Party work after 1942 had on the average been born in 1914 and had joined the Party in 1942.

To be sure, not all the obkom first secretaries had the technical experience of those in the most industrialized oblasti. Indeed, in the other oblasti the number of graduate engineers among the obkom first secretaries actually declined from 1957 to 1962.

Although many obkom first secretaries still were not industrial specialists, the Party officials specializing in industry continued to be

Table 10. Background of rural obkom first secretaries, April 1957 and September 1962.

Officials	Year	Average year of birth	Average age of entry into Party	Proportion with engineering education
First secretaries of most important agricultural oblasti, RSFSR	1957 (N = 25)	1909 (N = 25)	24 (N = 25)	6 of 25
	1962 (N = 25)	1914 (N = 25)	24 (N = 25)	3 of 25
First secretaries of other non-industrial oblasti, RSFSR and Ukraine	1957 (N = 57)	1908 (N = 47)	24 (N = 47)	8 of 47
	1962 (N = 52)	1912 (N = 52)	24 (N = 52)	7 of 52
First secretaries, oblasti of other republics	1957 (N = 48)	1911 (N = 34)	25 (N = 33)	2 of 33
	1962 (N = 41)	1915 (N = 39)	25 (N = 38)	4 of 38

chosen from among those with higher levels of technical competence. In the union republics (where the available information is most complete), this phenomenon is particularly noticeable. Only three of the republican first secretaries in September 1962 were engineers, but lower officials in the republican capital had a much more impressive background. Career data has been found on twelve of the men who were industrial secretaries in the republics at this time, and nine of them can be identified as having risen above the plant director level in industrial or construction administration.[59] The other three included a former plant director, a head of a geological expedition, and an engineer who had been in Party-industrial work since 1938.

Biographical information on the obkom secretaries for industry is very limited, but there is no reason to believe that these men were less qualified in 1962 than they had been in early 1957. For example, in Sverdlovsk, Cheliabinsk, and Dnepropetrovsk (where the first secretaries had left industrial administration while still far below the directoral level), one of the lower obkom secretaries had headed a coal or iron ore trust (or combine) as late as 1955.[60] In Kharkov and Karaganda (where the first secretary had been a high industrial administrator), one of the lower obkom secretaries had been Party secretary at a major enterprise and was in lower managerial work prior to that time.[61] There is no way of knowing whether it was usual to name an engineer with high managerial experience and one with longer Party experience to the obkom secretariat in an industrialized oblast, but this pattern is a logical one in many ways.

One reason to suspect a rising level of technical competence among the obkom secretaries specializing in industry is the very striking rise in technical competence occurring among their counterparts in the gorkomy and urban raikomy. Because these lower officials were usually selected by the obkomy, the leadership felt compelled to enunciate its policy with respect to them at Party gatherings, and this policy was quite clear-cut. In the words of Aleksei Kirichenko, "At the present time life has brought forward the demand that there be more specialists and experts of different branches of the economy among the supervisory Party, Soviet, economic, and trade union personnel. . . . For example, in a city where machinebuilding is the predominant industry, it is important that the gorkom secretary either be a specialist in the field or an experienced machinebuilder (*praktik-mashino-stroitel*) who knows his business well." [62]

This is one situation in which actual practice corresponded closely to announced policy. By 1959 it was asserted both in Kharkov and Leningrad that "almost everywhere [in the Party apparatus] the people dealing with industrial questions have a technical education." [63] In Kharkov, with nine raiony, sixteen of the raikom secretaries were engineers; [64] in Leningrad, with twenty-one raiony, there were thirty-three engineers among the raikom secretaries. [65]

In the less important industrial centers, the percentage of engineers among the Party secretaries was apparently not as great as in Kharkov and Leningrad. Even in Dnepropetrovsk oblast only twelve of the nineteen first secretaries of the gorkomy and the urban raikomy (and a similar number of the second secretaries) were engineers in 1959. [66] Yet these statistics themselves are not unimpressive, and the percentage of engineers among the Party secretaries clearly rose even further after 1959.

There is little information about the level of technical qualifications among the instructors, but in Leningrad, at least, the 1955 criticism of the industrial-transportation department officials was taken to heart. In 1958 the various industrial departments of the Leningrad gorkom had twenty-five responsible officials, twenty-three of whom were engineers and two, technicians. The seven responsible officials of the industrial-transportation department of the Lenin raikom included six engineers and one technician, and an analogous situation is said to have existed in the other important industrial raiony of the city. [67]

There are, of course, great variations in the technical qualifications and administrative experience of men with an engineering diploma. Some of those entering Party work in the sovnarkhoz period had become Komsomol secretary of their engineering institute (perhaps after political work in the army during the war) and had either spent years in Komsomol work or had been directed to organizational-political posts in the Party apparatus. For example, the first secretary of the Moscow gorkom from 1961 through 1966 (N. G. Egorychev) and the first secretary of the Kiev gorkom from 1960 to 1962 (V. I. Drozdenko) both fit this pattern. [68]

Whereas these "political engineers" were found fairly frequently among the gorkom first secretaries and the organizational secretaries of the Party committees, they were quite rare among the officials specializing in industry. Little information is available on the background of the instructor or the raikom secretary for industry, but the gorkom secretary for industry often had very substantial managerial experience. In the union republics, for example, significant administrative personnel can be identified among the secretaries in eleven of the capital gorkomy in 1962. They included six factory managers (all at important plants in the city), three high construction administrators, one high railway administrator, and one plant chief engineer. Many of the men with this background were given the power and status of the first secretary.

In November 1962, the bifurcation of the Party apparatus created conditions in which Khrushchev's policy of increasing the technical qualifications of Party secretaries could be carried through to completion. A year after the reorganization, eighty-two of eighty-four first and second secretaries of industrial obkomy and kraikomy in the RSFSR were industrial specialists. In Kemerovo oblast fifty of the eighty-four secretaries of the gorkomy and urban raikomy had higher technical education.[69] Since one third of the secretaries handled ideological matters and would not be expected to be engineers, the percentage of engineers among the first secretaries and organizational secretaries was quite high even at this level.

There is no comprehensive information about the type of engineers selected to work in the industrial Party organs, but the first secretaries of industrial obkomy were selected from posts normally staffed by men with substantial technical experience. Thus of the forty-two first secretaries in the RSFSR, eight had been obkom first secretaries immediately prior to assuming their new position, eighteen had been lesser obkom secretaries (at least five of them second secretary and at least three lower secretaries specializing in industry), four had been oblispolkom chairmen, three had been sovnarkhoz officials, three had been gorkom first secretaries, and one had been a gorispolkom chairman.[70] (The earlier position of five cannot be identified.) More complete biographical information is available on twenty-four first secretaries of the industrial obkomy, and of this group twelve had once been director of an enterprise and twelve had never held this post.

In the Ukraine, a greater percentage of first secretaries of industrial obkomy (eight of nineteen) had been obkom first secretary prior to the reorganization, and only two of the eleven industrial first secretaries for whom biographies are available had reached the level of enterprise director.[71]

Almost no biographical information is available about the men who became gorkom, raikom, and zonal production committee first secretaries in the larger republics after 1962, but in the smaller republics a substantial number of gorkom first secretaries in the medium-sized cities had been enterprise managers directly prior to assuming their Party post. This pattern was not universal, and some of the larger cities (for instance, Tallin and Tashkent) had a first secretary who was a young Komsomol official without either industrial or Party experience and, at least in the Tashkent case, without engineering education. (In such cities the secretaries specializing in industrial questions had managerial experience.)

Despite the number of managerial personnel transferred into the Party apparatus, during the sovnarkhoz period, the local Party organs still remained at somewhat of a disadvantage vis-à-vis the industrial hierarchy. The directors of the very largest plants still (with a few exceptions) were promoted into the sovnarkhoz rather than into the Party apparatus, and, as a consequence, the top industrial administrators had personal authority that the managers among the secretaries of the local Party organs usually could not match. The managers who entered Party work usually had directed plants that were important, but not quite important enough to give them reasonable hope of rising directly to the ministerial level. They often were men for whom responsible Party work might offer an attractive alternate route to higher levels.

Even more significant is the fact that the top administrators had a much larger staff than the secretaries. After Khrushchev's removal it was asserted that even a sovnarkhoz like Leningrad found it difficult to provide systematic guidance to the many industries under its control, despite a staff that probably numbered over a thousand men.[72] If so, the twenty-five officials of the industrial departments of the gorkom must have found it even harder to supervise the city's industry systematically.

The Post-Khrushchev Period

When one examines the personnel policy followed in the first years of the post-Khrushchev period, the first impression received is that of great continuity. When one looks, for example, at the obkom first secretaries on the 1966 Central Committee and Auditing Commission, one finds that over 70 percent of them were already at that level of the hierarchy by the fall of 1961 and that another 15 percent of them had become obkom first secretaries by the summer of 1963. This is a striking figure, particularly given earlier Soviet practice and the cataclysmic organizational and political changes which had occurred in this five year period. (In contrast, less than one third of the obkom secretaries on the 1961 committees had reached the level of obkom first secretary at the time of the Twentieth Party Congress in 1956.)

The stability in the ranks of the obkom first secretaries continued in the first two years following the Twenty-third Congress. Even after the oblast Party conferences in the winter of 1967–68 there had been only four changes among the first secretaries in the twenty-five most industrialized oblasti, and in one of the changes the first secretary in one of the twenty-five oblasti moved to another oblast in the group. The number of first secretaries removed in the other 59 oblasti (and autonomous republics) of the RSFSR was nine, and the number in the 60 other oblasti of the non-Russian republics was eight. As a result, the tenure of the average obkom first secretary on April 1, 1968, was much longer than it had been at comparable dates after the Nineteenth and Twentieth Party Congresses. Only in small part do the longer tenures shown in Table 11 result from the bifurcation of the Party apparatus. A very large majority of those with over five years tenure in 1968 had been first secretary of their obkom before November 1962.

Even when there were changes in personnel after the removal of Khrushchev, the level of technical competence of the Party officials showed relatively little decline, except perhaps among certain categories of officials. *Pravda* declared editorially that "knowledge of production and economics is as necessary to a Party official as air," [73] and the industrialized areas continued to have Party secretaries with an industrial background. In September 1962, nineteen of the obkom

Table 11. Tenure of obkom first secretaries (by percent).[a]

Oblasti	January 1, 1955	January 1, 1958	April 1, 1968
25 most industrialized oblasti			
0–1 year	12	36	8
1–3 years	44	16	28
3–5 years	24	24	16
Over 5 years	20	24	48
Other oblasti, RSFSR			
(N = 50–59)			
0–1 year	18	20	8
1–3 years	30	39	17
3–5 years	30	11	14
Over 5 years	22	30	61
Other oblasti, Ukraine			
(N = 17–18)			
0–1 year	18	6	6
1–3 years	53	47	28
3–5 years	29	6	6
Over 5 years	0	41	61
Oblasti of other republics			
(N = 36–45)			
0–1 year	21	13	11
1–3 years	48	48	17
3–5 years	18	18	30
Over 5 years	12	20	42

[a] Oblasti that had not existed for five years at a particular date were not included. A few oblasti (particularly in 1955) are not included because of lack of information.

first secretaries in the twenty-five most industrialized oblasti had an engineering education, and seven of them were former enterprise directors. In mid-1966, nineteen were engineers, two were graduates of a physics-mathematics department of a university, and two more graduates of industrial technicums. Nine were former enterprise directors.[74]

Five of the six first secretaries of the most industrialized oblasti who first reached this level during the post-Khrushchev period had an industrial background. One (Degtiarev) had been the chairman of the Donetsk sovnarkhoz (and head of a coal trust earlier); a second

Table 12. Background of obkom first secretaries, June 1966.

Officials	Average year of birth	Average age of entry into Party	Proportion with engineering education
First secretaries in most industrialized oblasti, RSFSR and the Ukraine (N = 25)	1916 (N = 25)	26 (N = 25)	19 of 25
First secretaries in most important agricultural oblasti, RSFSR (N = 25)	1914 (N = 25)	25 (N = 25)	4 of 25
First secretaries in other oblasti, RSFSR and the Ukraine (N = 52)	1914 (N = 52)	25 (N = 52)	11 of 52
First secretaries in other oblasti (N = 37)	1919 (N = 37)	25 (N = 37)	4 of 37

(Golovchenko) had been Party secretary at the Kharkov Tractor Works before becoming head of the machinebuilding department of the Ukrainian Central Committee (with eight years of managerial work before being named to his first Party post); a third (Vashchenko) had been Party secretary at the Kharkov Transportation Machinery Works (with twenty years prior technical-managerial work); a fourth (Katushev) had been Party secretary at the Gorki Auto Works (with six prior years of design work); and the fifth (Smirnov) had worked for twenty years in the textile industry, the last four as head of the glavk of the cotton textile industry of Ivanovo oblast. The sixth new secretary (Vsevolozhskii) in these oblasti had worked for approximately five years as a technician in industry, but the major part of his career was spent in the Komsomol and Party apparatus.[75]

In Leningrad, at least, the reunification of the Party brought no perceptible decline in the educational level of the lower Party officials. In 1965, all fifty-two secretaries of the raikomy in the city had higher education, and forty of them were "specialists of industry"; in the Leningrad obkom and gorkom all the instructors of the branch departments had "higher engineering-technical education." [76]

There is little comprehensive information about the gorkom and raikom officials in other cities or about the republican and obkom officials specializing in industry. Hence, it is impossible to make any conclusive comparisons between them and the men holding similar posts in the Khrushchev period. However, an examination of the biographies of the gorkom first secretaries in fourteen of the largest cities of the RSFSR and the Ukraine in 1966 reveals a very considerable technical expertise. Thirteen of these men were engineers, and only three of the fourteen were former Komsomol officials. Despite their relative youth (their average age was 44), nine had at least a decade of engineering-managerial experience in industry, construction, or railroad transportation before being transferred to Party work, four of them having been enterprise managers. The six named gorkom first secretary for the first time after Khrushchev's removal included four with at least a decade of industrial experience. [77]

In the other republics, the situation in 1966 was rather different. In twelve capital gorkomy (excluding Frunze because of lack of information), the first secretaries were younger (average age — 41), and only one had substantial managerial experience in industry. Four were Komsomol officials without engineering education; the others were men whose work experience had been predominantly in the Party apparatus — usually, to be sure, in Party posts basically oriented toward industry. [78]

However, if the republican capitals are at all typical, then one can say at a minimum that the leadership still seeks to ensure that each urban center has at least one secretary who has held a high managerial post in industry or construction. Both in Vilnius and Frunze the republican secretary for industry is a former republican minister of construction, but in Tashkent this secretary is a former director of a very large industrial enterprise. In Minsk the obkom second secretary once was a plant chief engineer, and in Erevan the gorkom second secretary is a former plant director, and so forth. (The number of managerial personnel among the Party officials in a republican capital is not necessarily limited to one; in Baku the republican secretary for industry is the former head of the Azerbaidzhan Oil Combine while the gorkom first secretary is a former plant manager.)

The one major change apparent in personnel policy involves the gorkom first secretaries. Frequently in the past, a plant director with little or no Party experience might be appointed directly to this post, a practice that now seems to have been largely abandoned. Of the nineteen men who were first selected gorkom first secretary in 1965 or 1966 (and whose biography is known), only two came directly from a managerial post, and only one had no previous Party experience.[79] A number of former managers among the gorkom first secretaries (particularly in the smaller cities) have been removed.[80] Such men, it is now stated, often had insufficient experience to handle the numerous nonindustrial duties of a first secretary.

Because there now exists a fairly large reservoir of former managerial personnel with considerable experience in Party work, the impact of this policy change has thus far been relatively limited, except probably in the gorkomy of the smaller cities. However, assuming that the industrial functions of the Party organs are not reduced (and it is likely that they will increase as — and if — authority is delegated from the ministries to the plants), there will be a need to infuse new technical expertise into the Party apparatus as time passes. It will be interesting to see how the problem is solved.

It may be that the leadership will choose to rely in large part on managerial personnel drawn into Party work at an earlier age — for example, shop heads, chief mechanics, or even lower officials who become Party secretaries in large plants and then move into higher Party work. Or perhaps they will draw first secretaries from among plant managers who have previous Party experience, ensuring that a sufficient number of managers have such experience. The new first secretary of the Kharkov gorkom, for instance, was director of the Kharkov Ballbearing Works immediately prior to being named gorkom secretary, but at an earlier stage of his career he had been a raikom secretary.[81] The new director of the Ulianovsk Auto Works is an engineer who had been raikom first secretary in one of the oblast's most important rural raiony, and conceivably his appointment represents an attempt to groom him for higher Party work.[82] Or perhaps the leadership will be less concerned with managerial experience among the first secretaries, being content to ensure that the secretary for industry has such experience and that more authority in industrial decision-making is delegated to him.

Whatever the career patterns of newly promoted Party officials, they continue to deal with plant and ministerial officials with long experience in industrial management. The pattern of stability in the ranks of the most senior industrial and construction administrators is particularly striking. Despite much talk of a new relationship between the ministries and the plants and of the increasing importance of economics in industrial decision-making, the new ministers were chosen from the same type of engineer-manager who had dominated the ministries for over two decades.

In fact, to a considerable extent, the new ministers were the very men who had held top posts in the ministries a decade earlier. Of the thirty-three USSR industrial and construction ministers appointed in the fall of 1965 (and without exception still in their post in February 1968), twelve had been USSR ministers in 1957. Another ten had risen to the level of deputy minister by that time, four had become glavk heads, and one was the RSFSR minister for his branch of industry. Two of the new ministers had been plant directors in 1957, one the head of an oil combine, one a plant chief engineer, one an obkom first secretary, and one the head of the construction department of the Central Committee.[83] Eighty-eight percent of the 1965 ministers had been at the level of enterprise director or higher for at least fifteen years, 55 percent for at least twenty years.[84] Surprisingly, the "post-revolutionary professional" who began rising into high industrial positions in the late 1940's still provided only 58 percent of the ministers, the others having biographies that correspond to earlier patterns. (Thirty-six percent of the 1957 ministers had the background of the "post-revolutionary professional." [85])

The continuity in the ranks of the ministers is reflected strikingly in the relative similarity of the early biographical data of the 1965 ministers and of that of their predecessors.

Very little information has been published about men becoming plant managers in the post-Khrushchev period, but in the 170 most important enterprises the directors usually remain men of very considerable experience. While the average tenure of the directors on Janu-

Table 13. Background of industrial and construction ministers, 1941–1965.[a]

Date	Average year of birth	Average age of entry into Party	Average year of college graduation
June 1941 (N = 28)	1901 (N = 23)	22 (N = 22)	1931 (N = 15)
March 1946 (N = 30)	1902 (N = 27)	22 (N = 26)	1931 (N = 18)
October 1952 (N = 28)	1904 (N = 27)	25 (N = 24)	1932 (N = 19)
April 1957 (N = 35)	1906 (N = 28)	27 (N = 28)	1933 (N = 23)
October 1965 (N = 33)	1909 (N = 33)	27 (N = 33)	1935 (N = 33)

[a] The Chairman of Gosstroi (the State Construction Committee) and the Chairman of the State Supply Committee (when it existed in 1952 and 1965) are included in these tables.

Those ministers who did not graduate from an institute are excluded from consideration in calculating the average year of graduation. There were 6 such men identified in 1941, 6 in 1946, none in 1952, 3 in 1957, and 2 in 1965. The two 1965 ministers without higher education — A. A. Ishkov and V. P. Zotov — had been ministers since before World War II (except for the period 1950–1953).

ary 1, 1967, was less than on January 1, 1962 (47 percent had spent at least five years as director of their plant, compared with 56 percent in 1962 [86]), this figure is not an accurate reflection of the trends with respect to the experience of these officials. Much of the managerial turnover had occurred at the time of the industrial reorganization in 1965, and a number of the "new" directors were men from the sovnarkhoz — men with even more substantial experience than their predecessors.

The age information available on forty-seven of the 1967 directors of the 170 most important plants suggests that the average age of these men continued to increase in the post-Khrushchev period. Eighty-one percent of these directors were at least fifty years old, compared with 47 percent in 1958 and 75 percent in 1962. Forty-nine percent were at least fifty-five years old, compared with 13 percent in 1958 and 35 percent in 1963.

Table 14. Age distribution of plant directors in the 170 most important plants (by percent).[a]

Age	1958 (N = 53)	1963 (N = 55)	1967 (N = 47)
60 and over	4	9	23
55–59	9	26	26
50–54	34	40	32
45–49	42	16	6
40–44	9	4	6
Under 40	2	5	6
Average age	49	52	54

[a] The four-year interval between 1963 and 1967 means that the 1967 percentages are based on different year of birth categories than those of 1958 and 1963 (for example, 1908–1912 rather than 1909–1913). Comparable categories would produce the following results for the 47 directors in 1967: Before 1904 — 4 percent; 1904–1908 — 21 percent; 1909–1913 — 28 percent; 1914–1918 — 28 percent; 1919 and over — 19 percent. (See Table 7.)

To some extent, the available data may exaggerate the percentage of older men among the 1967 directors. (A man who has been a director or sovnarkhoz official for a decade has had more of an opportunity to have his biography published in central sources.) However, much of the data was obtained from a source not subject to this particular bias — the directors elected to the USSR Supreme Soviet and those elected to the republican and oblast soviets in 25 oblasti.[87] An examination of the 134 directors in this sample reveals an age distribution for the directors of the largest plants which is very similar to that shown in Table 12, but a rather different age distribution for other directors, particularly those of the smaller plants.

As one examines the background of the senior industrial administrators, particularly the ministers, one wonders if these men have the flexibility to create a ministerial system in which the plants are given much greater autonomy in decision-making. As one notices the average age of ministers appointed in 1965 and without exception still in their post in February 1968 (an average age of 59 in 1968), it does not seem reckless to predict a substantial turnover within their ranks over the next five years. It will be interesting to see whether the new industrial administrators will simply be younger "post-revolu-

Table 15. Age distribution of plant directors among 1967 deputies to the USSR, republican, and oblast soviets (by percent).[a]

Age	The 170 most important plants (N = 31)	Defense plants (N = 18)	Other large plants (N = 43)	Other small plants (N = 42)
60 and over	23	17	7	10
55–59	23	28	30	12
50–54	32	28	23	21
45–49	6	22	21	21
40–44	10	6	9	14
Under 40	6	–	9	21
Average age	53	53	51	49

[a] The source of these data and their reliability are discussed in note 88. The 85 plants not included in the first two columns were divided into half on the basis of my personal (and far from infallible) judgment about their relative size. The failure of several of the columns to total 100 percent is the consequence of rounding.

tionary professionals" or whether the economic reforms will be associated with a new type of manager — one without the engineering education and the production background which has become so familiar. As of yet, there is no sign of any such change.[88]

Until really substantial changes take place, however, the situation remains much as it has been throughout the post-war period. The local Party organs continue to contain men with very substantial technical competence. In any significant urban center there are certain to be responsible Party officials who have the background necessary to understand the technical policy of local plant managers, to judge the technical meaningfulness of managerial investment programs or suggestions advanced by lower employees, to evaluate in a general way the technical competence of candidates for managerial posts, and to advance suggestions themselves with respect to the region's economic development. If conflict on a purely technical question arises between these Party officials and the leader of an important plant, glavk, or ministry, the Party officials are sufficiently qualified that their opinion will be considered by those at higher levels. Yet, in such a conflict the Party officials still remain at a disadvantage. Even if the top Soviet industrial officials may not be ideally equipped to carry through any revolution in industrial planning and administration, they remain men with great technical authority, and they remain very formidable opponents in bureaucratic struggles on planning and technical questions.

IV. Soviet Administrative Theory: (1) Edinonachalie and the Primary Party Organization

It has long been clear that top policy decisions are made within the central Party organs, but a number of seeming ambiguities and inconsistencies in Soviet administrative theory have made it quite difficult to understand the relationship between the lower Party apparatus and the industrial administrators. The Party apparatus has been assigned the duty of supervising and controlling the state administration, but the mandates and powers of the two hierarchies appear ill-defined and overlapping.

The Soviet legal and academic discussions of industrial administration seem to call for a strict line of command with single and undivided responsibility in the hands of the administrator at each level. Both the ministers and the plant directors are to perform their duties in accordance with the principle of *edinonachalie* (one-man management and control) — a principle that "demands the complete subordination of all the employees in the productive process to the will of one person — the leader — and his personal responsibility for the assigned work." [1] According to one authority, the managers enjoy "the right of decision" on all questions within their organization's jurisdiction,[2] and the official description of their authority seems sweeping indeed: "[The directors are] the fully empowered and individual leaders of the productive-economic activity of the enterprise, [and] they answer completely for the results of the work of the enterprise." [3]

But Soviet theory also contains equally emphatic statements that "the leading and directing role of the Communist Party is the foundation of Soviet state administration" [4] and that "not one important question is decided without supervisory instructions from the Party organs." [5] The primary Party organization in the factory has been granted the power to *kontrolirovat* (check or verify) the activity of the plant management, and its decisions are said to be "obligatory for each Communist" (presumably including the director).[6] The local Party organs — even the gorkom and the raikom — "are called upon to check on the activity of the economic organizations and to direct their work." [7]

The statements about the authority of the Party organs do not seem to be formal generalities. The Soviet press repeatedly contains matter-of-fact statements that particular Party organs have "obligated" a manager to do something or that they have removed him from his work. One gorkom secretary summarized his situation very succinctly: "The gorkom has enough rights. The use of some of them can put any director in his place." [8]

Clearly there is a need to explore these apparently conflicting sets of statements about the Party-state relationship and to attempt to clarify the ambiguities in them as much as possible. What actually is the intended power relationship between the Party officials and the industrial administrators? To what extent, if any, have the Party officials been granted the formal authority to force the industrial administrators to accept their will?

The Authority of the State Official: The Limited Meaning of Edinonachalie

For a Westerner the most unfortunate aspect of Soviet administrative theory is its failure to use familiar concepts in discussing familiar administrative problems and situations. To a large extent the problem is one of language. For instance, the word "policy" and the phrase "policy implication" are covered by the Russian word *"politicheskii,"* a word usually translated into English as "political"; or, the phrase "delegation of authority" has no easy Russian equivalent. Consequently, in grappling with the problems of "delegation of authority" and "the policy implications of administrative decisions," Soviet administrative theorists have often used language that has often been understood by Westerners to mean a chain of command far clearer and an allocation of power far broader than the Soviet leaders ever intended. In particular, the concept of edinonachalie has a much more limited meaning than the usual English translation would indicate.

Although all lower officials work within the framework of higher policy, Soviet administrative theory implicitly recognizes that the decisions delegated to each level often may entail policy considerations, and it attempts to distinguish between these decisions and those that are truly routine. The sweeping statements in the legal documents and textbooks about the authority of the state official pertain almost exclusively to the location of the power to take "non-policy" decisions and the power to issue the formal decrees by which all decisions must be implemented; these statements do not imply that the "policy" decisions at a given level are within the sole jurisdiction of the one-man manager.

For this reason edinonachalie is — and always has been — a very limited concept denoting only three things:

First, hour-to-hour, day-to-day decisions of a fairly routine nature are to be made by a single man, the one-man manager. He need not clear each of these routine decisions with the Party or trade union organizations.[9]

Second, important decisions can and must be influenced by groups other than the industrial managers (notably the Party organs), though every such decision must be formally implemented by a governmental organ — specifically by the man or institution having the legal, formal authority to do so. This aspect of Soviet administrative theory is epitomized in the famous demand that the Party organizations desiring some action must work "through" the state organs, not "apart from them."[10] Even when a Party organization has been granted the power to make a particular kind of decision, it cannot issue the necessary formal decree itself but must compel the appropriate governmental official or agency to do it.

Third, an employee is obligated to obey any order or instruction emanating from his formal administrative superior. He has no right to appeal to any Party or trade union organization to have a specific command countermanded, or at least he has no such right of appeal if the command requires immediate execution. Of course, the question of the illegal order raises problems in Soviet administrative theory as it does in any realistic administrative theory and in any bureaucracy. As the Weberian ideal-type of bureaucracy correctly indicates, the legitimate authority of an administrative official tends to be limited to the functions associated with his office and to be restricted by the rules that define the office. In any organization — even those like the military which stress the need for discipline — there obviously comes a point when a subordinate has the obligation to disobey his superior. To use an extreme example, if a plant director ordered a foreman to kill a lazy worker as an example to other workers, Soviet authorities would scarcely excuse the foreman if he carried out this order. Edinonachalie has the connotations usually found in organizations with emphasis on discipline: insubordination is justified only when the orders are extremely improper and even then the burden of proof is placed on the man who decides to carry out a "Caine mutiny."

The meaning of edinonachalie is well illustrated in a practice sometimes mentioned in the Soviet press. If the drive for plan fulfillment at the end of the month becomes very frenzied, many managerial personnel are willing to take extraordinary measures, including the use of design engineers for such tasks as unloading vital supplies. Even though this practice has been severely criticized by the Party leadership, an engineer receiving such an order from his superior is obligated to carry it out. This is the essence of edinonachalie. Nevertheless, the engineer does have the right and even the duty to protest later through the Party organization and to demand that the manager be punished and forbidden to repeat the practice in the future. Of course, the effectiveness of the protest will depend on the attitude of higher authorities (particularly the Party organs).

On questions with policy implications, however, the manager should discuss the alternatives with Party officials before a decision is taken and he should secure their approval. Or, conversely, if Party officials believe that a managerial decision has policy implications and is being decided incorrectly, they have the duty to intervene.

As any reader familiar with the long Western discussion about "policy" and "administration" can well imagine, Soviet theorists have had considerable difficulty defining concretely the difference between a question with policy implications and a routine question requiring no Party involvement. Although lower Party officials themselves have inquired as to "what kind of questions should be decided by the soviet organs and what kind by the Party organs," they have been answered by the foremost of Soviet theorists that "it is impossible to give a recipe or some sort of catalogue." This official, the head of the Party life department of *Pravda,* cautioned that in certain cases there could be questions which seem minor at first glance, "but which in reality should be raised to the level of important political significance." [11]

The inability to define a lower-level "policy question" with precision inevitably means a certain ambiguity in the Soviet administrative system, but it is an ambiguity that in one form or another is inherent in large-scale organization everywhere. For the sake of convenience one can simply define a lower-level policy question as one on which two technically qualified persons, each working within the framework of central directives and rules, might still arrive at a different decision. In practical terms a policy question becomes one on which a Party secretary differs with the decision advanced by the manager or believes it necessary to advance a suggestion himself. The "political maturity" of the Party secretary becomes defined as an ability "to pick out the most significant matters from among the mass of current business." [12]

It must be freely admitted that the interpretation of edinonachalie advanced here is not the traditional one, and it is difficult to prove its correctness conclusively. The interpretation does "work," however, in the sense that it explains a considerable body of data that otherwise must be dismissed as inexplicable or deliberately confusing.

First, the interpretation fits the history of the concept of edinonachalie. Edinonachalie was not invented by Stalin as he moved to reduce the independence of the Party apparatus that had placed him in power; rather it was vigorously advocated by Lenin in the first months after the Revolution — a period when he surely had no desire to limit the authority of lower Party officials.

When quoted in the abstract or in a contemporary Soviet source, there seems to be a categorical quality to an assertion by Lenin that *"incontrovertible subordination* to a single will is unconditionally indispensable for the success of work . . . [in] large-scale industry." [13] Yet, in the context of early 1918, such statements surely were not an appeal for a plant manager who would be an independent decision-maker subject only to higher administrative authorities. They are much better understood as an attempt to combat the utopian interpretations of workers' control and trade union control prevailing in this period (and encouraged by Lenin's own prerevolutionary slogans). [14]

From this perspective the advocacy of edinonachalie and "incontrovertible subordination to a single will" represented little more than Lenin's conviction that the complicated processes of industry would require planning, coordination, and labor discipline under socialism as well as under capitalism. Although the worker would have to accept orders from a directing figure, Lenin had no intention of suggesting that the orders of the "single will" would be based on the manager's independent decisions. It is for this reason that the early debate about edinonachalie hardly touched on the question of the role of the Party.[15]

Second, the interpretation explains the repeated insistence of Soviet spokesmen that edinonachalie is not incompatible with a vigorous role for the Party organs and the masses in decision-making. Again and again they assert that "edinonachalie does not mean . . . personal power (*lichnaia vlast*)."[16] Even in 1965 (a year in which the Soviet press was stressing the dangers of excessive Party involvement in administrative matters), Soviet leaders were careful to emphasize this point. In the words of N. G. Egorychev, the first secretary of the Moscow gorkom: "Many questions about the work of the enterprises which earlier were within the jurisdiction of the higher organs now will be decided on the spot. This does not mean, of course, that the director will decide everything personally. The widening of the rights of the enterprises — this is first of all the widening of the rights of the collectives."[17]

Similarly, after stating in 1965 that "the role of edinonachalie in production is now growing very greatly," even Aleksei Kosygin, Chairman of the Council of Ministers, added the following qualification: "Edinonachalie should be organically connected with the widest participation of the workers and white collar employees in the discussion of the most important questions of the economic life of the enterprise and the administration of production. . . . The role of the collectives of the enterprises, of the plant public should be raised to a high level in the resolution of questions dealing with planning, the mobilization of internal reserves of production, and the evaluation of the results of the work of the officials and the rewards to be given them."[18]

Third, the interpretation corresponds with the examples used by Soviet spokesmen to illustrate the importance of edinonachalie. When Party organs are criticized for interfering in the business of management, the examples almost always involve very minute details rather than questions of any significance. Thus, one Party handbook argues against excessive Party interference in the following terms: "What would happen if the raikom(!) told a collective farm chairman where to send a particular tractor or instructed the shop heads of an enterprise as to which worker should be placed on a particular operation?" [19] Similarly, the post-Khrushchev criticisms of local Party organs that usurped the functions of the administrative organs almost invariably deal with Party organs deciding such questions as the detailed nature of traffic rules, the location of a street sign, the method of street cleaning, or the schedule for digging the foundation of a building.[20] It is particularly instructive to note that when "such a style of work" is criticized, the reason given is that "it does not permit the political leader to concern himself with his real job — the resolution of the important problems which are within his competence." [21]

Finally, the interpretation offered here makes sense of one of the most puzzling paradoxes in Soviet administrative theory: the repeated instruction to Party organs to strive "to strengthen edinonachalie" and repeated assertions to the effect that "the Party committee of the plant, in using its right of verification (*pravo kontrolia*), is strengthening edinonachalie." [22] If edinonachalie implies autonomy for the manager in decision-making, the latter quotation obviously contradicts other statements about the role of the Party, and in some formulations it becomes ridiculous; but, if edinonachalie has the more limited meaning suggested here, then the strengthening of edinonachalie can mean little more than the strengthening of labor discipline — a much more understandable demand.

The Role of the Primary Party Organization and Its Secretary

The secretary of the primary Party organization is assigned a diversity of roles, and his relationship to the chief administrator of an enterprise or institution varies considerably from one role to another. A number of his responsibilities engender little conflict with the chief administrator, but rather create a situation in which he can be viewed as "only the assistant of the [economic] leaders." [23] If the Party organization does an excellent job of conducting ideological work among the labor force and of supervising the trade union and the "public" institutions designed to maintain order (the comrade courts, the peoples' guards, and the house committees), the manager may be quite enthusiastic, believing that "the better the ideological-educational work is established, the better [labor] discipline will be." [24]

In carrying out his other responsibilities, however, the secretary of the primary Party organization can have a far different relationship to the manager. If the Party organization is located within a governmental administrative office (a planning organ, ministry, sovnarkhoz, or department of a soviet), its secretary has no right to interfere in policy decisions, but he does have the duty to ensure that decisions are made smoothly and that there does not develop a "bureaucratic" atmosphere with red tape, toadyism, and excessive self-satisfaction. [25] Moreover, of course, he is in a position to inform higher Party officials of any wrongdoing within his institution. Indeed, in calling for a reestablishment of the ministries, Brezhnev took care to demand the selection of well-qualified Party secretaries for these organizations, saying, "The Party committees of the ministries should periodically inform the Central Committee about the conditions of work of the Party organizations." [26]

If the Party organization is located within a plant, a construction site, or a design bureau, it is assigned the so-called *pravo kontrolia,* the right to check on the substance of managerial decisions. [27] It is quite clear that the *pravo kontrolia* can involve the Party organization deeply in decision-making and in conflicts with the plant director, but the precise meaning of this phrase is not clear at first glance.

Part of the difficulty in understanding the *pravo kontrolia* stems from the fact that the word *"kontrol"* does not really reflect the real nature of the work of the primary Party organization. *Kontrol* has entered the Russian language from the French and has a much more limited meaning than the English word by which it is usually translated. The English verb "control" can often imply the providing of policy direction, but *kontrol* has more the connotations of the word "controller." Consequently, the phrase *"pravo kontrolia"* conveys the impression of a primary Party organization checking, verifying, inspecting the work of the manager and enforcing his adherence to laws and plans established elsewhere. [28]

However, the role of the primary Party organization and its secretary is stretched far beyond the literal meaning of *pravo kontrolia* by the nature of the instructions and directives that the plant receives from higher Party and state organs. In the first place, the responsibilities of the manager are defined very broadly. He is ordered not simply to fulfill a plan assigned him, but to help draft a very taut plan, to over-fulfill it by a maximum amount, to do so with optimal efficiency, and to continue to improve the production processes as rapidly as possible.

In the second place, the manager is given a multitude of plan indicators and regulations that cannot possibly all be fulfilled.[29] Much of his job is to decide to what degree violations of individual regulations and indicators will be required to fulfill his overall plan (and to what extent they will be excused if this overall plan is fulfilled). This phenomenon tends to be the rule in all large-scale organizations, but it has been exacerbated in the Soviet Union by the extreme tautness of the plan in relation to resources and by the resulting low levels of inventory accumulation. When there are mistakes in the planning of supply deliveries or when a supplier fails to meet his delivery date, the manager is driven to improvisation.

The impact of these conditions on the role of the manager has long been recognized. Because the manager has no precise set of rules and regulations to follow, he has much more room in which to maneuver than might be expected for an official low in a very centralized hierarchy. Indeed, one American authority, David Granick, devoted one entire chapter in his book to the subject, "Plant Management's Independence," and he concluded that the plant manager has so much freedom of action that he cannot rightfully be called a bureaucrat in the Weberian sense of the term.[30]

The nature of the Soviet planning system has not only left the manager with some freedom of action vis-à-vis his superiors, it has also had a major impact on the nature of the *kontrol* exercised by the primary Party organization. Because there is no precise plan or set of regulations, the *kontrol* cannot be a routine "verification of performance" in the usual sense of that phrase. If, as one Party secretary expressed it, regulations are broken continuously "for the sake of production," [31] the Party secretary cannot be an official who merely checks off regulations that have been violated. To be sure, he and his organization must be interested in machinations and law violations of a gross character, but their basic role must be much broader. In checking the overall preformance of the enterprise, the organization inevitably becomes involved in policy-making, if for no other reason than that the mere choice of the indicator or regulation to emphasize constitutes a decision of significance.

Soviet theorists freely admit — and actually insist — that the primary Party organization's role is indeed broader than simple verification. Repeatedly Soviet spokesmen assert that "the correct use of the *pravo kontrolia* of administrative activity presupposes not a mere recording of deficiencies, but their prevention (*preduprezhenie*)." [32] Consequently, it is not surprising that the official Party handbook is filled with demands that the Party organizations "raise questions about production," "recommend various measures," "advance different problems before the administration," and so forth. [33] Indeed, a post-Khrushchev summary statement on the primary Party organization states flatly that the organization can "express its opinion on any question of the activity of the enterprise and give recommendations in accordance with Party documents and Soviet laws." [34] This expression of opinion is not to be a formality; it is considered normal and praiseworthy that the manager and the secretary regularly "argue about questions of principle." [35]

In short, the right of *kontrol* entails both the right to check *after* a decision has been made, and also, more importantly, the right to participate intimately in policy-making *before* the decision is made. It means that the Party committee or bureau of the primary Party organization is the real board of directors of the plant — the place where the top administrative officials together with the Party secretary, the trade union chairman, and a few workers, discuss the major questions facing the enterprise and make the decisions concerning them. [36]

Although the Party bureau is primarily an "inside" board of directors (that is, composed of men from inside the plant who are subordinate to the manager in their daily work), it does contain at least one man who is always supposed to maintain a position independent of the manager — the secretary of the Party organization. Of course, the crucial question is: what happens when this official and the director do, in fact, "argue about questions of principle"? In cases of disagreement, do the Party organization and its secretary have the authority to compel the manager to accept their position?

There are, unfortunately, few other matters on which there are so many contradictory authoritative statements as on the proper relationship between the manager and the plant Party secretary. The word *kontrol* tends to deny the primary Party organization the authority to provide policy direction to the manager, and, in fact, Soviet officials (for example, Zhdanov, when he introduced the concept of *pravo kontrolia* in 1939) have warned that the Party organizations should not "take on themselves the improper functions of *leadership* (*rukovodstvo*) in economic matters." [37] Other Soviet spokesmen, however, have spoken of the "leading (*rukovodiashchaia*) role" of the primary Party organization in the enterprise or of its "providing of political leadership (*rukovodstvo*)." [38]

One Soviet source may state that "a decision taken [by the Party meeting] is obligatory for the whole Party organization and for each of its members." [39] Yet, in another place, Party officials are warned that there should never develop a situation in which "it is not the director who supervises the enterprise, but the Party organization which commands the director." [40] They are told that "the Party organization and its leaders cannot directly give any operational instructions concerning production work, [nor] . . . can they even demand that the director . . . clear his orders and commands with them." [41]

In the realm of personnel selection one authoritative spokesman has declared in *Partiinaia zhizn* that the primary Party organization, unlike the local Party organs, need not establish a nomenklatura of key personnel, whereas another authoritative spokesman has demanded that the Party organization "interfere and prevent the mistake" if an undeserving candidate is promoted. The latter official added that "the decisions, suggestions, and recommendations [of the Party organization] are obligatory for [the director], if they are in full correspondence with Soviet legislation." [42]

Perhaps the strangest formulation of all appeared in an attempt by *Partiinaia zhizn* to clarify the situation for a confused employee. The director at his plant acknowledged that the sovnarkhoz and the Party obkom could obligate him to take action, but he objected to efforts of the primary Party organization to do so. The employee wrote to the

Central Committee journal for clarification, and received the following answer: "Factory director, comrade Razumovski, makes a mistake if he thinks that only higher-standing Party and economic organs can obligate him [to take action]. . . . But it would be incorrect [for the primary Party organization] to abuse its authority by addressing the director in such categorical phraseology as 'to obligate,' 'to propose,' 'to demand.' " [43]

The contradiction among many of these statements seems blatant indeed, and Razumovski's questions (and others like them) indicate that lower Soviet administrators themselves are not always clear about the proper relationship of the Party organization to the plant management. Yet, even on this point Soviet administrative theory is actually not so ambiguous as appears on the surface.

The explanation for some of the apparent paradox in Soviet discussions of the authority of the primary Party organization can be found in the peculiar phraseology used to describe edinonachalie. For example, the assertion that the primary Party organization "cannot *directly* [my italics] give any operational instructions" is surely a reflection of the Soviet insistence that Party officials work through the duly-constituted governmental officials in carrying out their decisions. The prohibitions against commanding the director and against forcing him to clear his orders with the Party organization are also expressions of the Soviet belief that managers should be permitted to make minor day-to-day decisions on their own. (The word "command" — *komandovat* — tends to connote an excessive ordering around of people, particularly on detailed matters.)

A second partial explanation for the ambiguities in statements about the primary Party organization lies in the diversity of the types of decisions that the primary Party organization may take. Zhdanov's reference to "the improper functions of leadership *in economic matters*" (my italics) reminds us that other decisions of the Party organization deal with various intra-Party matters. Here the authority of the organization and its secretary may be unchallenged.

Even within the economic sphere itself there are many kinds of decisions that may be taken. If the local Party organs issue a *formal* decision about an enterprise, the decision is often directed at the primary Party organization rather than solely at the management. The decision is then echoed by the primary Party organization, its decision obligating all Communists to carry out the different points decreed by higher officials. In such cases there is no questioning the obligatory nature of the "decision of the primary Party organization" for the manager.

There are other decisions of the primary Party organization so general that it would seem strange if the word "to suggest" were to be used instead of "to obligate." In 1952, for example, "the Party committee [of the giant plant Elektrosila] obligated comrade Shevchenko [the director] to be attentive to the workers, to have more contact with them, to take into account criticism which comes from below." [44] A similar obligation was stated in 1965 by the Party conference of the Tbilisi Electric Locomotive Works: "A decision was taken which obligates the Party committee and the Communists: To raise the level of the technical leadership of production. To devote serious attention to the scientific organization of work. More boldly to introduce new techniques and progressive technology into production. . . . To strengthen labor and production discipline, to obtain a rise in labor productivity, to guarantee rhythmical work, to lower costs, and to raise the quality of production." [45]

If it were categorically denied that the Party organization has the right to obligate the manager, then the general decisions quoted above, as well as those on intra-Party matters and those embodying higher Party decisions, could not have been phrased as they are. When the editorial board of *Partiinaia zhizn* states that the director can be obligated by the primary Party organization but that the organization should not abuse its authority by using the word "to obligate," it is possible (or even probable) that it is tacitly differentiating between the type of decision we have been examining and those that deal with specific production questions.

A third step in understanding the role of the primary Party organization and its secretary lies in making a distinction that Soviet theorists are frequently eager to blur. If one examines closely two contradictory statements about the primary Party organization, it is often found that one statement refers to the powers and functions of the Party organization as a whole, whereas the other actually describes the powers and functions of the secretary alone.

Although the primary Party organization is assigned the right to check the work of management, it must never be forgotten that, in fact, the organization itself contains nearly all of the top members of management, a large percentage of the junior managers, and most of the best workers. Thus, it literally must be true that the 9,500 Communists of the Gorki Auto Works, for example, "are the nucleus of the collective, its advanced part . . . [and] everything that is done at the plant is connected with them." [46]

Even from an empirical point of view, therefore, the Party organization as a whole (including the managerial team) occupies a special position in relation to the enterprise employees who are not Party members. In Party theory they are described as the local vanguard of the proletariat, and their relationship to the local proletariat is depicted in the same terms used to depict the role of the Party vis-à-vis the national proletariat.

It is in this light that the really sweeping statements about the "leading" role of the primary Party organization are almost always to be interpreted. They refer not to the relationship of the Party secretary to those Communists who occupy the top administrative posts in the enterprise, but to the relationship of all Communists to the enterprise as a whole. This is vital to understand if a very frequent type of Soviet press report is not to be misinterpreted. Take, for example, the assertion that "the Party committee [of the Orekhovo-Zuevo Cotton Combine] . . . skillfully directs the efforts of the Communists, of the 26,000-man collective in finding and using the internal reserves, in perfecting production, in raising productivity of labor and profitability." [47] This statement does not necessarily imply any limitation on the role of the top managerial officials, for they are among the most important members of that Party committee. It means simply that the major plant decisions are made — or formalized — at a meeting of the plant's "board of directors"; it does not necessarily mean that the Party secretary has had any real impact on the decisions.

Much of the Soviet discussion of the primary Party organization, however, is implicitly based on a much narrower conception of the organization — that is, of the Party secretary at the head of the rank-and-file members. The whole concept of *pravo kontrolia* implies a

Party organization apart from the top administrators of the plant, and in practice it tends to refer to the role of the Party secretary.

Because of the democratic mythology surrounding the primary Party organization, Soviet administrative theorists sometimes find it awkward to discuss the legitimate authority that the leadership really intends to be vested in the Party secretary.[48] However, many of the narrow definitions of the organization are written with the secretary in mind. When Zhdanov denies that the primary Party organization is to provide leadership to the management, when *Partiinaia zhizn* states that it would be improper for the primary Party organization to use the words "obligate" or "demand" in its decisions, they are thinking primarily of the Party secretary.

All Soviet officials interviewed in 1958 and 1962 agreed that both in theory and in practice the powers of the secretary are limited to those of persuasion and of appeal to higher officials, and that the secretary cannot (without the support of higher officials) force the managers to accept his opinion on policy questions. Those interviewed stated that the decision of a meeting of the primary Party organization or its bureau usually does not bind the manager unless he has concurred in the decision. Even a non-Party director of a textile factory insisted that the primary Party organization would take no decision concerning the economic side of the enterprise's life without clearing it with him first.

The interviews indicate that if there is disagreement between the director and Party secretary the secretary's only recourse is appeal to the local Party organs for support. However, one authoritative post-Khrushchev statement about the primary Party organizations suggests that in the realm of personnel selection, at least, it is the director who must take the initiative if he is not to be bound by the opinion of the Party organization. After asserting that the Party committees' "decisions, proposals, and recommendations are obligatory for the [director]," this statement continued, "If the economic leader . . . considers the decision of the Party organization mistaken, he should turn to a higher-standing Party organ and ask it to correct the mistake of the Party organization and to annul its decision." [49]

It is not certain whether the burden of making the appeal has been placed on the director only in the post-Khrushchev period or whether it actually represents a long-standing operating procedure. In fact, the statement does not make clear whether this procedure applies to all decisions of the primary Party organization or just to those involving personnel changes. Another 1965 *Partiinaia zhizn* statement about the primary Party organization defines its role in such a way as to suggest that it still may be compelled to initiate most of the appeals in cases of disagreements with the manager: the Party organizations should, the statement demanded, "work out effective recommendations for the administration and *place important problems* before higher-standing Party organs." [50] The three italicized words were in heavy dark print in the original.

Whoever must make the appeal to the local Party organs, neither the director nor the plant Party secretary can force the other to accept his opinion without the support of higher Party officials. As a result, the essential image of the relationship of the director and the Party secretary emerging from Soviet administrative theory is that of a policy-making team within the enterprise. These two officials, together with the trade union chairman, are to form a three-man directorate — the triangle (*treugolnik*), a term from the 1920's still used today.[51]

Within the policy-making team the director is primarily responsible for day-to-day decisions, but when broader questions arise he must discuss them fully with the secretary, and the two must find a common language, an *obshchii iazyk*. On certain questions dealing with dismissals, housing distribution, and so forth, the agreement of the trade union chairman is also required, but he is closely supervised by the Party secretary and is scarcely an independent power center within the plant.

It is safe to say that the relative influence of the director and the secretary varies from enterprise to enterprise, depending on the respective personalities and abilities of the two men.[52] No doubt it is also safe to say that most frequently the director is first among equals, both because he has been granted higher prestige and pay and because he is in charge of day-to-day administration.[53] It is perhaps enough to point to the fact that a secretary of the primary Party organization on the rise may be promoted to the directorship of his plant (and is in a significant number of cases), but the director never becomes the plant Party secretary.[54] Nevertheless, the mere existence of a right of appeal for the secretary is surely a powerful factor ensuring a role for him, even when that right is not exercised.

The Soviet leaders have realized that the establishment of a policy-making team within the enterprise can create difficulties, and they have taken a number of steps to avoid them. To prevent one member of the team from becoming dominant, they have a tendency to alternate the emphasis placed on edinonachalie and active Party participation respectively, presumably thereby helping to counteract any trend toward an imbalance.

For reasons to be discussed in later chapters, the more serious danger has been that of domination by the director over the Party secretary rather than that of the secretary over the director. For this reason the leaders have emphasized the necessity of maintaining the secretary's independence from the director. Besides forbidding the secretary to accept premiums from the director, they have also sought to ensure that the secretary receives all the information he needs. He may demand any information or documents from the director, and the rank-and-file members have been ordered to report any defects to him (and to higher Party organs).[55]

During the last decade several additional measures have been taken to institutionalize the flow of information to the secretary. In 1959 there were organized formal commissions composed of workers, engineers, and lower administrators to assist the secretary in checking the performance of the administration in such areas as product quality, production cost, fulfillment of inter-regional deliveries, and so forth. Since 1962 these commissions have been supplemented by "posts of assistance to the Committee of Party-State Control" (later termed "posts of assistance to the Committee of Peoples' Control").[56] As the title implies, these posts are part of the Party-State Control or now Peoples' Control hierarchy, but they are subordinate to a deputy secretary of the primary Party organization.[57] Because the raion Party-State Control Committee had but one paid official (its chairman),[58] the subordination of the posts to the primary Party organization seems more meaningful than that to the control hierarchy and seems to determine the primary role of these institutions.[59]

The Soviet leaders use a number of devices to thwart the development of irresponsibility and indecisiveness in this system. They hold the manager and the Party secretary strictly responsible for results (basically the same results in both cases) and then give them an extremely difficult plan to fulfill. In this way the two men are given to know that any poor results ensuing from a failure to work together effectively will bring their prompt removal. Another device is the insistence on edinonachalie — the insistence that orders be carried out along the administrative line and that the administrator have authority to carry through action he thinks is needed immediately. Finally, the local Party organs are given the right and the power to settle any conflict that arises between the administrator and the Party secretary and cannot be resolved by them.

Conclusion

The Soviet leaders do seem to have avoided a system rife with irresponsibility, but the administrative arrangements within the Soviet plant are rather complex, and to understand the reasons that underlie them is a crucial part of understanding the role of the primary Party organization.

In the West there has been a tendency to explain the primary Party organization as an attempt by the leadership to solidify its political control, to mobilize the workers, and to curtail illegal activity on the part of the managers. Undoubtedly these are important factors. The secretary is, of course, a useful political check within the enterprise, and the organization serves as an excellent instrument for mobilizing the energies and loyalties of the labor force. Moreover, the existence of the organization and its secretary surely makes the leadership more disposed to accept the necessary but quasi-legal maneuvering that Granick and Berliner have described, for they reduce the danger that the maneuvering will be undertaken purely for reasons of private gain.

Yet, the rationale for the present role of the secretary of the primary Party organization goes beyond the desire to establish a control system in the limited sense of that term. The Soviet leadership seems to believe quite deeply that a Weberian-type of organizational structure with a clean line of command and clearly defined spheres of competence is not, in fact, the best form of organization for producing optimal decisions from a rational-technical point of view. It assumes that a two-headed leadership of enterprises located at lower levels of the hierarchy helps the administrative system to avoid several serious problems endemic to large-scale organization.

The first of these problems is the amount of discretion that in practice tends to accrue to administrative officials at lower and middle levels of the organization. The Weberian model implies that decisions within a bureaucracy can always be made correctly and predictably by any technically competent official supplying rules determined by higher policy-makers, but Western social scientists have long realized that this is not necessarily the case, particularly in administrative situations (such as found in industry) where many decisions are not routine.

In theory the development of a perfect incentive system might provide a set of "rules" that would ensure that the "independent" decisions of the administrators conformed either to the specific preferences of the leaders or to their generalized desire for efficiency and growth. However, such an incentive system is difficult to achieve within a hierarchical order. The establishment of a measure for success may distort decisions, as the administrators come to focus on the indicator rather than the goal behind it.[60] Moreover, the existence of many diverse units in a hierarchy (particularly in the Soviet Union where all organizations are really part of the same hierarchy) makes it quite difficult to ensure that the incentives in the different units do not lead to conflicting actions.[61]

The problem of policy discretion in the hands of lower officials is complicated by the possibility that the training of these officials may not prepare them well for its exercise. A number of Western authorities have expressed concern about the habits and techniques a future executive develops in his first, more detailed jobs and about the isolated environment in which he works (Peter Drucker speaks of the environment in the corporation as being that of a monastery). The fear is that this environment tends to produce parochialism and a mechanical attitude toward men that may seriously limit the executive's effectiveness as he rises to posts in which more and more policy-making is involved.[62]

Soviet authorities on the Party-state relationship show a keen awareness of this problem. All the discussions on "democratic centralism," "Leninist principles of administration," and the advantages of "collective" decisions contain expressions of concern about the danger of one-sided, arbitrary decisions by administrators. On the surface, at least, the Soviet leadership worries less about these arbitrary decisions involving too much political independence than about the danger that they will not be well thought out and well rounded. In the words of one authority, "decisions taken by a single man are as a rule one-sided. They cannot take all aspects of a matter into account." [63] In the Soviet view the existence of the secretary and the bureau of the primary Party organization helps to mitigate this problem by increasing the probability that at least two top men at the enterprise level will consider questions relating to policy. In order to increase this probability further, the leadership has often called for the selection of a "team" with contrasting age and experience.[64]

A second problem of large-scale organization that the primary Party organizations seem intended to alleviate is the persistent inability of administrators to obtain all the information they need in order to make intelligent decisions. Few questions are so widely discussed in American administrative literature as that of the difficulty administrators face in receiving a proper "feedback" of information from lower levels and of the continual necessity for them to make decisions with insufficient information.[65]

There is no Russian equivalent to the word "feedback," but as early as 1923, Stalin manifested public concern about this problem when he objected to "a 'simplified' apparatus" with a straight line of command. Stalin declared that under such a form of administration "the ruler . . . receives the kind of information that can be received from governors and comforts himself with the hope that he is governing honestly and well. Presently friction arises, friction grows into conflict, and conflicts into revolts." [66] As this quotation indicates, the preoccupation with flow of information upward has had its roots in a fear of political unrest, but it is also connected with an interest in economic performance. Soviet administrative theory emphasizes the creative wisdom of individual workers, peasants, and white collar personnel, and it repeatedly refers to the economic advantages to be gained from utilizing their ideas.[67] Soviet sources insist that "a timely and frank word of the Party leader is the best assistance [for a good director] — one of the ways for avoiding possible mistakes." [68]

In many ways the primary Party organization is, in fact, very well designed to ensure that information does flow to those who need it. The higher Party officials receive from the enterprises independent reports filled with criticism and self-criticism, and are able to participate in the resolution of issues that have provoked major disagreement between the director and the Party secretary. Moreover, the existence of the primary Party organization guarantees that the director (and the secretary) will be provided with a steady stream of information about conditions and trouble spots at lower echelons of the enterprise and will receive alternative suggestions for action.

Without the type of field research that is not permitted, it is difficult to judge the extent to which the primary Party organization actually does solve these two problems. It is, of course, quite possible for a two-headed policy-making team to function in quite unintended ways. One does, for example, read of cases in which the Party secretary fails to participate meaningfully in decision-making, concentrating only on ideological work as long as the plan is fulfilled.[69] One reads of still other cases in which the conflict between administrator and Party secretary becomes very severe, particularly as the secretary attempts to assume powers that are not his.[70] Yet, managerial officials interviewed in the Soviet Union insist that these cases are exceptions. They insist that the Party secretary is usually consulted regularly and that normally the manager and secretary are able to find a "common language" without referring questions upward. This evidence is scarcely conclusive, but the fact does remain that, whatever the possibilities of chaos, the Soviet factories do produce goods and Soviet industry has been able to maintain high rates of growth for many decades.

V. Soviet Administrative Theory: (2) The Local Party Organs

Western scholars often speak of "the" role of the Communist Party in Soviet society and "the" relationship between the Party and the state. In certain contexts this phraseology is quite useful and helps to illuminate meaningful problems, but in other contexts such phraseology only serves to confuse our understanding of Soviet society. This is especially true in the case of the relationship of lower Party officials to governmental officials, for the relationship of the primary Party organization to the governmental administrators is really quite different from that of the local Party committees to the same administrators. Moreover, even the authority granted to the officials of the local Party organs can vary immensely, depending on the position of these officials and the level of governmental administrator with whom they are dealing.

The Legitimate Authority of the Local Party Organs

In Soviet administrative theory the key variable in the relationship of any local Party organ to any state administrator is the territorial level at which the two are located. Whereas the local Party organs have a powerful position vis-à-vis state administrators at their territorial level or below, their position is quite weak with respect to the state organs located at higher territorial levels.

Soviet administrative theory actually has little to say about the relationship of the Party organs to the higher state bodies. Because Soviet theory emphasizes that the local Party organs should be especially concerned with long-range policy questions — questions that almost invariably require approval and financing from higher-level organs — it does imply that the Party organs will have rather substantial contact with higher planning and administrative bodies. Even during the Stalin period, *Pravda* stated that "the gorkom [and, presumably the other local Party organs] can and should raise necessary questions before any ministry and play the role of an initiator and stimulus." [1]

However, there is nothing in Soviet administrative theory to suggest that a Party official can obligate a higher state official to take action or that their interaction should properly be visualized as team decision-making. The higher state organs are under the policy direction of the Party organs at their level, and their decisions often embody higher Party directives. Consequently, it would clearly be a violation of the logic of Party discipline for a lower Party organ to have the power to compel higher state officials to take action or (except in certain prescribed cases that will be discussed later) to countermand orders given by higher state administrators to local officials.

The image of the interaction between a local Party organ and a higher state administrator which emerges from Soviet administrative theory is that of a supplicant-superior relationship. A Party committee can request that a higher official follow some course of action, it can appeal one of his decisions to higher Party officials, but it is not in any sense an equal with him. Indeed, on the average its requests and appeals cannot be guaranteed success. These requests usually must involve the allocation of funds, and here the local Party organ is really a competitor with a multitude of other lower Party organs and lower state officials for the limited resources at the disposal of the higher organs.[2] On purely technical questions (and these are fairly rare, for major technological innovation or product change requires appropriations), the local Party officials face the difficulties in dealing with a specialized hierarchy that were discussed in Chapter III.

The local Party organ has quite different powers and quite a different role in its relationship with the state administrators at its territorial level or below. In this case the position of the local Party organ is far stronger than that of the primary Party organization within the enterprise. The local Party organ is not called on simply to exercise *kontrol* over the administrators within its region but (in the words of one of the last *Pravda* editorials of the Stalin era) "to lead the soviet, economic, and public organizations . . . , to unite, to direct (*napravliat*), and to verify (*kontrolirovat*) [their] activity." [3]

This difference in the role of the local Party organs and the primary Party organization is expressed succinctly in a 1940 *Pravda* editorial: "Checking (*kontrol*) . . . by the plant Party organization in a given case is combined with correct and capable leadership (*rukovodstvo*) of the plant from the side of the Leningrad gorkom — daily leadership which is concrete and deep." [4] "Plant" and *"rukovodstvo"* were the only two words in this editorial that were in heavy black print.

Napravlenie (direction) and *rukovodstvo* (leadership) have come to signify a number of concrete roles that will be discussed in the latter half of this chapter, but it is vital to understand that they do imply great authority for the local Party organs. *Kontrol* implies the absence of an authority to obligate an administrator to take a particular policy decision; *rukovodstvo* denotes the presence of that authority. This authority legally derives from the relationship of the local Party organ to the primary Party organization defined in the Party Rules — specifically from the clause speaking of "the unconditionally binding nature of the decisions of the higher (Party) bodies upon the lower ones." [5] Because the important administrative personnel are Party members and are enrolled in the primary Party organization at the place they work, they too are subject to the decisions of the local Party organs supervising their primary Party organization.

The authority of the local Party organs is not simply symbolic, and it extends far beyond intra-Party matters. The local Party organs have the authority to do much more than merely provide general ideological and inspirational leadership to the industrial managers. The "leadership" that Soviet administrative theory demands from them is associated with the job of a chief executive, and the authority it grants them is similar to that of a chief executive. Indeed, the best translation for *rukovodstvo* when applied to the local Party organs is "executive leadership."

Of course, in directing the work of the enterprises, the local Party organs have been obligated to conduct themselves in accordance with the principles of edinonachalie. This is the meaning of the statute in the Party Rules that requires the Party organs "not to supplant (*podmeniat*) the soviet, trade-union, cooperative, and other public organizations of the toilers, not to permit a mixing of the functions of the Party and other organs or unnecessary parallelism in their work." [6]

103

This is the meaning of statements that "the Party organs cannot take on themselves the functions of direct administration," that there should be no "detailed interference of the Party committees in the work of the economic organs and their leaders." [7]

These assertions — and others like them — have often been interpreted as representing a limitation on the authority of the Party organs, but such an interpretation is mistaken. Precisely the same language is used by Soviet administrative theorists when they discuss delegation of authority from a superior to a subordinate in the state apparatus: "In providing general leadership to the organs subordinate to them, the higher administrative bodies do not supplant (*podmeniat*) them." [8] When this language is used in discussions of the local Party organs, it is little more than a demand for delegation of authority on minor questions, a demand that a prefect should not interfere in every *detailed* decision taken by the technical administrators within his area.

The essence of the proper relationship between a local Party organ and an industrial administrator within its area is best summarized in a 1957 statement by the second secretary of the Sverdlovsk obkom about the relationship of the obkom and the newly created sovnarkhoz. After asserting that "the oblast Party committee should not and must not supplant [the sovnarkhoz]," the second secretary continues: "The impression might be created that our Party organ takes on the role of a passive inspector. . . . In actuality, this is not so." He then makes the crucial distinction: "There is a line where concrete, operational leadership of the enterprise ends and where economic policy begins." [9] Even though the Sverdlovsk sovnarkhoz was then headed by a former USSR minister — a candidate member of the Party Central Committee [10] — the secretary made it clear that questions involving "economic policy" should not be left to the sovnarkhoz to decide. The secretary's distinction has general applicability to the relationship between any local Party organ and a state administrative agency at its territorial level or below.

Although *rukovodstvo* and *napravlenie* have implied great authority for the local Party organs, not all Party officials share equally in this authority. In theory, it is the Party committee or bureau, acting collectively, that has the power to obligate a state institution within its jurisdiction. In practice, the first secretary of the Party committee, although officially the instrument of the bureau, can usually exercise the authority of the committee. It is he who is "the boss," "the head," "the highest authority." [11] In short, it is he rather than the committee who is the real prefect.

The lower secretaries of the Party committee and the heads of the departments have a far weaker position vis-à-vis the state administrators. On many minor questions, they may be delegated considerable authority and their word is often accepted as final.[12] Yet, although the lower Party officials may mediate a dispute that is brought to them or may give advice that is accepted, they cannot compel an important industrial official to take action unless they have the backing of the first secretary. In essence, the lower Party officials serve as assistants to the first secretary, providing him with a source of policy advice independent of the state administrators and helping to resolve those conflicts that require little more than mediation.

In fact, the first secretary has two sets of subordinates for each sphere of the economy — one in the Party organs and one in the governmental agencies — and those in the Party organs often have status and power inferior to those in the industrial organs. For example, the position of the head of the industrial-transportation department of an obkom or republican central committee was markedly inferior to that of the sovnarkhoz chairman from 1957 to 1962. At the very best the secretary for industry had status equal to the sovnarkhoz chairman, and often he did not achieve this equality.[13]

Similarly, the director of an important plant often may have greater stature and authority than a lower official of a local Party organ. For example, in the mid-1950's the large Kokhtla-Iarve Shale-Processing Combine was headed by A. N. Lebedev, a full member of the Estonian Central Committee. The first secretary of the gorkom dealt with Lebedev regularly, but the head of the industrial-transportation department was even afraid to talk with him. "What would happen," she asked, "if I were to step on his sore corn?" [14]

The relationship of the local Party organs to local state administrators is complicated not only by the inner structure of the local Party organs, but also by the subordination of local administrators to a centralized functional hierarchy. Although a Party official may speak of deciding questions of "economic policy," there are many such questions whose final resolution is not made at the local level. Instead, the manager receives direction from his superiors located at a higher territorial level — superiors whose position vis-à-vis the local Party organs is quite strong.

Certainly the dual subordination of local administrators both to the local Party organs and to their own specialized hierarchy places many severe limitations on the real ability of the Party organs to influence the behavior of the lower industrial administrators. Not only may the higher industrial authorities give directives to their subordinates, but the local Party officials must gain the approval of these higher authorities if they attempt to promote any technical innovation requiring the expenditure of significant funds. The difficulties that the local Party officials face in this respect are not peculiar to the Soviet Union; they have been encountered by prefectoral officials throughout the world as the specialized hierarchies have become more numerous and more technically competent.

Yet, despite the practical limitations on the authority of the local Party organs, it is still meaningful to insist that they have the authority to obligate local managers to take action. Paradoxically, the very multiplicity of regulations, plans, and directives flowing down the different governmental lines of command into a locality has widened the scope of action of the local Party organs very substantially. All these plans and instructions ultimately derive from the policy of the same Party leadership, but they inevitably come to contradict each other to some extent as Party policy becomes associated with different departmental emphases and self-interests. Because of these contradictions and divergencies, many conflicts inevitably arise among local administrators.

It is precisely when the actions of one specialized hierarchy begin to interfere with the work and interests of other hierarchies and groups that a *politicheskii* question emerges. It is here that the local Party organ has the authority to countermand an administrative order or regulation and to obligate an administrator to take action. It may decide (in fact, be forced to decide) the relative priority of two plans or directives; it may demand that one institution help another in certain cases; it may authorize an administrator to disregard a particular regulation.

If such a decision need not be carried out immediately or if it applies to the resolution of a whole series of conflicts, a dissatisfied local administrator may appeal to his superior and that superior may attempt to have the decision overruled by the Party organs at his level. However, if the decision requires immediate execution and the manager has the ability the carry it out, there are very few circumstances in which he could or would refuse to obey.

It should be strongly emphasized that this authority relationship of the local Party organs to the administrators within their districts is not an innovation of the Khrushchev period. As the 1940 and 1953 *Pravda* editorials that have been quoted indicate, the local Party organs also had the mandate to lead and direct the work of their area's administrators during the Stalin era. In the words of Georgii Malenkov, "The city and oblast Party committees, together with the people's commissariats, are obligated to bear responsibility for the work of *all* industrial and transportation enterprises of the city and oblast." [15]

Often when a local Party organ neglected large-scale industry or industrial construction projects, it would be subjected to strong official criticism. A 1947 *Pravda* editorial summarizes a Central Committee decision dealing with one such obkom: "The Central Committee noted that the Zaporozhe obkom hasn't understood the political significance of the construction project [the reconstruction of Zaporozhstal] and that the obkom first secretary, comrade [Leonid] Brezhnev, leads the construction site superficially. The obkom officials say that they are assigning much attention to agriculture. And so it should be . . . But does this mean that a most important construction site can be neglected? Not in any case." [16] Comrade Brezhnev seems to have corrected his errors, and in the mid-1950's was named the Central Committee secretary in charge of industry.

Repeatedly in the last years of Stalin's life, one can find matter-of-fact statements in the Soviet press indicating great authority in the hands of the local Party officials. Chapter IX contains a number of such statements, and perhaps one example from 1947 will suffice to illustrate this common phenomenon: "The [Kharkov] obkom bureau obligated the head of the Southern Heavy Construction Trust (comrade Sodenkov), the head of the 3rd construction trust (comrade Gladkov), the secretary of the Party organization of the 3rd construction administration (comrade Repetia) and the subcontracting organizations . . . [to finish the construction] of the mechanical-assembly shop [of the Kharkov Tractor Works] by June 1, 1947." [17]

The Southern Heavy Construction Trust was subordinate to an All-Union ministry, and its Party secretary was a Party Organizer of the Central Committee.

To say that the basic Soviet definition of the Party-state relationship at the lower levels has been marked by a great deal of continuity is not to say that the influence of the local Party organs on Soviet decision-making has remained stable. When middle-level industrial administrators were moved into the oblast with the creation of the sovnarkhozy, the local Party organs (especially the obkomy) were obviously in a position to influence their decisions far more than when they worked in the ministries in Moscow. Likewise, when the amalgamation of the economic regions raised the sovnarkhozy above the oblast level, the principles defining the Party-state relationship dictated a significant reduction in the influence of the obkom on sovnarkhoz decisions.

There are many other factors that also result in variable influence of the local Party organs. When, as in the case of the Smolensk obkom in the 1930's, the Party officials in an area are judged primarily on the basis of the performance of one sector of the economy (in the Smolensk case, flax production [18]), the influence of the Party officials may be quite selective as they concentrate their attention on the state administrators in charge of that particular sector. When, as in Saratov oblast in 1959, the Party leadership removes a first secretary with long experience in agricultural regions and replaces him with a former plant director who had been in industrial management until the age of forty,[19] the meaningfulness of the supervision over the two branches of the economy will obviously change. (In fact, in the Saratov case that was precisely the reason for the change.) [20]

The important point is that the Party leadership has changed the influence of the local Party organs not by redefining the basic Party-state relationships, but by changing the technical qualifications of the Party officials, by changing the relative priority of the plan fulfillment in different sectors of the economy, by changing the territorial level at which particular administrators are located, by dividing the Party into industrial and agricultural components to allow Party officials more time for each branch.[21]

The Roles Assigned the Local Party Organs

To state that the local Party organ and its first secretary have the authority of a chief executive, of a prefect, is only to begin an analysis of their role vis-à-vis the industrial administrators in their area. There is not one superior-subordinate relationship, but rather a great number of them. At one extreme the superior (as in the case of many American baseball owners) may permit his subordinates almost complete freedom in decision-making, reserving for himself little more than the right to dismiss the subordinate if results are not satisfactory. At the other extreme the superior may (as in some foreman-worker relationships) provide detailed daily instruction and direction to the subordinate. Between these extremes are a series of intermediate possibilities.[22]

Unfortunately, because Soviet literature on the work of the local Party organs nowhere contains a systematic analysis of the proper role of these organs, one is compelled to rely on a great number of individual statements and criticisms that define a wide variety of roles, not all of them mutually reconcilable. The purpose here is simply to describe each of these roles as it emerges from Soviet administrative theory. Subsequent chapters will discuss the way in which each has been performed in practice and how inconsistencies among them seem usually to have been resolved.

Representation of the Party and Maintenance of Political Stability

Traditionally the most important function of a prefect or a prefect-like officer has been the preservation of law and order — the preservation of political stability — and normally he has had very wide-ranging authority for this purpose. Napoleon originally conceived of the prefect as an *empereur au petit pied,* and in Europe he has continued to be "the" representative of the government at the provincial level.[23] Similarly, in the colonial areas the district commissioner was the direct embodiment of the Mother Country.[24]

Soviet administrative theory seldom discusses such a prefectoral role for the local Party organs in explicit terms, but the Party officials obviously are seen as "the" representative of the Party in the area [25] — "the best people of the Party" [26] — with broad responsibility for defending "the pure name of the Party" and "its great cause." [27] The responsibility of the local Party organs for political stability is made abundantly clear. The first Party Congress to define the role of the local Party organs — the Eighth Congress held in 1919 — declared flatly that "the Russian Communist Party should win for itself undivided political domination (*gospodstvo*) in the soviets and practical control over all their work." [28] Since then, the Party organs have repeatedly been warned to lead a relentless struggle against "counter-revolutionary elements," "bourgeois nationalism," "manifestations of bourgeois ideology," and so forth. The seriousness with which the leadership takes this responsibility is indicated by the speedy removal of Party officials whose area is the scene of political disorder.[29]

In order that they may adequately carry out these duties, the local Party organs have been given a very broad mandate. The Party Rules obligate the Party member to report to the Party "any actions which harm the Party and the state," [30] and there is the clear implication that the Party organs should act on these reports. The Party Rules state that the Party organs "conduct within the boundaries of the republic, krai, oblast, city, and raion all work [necessary] for the achievement of the policy of the Party." [31] Consequently, as Party spokesmen frequently declare, "there is not a [single] question in the economic, cultural, and public life of the district in which the Party organ would not be interested." [32]

Inspirational Leadership and Mobilization of the Masses

The maintenance of political stability is one of those duties far from precise in its implications. To achieve it, one may use police power or may mediate group conflicts by concessions to the most dissatisfied groups. Inevitably, however, it must include efforts to maintain and strengthen the legitimacy of the existing political system.

From this point of view alone it is not surprising that Soviet spokesmen emphasize the responsibility of the local Party organs to mobilize support for the regime and its programs. Any Central Committee decision on ideological work will speak of "the forming of a Communist world view among the workers; the overcoming of survivals of the past in the consciousness and behavior of the Soviet people; . . . the training of the people in the spirit of Soviet patriotism and socialist internationalism; a decisive struggle against anti-Communism and all forms of bourgeois ideology; . . . [the training] of all Soviet people in a spirit of love and respect for the glorious Armed Forces of the Soviet Union; . . . the ensuring that the Program of the Communist Party of the Soviet Union will be brought into life." [33]

In mobilizing popular support, the local Party officials are not to limit themselves to agitation and propaganda activities. Like the traditional Western politician, they are also supposed to win the support of the citizens by convincing them that the Party is defending their interests. Although the leadership has long thought it necessary to give the highest priority to the "long-range interests" of the workers — that is, to the expansion of industrial production — it has also called on the local Party organs to look after the short-term interests of the workers as well. In Central Committee decrees on Party work in industry one almost always finds points that obligate the Party organs, "To display a more sympathetic attitude towards the needs of the working people and to take measures for further improving cultural and welfare services . . . paying particular attention to insuring the absolute fulfillment of the established plans of housing construction; . . . to guarantee the strict carrying out at the enterprises of all necessary measures for labor safety." [34]

In addition to showing concern for workers in general, the lower Party officials should also work to convince the workers that the Party is interested in them as individuals. In this role the secretary is to humanize the governmental process, correcting injustices perpetrated by insensitive bureaucrats and serving as "the ultimate dispenser of mercy and patronage." [35] Those who have studied the images of ideal Party secretaries in Soviet literature have discovered that this role is much emphasized there. Vera Dunham, for example, writes that Soviet literature "has made a great fuss about a Party leader's 'communion' with and 'love' for people. To take care of people is one of his main jobs." [36] Peter Bridges likewise finds that the good Party secretaries (that is, those not exposed and removed by the end of the book) were almost invariably kindly father-types.[37]

A long quote from the official handbook for Party officials gives some sense of the magnitude of the demands placed on the secretary by this conception of the Party:

> Of no small importance for the success of [his] work is the degree to which the Party leader maintains intimate and constant contact with Communists and non-Party people, the degree to which he is accessible to people.
>
> . . . First of all, the leader should himself seek meetings with people and should go to the places where they are located: the plants, the factories, the kolkhozy, and the institutions. A Party leader must not limit his presence to general meetings, to conversations with the factory director or the kolkhoz chairman, or to a fleeting trip through the production sections. Instead, he must establish contact with rank and file workers, collective farmers, and specialists. Otherwise there will only be the appearance of contact with the masses.
>
> . . . In this respect it goes without saying that there are different demands on a raikom secretary than on a secretary of the obkom. But each Party leader should go into the enterprises and the institutions — there where the fate of our economic plans is decided, where the basic mass of the working people are located. He should not go there for form's sake, but in order to talk with the people and to listen to their remarks and suggestions.
>
> . . . The quality of a leader is also judged by the degree to which he becomes acquainted with the letters of the working people . . . It is difficult to understand references to insufficient time or to being loaded down with other, more important matters when this work is discussed. . . . This is work with people. And what can be more important to a leader than work with people, meetings with them, and frank conversations which will help the leader to lead correctly.
>
> . . . Every real leader considers such work his indispensable obligation. The Party removes from supervisory work those who forget about it.[38]

At times the responsibilities of the local Party organs toward individual citizens and Party members take on a pastoral character. The

112

Party committee office has been described as a place where people can legitimately "come simply to ask advice on some personal matter or to hear an encouraging word," and the Party secretary a man who may be called on "to smooth out details of family life." [39] Although these purely pastoral functions are performed more consistently by the primary Party organizations, the local Party organs are also supposed to engage in them.

Although the mobilization activities of the local Party organs should be directed in large part toward development of political support for the regime, the Party organs should also carry on ideological work specifically directed toward fulfillment of the economic plan. In the 1963 Central Committee decision on ideological work, one finds a comprehensive list of the different Party duties in this realm: "It is necessary to instill in each worker a clear understanding of the fact that ensuring a high productivity of labor is a national task and the chief condition for the building of communism, to develop widespread socialist competition, to introduce progressive experience, to surround the heroes of labor with honor and respect, to struggle against a bureaucratic relationship towards the creative initiative of the working people, and to raise all the forces of society in a struggle against parasites, drunkards, and loafers." [40]

In seeking to mobilize the energies of the citizens for the fulfillment of the economic plan, the local Party officials should strive to inspire those who work in the area as well as to indoctrinate them. A *Pravda* editorial declares that "it is the duty of each Party official, whether great or small, to introduce a spirit of enthusiasm and of creative labor into the production group." [41] The Party secretary must have "the ability to find a path to peoples' hearts"; he must be "a real man of the people (*massovik*) who knows how to work with fire (*gorenie*) and how to transfer this fire to the group in which he acts." [42] Although much of this effort is to be directed toward the stimulation of enthusiasm among the workers, the Party organs also have similar responsibilities toward managerial personnel at all levels. [43]

Personnel Selection

If one of the local managerial personnel does not prove to be sufficiently inspired in the performance of his duties, the local Party organs are in a position to do more than simply intensify their ideological work. They normally have the authority to replace such an official with another who works with more fire. Indeed, they have a duty to do so. Since the early 1920's one of the key responsibilities, if not *the* key responsibility of Party organs at all territorial levels has been the "selection and distribution of supervisory personnel." [44] In the words of one of the foremost Soviet authorities on Party work, "The Party could not lead the work of the soviet, economic, and public organizations nor could it direct all sides of the state, cultural, and economic life of the country if it did not have the possibility of placing personnel in accordance with political and economic problems." [45]

One aspect of the personnel responsibilities of the local Party organs is the general maintenance and strengthening of educational, technical, and moral standards in personnel selection throughout the governmental service. Repeatedly, for example, the local Party organs have been instructed to strive for an increase in the number of college-trained engineers in technical and managerial positions.[46]

However, the responsibilities of the local Party organs in personnel selection go far beyond general supervision. In two types of situations, the local Party organs are required to give their formal consent before personnel action can be taken. First, if a member of the Party holds a job, he (and his superior) must seek the agreement of the local raikom (or gorkom if there are no raiony in the city) before he leaves the job. Second, if an administrative post has been considered sufficiently important to be placed within the formal jurisdiction of a local Party organ, that Party organ must give its "confirmation" before any personnel action can be taken with respect to that post.

The requirement that a Communist receive the permission of the lowest Party organ before changing his job comes from Lenin's original conception of a Party member. The Party member is still viewed somewhat as the professional revolutionary of *What Is to Be Done;* he is to be a man who has given his life wholeheartedly to the Party and who is completely at its disposal. He "does not have the right to move from place to place at his own discretion or change his work as he thinks best. He can do this only with the permission of the Party organization." [47] From at least 1946 to 1954, it was the obkom, kraikom, or the republican central committee in an oblastless republic whose permission was required. Even in this period, however, the real decision was usually made by the raikom or (in cities without raiony) the gorkom, and in 1954 these institutions were granted the authority to permit departures of local Communists themselves.[48]

Control over a Party member's movements is enforced through the procedures by which Party membership is registered. Each Communist has not only a Party card that he himself carries, but also a registration card kept on file at the raikom of the district in which he works.[49] When the member changes jobs, his card must be transferred or (if his new job is in the same raion) updated. The raikom has the right to object to the removal of a man if it thinks his absence will have a serious impact on production — and it has this right even if the man's economic department has ordered his transfer. Indeed, the rules require the signature of the first secretary himself before the move is approved.[50] In those cases when the economic department disagrees with the raikom's objection, the question is settled by a higher Party organ.[51]

A far more important control on personnel selection is the stipulation that personnel in a number of administrative posts cannot be changed without a particular Party organ confirming the action. Each local Party organ has been given a list of positions — its *nomenklatura* — and must give its approval before the occupant of a listed post is removed or a replacement named. The nomenklatury or lists of the various Party organs are quite broad and include not only the directorships of all significant factories, but also many lesser managerial posts in the most important enterprises.

The term "nomenklatura" is a general one; a state administrative office also has a nomenklatura — a list of positions for which it has the authority to make personnel changes.[52] Consequently, any important administrative post will normally be within the nomenklatura of both a Party organ and a state organ, and hence both must be involved before a personnel change can be made final. (In this book, however, the word "nomenklatura" will always refer only to Party nomenklatura.)

In accordance with the canons of one-man management, the Party organs cannot formally appoint or dismiss an official within their nomenklatura (except one in a nonelected post within their own apparatus), but instead they are given only the power to "confirm" an action taken by the formally constituted administrative body or the electorate (if the post is formally an elected one). In practice, as will be seen in Chapter VII, the role of the local Party organ can be much more active than the word "confirm" implies, for the Party organs should participate in personnel decisions long before the "confirmation" stage is reached. Indeed, the initiative with respect to a personnel change is frequently taken by the Party organ, and in operational Party theory it often should be.

Although the Party organ should concentrate its attention most directly on the posts in its nomenklatura, the Party leadership has declared that "this does not mean that work with personnel of other categories can be neglected." [53] In order to try to guarantee that the Party organs pay attention to other personnel, the leadership has given each Party organ a second list of positions — the *uchetnaia nomenklatura* or accounting list. The Party committee's confirmation is not required when changes are made in positions on its *uchetnaia nomenklatura,* but it must be informed of any changes in them. The purpose of this list is to keep each Party organ acquainted with a secondary group of officials in the area so that it can "study these people attentively," "follow their growth," and "create a reserve fund from which to promote new officials." [54] (The existence of the *uchetnaia nomenklatura* means that an important state official may be in the regular nomenklatura of one local Party organ and in the *uchetnaia nomenklatura* of another Party organ at a higher level.[55])

Verifying Performance and Providing Policy Guidance

In democratic governments local Party organs frequently play a major role in advancing candidates and in selecting personnel for patronage posts, but they often take little responsibility for and little interest in the decision-making activities of these men once they are in office. In the Soviet Union, however, this is not the case. Even in the Stalin period nothing has been so condemned as those local Party organs that simply provide "leadership in general." [56]

With the possible exception of ideological-mobilization work and personnel selection, no responsibility of the local Party organs is more discussed than that of their checking the performance of the area's managers, correcting their mistakes, and providing policy guidance. To be sure, the governmental supervisors of local managers also have this responsibility, but there is never any suggestion that this might limit the Party organs' participation in these activities. In fact, the awkward 1962 reorganization of the Party was officially justified on the grounds that it would give the local Party organs the time necessary to fulfill this responsibility more thoroughly.

During Stalin's lifetime Soviet spokesmen could be particularly blunt in explaining the necessity for the local Party organs to check on the performance of plant managers, to report any defects, and to enforce strict observance both of the letter and spirit of the law and plan. "Experience shows," one Soviet writer stated, "that the best officials left to themselves without control and verification of their activity . . . begin to become corrupt and bureaucratized." [57] In recent years Soviet discussions are usually not quite so direct, but the Soviet leaders continue to demand that the local Party organs help local industrial officials to avoid this fate.

The local Party organs have been given a number of tools with which to verify the performance of the managers. The departments are provided with instructors to seek information about conditions in the field; the primary Party organizations can be required to submit written protocols about their meetings as well as other more specific information; [58] and the rank-and-file members are obligated by the Party Rules "to speak out against any actions which harm the Party and the state and to inform the Party organs, right up to the Central Committee, about them." [59] Indeed, during the Khrushchev years the Party organs were given still other instruments for verification. In 1959, as has been noted, commissions were created under the primary Party organizations to assist in this task; in 1962 a Party-State Control Committee was created and given the duty to conduct its own investigations — investigations based in part on its wide network of "posts" in industrial plants.

Although the local Party organs are required to collect information partly in order to keep the higher Party organs informed,[60] the main purpose of this activity, according to Soviet spokesmen, is to provide the basis for corrective action. One of the words that appears most frequently in discussions of the relationship between Party secretaries and industrial administrators is *trebovatelnyi* — "demanding" or "exacting" — and it is repeatedly used to describe the proper attitude of the local Party organs in maintaining the strictest Party and state discipline by the administrators.

The endless demand that the Party organs *vospityvat* (train or educate) the industrial administrators also refers largely to the inculcation of high standards of legality and good discipline. Thus, in a Soviet book entitled *The Leninist Principles of Selection, Distribution, and Training (Vospitanie) of Personnel,* the section on *vospitanie* contains very little discussion of propagating Marxist-Leninist philosophy. Instead, its author concentrates on "the training of personnel in the spirit of high responsibility for the business entrusted to them." He declares that "correctly to train (*vospityvat*) personnel means to make high demands on officials . . . and openly to indicate [to them] the mistakes and neglected areas in their work." [61]

The enforcement of legality should not be limited to the letter of the law and plan; the spirit of the law is also important. The local Party organs are told to concern themselves with all the semi-illegal activities of managers so fully described by Joseph Berliner — the seeking of a lower plan, the inflation of requests for supplies, the hoarding of supplies, the sacrifice of quality and of individual plan indicators in the interests of fulfilling the plan for gross production, and the use of influence, personal favors, and "pushers" to cut corners in supplies procurement. The Party leadership professes to believe that the local Party organs are especially well equipped to prevent these various types of "localism" because of "the fact that [they] are independent [of the state agencies], that they are not tied by departmental interests." [62]

In addition to insuring observance of legality, the local Party organs are directed to provide policy guidance when "questions of principle" arise. They must not only "control" the enterprises but also "lead" (*rukovodit*) them, and the "questions of principle" on which leadership is to be exercised can be quite specific. As the first secretary of the Minsk gorkom emphasized in 1967: "The formula 'do not supplant' does not at all mean that the Party committee can walk away from economic questions. I am speaking not only about the large, long-range problems, but also about the daily matters with which the working collectives live. Can the Party organ stand aside if the work at an enterprise is not going well? No, it cannot." [63]

In Party theory the greatest emphasis on local Party participation in concrete decision-making is, however, placed on what the Minsk first secretary called "the large, long-range problems." The local Party officials are depicted as men freed from the time-consuming details of operational administration, who can concentrate their efforts on the most important matters. Like the board of directors in an American firm, like the Policy Planning Staff of the United States Department of State, the local Party organs are supposed to be the reflective bodies which rise above the pressures of today and provide the general policy direction to those who are enmeshed in those pressures.

In the words of Lazar Slepov, "The obligation of the Party organs is to pick out the fundamental questions and to concentrate the attention of the Party, soviet, and economic organizations on them. They should keep in view first of all questions such as: In what direction should things be moving? What is indispensable to develop in a given . . . region? What should be the mutual interrelationships between different branches of the economy? . . . What measures must be carried out to put the reserves [of the economy] into operation and to achieve the best results?" [64]

Because long-range considerations in industry are so closely connected with technical progress (and because the Soviet incentive system sometimes makes technical progress unrewarding for a manager), official spokesmen also emphasize the role of the local Party organs in promoting technical innovation. No action earns a Party organ such fulsome praise in the press as its intervention to force a cautious administrator to introduce an invention or new work-technique. It is no accident that the conflict between an energetic Party secretary and a conservative manager over the question of technical innovation is one of the most recurrent themes in the Soviet novel on contemporary industry.

Area Coordination and Resolution of Group Conflicts

Conceptualizing a prefectoral type of organization, one thinks first of the maintenance of law and order and then (particularly in the setting of a fairly well-developed system of technical services) of the coordination of the various governmental officials in the area. It is generally recognized that in modern conditions the latter function becomes much more important than the former.[65]

However, an examination of Soviet statements about the proper role of the local Party organs discloses relatively little about area coordination. To be sure, there are a few general statements about the duty of the local Party organs to "unite" and "coordinate" the activity of "all the Soviet, economic, and public organizations," [66] but these are relatively rare. Far more usual are complaints that the Party organs intervene too much in the resolution of conflicts among local officials, particularly those involving the relative priority of supply deliveries. When an article in the Soviet press reports that a local Party organ is acting as "an intermediary stage between different economic organs," [67] it scarcely does so in order to praise.

The warnings against excessive involvement in interdepartmental disputes (particularly on questions of supplies procurement) have been harsh enough for some to conclude that Party participation in these activities is viewed as illegitimate by the Soviet leadership. These Soviet warnings should be evaluated with perspective, and their significance should not be exaggerated. Even the warnings against involvement in supplies procurement are directed against *excessive* involvement, and throughout the post-Purge period they have been counterbalanced by the repeated demand that the Party organs ensure that "cooperating" factories time their deliveries correctly. In the words of a 1941 *Pravda* editorial, " 'All plants, factories, mines, and railroads are obligated to fulfill the plan.' The realization of this demand depends in significant measure on how well the economic ties between enterprises are adjusted, on how well their work is coordinated. . . . Practice shows us serious deficiencies in the work of cooperating (*kooperirovannye*) enterprises. Often we meet with a case in which, for example, a machine tool plant which has prepared a complex machine tool cannot deliver it to the customer because of the absence of some insignificant part. . . . In the establishment of efficient work of cooperating firms, much depends on the local Party organs, which are obligated to know which branch of industry, which plants or factories are cooperating with this or that enterprise in its raion, oblast, krai, or republic." [68]

A 1967 *Pravda* editorial was more succinct. Calling for the expansion of the use of contracts in supplies procurement, the editorial added, "It is indispensable to strengthen Party control over the fulfillment of contract obligations." [69]

The limited nature of the warnings against involvement in supplies procurement can be clearly seen in the Soviet press response to a local Party organ failing to intervene to expedite the delivery of some urgently needed supply. Thus, when a group of officials in Minsk once blamed their plan nonfulfillment on the tardy delivery of parts from Tambov, a Soviet editorial writer retorted sharply, "If the Minsk people had placed this question before the Tambov Party organization in time, such a disruption would not have occurred." [70]

The more general responsibility of promoting regional *soglasovanie* — the smoothing out of differences, the achievement of interdepartmental agreement — is recognized even more explicitly and frequently in the call on the local Party organs to "unite" and "coordinate" the governmental agencies. As has already been mentioned, industry, construction, and transportation have largely been supervised by organizations (at least below the republican level) administratively independent of the soviets that coordinate other spheres of life. When conflicts develop in the directives or interests of the separate administrative hierarchies, there is frequently no nearby state agency that can resolve them. Consequently, as one Party official asserted in 1956, "Understandably there are not a few questions which leaders of the Soviet and economic organizations are compelled to take to the obkom, and we are obligated to take the necessary measures to solve them." [71]

In late 1965 the first secretary of the Cherkassy gorkom summarized very concretely one aspect of this role that the "gorkom has to assume": "In our city there are four construction trusts and over thirty sub-contracting organizations. As a rule, they are subordinated to different departments, but they work on one project. Since there is not an economic organization in the city which could coordinate their activity, the Party gorkom has to assume that role. The officials of the industrial-transportation department and the gorkom secretary who handles industrial questions continually coordinate (*soglasovaiut*), 'settle' (*utriasaiut*), and call economic leaders to conferences." [72]

Although Party leaders and officials have recognized the general legitimacy of local Party participation in detailed coordination work, there have been differences over the proper extent of this participation, a difference which came out clearly in an interchange published in *Pravda* in 1967. In February, G. V. Kolbin, the first secretary of the Nizhnii Tagil gorkom (and an engineer with a dozen years in engineering and managerial work [73]) wrote an article condemning excess Party involvement in detailed managerial work. He acknowledged that "willingly or unwillingly" the gorkomy must try "to settle 'conflicts' between builders and customers," but he expressed considerable dissatisfaction with this role.[74] In July a plant manager writing on the same subject referred to the Kolbin article and indicated his disagreement: "I cannot agree with comrade Kolbin at the point where he regrets that the gorkom 'willingly or unwillingly' has to interfere in the resolution of this kind of question. My opinion is that contacts of the Party and economic leaders should be as systematic as possible."

> Surely is not the Party official and the Party committee obligated to help the industrial administrator (*khoziaistvennik*) and the specialist to find the correct solution to a difficult production problem? . . . [What if the administrator] encountered red-tape in higher economic organs, in a word, could not achieve the necessary results? Can the Party organization of the enterprise and the [local] Party committee stand aside? No, they cannot. . . . If such a practice qualifies as supplanting, if it is called "current details" (*tekuchka*), then what does Party help to the economic administrators mean? . . . In my opinion there is nothing shameful if the Party gorkom sometimes "appraises the lists of construction projects (*titulnye spiski*) and

brings them into harmony with the plans of the enterprises and with the financing." [75]

This disagreement between the gorkom secretary and the plant manager is not an isolated one. Often Westerners conceive of a struggle between the Party apparatus and the managers in which the Party officials incessantly attempt to interfere in managerial affairs and the managers persistently resist this intervention. As the above disagreement suggests, however, this conception is much too simple. The essential question has been — what kind of Party intervention? Many Party officials have found deep and continual involvement in supplies procurement and construction coordination "shameful" for the "leading organ in Soviet society," but most managers have understood the need for this assistance and have welcomed it. Men such as the Nizhnii Tagil Party leader have believed that the Party officials should concentrate more attention on "policy questions" — for example, the nature of the plan and of the technical policy — but the managers have surely been less eager for this type of local Party intervention.

This particular disagreement is, I think, at the heart of the so-called Party-state conflict which has even engaged members of the Politburo. The basic conflict on this question between Malenkov and Zhdanov — and particularly between Malenkov and Khrushchev — did not involve the question: should the Party organs concentrate their attention on ideological-organizational work? Rather, it centered on the preferable type of Party involvement in managerial affairs. Malenkov adhered to the managerial position as expressed in the director's article just cited, while Zhdanov and particularly Khrushchev adhered to the position of the Nizhnii Tagil first secretary. The 1962 reorganization of the Party apparatus was not intended to involve the Party organs in administrative details, but to give them time for other functions.[76]

On this question — as on so many others — the post-Khrushchev Party leadership seems to have adopted a compromise position. However, in reuniting the Party apparatus, they did recognize the coordinating role of the local Party organs very explicitly. It was acknowledged that "the oblast is a single living organism where industry, agriculture, and the sectors serving them are intimately intertwined and interconnected" [77] and that the unified Party organ had been a vital instrument in uniting it. In particular, an editorial in *Partiinaia zhizn* referred with very considerable understanding to this function served by the Party organs prior to 1962 and strongly implied that one of the main purposes of the reunification of Party apparatus was to permit the function to be served once more: "[Prior to 1962] the administrative divisions of the country had been changed. The names of the organizations had been changed. But always within the boundaries of this or that administrative unit, there was a single Party organization which embraced all of the given area. The Party organ in this area united and coordinated the activity of all the Soviet, economic, and public organizations. It led and bore complete responsibility for all sides of the political, economic, and cultural life. Each Party committee . . . saw the outlook for the development of the krai, oblast, or raion as a whole and could distribute personnel correctly and more rationally." [78]

The Dilemmas of the Party Organs

As one surveys the roles and work load of the local Party organs, one is struck by the great breadth of their responsibilities. These organs have been given a span of control unparalleled in the Western world. They are literally responsible for every kind of political, economic, and cultural activity within their area. Even from 1962 to 1964, when agriculture and other rural activities were assigned to special agricultural Party committees, the industrial Party committees had the duty of supervising not only all industrial plants within their respective areas, but also all construction, transportation, urban trade, urban education, urban cultural life, and so forth. It is not surprising that Khrushchev could provoke "gay animation" among the audience at the November 1962 session of the Central Committee by declaring, "Under present conditions the [obkom] first secretary requires almost the whole day just to receive the other obkom secretaries — and when does he find time to work!" [79]

As if this were not enough, they have been assigned a multiplicity of roles, many of them mutually contradictory. Even leaving aside nonindustrial responsibilities, the Party secretary must serve as chief industrial executive, political boss, and head of the trade union council in an area the size of a county, city, or state. He is detached from operating responsibilities so that he can engage in long-range thinking and planning — and yet he has very detailed duties in verification, coordination, and supplies procurement. He is an executive who must intervene to protect citizens from injustices by the very bureaucracy that he is leading — and he must do so without undue interference in the detailed administrative work of the officials of this bureaucracy. In addition to all this, he must travel widely in order to have many heart-to-heart conversations with the workers.

The multiplicity of roles and the large span of control has created a work load for the local Party organs that has greatly affected their relationship with the local industrial administrators. Inevitably, the work of the local Party organ must assume what Khrushchev called a "campaign character." However deeply a local Party organ may involve itself in a particular industrial decision, there cannot be enough time to intervene consistently throughout the district. Whatever happens on a particular decision, there must on the average be a considerable amount of autonomy for the state officials. Moreover, the work load also must inexorably force the local Party organs to choose among the roles assigned them. Even if there were no contradictions among these roles, the pressure of time would prevent full realization of all of them.

The rest of the book will be concerned with ascertaining how, in fact, the Party officials resolve the dilemmas of their position. Which roles do the local Party organs tend to emphasize and which do they tend to ignore? How is each of them "reinterpreted" by the pressure of events?

VI. Mobilizing the Population

To a Westerner one of the most striking features of Soviet society is the degree of the concern of the leadership with the world-view of its citizens. All political leaders are interested in developing support for their political program, for the political institutions of the society, and in general for law and order, but few would set for themselves any such goal as "the forming of a scientific world-view based on Marxism-Leninism as a complete, well-balanced system of philosophical, economic, and social-political views in all the working people of Soviet society." [1] And even fewer would take so many different kinds of action to achieve this goal.

As representatives of the Party in the area, the local Party organs are obligated to help in the realization of this ideological program. Their ideological work includes supervision of education, publishing houses, the press, radio and television, local theater, and so forth. However, as much of the ideological work is ultimately carried out by the primary Party organizations and as these organizations are based on the members' place of work rather than on their place of residence, the local Party organs in urban areas find that a large proportion of their ideological work must be conducted within the industrial enterprise. This chapter will not deal with the total mobilization program of the local Party organs, but will be concerned only with the work carried on through the primary Party organization, specifically the primary Party organization of the industrial enterprise. The first part of the chapter will describe the program, and the second half will be devoted to the specific role of the local Party organs in conducting it.

The Mobilization Program

In the Soviet Union the importance of the place of work as a center for political socialization is undoubtedly declining with the development of the mass media, but the factory still remains the scene of a very considerable amount of ideological activity. As the prerevolutionary Party cells were originally formed in the place of work, the establishment of one-Party rule (coupled with the Leninist conception of the need to raise the level of "consciousness" of the workers) made it virtually inevitable that the cells would continue to try to mobilize support for the Party and its program. This practice has persisted because it meets important needs of the industrialization drive.

One of the major consequences — and prerequisites — of the industrialization drive has been a mass influx of peasants into the city and into factory life. These persons have been imbued (particularly in the thirties) not only with alien political values, but also with the familiar set of "traditional values" that have hindered the performance of new industrial laborers everywhere. In the factory, all of the newcomers could easily be "embraced" by ideological work and embraced on a face-to-face basis rather than by more abstract — and more expensive — means of communication. Moreover, in the factory, ideological work could be easily linked with specific appeals for greater productivity and with general attempts to inculcate the discipline and the achievement-oriented norms required in industrial society.

Within the factory a wide range of methods has been used to increase the exposure of the workers to the themes emphasized by the Party. Lower Party officials have been permitted considerable amounts of freedom in developing new forms of ideological work, and one constantly finds press reports about experiments that have worked well in some plant or area. The lower Party officials may organize an economic lecture series to propagate specifically industrial information, or they may establish at the enterprise special councils or commissions on atheism.[2] All Party committees are obligated to conduct campaigns to increase the percentage of employees who subscribe to newspapers [3] or who are engaged in adult education at night, and some have organized radio networks throughout the shops so that special news or appeals may be transmitted to the workers without taking them from their place of work.[4]

Since 1929 the most widespread mobilization program has been the organization of "socialist competition" among workers, brigades, shops, plants, and even districts or cities.[5] The competition can involve almost any aspect of factory work — fulfillment of plan indicators, lowering of costs, the number of rationalizers' suggestions, the speed at which orders for a high-priority project are completed, and so forth. It very often entails assuming "socialist obligations" to overfulfill the plan by a certain percentage and to do this with even more economy than the plan indicators require.

Socialist competition is normally depicted as a voluntary form of social activity that springs spontaneously from the collective itself. In the ideal case a worker will see a problem and will propose competition to resolve it; his fellow workers will see the wisdom of this proposal, will accept it, and will respond energetically in fulfilling the obligations embodied in it. The competition is often formalized with great ceremony, and boards may be erected on which the progress of the competition is recorded. Banners (and in some cases more material rewards) may be awarded to the victors. The competition implies a winner and striving for victory is obviously seen as a meaningful incentive, but the use of the adjective "socialist" in front of the word "competition" is supposed to mean that the competition is not of a selfish nature. Rather, two competing individuals or groups are called on to help each other by exchanging ideas and experiences about the most effective production techniques.

Despite the supposedly voluntary nature of socialist competition, the number of employees engaged in it is so large that one strongly suspects that the work of the Party and trade union organizations in leading it goes far beyond mere persuasion. (In both 1949 and 1965, some ninety percent of the workers, engineering personnel, and white collar workers in the Soviet Union were said to be engaged in socialist competition.) [6] In fact, the Party and trade union organizations in the plants are instructed to ensure widespread competition among their workers.

There is reason to think that the Party organs not only organize socialist competition but also control it. The reporting of Stalinist socialist competition often conveyed the impression of workers presenting impossible obligations to put pressure on conservative managers, but it is unlikely that the competition was ever this "unorganized." Moreover, in recent years there has been explicit recognition of the need for "objectivity" in the obligations, and, by implication, the role of the Party officials in preserving this "objectivity": "A reporter, having heard about [the ship] Vostok, asked a foreman: 'Will you finish it ahead of schedule?' This man, not being well-informed about the planned schedule, answered, 'We will try.' And the next day the Leningraders learned that 'having taken on themselves a heightened obligation, the collective of the Admiralty Works unanimously . . .' This incident alarmed the secretary of the Party committee, comrade Poliakov. How could he not be agitated? In order to finish the Vostok ahead of schedule, it would be necessary to take workers from other ships, and thus hold up their planned delivery. Why? For what reason? The chief thing is that it is unprofitable. 'And we won't do this,' said the secretary." [7]

The direct supervision of the socialist competition is the responsibility of the primary Party organization in the plant, but the local Party organs have the duty of ensuring that the socialist competition remains vigorous in all the plants. In addition, the local Party organs also should pick out specific innovations in individual plants and see that these "initiatives" (*pochiny*) are taken up throughout the area. At times such an "initiative" will be supported by higher Party organs and will become the subject of a major nationwide movement. During the sovnarkhoz period campaigns were built around an "initiative" of Nikolai Mamai, a coal-mine brigadier who called for the production of one ton of above-plan coal per shift, and around that of Valentina Gaganova, a brigadier in a textile plant who volunteered to lead a "lagging" brigade and to raise its productivity.[8] (Both Mamai and Gaganova were elected to the Central Committee in 1961 as a result of their "initiatives.")

The most famous of all these campaigns was the Stakhanovite movement that began in 1935 and continued until shortly after Stalin's death.[9] The movement was named after a coal mine foreman, Stakhanov, who reorganized the work methods of his crew so that in one day they were able to dig 102 tons of coal instead of the usual norm of 7 tons. At its core the Stakhanovite movement continued to have as its ideal this type of rationalization of the work processes by the workers themselves. The Stakhanovite was to improve his own skills, try to develop production shortcuts, and, most important, teach these skills and shortcuts to the poorer workers. Moreover, he was also encouraged to suggest more important changes to the managers and to fight for their introduction. "Production conferences" and other types of meetings continued to be held to provide a formal setting for making these suggestions.

The Stakhanovite movement became a mass one, and by July 1, 1939, 33.8 percent of the labor force were Stakhanovites.[10] At an advanced plant like the Leningrad Optics-Mechanical Works, as many as eighty-three percent of the workers might be Stakhanovites and shock workers. The number of Stakhanovites continued to rise: in 1951 seventy percent of the workers in an industrialized raion in Yaroslavl had been given this title.[11] In the process the term "Stakhanovite" came to be applied to almost any efficient worker and thereby (hopefully) to serve as a widespread status symbol and a moral incentive for laggards.

The major successor to the Stakhanovite movement (and the most important effort to mobilize the energies of the workers in the post-Stalin period) has been the drive to promote "brigades of Communist labor" and "plants of Communist labor." [12] In many ways the "Communist labor" movement has had the same goals as the Stakhanovite movement, and it has called on the worker to undertake much the same kind of action. In its emphasis, however, it has tended less to encourage the type of one-day record that Stakhanov set (and that many tried to emulate in their own industry or enterprise), and instead has tended to stress the quality of work. Indeed, the movement is also concerned with the "quality of life" as well as with production goals, and has attempted to foster a more comradely, more pleasant industrial enterprise.

Like its predecessor, the campaign for "Communist labor" has demanded that the good worker improve not only his own work but also that of his less efficient comrades, and, in focusing on the brigade, it attempts to give the good worker a psychological incentive to do this. As misbehavior or inefficiency on the part of one member of the brigade can cause the entire brigade to lose its title and banner, the leadership has hoped that the conscientious members of the brigade will be motivated to bring severe pressure to bear on those members who might "shame" it.[13]

Whatever the success of the Communist labor movement in achieving its goals (and there have been complaints of formalism in its organization), it clearly has succeeded in achieving a mass character. By the spring of 1963, twenty-one million persons were competing in the movement of Communist labor, including seventy percent of the "toilers" in the metallurgy, chemical, energy, and textile enterprises. By the summer of 1965 the number of competitors had risen to thirty million.[14]

One of the means of promoting socialist competition — and a strikingly unique feature of Soviet ideological work — has been the use of "agitation" (*agitatsiia*), the attempt to convey relatively simple ideas on a face-to-face basis. Initiated at a time when literacy and the mass media were not sufficiently developed, agitation even today is called "one of the most important (*vazhneishee*) means of Party communication with the masses, a tried and true method of persuading the working people and of explaining the policy of the Party to them."[15]

To a Westerner visiting a Soviet plant, the most noticeable form of agitation is "visual agitation"— the use of placards, banners, signs, and bulletin boards aimed at improving the worker's political consciousness and/or mobilizing his energies for the improvement of production.[16] At the entrance to the factory and in its main entrance hall the worker usually sees a large banner proclaiming dedication to the Party and to certain of its main goals (for instance, "We will fulfill the decisions of the Twenty-second Party Congress"). Scattered through the factory are smaller placards pledging fulfillment of the plan or of socialist obligations, raising of labor productivity, maintenance of quality standards, and so forth. In one spot there may be some graphic indicator (a thermometer, for example) showing the extent to which the Komsomol have fulfilled their socialist obligation to save the enterprise money through economizing and the introduction of innovations.

Associated with this exhortative agitation are a number of visual indicators of approval or disapproval of the work and behavior of individual workers — indicators which, it is hoped, will stimulate better performance by all the workers. In the factory yard or main corridors there are certain to be pictures of workers who have overfulfilled their plan by the greatest amount. At many of the machines will be little signs indicating that this worker is "a shock-worker (*udarnik*) of Communist labor" or that this group is "a brigade of Communist labor." There will also be bulletin boards containing "lightning bolts" (*molniia*) directed at persons responsible for defects, and caricatures of these persons may be posted there. There may also be public lists of the percentage by which each worker either overfulfilled or under-fulfilled his norms.

The other major form of agitation within the plant has been oral agitation — the attempt to convey ideas to workers on a face-to-face basis by a person with whom they are familiar. Individual oral agitation has been a many-sided activity. It has involved reading aloud an important article or speech from the newspaper, the delivery of a fif-teen to twenty minute talk on a timely subject,[17] or the attempt to persuade an individual worker on an individual basis that he is mis-taken either in his beliefs or in his conduct.

The themes raised in an agitation session can be very diverse. In December 1963, for example, the following were suggested as desir-able subjects for agitation work during the month: (1) putting the decisions of the December plenum of the Central Committee into life; (2) the participation of the workers in the compilation of the five-year plan; (3) improving the quality of output; (4) using the capacity of the machines completely; (5) cleanliness at the workers' place; (6) the shirker — a shame for the collective; (7) the inter-national situation; and (8) training children in the family.[18] Other themes that have often been discussed are the advantages of high norms for the workers, the evils and errors of religious beliefs, the revolutionary and wartime traditions of the local plant and area, and, of course, the need to assume higher socialist obligations and to ful-fill them.

As Inkeles points out, Lenin rejected the idea that agitation would primarily be a call for action,[19] but the examples cited indicate that agitation usually does have an immediacy which is associated with a call for action. Even the nonproduction themes tend to center on cur-rent policy or current events rather than on more general ideological subjects (except in the case of religion), and agitators are usually in-structed to end their discussions of nonproduction questions by draw-ing concrete implications from them. A talk about "American imperialism," for example, may be concluded with a reminder about the need to sacrifice or to work hard, and it may turn out that improved quality in the products of the local shop will constitute a major blow at "international reactionary circles."

The scale of the agitation effort in the Soviet Union is difficult to gauge, in large part because of the scarcity of comprehensive statistics. However, the effort clearly has fluctuated very considerably depending on the campaign being conducted by the Party leadership and on the energy of local Party officials. Thus, at the Krivoi Rog Steel Plant (8,300 workers in the summer of 1958) there were 134 agitators in 1958, but 1,172 in 1962.[20] Although this increase was partially a product of expansion at the plant during this period, it primarily reflected the differing intensity of local Party interest in agitation in the two periods. It is quite likely that the ratio of agitators to workers in Krivoi Rog in 1958 and 1962 represent the upper and lower limits of these ratios in large-scale Soviet industry. A more typical example is probably that of the Dnepro Special Steel Plant (Zaporozhe) in 1957: 11,000 workers and 550 agitators. But because the agitators should be concentrated in certain crucial points in the plants, the Odessa Steel Rolling Plant may not have been completely atypical in having one agitator attached to each three to four men "in a series of shops." [21]

The scale of the agitation effort is also difficult to estimate because of changes which have occurred in the program in recent years. As has been increasingly recognized, agitation in its simpler forms was far more appropriate for a poorly educated population than a well-educated one. In the words of a leader of a brigade of Communist labor, "How long can adults, [politically] conscious people, continue to be considered part of the barely conscious, 'unreached masses'?" [22] One of the first — and quite widespread — responses to this problem was a formalistic approach to much of oral agitation. By limiting agitation to the reading aloud of a newspaper article and by treating it as an unfortunate chore rather than a serious attempt at instruction, the agitator could reduce the strains which agitation might otherwise place on his relationship with his fellow workers. The following newspaper report undoubtedly illuminates a very frequent occurrence:

At times you open a newspaper and you see a photo — three men listening to a fourth. And the title: an agitator reads the newspaper to the workers.

. . . It is the dinner break. Some hurry to the dining hall, others unwrap a package with sandwiches, others gather in small groups and discuss something. Each is going about his own business. Only one man is looming in the section. He is the agitator. Yesterday he had been called into the Party bureau, and "shaped up" (*snimali struzhku*): why, you haven't conducted a reading-aloud session for a long time! Today it is necessary to organize one at any cost. And he approaches the worker at the neighboring machine:

"Friend, let's gather five people, and I will read you the paper."

The worker raises his head in surprise.

"Don't you see that I am busy with this? Or do you consider me illiterate?"

The agitator hurried to another machinist and received the answer:

"Why are you bothering me? I want to eat and to rest. This evening I will read the paper with a pencil in my hand. I have a test at the technicum . . ."

The agitator finally rounds up five men, and he reads so quickly that you don't gain an understanding of the words. [After all], there was little time left. One man is eating his sandwich, another looks at the ceiling, the third thinks about his own concerns. And this is how the photo-reporter catches them.

Thus there appears a picture in the newspaper. Thus, a checkmark is placed after the name of the agitator, and a new figure is entered into the summary data of political-mass work of the Party committee: a certain number of people were reached.[23]

The growing difficulties associated with agitation have finally produced a major change in the program. A greater use has been made of "mass forms of agitation" — particularly meetings and question-and-answer sessions [24] — and individual agitation has become increasingly specialized. The Twenty-third Party Congress emphasized the need to base agitation on "information widely and systematically delivered to the population," and the means chosen to achieve this goal has been a new type of agitator — the *"politinformator"* [25] (the political communicator). The politinformator is an agitator who specializes on a particular type of question. For example, the 219 politinformators at the First Ballbearing Works in Moscow in late 1967 were divided into three groups: 67 on economic questions, 65 on international affairs, 87 on questions of Communist morality.[26] They are to be "qualified men, widely knowledgeable on a given subject, who regularly receive and deeply illuminate the freshest information on a particular circle of questions." Consequently, there is no pretense that the politinformator is to be a fellow worker; rather he is to be selected from among "the supervisory Party, soviet, trade union, and economic officials and from the engineers, teachers, doctors, agronomists, and other specialists who have proven themselves in political work."[27] A politinformator does not restrict his activity to one particular section or shop, but speaks or leads discussions on his subject in a variety of locations.

The relationship of the politinformator to the rest of the oral agitation program remains uncertain. One Party member asserted in a letter to *Pravda*, "It has become clear that this is not an experiment, but a seriously thought-out liquidation of the institution of the agitators." However, the deputy secretary of the First Ballbearing Works in Moscow, who was given the assignment of responding to this letter, vigorously denied the charge and indicated that at his plant the *agitkollektiv* (the group of agitators) continued to exist side-by-side with the group of politinformators.[28]

To a considerable extent, the question is a semantic one. In an interview in the summer of 1967, a deputy editor of the Rostov newspaper *Molot* (the deputy editor in charge of articles on propaganda-agitation questions) asserted that the politinformator's work was still considered agitation, in contrast to that of the *dokladchik* (reporter), *lektor* (lecturer), and *propagandist* (propagandist) which is considered propaganda. Moreover, he stated that workers and lower managerial personnel (such as brigadiers or foremen) still served as agitators, but that they no longer held formal agitation sessions. Rather, as men who are almost always Communists, they have the responsibility of "agitating" informally every day, of "helping to lead conversations in the correct channel" (the editor's phrase). In these senses, oral agitation continues to exist. However, as far as the type of oral agitation usually described in Western textbooks is concerned — that is, the formal sessions involving face-to-face contact between the worker and someone he knows personally — the letter in *Pravda* was correct in pointing to a major change in the agitation program. That oral agitation in this sense has been explicitly judged relatively inappropriate in a modern industrial society is a fact of considerable importance for communications theory.

Another type of Party mobilization-ideological work has been the system of adult political education. In order to cater to the different education levels among the population, the Party leadership has established three educational levels within the system. Prior to 1965, there were the elementary "political school" (*politshkola*) for those with little political knowledge, the "circles" (*kruzhki*) for those with an intermediate background, and independent study (coupled with seminars) and "universities of Marxism-Leninism" for those with higher levels of education. In theory, the system of adult political education was well differentiated, permitting the citizen to specialize in questions that interested him most. Among the more common subjects offered at various times have been Party history, the biography of Lenin (and, earlier, the biography of Stalin), Marxist-Leninist philosophy, political economy, concrete economics, or current politics.[29]

In 1965 the new Soviet leadership attempted to develop a more systematic and long-term education program. The elementary program was to consist primarily of a two-year political school, and the secondary program of a four-year school on the bases of Marxism-Leninism. The program of higher education was to be more varied in order to meet the differing needs at this level. The student could choose a university of Marxism-Leninism, a city school of the Party economic *aktiv,* or a division of the Higher Party School. The subject matter of each of these programs was to be a comprehensive survey of the political and economic questions earlier presented separately in the various circles and seminars.[30]

Throughout most of the post-Purge period, the adult political education program has been an elitist one, aimed primarily at the Party member. Thus, in the 1957/58 school year there were 6.2 million persons enrolled in the system of political education and only 900,000 of them were not Party members. From 1957 to 1964, however, a major effort was made to turn the adult political education program into a mass form of ideological activity. In 1958/59, there were 6.7 million students (including 2.2 million non-Party); in 1959/60, 12.9 million students (including 6.8 non-Party); in 1960/61, 19.1 million students (including 12.7 million non-Party); in 1961/62, 22.6 million students (including 15.5 million non-Party). By the 1964/65 school year the number of students had risen to 26 million students, and at some enterprises 80 percent of the employees were engaged in this activity.[31]

The broadening of the political education system would seem to have been a logical response to the growing anachronism of traditional forms of oral agitation, but apparently the problem of finding an adequate number of qualified instructors and leaders proved to be unsolvable.[32] The post-Khrushchev leadership returned to the earlier policy of elitist enrollment. In the 1965/66 school year the total number of students in the program was reduced to twelve million, 75 percent of whom were Party members. In 1966/67 the number of students rose to 13.5 million, but, as prior to 1957, it continued to approximate the number of Party members.[33] (It should be added, however, that there continue to be programs for non-Party members: 10 million were enrolled in the Komsomol political education system in 1966/67, 11 million in people's universities, schools of Communist labor, lecture courses, and so forth.) [34]

It is too early to judge the success of the post-Khrushchev program of political education, but in the past the program has often looked quite different in practice than on paper. Despite the insistence that a man voluntarily choose the subject that interests him most, the program has taken on a campaign character. In the Stalin period great emphasis was placed on Party history (based on the famous *Short Course of the History of the Communist Party*) and the biographies of Lenin and Stalin (particularly the latter).[35] As Suslov complained at the Twentieth Party Congress, each year the student would study the Bund once more.[36] Beginning in 1957, however, the leadership ordered a massive expansion in the study of economics (both "concrete economics" and "political economy") and, later, in the study of "current politics." By the end of the Khrushchev period only 29 percent of those in political education were studying philosophy, political economy, "scientific Communism," or Party history.[37] In the 1961/62 school year over half of all students in the system were "mastering economic knowledge." [38] Moreover, often the entire program was suspended so that all of the students could study the most recent Party decisions.

Despite the talk about a more systematic program, the post-Khrushchev leadership does not seem to have eradicated the tendency toward the use of campaigns in the system. The emphasis swung very strongly toward the study of "political" subjects during the first year under the new program. Thus, in the 1965/66 school year 70 percent of the students in the program in Leningrad oblast were studying philosophy, political economy, "scientific Communism," or Party history.[39] After the beginning of the school year, however, the leadership decided that it was vital to explain the economic reforms and the new planning techniques to the managerial personnel, and all or nearly all of them were enrolled in economic study.[40] Three different courses were established — one for the top plant managers, one for the middle-level managers, and one for the lower supervisors — and in Leningrad alone they came to embrace 100,000 men.[41] Although this study apparently was supposed to supplement the regular program of adult political education, in practice it frequently seems to have supplanted it.

In addition to its frequent failure to provide a free choice to the potential students (or perhaps because of this failure), the system of adult political education has been marred by a great many deficiencies. One reads of low attendance, of poor and formalistic teaching, and of an unwillingness of many students to do any reading. Those engaged in independent study may do little at all, for they are usually men of some standing and "at times it is inconvenient (*neudobno*) to check [on their study]: they are not children." [42]

In part, these deficiencies result from the great difficulty in recruiting competent and interesting teachers to staff the various courses, but they also seem inherent in the system itself. The economics courses may be of great interest (particularly when they deal with a new planning system), but those on current politics and political subjects are apt to be particularly valueless to the very persons enrolled, especially if (as is usual) they are taught on a superficial level. Since 90 percent of those in the adult political education program at a major plant may be Communists,[43] the students are already committed to the Party and presumably are acquainted with its philosophy, history, and program. Some of the workers and farmers among the members may need political instruction, but, given the rising educational level of Party members, a great many of the students have already received more sophisticated instruction in the regular educational system.

It is likely that managerial-engineering personnel receive their greatest benefit from the Party ideological program not by studying in the adult political education courses, but by teaching in the courses and serving as agitators. The number engaged in this activity has been very large. Thus, in 1952 it was reported that over 75 percent of the engineers and technicians at a major Ivanovo plant were agitators, lecturers, and propagandists, and this figure may not be atypical for engineers in production.[44]

At a minimum, requiring managerial personnel to engage in agitation-propaganda work ensures that they do not absorb themselves completely in technical work and that they keep informed on national and international affairs. As one plant director stated in complaining about political work, "In order to answer questions, you have to know a lot yourself and to be well informed on all events." [45] Even if acquaintance with the national and the international scene may have little relevance for decision-making at the plant level, it may be valuable schooling for those who will rise higher. Even beyond this, the agitator and propagandist must face many of the more practical concerns and problems of the workers, and these can furnish a very valuable perspective indeed for the manager.

Besides broadening the manager's perspective, political work is also said to develop certain skills in dealing with people that are quite useful in managerial work. Thus, the director of a major plant in Kazakhstan, in talking about a shop head who at first had great difficulties in his post, pointed directly to the value of agitational-propaganda work in helping him adjust to supervisory work:

I knew well that this man loved books in his specialty and that he followed technical innovations. But he had no taste for political study. I think that this is precisely why it was so difficult for him to talk with people and to lead them skillfully. Why, work with the collective is impossible for a leader without a deep and systematic mastery of the knowledge of Marxism-Leninism and the application of it in practice.

Serious independent study widened the political horizon of [the shop head]. And the man came to feel the confidence in himself which the leader of an important workers' collective needs but which he had previously lacked. Now the head of the shop . . . is himself a propagandist and a leader of an agitators' cell. He appears before the workers with lectures and reports.[46]

One need not agree about the importance of a mastery of Marxism-Leninism to recognize that the development of the ability to explain it to others might, indeed, help to develop a vital ability to communicate in general.

The Role of the Local Party Organs in Mobilization Work

The Soviet press incessantly discusses the ideological-mobilization work of the Party apparatus, and the scholar faces few problems in outlining its features. Yet, although it is easy to describe the program, the precise nature of the role of the local Party organs in carrying it out is less clear. In particular, it is difficult to determine the extent to which the bureau, the first secretary, and the Party officials specializing in industry find their energies absorbed in this activity.

The local Party organs are responsible for overseeing ideological-mobilization work, and this requires a considerable amount of time. Many of the ideological-mobilization activities of the local Party organs are related to industry only in the most peripheral way, if at all. Thus, the Party Rules stipuluate that the local Party organs have a direct role in selection of the editor of the local newspapers, and they also confirm the editorial collegia of these newspapers.[48] Officials of the local Party organs also serve as chief censor in the literary-cultural field and the chief enforcer of *partiinost* in the schools and universities. They also must make many concrete "ideological" decisions, such as the relative priorities in school construction, the number and location of new theaters, and so forth.

The local Party organs should, of course, also supervise the ideological-mobilization work conducted within the factory. They must make certain that each plant has enough agitators, propagandists, and students in political education, and they should ensure that the work of these men is carried out in a lively, meaningful manner. They should "be constantly interested in the course of competition in the industrial collectives and help to develop it where it is weak." [49]

In addition, the local Party organs should provide concrete assistance to the primary Party organizations in carrying out the ideological program. They must play an active role in recruiting propagandists and lecturers who come from outside the plant (for example, the secondary school or college teachers, who are often used in the circles on Party history, Marxist-Leninist philosophy, and so forth). [50] They must conduct schools, conferences, and seminars to train agitators and propagandists and to keep them informed about current policy. [51] They may even provide such services as organizing excursions for agitators. For example, the agitators of a raw materials plant may be taken to the plant using their product so they may be able to speak more concretely of the reasons for maintaining quality standards. [52]

In more direct mobilization work, one of the most frequent responsibilities of the local Party organs is endorsing the various *pochiny* — initiatives. However, this is not the limit of their activity. A campaign to develop the movement for Communist labor can require a great deal of organizational work: "The Moscow city committee of the Party constantly studies the way in which competition for Communist labor is practiced and the degree to which it is regularized. For this purpose there have been created under the Party raikomy commissions, staffs, and technical-economic councils with numerous sections. There have been conducted mass reviews, raids, conferences, meetings, and raion evenings for the exchange of experience." [53]

In addition, the Party organs are responsible for establishing "schools of advanced experience," "schools for innovators," and so forth. (During the Stalin period these were often called "Stakhanovite schools." [54])

Finally, the local Party organs may also play a major role in determining the themes used in agitation-propaganda work and in deciding the plan indicators or the orders on which socialist competition should be focused. Frequently they simply transmit to the primary Party organizations the decisions already made at higher levels, but at times they may manifest some independence. This is particularly true of socialist competition directed at giving special attention to the orders for a particular construction project or at economizing on the use of a local material or utility service temporarily in very short supply.[55]

It is quite obvious that officials of the local Party organs are concerned with supervising the ideological-mobilization program, but the real question is — which officials? As noted earlier, each local Party organ has a special secretary for ideological questions and an agitation-propaganda department. In recent years it often has also had an ideological commission that draws on the "public" for assistance. In addition, each local Party organ has an organizational secretary concerned not only with the selection of lower Party and soviet officials, but also with many aspects of mobilization work (including those led directly by the trade unions and the Komsomol). The oblast Party organs have a House of Political Education with a library of political literature (for example, the Leningrad library had 100,000 books on Marxist-Leninist theory in 1955); [47] lower Party organs have a cabinet of political education to perform similar functions.

Clearly the ideological secretary and the agitation-propaganda department devote much attention to ideological-mobilization work. (Even they, however, are probably far more concerned with the school construction schedules and with appropriations politics than with the adult political education program.) But what about the bureau, the first secretary, and the officials specializing in industrial questions? How intense is their interest in the ideological-mobilization program?

As far as the Party officials handling industrial questions are concerned, the evidence is quite overwhelming: these men have a relatively minor connection with ideological-mobilization activities. When the Party leadership attempted to abolish the departments in the raikomy and gorkomy in the latter half of the 1950's, one of the major reasons given was the previous lack of coordination among the industrial-transportation, agitation-propaganda, and organizational departments. Specifically the officials of the industrial-transportation departments were said to be unconcerned with organizational and ideological questions at the plant,[56] and the opponents of the reorganization did not dispute this point. Another indication that the industrial-transportation department has had no real responsibility for mobilization work is the frequent statement that the officials of these departments seldom deal with the secretaries of the primary Party organization.

In 1967 a Party official acknowledged that "at one time" the industrial officials had had only a minor role in organizational-ideological work: "At one time the opinion was widespread that only two departments of the obkom should concern themselves with strictly Party work: the organizational-Party work department and the propaganda-agitation department. Many looked on the branch departments as offices to which they should turn on 'purely' economic, production questions. There was a portion of the truth in this opinion." [57]

The Party official asserted that this situation no longer prevailed, but as we shall see in Chapter X, such assertions have been made frequently in the past and have proven to be pious hopes.

It would, however, be wrong to say that the industrial officials in the Party apparatus have absolutely no contact with the mobilization program. The bureau sessions provide the setting for a good deal of interaction among the specialized secretaries, and the industrial secretary surely participates in discussions about ideological-organizational work in industry.[58] He also has a role (or at least hopes to have a role) in determining the relative priority of construction projects and of plan indicators, and hence he undoubtedly takes part in the decisions about the focus of some of the socialist competition. Moreover, when there are meetings formalizing city-against-city competition, when there are conferences for agitators or for participants in the movement for Communist labor, the industrial secretary (or, less frequently, the head of the industrial-transportation department) is often called on to speak about the area's economy and to insist on the need for increased productivity. But beyond this, the industrial officials do not appear to be meaningfully involved in the ideological-mobilization work.

The role of the bureau and the first secretary in mobilizing the population is much more complex and much more difficult to summarize. As the prefect, the first secretary has a very definite responsibility for the prevention of unrest. Any program increasing the population's commitment to the regime, its tolerance of local conditions, or its dedication to the fulfillment of the plan cannot but arouse interest in the first secretary. However, the question a first secretary formally or informally must ask himself (and answer) is: To what extent does the ideological-mobilization work [as described in this chapter] contribute directly and immediately to a more contented, productive population? Or, more to the point, will time devoted to this activity contribute as much to the achievement of this goal as time spent in other ways?

The evidence is strong that throughout the post-Purge period many first secretaries have had serious doubts about the relative urgency of industrial mobilization work. Again and again one reads of formalism in this work — of Party officials being interested only that plant officials be able to report quantitative indications of success (for example, the number of agitators and of people reached), of the bureaus approving "initiatives" and socialist obligations automatically, of Party officials assuming that ideological work must have been done well if the plan is being fulfilled. In the words of one plant manager, "There arrives, let's say, a gorkom secretary, a head of a department, or an instructor. He passes through the plant and looks at the visual agitation [placards, banners], which he takes to mean that mass political work is organized fairly well. And if the plan is being fulfilled, then in general everything is all right." [59]

Of course, when the Party leadership issues a special decree on ideological work (especially if it is associated with a Central Committee session) or when it endorses a new nationwide "initiative," meetings must be held and planned, and measures must be taken. Inevitably this requires some attention from the bureau and the first secretary. Yet, the Soviet press repeatedly reports that even in these cases their interest usually wanes rather quickly. The response of the leaders of one city Party committee to the "Communist labor" campaign is probably quite typical:

At first the Tiraspol Party gorkom was concerned a great deal with the organization of the competition. These questions were discussed at plenary sessions of the gorkom, at meetings of the Party *aktiv,* and in the primary Party organizations. Meetings of the advanced workers were called. In 1961 a city economic conference was conducted to exchange experience on the competition for Communist labor. But with the passage of time the leaders of the gorkom gave less attention to this important matter and ceased to occupy themselves with organizational work. The leadership of the competition to turn Tiraspol into a city of high productivity of labor, of advanced culture, and of model order was delegated to the ispolkom of the city soviet, and there they limited it to the organization of better services and amenities in the city (*blagoustroistvo*). Thus, the chief thing in this competition — the struggle for Communist labor and the instilling in the workers of a spirit of steadfast observance of the moral code of a builder of communism — was lost from view.[60]

These complaints could be multiplied many times over, and there are many indications that they do not merely represent isolated cases. Whenever there is a Party reorganization, it is freely admitted that formalism in organizational-ideological work was an inherent feature of the old system. The new reorganization, it is said, will permit (or is permitting) the Party organs to concentrate its attention more fully on this neglected sector of work. But when the new organizational forms are in turn changed, once more one reads that they too had led to formalism in this realm: "Earlier it often happened that . . ."[61]

Although there have been increasing numbers of complaints that the rising educational level of the population makes much agitation-propaganda work rather anachronistic, the tendency for the first secretary and the bureau to neglect it is not a new one. In reading Merle Fainsod's discussion of the main concerns of the bureau of the Smolensk obkom during 1936, one is struck by the almost total absence of any mention of ideological work. (Indeed, the words "agitation" and "propaganda" do not even appear in the index of the book.) The obkom bureau did play "an active role in planning meetings and campaigns to popularize the Stakhanovite movement" (which had begun in the previous year), but it is clear that this was far from being the first secretary's primary concern.[62]

The Soviet leaders — and, even more frequently, Soviet newspaper reporters — make continual public demands that more attention be given to mobilization-ideological work, but the reasons for its relative neglect are not difficult to discern. Although the Party leaders speak much about the importance of this type of work, they do not support their words with action. As observed previously, the first secretaries are normally not chosen from among "the ideological specialists," and relatively little is done to "develop a taste for ideological work" in them once they are in office.[63]

Rewards and punishment for a first secretary seem little connected with imaginative ideological-mobilization work; rather, it is the degree of achievement of the goals of this work (a committed population and plan fulfillment) that furnish the basis for judging a Party secretary, regardless of how the goals are achieved. In 1933 the first secretary of the Smolensk obkom grasped the essence of the matter: "We are a flax oblast," he wrote to the raikom first secretaries, "and the Central Committee completely correctly will make demands and evaluate our work precisely on the basis of the successful fulfillment of this work. . . . Everything will be canceled out if there is a failure in the flax sector." [64] The Smolensk secretary took this situation for granted; in 1966 the first secretary of the Cheliabinsk obkom was critical of a similar criterion used in judging the Magnitogorsk gorkom: "How is the work of the Magnitogorsk Party organization sometimes evaluated? Often as if the single measure of it is tons of above-plan iron and steel and the quantity of metallurgical units built." [65]

It is often instructive to examine the fate of Party officials involved in ideological work which is particularly successful or unsuccessful. For example, the great increase in the number of agitators at the Krivoi Rog Steel Plant between 1958 and 1962 has been mentioned. Unfortunately, it is not known precisely when the increase took place, but one fact is clear. The first secretary of the Dnepropetrovsk obkom (Shcherbitskii) who had permitted the number of agitators in one of the most important plants in the oblast to drop to one per sixty-two employees (and who had permitted similar neglect in other aspects of ideological work) was in December 1957 named a secretary of the

Ukrainian Central Committee — one of the two secretaries to handle industrial work. (Later, he became chairman of the Ukrainian Council of Ministers.) His successor (Gaevoi), who held the job from 1957 until 1961, was promoted to the same post in the Ukrainian Central Committee. The obkom first secretary (Tolubeev) in December 1962 — when the level of ideological work was so fulsomely praised — was demoted to the position of obkom second secretary in the summer of 1963. The man who had been first secretary of the Krivoi Rog gorkom since 1955 (Oleinikov) continued in his job until he was named industrial secretary of the Dnepropetrovsk obkom in the post-Khrushchev era.[66]

The most basic problem with ideological-mobilization work — the problem explaining the failure of the first secretaries (and the leadership) to give it the highest priority — is that it actually has a rather marginal impact on the degree of plan fulfillment or popular disaffection, at least in immediate terms. Active intervention by a first secretary in this work has an even more marginal impact.

In the 1920's there was a need to establish an ideological network, and the first secretary had a quite important role to play in this undertaking. Hence it is not surprising that an old teacher can recall nostalgically that in the early years "the teacher enjoyed the attention and care of the rural and city leaders." [67] Now that the basic organization has been created, however, now that there are trained and trusted men (many with experience in Party work) occupying the key local posts in the press, the educational and cultural administration, and the trade unions, the delegation of much of the ideological-mobilization work to them becomes a real possibility.

Under these conditions there are many ways in which a man with the authority of a first secretary can more profitably promote political stability and plan fulfillment than by directing ideological activities. Indeed, certain of the steps that may be taken locally to further the achievement of these goals can be effectively carried out only by a man with his authority. It is only the first secretary, for example, who can try to control unrest among the youth by ensuring that the local plant managers overcome their reluctance to hire teen-agers. It is only the first secretary who can journey to Moscow for a week and have a reasonable chance of persuading higher authorities to appropriate money for a sports stadium or to allocate additional supplies to a local plant. It is only the first secretary who has the perspective to decide whether political stability requires that the construction of a local movie theater be given temporary priority over an industrial project.

Although a decision on replacing a director or on priority in production scheduling or in supply deliveries might be delegated to other men, these are decisions likely to have a substantial impact on political stability and plan fulfillment. A day spent by the first secretary in consultations on such a decision may produce far more direct results than a day spent in consultations on the agitation work at a given plant. Or, conversely, a poor decision on an important appointment or on construction priorities can have far more disastrous consequences than a poor decision on agitation work. In these circumstances a first secretary would be acting irrationally if he concentrated his efforts on ideological-mobilization work.

In large part the first secretary surely does not make a conscious decision that he will neglect ideological work in a particular week. No doubt, this is one of those responsibilities about which he always says to himself, "This week I will have to give a bit more attention to that." But, as Merle Fainsod noted with respect to the Smolensk obkom,[68] the problems stream in. In the industrial field alone there can be no delay in deciding the construction priorities, in expediting an urgently needed delivery, in responding to the ministry's proposal of a candidate for a vacant directorship, and so forth. If a "ChP" (extraordinary occurrence) takes place at a factory (an explosion, a workers' strike over an increase in the norms, even plan non-fulfillment), action must be taken at once. Except when a Central Committee decision on ideological questions makes holding a local plenary session on that subject the current imperative, ideological and mobilization work can slip from mind.

VII. The Selection of Personnel

One of the surest indications of the extent of the local Party's involvement in the administrative life of its area is its role in personnel selection. If the local Party organs had no responsibilities in this realm or if they simply checked on the political reliability of candidates for administrative posts, one would be quite justified in suspecting that their role went little beyond a general attempt to lead and to mobilize and perhaps to provide their good offices for mediation purposes. In fact, however, the meaningfulness of the local Party organs' leadership is greatly strengthened by the fact that they can remove many administrators within their area and that they have a key role in the appointment of a successor. There was quoted earlier the statement by a Soviet spokesman that the Party could not "direct all sides of the state, cultural, and economic life of the country if it did not have the possibility of placing personnel in accordance with political and economic problems." [1] The quotation can be reversed; because the local Party organs do have this "possibility," they are indeed in a position to "direct all sides of the state, cultural, and economic life" in the area.

Personnel selection cannot, of course, be a mechanized process of Party dictation, for it is important that a man selected for a job be willing and even eager to do it and that he be able to work smoothly with those above and below him in the hierarchy. Consequently, the lines of influence in personnel selection are subtle and difficult to trace, and the informal aspects of this activity are more important than the formal ones. The second part of this chapter is devoted to a discussion of the local Party organs' complex role in the informal process of personnel selection, but a prerequisite for that discussion is an understanding of the formal rules and procedures that guide their work.

Formal Party Controls over Personnel Selection:
The Nature of Party Nomenklatura

Held responsible for the performance of every official and every enterprise, the local Party organ must be ready to take personnel action if performance seems to be suffering. It can be involved in selection of an important plant director, provision of a plant with a rank-and-file engineer, recruitment of a special work gang for a construction site, or maintenance of standards of technical competence in the general hiring procedures.

In carrying out these responsibilities, the local Party organs generally have the same authority relationships with industrial administrators as they have on other questions. That is, if a local industrial official is formally selected by an administrative organ at a higher territorial level, then the local Party organ may be consulted, it may suggest and appeal, but it cannot compel the administrative organ to take action. If the appointing administrative organ is at the same or a lower territorial level, the local Party organ can usually compel it to dismiss an official and to name a particular man as his successor.

As is the case with its other responsibilities, the local Party organ may choose to intervene in the selection of a particular official, or it may defer to the judgment of the responsible administrative officials. As noted in Chapter V, however, there are two types of situations in which the local Party organ is obligated to give its consent before an official may be removed or his successor appointed. First, any Party leader working in any post, however small, must obtain the permission of the local raikom (or gorkom if there are no raiony in the city) before leaving his job. Second, there are a number of administrative posts considered to be of sufficient importance to warrant special attention from the local Party organs. If a post has been placed within the nomenklatura (the official list of posts) of a particular Party organ, that Party organ must give its "confirmation" (*utverzhdenie*) before any personnel action is taken with respect to the post.

As mentioned earlier, the nomenklatury of the various Party organs contain a wide range of positions in the governmental hierarchy, the Party committees, and the other "public" organizations (particularly the trade union and the Komsomol). Thus, in early 1966 the

Riga gorkom had 662 posts on its nomenklatura: 253 in the Party and soviet organs, 83 in the ideological organizations, 85 in administrative and trade-financial organs, 71 in education, 61 in construction and municipal services, and 107 in industrial administration (basically directors, chief engineers, and heads of personnel departments).[2]

The only other recent discussion of the number and distribution of posts in Party nomenklatura involved the gorkom and raikomy in Moscow in 1958. At that time the gorkom and raikomy together had more than 17,000 supervisory officials in their nomenklatury. Around 3,000 of these positions were in economic administration, over 1,200 were in the city and raion soviets, and over 9,000 were within the Party itself. It is worth noting that in 1956 there were 7,928 primary Party organizations in the city.[3]

Soviet sources are very reticent about divulging the distribution of industrial positions among the nomenklatury of the different local Party organs, and for information about this point, one is forced to rely on scattered references in the Soviet press and on interviews. Unfortunately, the distribution of posts among the Party organs changes from time to time,[4] and some of the individual examples cited may no longer be accurate. However, there is no evidence of major changes in the practices and patterns of Party nomenklatura in the 1960's, and the discussion here should continue to be relevant for the present period.

In most basic terms, the distribution of posts among the nomenklatury of the Party organs has always depended on the estimate by the Party leadership of the relative importance of the posts. Once the leadership has established this ranking, it distributes the posts on the principle: the more important the post, the higher the level of the Party organ in whose nomenklatura it is placed. As might be expected, this practice has made the level of Party organ in whose nomenklatura a post is located a very important status symbol for its occupant,[5] and even in an interview with a foreigner a plant director may speak with distinct pride when he states that *his* post is in the nomenklatura of the All-Union Central Committee.

During the Stalin period the distribution of posts within Party nomenklatura was quite centralized. In Smolensk of the 1930's, none of the directorships of plants of the All-Union Peoples' Commissariats were in the nomenklatura of the obkom, and this may have been the normal situation throughout the Stalin period. After the late 1930's, the secretaries of the primary Party organizations of the large plants were also placed in the nomenklatura of the All-Union Central Committee, and, in fact, they were called "Party Organizers of the Central Committee" (*Partorg TsK*) to emphasize their relationship to the center.[6]

By the late 1950's, there had been considerable decentralization in Party responsibility for personnel selection. The post of Party Organizer of the Central Committee was abolished in 1956 in order to "raise the responsibility of the local Party organs for the work of the important enterprises and the most important institutions,"[7] and the number of plant directorships within their nomenklatura was also increased. In 1958, only ten plant directors in Minsk (less than three percent of the total) remained in the nomenklatura of the All-Union Central Committee, and another forty to fifty were in the nomenklatura of the republican Central Committee.[8] In Belorussia — and in the smaller republics — there was only one sovnarkhoz, and hence the republican central committee was the only local Party organ in a position to supervise it. In the RSFSR and the Ukraine, where there were a number of sovnarkhozy, the obkomy undoubtedly had jurisdiction over many posts similar to those in the nomenklatura of the Belorussian Central Committee, and the Bureau of the Central Committee for the RSFSR and the Ukraine Central Committee were probably given responsibility for some of the posts that in Belorussia were in the nomenklatura of the USSR Central Committee. One indication that this was, in fact, the case is the inclusion of a number of sovnarkhoz officials in the nomenklatury of the obkomy in the larger republics, at least prior to 1962.[9]

In addition, a number of significant plant directorships were even placed in the nomenklatura of the gorkomy in the large cities. To be sure, most of these plants seemed to be in light industry, but they included a modern knitted goods factory in Kiev with 2,000 workers and a plant in Tbilisi that packed 24 percent of the tea in the USSR.[10]

Yet, even the sovnarkhoz period did not produce rampant decentralization in personnel selection. A very considerable portion of industry continued to be supervised by men within the nomenklatury of the All-Union and republican central committees. Although only three percent of the directorships in Minsk were in the nomenklatura of the All-Union Central Committee, these plants probably employed about one third of the city's industrial labor force. The forty to fifty plants whose directorships were in the nomenklatura of the Belorussian Central Committee probably embraced nearly 50 percent more of the city's factory workers.[11] Even if many of these posts would have been in the nomenklatura of the obkom in the RSFSR or the Ukraine, it should not be forgotten that the oblast is a unit the size of an American state.

The Party committees closer to the plant level — the raikomy and the small gorkomy — have never been given the authority to confirm changes of directors in the important plants. The only directorships in their nomenklatury have been small local plants, especially those usually supervised by the local soviets. However, their nomenklatury have included a number of lower managerial positions within the larger enterprises. For example, in the Minsk Ballbearing Works — a plant whose director and chief engineer both were in the nomenklatura of the All-Union Central Committee in 1958 — the shop heads (*nachalniki tsekhov*) were in the nomenklatura of the local raikom.[12] In several light industry plants in which the director was in the nomenklatura of a gorkom, the so-called *glavnye* — the chief engineer, the chief designer, the chief accountant, and the chief mechanic — were in the nomenklatura of the raikom.[13] In these plants the post of shop head was considered too unimportant to warrant inclusion in the Party nomenklatura.

Another set of positions placed within the nomenklatury of the lower Party organs are the key "elected" posts within the factory — the Party secretary, often the trade union chairman, and perhaps even the Komsomol secretary. Because Party responsibility for posts supposedly elected from below poses some awkward problems for Soviet theorists, there has been very little discussion of their distribution among the various local Party organs. It is often implied, however, that the local Party organ directly above the primary Party organization has special or even sole responsibility for the position of secretary of the primary Party organization. The official Party handbook, for example, has one section entitled "The role of the raikom in selection of secretaries [of the primary Party organizations]," [14] and it gives no hint that any other Party organ is involved. This statement in the handbook (and many others like it) are strong evidence that a great many Party secretaries are within the nomenklatury of these lower Party organs. However, a 1966 article refers to secretaries of the primary Party organizations that are in the nomenklatura of the obkom, and a 1967 article reports that in Donetsk oblast the secretaries, bureau members, and responsible officials of the obkom "as a rule . . . help to prepare the report-election meetings . . . at important industrial enterprises." [15]

There are many statements in the Soviet press to indicate that the lower Party organs also have responsibility for the trade union chairmen in the important plants. One reads, for example, that "Comrade Ponomarev criticized the [Dzhalal-abad] gorkom for incorrect selection of primary Party organization secretaries and chairmen of the trade union committees." [16] Indeed, their role in the selection of the trade union officials can be quite decisive. [17]

Whatever the precise nature of the distribution of important industrial posts among the various organs of the Party apparatus, it is obvious that the important posts are in the nomenklatura of some Party organ. The essential question is: what role do the nomenklatury imply for the local Party organs? Officially the local Party organs have the right only to confirm or to reject personnel changes taken by other organizations, and one might suppose that they reject candidates only in cases of political unreliability. If this were the case, the existence of the Party nomenklatury would probably have little significance in an age when most officials in nomenklatura posts are Communists who have been raised in Soviet society and who are being employed or removed by other Party members in the higher state apparatus. However, although formal Party theory may refer only to a right of confirmation, Soviet sources indicate clearly and officially that the confirmation does not imply Party passivity or preoccupation only with political reliability.

The discussions of staffing the sovnarkhoz in 1957, for example, often seemed to imply that the state organs — even the All-Union and republican council of ministers — had almost no part in selecting their subordinates in the industrial administration. According to one authority, *"all* [my italics] the complex and large-scale work connected with the selection and distribution of personnel in the sovnarkhozy was carried out by the Central Committee of the Communist Party of the Soviet Union and by the local Party committees." [18] Another authority was more specific: "The basic supervisory personnel of the sovnarkhozy — the chairmen, deputy chairmen, a significant part of the administration and department heads — were selected (*otobrany*) by the Party Central Committee from the best, most experienced officials of the former ministries and particularly from among enterprise directors. Not a little was done in the selection of sovnarkhoz personnel by the local Party organs. For example, in Kemerovo oblast only 26 of 629 sovnarkhoz officials were sent from Moscow and other centers, while the rest were selected (*podobrany*) by the Party obkom on the spot." [19]

The Party press continues to use phraseology suggesting that the 1957 practices were not completely abnormal and that the Party organs often do more than "confirm" nominees from the state organs. It may, for example, be stated in a matter-of-fact, even laudatory manner that some particular Party organs "promoted" (*vydvinul*), "decided to remove" (*otstranit*), "discharged" (*snialo*), or "freed from work" (*osvobodilo ot raboty*), some individual administrative official.[20]

In the last year of the Khrushchev period one Central Committee official actually defined nomenklatura not as those posts requiring Party confirmation, but as "the circle of positions, the promotion (*vydvizhenie*) to which is carried out (*proizvoditsia*) by the appropriate Party committee." [21] A year after Khrushchev's removal, another Party spokesman flatly declared, "As is well known, the leaders of the enterprises are confirmed in their post on the recommendation of the Party organs." [22]

The Informal Role of the Local Party Organs in Personnel Selection

To speak of the powers implied in the registration procedures and the nomenklatura is not to define the actual role which the Party organs play in personnel selection. For that, it is necessary to examine a series of concrete situations.

Not all kinds of Party participation in personnel selection are associated with the exercise of control over important administrators. In many cases the local Party organs intervene in personnel selection only to help administrators to fulfill their plan or to help Party members find work. It is taken for granted, for example, that a local Party organ (particularly a gorkom or raikom) will assist an enterprise that is seeking a particular type of specialist or even a large number of workers. The major Soviet study of the local Party organs reports that "if a plant director needs, for example, an employee for the supply department, he turns to the Party obkom or gorkom." [23] Similarly, the head of the industrial-transportation department of the Vladimir gorkom has noted that the enterprise administrators "constantly turn to the gorkom with requests to find suitable specialists of the most diverse kinds." [24] The official accepted this practice unquestioningly. Her only complaint was that the plant administrators were not sufficiently interested in hiring economists, for that was the only type of specialist never sought from the Party organ.

In this role the local Party organs are providing a service both to managers and to Party members, and are acting as a kind of personnel clearing house or (in the words of a Soviet authority) a "labor exchange." [25] Because they must consent to any change in employment by a Party member, the local Party officials inevitably have comprehensive knowledge of recent job vacancies and of the employment situation at various enterprises. There has been no employment agency in the Soviet Union, so it is not surprising that unemployed Party members have turned to the Party organ for information about appropriate openings. This natural tendency has been strengthened by the feeling among some members, at least, that "it is uncomfortable (*neudobno*) for a Communist to go to personnel departments [of enterprises and institutions]" and that the raikom has the duty of getting them work.[26]

Whatever the reason, the effort expended on this kind of assistance to members and to the enterprises can be fairly considerable. In Tbilisi in 1956, for example, each raikom had dozens of temporarily unemployed Communists registered with it. "The overwhelming majority of them were demobilized soldiers of the Soviet army, people released from work because of the reorganization or liquidation of their institution or organization, or Communists who had moved to the raion for family reasons. . . ." [27] The raikomy sought to find employment for all these persons, and they did so with some success. A demobilized army officer without a specialty received the suggestion that he become an apprentice linotypist, and a spot was found for him at a local printing office; a man who had been released as head of an artel was induced to accept the job of shop head at another artel.[28]

Another type of Party work with low-level personnel is the shifting of workers temporarily from one place to another in order to ensure that high priority plans are fulfilled. The most obvious example of such temporary transfer is that which takes place at harvest time. During this period of the year there has been a chronic shortage of manpower on the farms (at least in relation to the existing level of mechanization), and the cities have habitually been called on to furnish assistance. The local Party organs may organize "volunteer" projects on Saturday and Sunday (*subbotniki* and *voskreseniki*) to help in the harvesting and unloading of part of the crop,[29] but it can also require the state and economic institutions to send help during working hours. Even an important heavy industry plant (in this case the Kalinin Railroad Car Construction Works) may have to send a dozen skilled workers and engineers to help harvest hay and four to five hundred of them to harvest potatoes — at the plant's expense.[30] The demands on the industrial plants do not seem as harsh as those on other institutions (a pedagogical institute may be completely closed for a month [31]), but they can be considerable. Despite a 1962 decree demanding a reduction in the scale of urban assistance in the harvest, the secretary of the Nizhnii Tagil gorkom noted later that the gorkom had been reproached by one of the plant managers: "When are the leaders of the enterprises called to the gorkom? In case of a failure in the plan or during the days of the harvest in order to help the village." [32]

The sending of the workers to assist in other tasks may be even more persistent within the city than it is between the city and countryside. A very comprehensive (if critical) survey of this practice in the city of Sterlitamak describes a situation that most probably is typical in the Soviet Union:

[From a letter of the head of personnel at the Sterlitamak Synthetic Rubber Works]: Why does the city soviet write to the directors of enterprises: "Assign eight men to the meat combine for a month." "Direct eight competent men for fourteen days to the city statistical inspectorate." "Send twenty specialists for a month to the Construction Administration No. 1 and 2 of the Ishimbai Housing Construction Trust," . . . Moreover each time it is suggested that the assigned workers be freed from their basic work but that they be paid by their original place of work. . . .

"Correctly written!" confirmed an official of the personnel department of the soda-cement combine, Comrade Mudryi. "Sometimes over one hundred men are occupied for weeks on the side, fulfilling different tasks."

The deputy director of the chemical works said, "There are months when fifty or more men are not at the works for several days. They are occupied at the construction sites and institutions of the city." [33]

It was the gorispolkom that was criticized for demanding this help, but as the gorispolkom by itself does not have the authority to enforce such demands, it is clear that the criticism was directed in a somewhat Aesopian way at the local gorkom.

In other cases it is the large plants and construction sites that are sent workers in an emergency. In 1941 Frol Kozlov, then the secretary of the Izhevsk gorkom, reported that the gorkom had called a conference of the directors and Party secretaries at the plants of local industry, and "arranged with them the assigning of a certain quantity of labor force to help the [Izhevsk] Metallurgy Works." In two weeks this temporary measure helped the plant to overcome its plan nonfulfillment. A decade and a half later it was stated (with no hint of criticism) that at one crucial stage of a large construction project in Groznyi, "the Party gorkom and raikom . . . helped to transfer approximately 200 metalworkers temporarily from the other enterprises of the city to the chemical combine." [34] Although both of these examples involved the transfer of personnel from one enterprise to another, the Party organs may also be able to render assistance to construction projects by organizing "volunteer" work-crews during the off-hours.[35]

In some respects shifting labor to the sections that need it most is relatively uncomplicated work for the local Party organs. It must entail some bargaining as various administrators present convincing arguments why they need more help or why they cannot afford to release workers for other projects, but in this bargaining process the participants are not equal. When the local Party organs are persuaded (or are told by higher officials) that a certain project or plant must be given emergency priority, they are in a position to use their power to decisively override objections. As one plant official stated in complaining about the number of workers that had to be sent to the farms, "That is the decision of the Party raikom, and we are obligated to fulfill it." [36]

In the selection of individual officials to posts important enough to be in Party nomenklatura, the bargaining process can become much more complex. Here it is not simply a question of directing two hundred workers to the type of job they are accustomed to performing, but rather one of seeking the individual who has the best qualifications for a particular job and who can work harmoniously with those whom he supervises and those who supervise him. In such a decision the relationships among local Party organs and industrial administrators can vary greatly, and the lines of influence can become quite tangled.

Changes in nomenklatura posts are least complicated in the selection of personnel for "elected" posts in the soviets, the primary Party organizations, and other "public" organizations. In these instances the Party organs have explicit authority to intervene, and the other interested persons occupy a very weak position vis-à-vis them.

In the case of the trade union elections, the Party Rules themselves provide the authority for decisive Party intervention. All Party members of the unions are required before election meetings to agree as a Party group on a candidate for chairman. All the Party members are then obligated to support the decision of the Party group at the meeting of the trade union itself. The Party Rules declare that the Party groups are "on all questions obligated to be strictly and unswervingly governed by the decisions of the supervisory Party bodies," [37] and Soviet sources frequently indicate that "all questions" definitely include the name of the man who is to be the leader of the trade union.

A very illuminating article in *Pravda Ukrainy* illustrates the powers of the local Party organs in this sphere and the methods they can use in exercising these powers:

> For three years Communist V. I. Priakhin worked as chairman of the trade union committee of the Odessa works "Kinap" . . . At the regular works trade union conference Comrade Priakhin was again elected to the trade union committee, and the Party bureau of the works recommended that he be reelected as its chairman.
>
> But when this question was placed before the session of the Party group of the trade union committee, the second secretary of the Ilichev raikom, Comrade Petrusenko, stated that Comrade Priakhin could not provide leadership to the works committee, and he suggested that Comrade Shimlovskii be elected to this post.
>
> "And if you do elect Priakhin," stated Comrade Petrusenko, "then the Party raikom will not confirm him."
>
> . . . The session of the Party group lasted for over three hours. Petrusenko got what he wanted: the Party group decided to recommend Comrade Shimlovskii as chairman.
>
> . . . Even before the session of the Party group of the trade union committee, Petrusenko had called the former secretary of the works Party committee, Comrade Ezerskii, and the head of the personnel department of the works, Comrade Klitsenko, to his office, and he had suggested that they "conduct work" (*provesti rabotu*) so that the members of the trade union committee would vote against Priakhin. After this, he called Priakhin himself to the raikom and stated to him:
>
> "Now we will have a plenary session of the trade union committee and I suggest that you withdraw your candidacy there."
>
> "Why?" asked Comrade Priakhin.
>
> "Because it is necessary," answered Comrade Petrusenko without giving any justification. [38]

The attitude of the newspaper correspondent toward Petrusenko's behavior is even more interesting than his description of it. Petrusenko was severely criticized for the way in which he interfered in the election, but not for the fact of his interference. He was condemned for being too rude, for ordering people around, for not explaining the reasons for Priakhin's removal, and for recommending a replacement who himself admitted that he was not qualified. However, there is the clear implication that if Petrusenko had "directly and frankly" pointed out the deficiencies in Priakhin's work, there would have been no trouble. The newspaper correspondent declared further that "it is clear that if the Party raikom had selected a candidate more qualified than Priakhin, then, of course, no one would have objected." [39]

This article demonstrates not only the great power of the local Party organ in these matters, but also inferentially that the Party organs are not in a position to demand that the electors accept their nominee automatically. Even when the Party secretary was determined to be quite arbitrary, he "got what he wanted" only after a session of the Party group which lasted for three hours. And, undoubtedly, he did so at fairly great cost. If the plant is to operate smoothly, if the trade union chairman is to serve the functions desired by the leadership, such incidents should be avoided. It is for this reason that the authorities emphasize the importance of persuasion and that many local Party officials are probably more willing than Petrusenko to yield to strong opposition at the local level.

The local Party organs' role in the selection of the secretaries of primary Party organizations is much the same as that in the selection of trade union officials. Although Party theorists stress the democratic nature of the election of these officials, they do not hide the very deep participation of the local Party organs in them. According to the official Party handbook, "it is forbidden to dictate the elections, [but] it is also forbidden to let them be conducted in an unorganized manner. . . . The raikomy and gorkomy are obligated to help the primary Party organizations to approach the elections correctly, and they should take care that the Communists elect as their secretaries politically mature members who are good organizers." [40] The local Party organ immediately above the primary Party organization in the hierarchy is obligated to send one of its officials to the election meeting of the organization, and this official "can take part in the discussion about whom it is necessary to elect as leader of the organization." [41]

As far as one can judge, the role of the representative of the local Party organ is normally decisive in determining the outcome of the meeting, and, indeed, the initiative in "recommending" a candidate usually seems to be in his hands. Frequently, the recommended candidate has worked outside the primary Party organization and has been brought in as a fairly explicit agent of the local Party organs. This may happen not only at the level of the plant primary Party organization, but even in the selection of secretaries of shop Party organizations within the plant. In one extreme case the secretary of a shop organization (at the Chernovitsky Machinebuilding Works) was changed eleven times in thirteen years: "You turn around, and the gorkom has sent a new secretary. . . . The Communists say, 'The gorkom's nomenklatura has arrived.' " [42]

Although the recommendations of the local Party organs are usually accepted as a matter of course, the attitudes of the local members may be taken into account. In fact, the ability of the members to express an opinion is safeguarded by the election procedures. The secretary himself is elected in an open ballot by the members of the bureau (or Party committee in a large organization), but the bureau (or committee) of which he too is a member is elected by the whole organization in a secret ballot that usually seems to be truly secret.[43] The nominations for the list of candidates are made openly (and surely in an "organized manner"), but the member apparently has a real opportunity to cross out names in secret and to blackball (*zaballotirovat*) a candidate who is too obnoxious. If half the members cross out the name of a candidate, he is defeated.[44]

Party officials have learned how to emasculate a secret ballot in general elections to the soviets, and some undoubtedly use similar techniques in carrying out Party elections. Nevertheless, the evidence indicates that the elections to the bureau of the primary Party organizations are not always meaningless formalities. Even during the late Stalin period a Party secretary at a giant plant (the Lugansk Locomotive Works) could be reelected despite a statement by the gorkom secretary that the gorkom did not recommend his reelection; and the director of an equally important plant (the Briansk Locomotive Works) could be blackballed even after the gorkom first secretary termed criticism of him "slander." [45] One may also read of secretaries of shop Party organizations being blackballed.[46]

It has not been possible to determine how often the wishes of the local Party organs are ignored by enterprise Communists, but it occurs with sufficient frequency to have provoked some agitation by Party secretaries for the abolition of the secret ballot. Those advocating this step (and they included the Tadzhik republican organization in 1961) [47] have claimed that it is necessary in order to prevent the "cowardly practice" of Party members sitting silently during the discussion of the nominees and then voting against them.

The specific instances of blackballing reported in the Soviet press usually have been directed not at new candidates suggested by the local Party organs, but rather at old officials whose reelection is being recommended by the raikom. In these cases the raikom has been basically satisfied with the secretary's performance and discovers to its surprise that its judgment is not shared by Party members within the plant. The local Party organ may decide to fight for its candidate and may demand that new ballots be cast,[48] but the normal reaction is probably to accept the blackballing as evidence of unhealthy working relations which are better corrected before they affect production.[49] A realization that the secret ballot provides useful information for the local Party organs must be one of the reasons that the Party leadership rejected the suggestion to abolish it.[50]

In dealing with "elected" positions, the local Party organs may encounter some rare difficulties with the electors, but their work is not complicated by conflict with the other power centers in Soviet society. When the local Party organs deal with the appointed positions within their nomenklatura — particularly the industrial ones — they find themselves in a far more complex situation. These positions are within the nomenklatura not only of the Party organs, but also of the industrial administrative organs, and these administrative organs may be located at a higher territorial level. Moreover, the greater importance of the purely technical qualifications of the candidates tends to require more consultation with those in the best position to judge these qualifications, and their opinion may be the determining factor.

Under these circumstances the variation in Party influence can be extremely great.

In some cases, for example, the local Party organs have obviously played a very limited role in the selection of important industrial personnel. In studying the Smolensk archives, Merle Fainsod concludes that the obkom "merely ratified appointments which were initiated in the hierarchy of the commissariats." [51] Under the ministerial system this must have been a fairly frequent occurrence, particularly for Party organs located in agriculturally oriented areas. Even after 1957, there surely were many positions in which various lower Party organs took little interest. Or, for one reason or another, they may have demanded that an official be removed but have left the selection of a successor to the appropriate industrial officials. When, for instance, the director of the important Minsk Ballbearing Works, himself a member of the bureau of the Minsk gorkom, stated in an interview that the local raikom did not interfere much in his selection of shop heads, his answer rang true.

The local Party organs do not, however, always defer to the wishes of the officials in the state apparatus. As the discussion at the end of the last section indicates, the participation of the local Party organs in this aspect of personnel selection may be very active, and it may be decisive.

Personnel action begins with the creation of a vacancy, and this may occur in a number of ways. The occupant may seek work elsewhere either by responding to a call for candidates for an opening or by maneuvering for a position through informal contacts; he may be promoted to a higher position within his own chain of command; he may be "pirated away" by another department.[52] A gorkom first secretary has complained about "some comrades of the higher-standing organs": "They call a specialist or enterprise director to the ministry or glavk and woo (*svataiut*) him to other work, and the gorkom officials know nothing about this." [53]

When a man seeks to leave for a better job (particularly when he is being promoted), there is little evidence that the local raikom would stand in the way, even though the member is supposedly at the disposal of the Party. Certainly the local Party organs do not seem to have been notably successful in preventing dissatisfied Communists from returning to Moscow from provincial jobs which they had been given in 1957, and there is even a report of a worker who, although a Party member, left his plant in a critical period because of his anger over the apartment he had received.[54]

Vacancies may also be created by the dismissal of an official, and this is far from a rare phenomenon in the Soviet Union. It is difficult to unravel lines of influence in the decision to remove a man, for it is likely to be made after a period of difficulties at the plant during which there undoubtedly have been long discussions about the reasons for the difficulties. In these circumstances, the possibility of inadequate management is probably in everyone's mind, and the manager's superiors themselves are probably not always aware of the process by which this vague possibility comes to be accepted as reality. The first deputy chairman of the Belorussian sovnarkhoz stated in a 1958 interview that most often (*chashche vsego*) it was the Party organ that took the initiative in replacing an incumbent of a position in its nomenklatura, but not surprisingly, he also reported that the initiative could, in practice, come either from the Party organ or the responsible governmental office.

If a local Party organ raises the question of removing an official from an administrative post within its nomenklatura and the responsible governmental supervisor disagrees, the issue is resolved according to the principles discussed earlier. If the administrative organ in whose nomenklatura a post is located is at a lower or the same territorial level as the Party organ responsible for the post, then the Party organ can usually force through its will. Thus, the first deputy chairman of the Belorussian sovnarkhoz stated that if a post was within the nomenklatura both of the Belorussian Central Committee and the sovnarkhoz, the sovnarkhoz was obligated (*obiazan*) to remove its occupant if the Party organ insisted.

When the responsible administrative organ is located at a higher territorial level, the local Party organ cannot compel it to take action. If there is a disagreement between two such bodies about a post in their nomenklatura, the question is referred to higher Party organs for resolution. Although the mutual desire for a harmonious working relationship should reduce the number of conflicts in which each side insists on its position, conflicts do occur. And when they do, the local

Party organ can no more count on the support of its Party superior than it can in policy disputes.

In 1967 there were still no reports of disagreements about personnel selection between the local Party organs and the new ministries. Prior to 1957, however, there were a number of such reports, each indicating that the local Party organ had been unable to secure the removal of a particular official. In one such case the bureau of the Zaporozhe obkom decided that the director of the Zaporozhe Transformer Works had "failed in his work" and called for his removal, but the ministry defended him. Even though *Pravda* joined the obkom in its criticism, the director was still in his post two years later.[55]

The raikomy too are not always supported by the gorkomy and obkomy. In one instance a raikom was dissatisfied with the work of a local construction trust and became convinced that much of the trouble stemmed from the fact that "the head of the trust, Comrade Razanov, drinks too much." When Razanov failed to respond to the raikom's warning, the raikom "decided to free him from his work." Apparently Razanov's superiors did not agree with this decision, for the question was taken to the obkom. As the raikom secretary complained, "the head of the industrial-transportation department of the obkom, Comrade Shmelkov, and the secretary of the obkom, Comrade Morgunov, did not support the raikom." In another case, a raikom's decision to fire a manager was appealed first to the gorkom and then to the obkom, both times without success.[56]

Particularly during the ministerial periods, the formal authority to make personnel changes has been centralized within the state apparatus, and the local Party organs usually have had to secure the consent of higher industrial or Party officials before removing an industrial administrator within their nomenklatura. The republican Party organs have had the authority to remove most of the managers supervised by the republican ministries, but the situation is quite different for the lower Party organs or for plants subordinate to All-Union ministries. It is possible that not only the director but also other key plant administrators are formally appointed by the ministry. It may even be that all industrial posts within the nomenklatura of the Party organs are also within the nomenklatura of the All-Union or the republican ministry. This would be a logical way to ensure that no serious problems arise from the practice of placing posts from a single plant within the nomenklatura of different Party organs.

Normally, an attempt by a local Party organ to remove an official within its nomenklatura is likely to prove successful. Even if higher administrative authorities still have faith in such an official, they are wiser to transfer him to another area than to permit an important subordinate to have poor relations with the powerful local Party organs. In fact, there are many complaints from Party officials that this is precisely what happens: "The leaders of some soviet and economic organs do not take the opinion of the Party organs into account in the selection of personnel, and they defend and appoint to higher posts officials who have been removed from posts for failing to cope with them. Thus, the former director of the polygraph combine was appointed to the post of head of the capital construction department of the flax- and hemp-working administration of the Belorussian sovnarkhoz, [although] in recent years he had twice been removed from posts by Party organs for not having coped with his work. The Belorussian Minister of Construction called to work in Minsk [a man called] Biriukov, who was recently expelled from the Party by the plenum of the Briansk obkom." [57]

Of course, such a complaint is not necessarily proof of venality on the part of the administrative officials; they may have evaluated the performance of their subordinate quite differently than did the local Party organs.[58]

The process by which a vacancy is filled seems to be somewhat more complicated — or at least more varied — than that by which it is created. As in analogous situations in the West, there is sometimes an heir apparent (probably the chief engineer) who has long been taken for granted as the successor when the old manager is promoted or retires. Indeed, a raikom secretary has asserted that one of the duties of a director is to prepare his own replacement.[59] But, sometimes a long search is necessary to find an acceptable candidate. Thus, it took over a year in 1962 and 1963 to select the first deputy chairman of the Moldavian Gosplan and a year to select a deputy chairman of the sovnarkhoz — both posts apparently in the nomenklatura of the republican central committee.[60]

The Soviet press has said very little about the relationship of the local Party organs and the post-1964 ministers in the selection of new personnel. As indicated before, several articles suggest a considerably more important role for the local Party organs than seemed to be the case prior to 1957. Certainly, it is difficult to recall any pre-1957 Party spokesman or official stating that "as is well known, the leaders of the enterprises are confirmed in their post on the recommendation of the Party organs." [61] When this question was explored in two interviews in the Soviet Union in 1967, both a newspaperman and an enterprise manager insisted that the Party organs normally have the initiative in the selecting of new directors. They indicated that the local Party organs usually advance a candidate and that the ministry then has the right of veto; if the ministry disagrees, the Party organs advance another candidate. If none of the candidates of the local Party organs is acceptable or if the Party officials are dissatisfied with possible local replacements, the ministry may submit a candidate from another plant for Party approval.

Surely, however, it would be a mistake to suggest too formal a structure to the process by which a new manager is selected. Undoubtedly, the final decision is normally preceded by considerable consultation with a variety of officials. For example, the lower Party officials may often be asked their opinion of candidates for posts in the nomenklatura of higher organs. Even prior to 1957, a heavy industry ministry might ask the gorkom in a small city for its evaluation of a candidate for a directorship not within its nomenklatura.[62] Such a practice seems even more common within the Party apparatus itself. One obkom first secretary acknowledged that "thanks to the constant businesslike contact which the gorkomy and raikomy maintain with the enterprises, we [the obkom] are in a position to judge correctly whether some comrade should be promoted or removed." [63] In 1965, the Riga gorkom formalized the process of consultation by establishing a "personnel commission" for decisions on posts in its nomenklatura. The commission was headed by a gorkom secretary and the head of the organizational department, and its membership varied depending on the specific post under consideration. The members included heads of other departments, instructors, and raikom secretaries as well as managers and heads of the personnel departments of the local enterprises and institutions.[64]

The Party organs are especially likely to rely on the advice of lower Party officials in those instances when the Party organ is geographically or organizationally distant from a post in its nomenklatura. It may even delegate the real responsibility for a post in its nomenklatura to lower officials. For example, a 1959 article in *Partiinaia zhizn* complained that "some obkomy and republican central committees . . . even independently transfer officials in the nomenklatura of the All-Union Central Committee without asking the consent of the Central Committee." [65]

Because infringing on a superior's prerogatives is always dangerous and must be especially so in the centralized Soviet system, it is hard to believe that such transfers would have taken place if the higher officials had not given the impression that this was permissible. Plant chief engineers in Minsk may be within the nomenklatura of the All-Union Central Committee, but the Central Committee secretariat surely has little knowledge of the candidates and probably relatively little interest in the posts, and it would be understandable if the real Party responsibility devolved to a lower level. Indeed, it may have become normal to give the local Party organs responsibility for selecting officials for important local posts in the nomenklatury of higher Party organs, the role of the latter often becoming more one of confirmation. This may now even be true of plant directorships in the nomenklatura of the Central Committee.

Within the industrial hierarchy too, a wider range of officials is usually involved in filling a vacancy than simply those of the organ with the official power of appointment. Whereas a chief engineer may be formally appointed by the ministry, those interviewed declared that the plant director would have a major role in the selection of his chief assistant, and, indeed, they insisted that he would have the right of veto over any unsatisfactory candidate.

Finally, the wishes of the candidates themselves are also taken into account in the selection process. It should be reemphasized that the official statements about the power of the Party over its members can create a misleading impression of the actual situation in the Soviet Union. Again and again, the Soviet press mentions Party members who have refused to accept a job that the local Party organs have suggested they take. In particular, there are many complaints about

169

the "offended ones," men who have performed unsatisfactorily in a post and who are then offered a lesser one. It may be months before the Party organs find a job that is accepted by such a man.[66]

In the Soviet Union, as is the United States, it may be costly for a man to decline a job offered by his superiors. Just as the young American corporation executive turns down a promotion to another city only if he is willing to forego further significant advancement, so a Communist in the Soviet Union undoubtedly pays the same price for a refusal. In addition, he also runs the risk of being expelled from the Party. In one case a man was expelled from the Party for refusing a promotion to a post for which he did not think he had the necessary qualifications, and he appealed to *Partiinaia zhizn* for support. The editors expressed doubt about the wisdom of expulsion in his particular case, but they clearly considered the action legitimate in general terms.[67]

A Soviet novel about the 1957 industrial reorganization probably presents a fairly accurate picture of the typical behavior of a Communist who is dissatisfied with a job offered him. The leading character, a young official in the Ministry of Coal Industry, is told by an official of the Central Committee secretariat that he has been assigned to the Donetsk sovnarkhoz. Unhappy over the prospect of leaving Moscow, he at first refuses the position. When the Central Committee official indicates that this decision would involve expulsion from the Party, the engineer asks for a few days to think it over. He and his friends gather like "conspirators" to decide who are "the necessary people who could help [him] to remain in Moscow." However, after unsuccessfully calling a number of persons, he finally decides that he must accept, and does so.[68]

There are many jobs in the Soviet Union and many institutions ready to hire a man who is reasonably qualified — even one who has been expelled from the Party. In the words of the Central Committee official in the novel just discussed, "A capable engineer will always find pleasant work for himself." [69] Although a recalcitrant member will often not be threatened with expulsion, a man who looks for more than just "pleasant work" can never forget that the important jobs are all within the nomenklatura of some Party organ and that the wrong decision can end all hopes for a truly successful career.

The Criteria of the Local Party Organs for Selecting Personnel

Throughout this chapter — and throughout this book — the role of the local Party organs in personnel selection has been discussed as a normal component of their executive responsibilities. It has been implied that the major criterion used by the Party organ in determining whether to appoint or dismiss an official is a rational-technical one — that is, whether his occupancy of a position will contribute to plan fulfillment and industrial growth. This implication needs to be discussed more explicitly and the qualifications to it presented.

It goes without saying that one of the original reasons for placing industrial posts within the nomenklatura of Party organs was a desire to maintain political control of industry. Like the policy of reserving a steadily increasing percentage of important posts for Party members, the establishment of the Party nomenklatura was a key step toward ensuring that "Soviet public administration is suffused with political content." It also was to guarantee the institution of a true "one-party administration." [70] An official or a candidate for a post who has allowed doubts to be created about his loyalty to the Communist regime will surely not occupy a significant administrative post for long, particularly now that there are many loyal men who can replace him.

In speaking of a political criterion for selection, however, one must always be clear about the meaning given this phrase. If an American official is said to be fired for political reasons, there are several quite different factors that may be involved. He may be fired because he is suspected of disloyalty to the American system; he may be fired because it is necessary to appease some angry element in the electorate that is calling for his removal or that will become increasingly hostile to the political leadership unless a scapegoat is found; he may be fired because his is a "patronage" post and his party or faction has been defeated.

If by "political criterion" one means insistence on a manager's loyalty to the Communist Party and the Communist system, then obviously the Soviet administrative system is thoroughly political. Not only loyalty to the Party but actual membership in it is required for an increasing number of administrative jobs. However, to state that the Party organs demand Party membership from a candidate is not to use the term "party" in the sense that it is normally used in Western discussions of political criteria. A demand that a Soviet administrator be a member of the Communist Party is "political" in much the same sense as the demand that the American administrator swear that he is *not* a member of the Communist Party. In both cases the basic question is one of loyalty to the system as a whole, and in both cases that loyalty — and the formal demonstrations of it — usually come to be taken for granted as the stability of the political system itself is no longer seriously challenged.

In the 1920's and early 1930's, the insistence on Party membership for a manager had a quite different meaning than it does now. Then a man was often named manager because of his Party membership (or more specifically his commitment to the Party and his organizational ability as demonstrated in command or political work in the Civil War); now a man is more likely to be made a member of the Party because he gives promise of becoming a good manager.

The major step that has changed the character of Party membership for the industrial administrator (and that has also changed the type of man becoming a Party member) has been the raising of the minimum age at which Soviet citizens — or, at least, educated Soviet citizens — are admitted to the Party. Although the Party Rules list the minimum age for admission as eighteen, even the most politically active men — the Komsomol leaders — frequently do not join the Party until their mid-twenties,[71] and potential industrial administrators are seldom permitted to join before their late twenties.[72] By following such a policy, the Soviet leadership is able to retain the old Leninist image of the Party member as a man who not only believes in the goals of the Party but who is willing to dedicate his life to their realization. By postponing the decision on admission until the candidates have worked for a number of years, the leadership is able to judge more effectively whether a man does indeed have the drive, the dedication, and the ability that will permit him to make a significant contribution to the Party's goals.

In industry, raising the minimum age for Party admission has meant that normally those engineers are admitted into the Party who have demonstrated a level of excellence in their job performance sufficient to suggest further promotion. This means that (in industrial management, at least) the men who come into the Party and who rise to posts reserved for Party members are in many ways similar to those who would rise to top industrial posts even if the Party did not exist. To be sure, like other Soviet citizens, they have undergone political socialization in the Soviet system, and many of their political-philosophical assumptions reflect this experience. (In fact, their acceptance into the Party indicates that they have been sufficiently socialized not to have shown "political immaturity" in their school and college years.) For this reason it is quite incorrect to state that "a shrewd and hard-working manager cannot be a convinced, sincere Communist." [73]

Yet, the most important fact for an understanding of the participation of these men in industrial decision-making (at least at the level of decision-making which is the prime concern of this book) is that the requirement of Party membership does not prevent the industrial administrator from being a man who has all the technical qualifications and organizational ability required for the job. On the contrary, as long as he was admitted into the Party after the Great Purge (and not at the front during the war), his membership is a sign that his superiors think that he has those qualifications.

The question remains, what about the other types of political criteria for personnel selection? Does the involvement of the local Party organs create a tendency for removal of officials who offend elements in the "electorate"? Does it mean that officials will be appointed or dismissed depending on their allegiance to one or another faction or leader within the Party?

These questions are, unfortunately, quite difficult to answer. The Soviet press has not chosen to explore them fully, and they hardly can be raised fruitfully in interviews. Hence, one is compelled to attempt only tentative answers to them. It is abundantly clear that officials at times are either appointed or removed to appease some powerful group; it is also clear that friendships with important Party officials can be an important factor in determining career success. What is difficult to judge is the relative importance of these factors, particularly in the selection of lower-level and middle-level industrial administrators. It is also difficult to judge whether these factors would, in fact, be less important if the local Party organs were not involved in personnel selection.

One can easily demonstrate, for example, that personnel decisions are sometimes made with an eye toward their effect on some particular group in Soviet society. The most important of these groups — and the one taken into account most frequently — is the higher Party apparatus. Like the higher Party officials themselves, the lower Party organs are likely to seek a scapegoat when failure occurs. By replacing a lower official, they are able to report to their own superiors that the cause of the difficulty has been discovered and that a new man who can produce results has been appointed. It is interesting to note that when officials of republican central committees mention that they have transferred a certain category of positions from the nomenklatura of lower Party organs to their own, they almost invariably justify their action by referring to an excessively high rate of turnover in the posts — a turnover that they say results from an attempt of lower Party officials to protect themselves by finding scapegoats for failure.[74]

Actions taken to appease other groups within society seem to be much less frequent, but they do occur. Plants in the non-Slavic republics almost always have at least a few non-Russians in the top management group,[75] and this probably is not always a chance occurrence. And in a slightly different context, every year there are reports of plant managers who have been removed because of lack of concern for working conditions, and so forth. Ilia Ehrenburg is probably right in his suggestion in *The Thaw* that the Party officials intervene in these matters only when the situation becomes disastrous or near to it.[76] Yet, when conditions do reach this stage, it is, no doubt, easier to sacrifice a manager (or simply transfer him) than to admit the nature of the pressure that caused him to act as he did.

The removal of the local Party organs from the process of personnel selection would not, of course, cause this kind of "political" factor to disappear. Industrial administrators know the value of a scapegoat, and they should be aware of the preconditions of good morale among the workers as well as the importance of morale for plan fulfillment. However, the Party officials' responsibility for political stability is likely to make them more sensitive to this type of "political" consideration than a "businessman" might be.

The third type of political factor — that of the possible importance of factional and personal connections — is the most difficult to assess.

Unquestionably, allegiance to a higher political leader often is a significant consideration in the selection of persons for many important posts in the Party and state apparatus. Similarly, frequent complaints in the Soviet press leave no doubt that at times officials are selected for reasons of friendship or kinship rather than for their technical-organizational abilities. But, as before, the question — just how important is this factor in comparison with other criteria for selection? Is it as important in the selection of industrial administrators as it is in the selection of high-ranking Party secretaries?

Although the evidence on this point is not very strong, it is possible that some of the Western conception of a neutral civil service has become accepted in the Soviet Union, at least in connection with the industrial administration. The Soviet industrial administrator cannot be neutral toward the Party or the Soviet regime (as the American civil servant is not neutral toward the American system as a whole), but he may be permitted or even expected to display neutrality toward the political struggles taking place *within* the Party. To be sure, like all important civil servants, the most important industrial administrators must participate when the political struggle concerns their specialty (as, for example, in the controversy over the relative priority of steel and chemicals in investment decisions). However, if the political leaders take for granted that the industrial administrators will take a "departmental point of view," there is no necessity for the question of political loyalty or disloyalty to be raised.

The strongest evidence that such a neutral attitude does exist in the Soviet Union can be found in the career patterns of the most important industrial administrators. As noted earlier, those who have risen to the rank of minister or deputy minister often have a length of tenure that would be most improbable were their fortunes to depend on the success of a particular Party leader or leaders.

Consider, for example, the dozen years from the spring of 1946 to the summer of 1958 — the period of the fall of Zhdanov, the Voznesensky affair, the death of Stalin, the fall of Malenkov, and the abolition of the industrial ministries. In the spring of 1946, there were thirty USSR ministers in the industrial and construction field, six of whom died in high office or shortly after leaving it. Eighteen of the remaining twenty-four held very important industrial-construction posts in the summer of 1958. Three of the missing six had risen above the ministerial level (where, of course, they were not immune to the vicissitudes of factional struggle), and a fourth remained an important plant director.

A similar pattern of stability is observable among the directors of the 170 most important plants, particularly if one accounts for the fact that they are middle-level officials subject to promotion into the ministries (or the sovnarkhozy). For example, one industry whose leader (I. F. Tevosian) apparently did become embroiled in factional politics was ferrous metallurgy. However, what happened after Tevosian was appointed Ambassador to Japan in 1956, apparently as a mild form of exile? It has been possible to identify the director in twenty-six of the thirty steel plants in the sample in early 1956. Despite the removal of Tevosian, despite the steel versus chemical conflict that raged during the sovnarkhoz period, fifteen of the twenty-six men still retained the same directorship six years later and six more had been promoted to a higher post in the sovnarkhoz (or, in one case, the planning organs). Two of the twenty-six had died while in office; only three had been removed without being given a higher position (or at least a higher position that has been identified).

If one examines the plants of the ministry with whom the Ministry of Ferrous Metallurgy was in conflict — that is, the Ministry of the Chemical Industry — one finds an almost identical situation. In early 1956, the directors can be identified at fourteen of the fifteen plants in the sample. In 1962, eight of them held the same position, and five had been named to a higher post in a sovnarkhoz. Only one was removed without being promoted.

Figures such as these prove little directly about the role of the local Party organs. The directorships of the 170 plants are surely within the nomenklatura of the Central Committee, and the local Party organs have nothing to do with the selection of All-Union ministers. However, the statistics are still suggestive. If the ministers and the directors of the largest plants usually can survive the changing fortunes of factional struggle, particularly if they could survive the defeat of the anti-Party group with its heavy representation among leaders of the Council of Ministers, it is difficult to believe that lesser industrial administrators would become deeply involved in factional politics. Not only would there seem to be no reason for this to occur, but the top administrators themselves should be able to provide considerable protection to those below them.

The evidence on this question should not be pushed too far. Even if technical and organizational ability (as manifested in the ability to fulfill the plan) are the prime criteria for selection, the career of an industrial administrator is apt to be furthered if those in important Party posts are familiar with his ability. (See the discussion of this point in Chapter XIII.) Moreover, to say that factional loyalty is not a significant factor is not to say that considerations of personal friendship are not significant. This factor never can be excluded in any bureaucracy, and it would be strange if it were not present in a society still fairly close in time to the traditional stage. (For this reason, it is not surprising that some of the most persistent criticism of personnel selection based on friendship is directed at the officials in the central Asian republics.)

Yet, the Party officials can never forget that they themselves are judged on the basis of plan fulfillment, particularly plan fulfillment in such an important sector as industry. It is one thing to appoint a friend to a relatively minor job in small-scale industry, for technically qualified officials are difficult to find for those posts in any case. It must be quite another matter when a post affecting the record of the region is concerned. In those cases, Party officials are likely to echo a proverb recited by Khrushchev: *Druzhba druzhboi, a sluzhba sluzhboi* (Friendship is friendship, but business is business).[77]

VIII. Types of Intervention in Production, Technical, and Planning Decisions

An outsider may look on the local Party organs primarily as a prefectoral institution that coordinates the activities of different plants and organizations, but Soviet spokesmen place their emphasis on work of the local Party organs that is related to individual plants or (from 1957 to 1962) to individual sovnarkhozy. They stress that the Party organs should provide policy guidance to the managers, promote technical innovation, enforce strict adherence to the law and the plan, and ensure that plans take into account all of the "reserves" of the plant or area.

Few assertions are easier to document than that the local Party organs have, in fact, often concerned themselves with these matters. Even before 1957 the local Party organs were "concerned with the basic problems of the development of industry and construction in the oblast"; they "examined the plans of the enterprises, supervised their fulfillment, and expressed to the ministries their ideas about the best way of using local reserves and resources." [1] After the creation of the sovnarkhozy it was everywhere stated that (to quote the first secretary of the Leningrad obkom) the local Party organs had begun "to lead the economy more concretely . . . to influence the work of the industrial enterprises and the construction sites more actively . . . to uncover and to use the reserves of production, to introduce progressive methods. . . ." [2] Similarly, one reads that the reunification of the Party apparatus in 1964 and the creation of the ministries has "noticeably increased the role and authority of the Party organizations and has strengthened their influence on all sides of life." [3]

Yet, at the same time the Soviet press contains numerous criticisms of the local Party organs which cast doubt on these general statements. The very quotation about the pre-1957 work of the Party organs cited above is followed by the statement that "speaking frankly, there was a great deal of formalism in this important matter." [4] Repeatedly, one reads that some Party organ has adopted a servile attitude toward a certain manager, that it has not been sufficiently demanding, and so forth. Even when the Party organs are "demanding," it may be in the wrong direction. Instead of fighting localism, for example, the Party officials may "compel the economic leaders [to take some action] favorable to local interests." [5]

This chapter and the next examine the set of responsibilities revolving around what might be called "purely industrial" intra-plant (and intra-sovnarkhoz) decision-making. An attempt will be made to ascertain the extent to which Party involvement in this realm is, in fact, meaningful, and to what extent the oft-stated defects in Party work represent typical patterns of behavior or are exceptions. The discussion is organized in two basic parts: this chapter surveys the concrete ways in which the local Party organs can be involved in production, technical, and planning decision-making; evaluation of the Party organs' performance of this role is contained in the next chapter.

Investigation Work

Whatever defects may exist in the work of the local Party organs, it seems incontrovertible that all Party organs have at least overtly shown considerable interest in intra-plant matters. They have, of course, been responsible for the fulfillment of the plan and for the correction of deficiencies reported by Party members and rank-and-file citizens. If things go wrong, the local Party officials know full well that they had better be able to produce documentary evidence that they have not been inactive or indifferent.

One universal manifestation of this interest in industrial questions has been a multitude of Party investigations of conditions in the area's factories. If the Party officials want information about a plant, the simplest technique at their disposal is to call the managers directly on the telephone, and they often do this, frequently bypassing the plant Party secretary. The obkom has a special telephone network to give it direct contact with the leading officials of the oblast, and the managers of the major plants are on this network. [6]

Another favorite method of obtaining information about a plant has been to summon the director to a bureau session to give a report. When an important plant fails to fulfill its plan, these visits normally become very frequent. When, for example, the Dzerzhinski Metallurgy Works in Dneprodzerzhinsk was lagging in 1955 and 1956, the gorkom and the raikom discussed it fifteen times within a year.[7] This took place during the ministerial period, it should be noted, and the plant was a very large one with a Party organizer of the Central Committee as its Party secretary. Similarly, when the Nizhnii Tagil Metallurgy Combine did not fulfill its plan in December 1966, this was considered a "ChP" (an emergency) and became the subject of a commission investigation and a two-hour discussion at the gorkom bureau.[8]

In certain cases a local Party organ may follow the practice of calling the area's important plant directors for frequent regular reports. The Lenin raikom in Krasnodar was criticized in 1965 for summoning the leading administrators to the bureau four or five times during a year,[9] and it is possible that this is fairly typical behavior for the lowest of the local Party organs.

Plainly the local Party organs do not rely completely on the economic managers for information about the local plants. When the Party officials simply want current production statistics (that is, the plant's own count, made before the official monthly report),[10] there is not much alternative to accepting management's figures, at least until the monthly report comes out. However, in other cases — even when the director is called to make a report — the Party organ can send its own officials into the plant to investigate conditions. The article that criticized the Lenin raikom in Krasnodar for requiring too many reports took for granted that each of these reports would be preceded by an investigation: "And, each time, naturally, investigations are carried out, commissions are sent, memoranda are written." [11] Indeed, the criticism of the raikom was based on the fact that the preliminary investigations were so time-consuming that they did not leave the raikom officials sufficient time for their other responsibilities.

Because their own staff is small, the Party organs have long followed the practice of drawing on outside help for their investigatory work. In recent years the policy of having "volunteer" (*vneshtatnyi*)

180

instructors and "public" councils and commissions attached to the local Party organs has provided a reservoir of outside specialists who can be used to supplement the full-time Party officials in this work.[12] Moreover, the local Party organs have also increasingly taken advantage of the rapid development of concrete sociology. Survey investigation has become almost the symbol of the scientific approach to problem-solving which the Party officials have incessantly been instructed to follow in the post-Khrushchev period. The obkomy have acquired "sociological laboratories" and "sociological commissions," apparently staffed in large part by volunteers, to help in the collection of necessary information.[13]

However, long before voluntary public assistance to the Party organs was emphasized as a campaign, the local Party organs had regularly called on outsiders for assistance in investigation. The normal way for these outsiders to be utilized has been through the creation of a "commission" or a "brigade," the size and nature of which has varied with the nature of the investigation. Sometimes a commission is selected completely or in large part from employees of the plant being studied. In these cases the raikom calls the secretary of the Party committee and instructs him "to form such and such a commission of such and such a composition to prepare a question for the bureau." [14] More frequently, the commission is composed completely or largely of outsiders. Occasionally, such a commission may not contain any Party officials,[15] but it seems normal for an instructor (or even a secretary) to participate in the work of the commission — and probably to head it.

The outside members of the commissions are chosen on the basis of the specialized knowledge needed in the particular investigation. When the Lvov Auto-Carrier Works was experiencing difficulties in 1956, for example, the commission was composed primarily of experienced industrial managers. When the Kharkov Tractor Works failed to build new machines and modernize the old ones as rapidly as possible, the brigade created by the obkom included the chief designer of another large plant and a professor of the local polytechnical institute.[16] When it was necessary for one obkom to determine the worth of a new invention, the commission was composed of the head of a research institute, an associate professor (*dotsent*) of an engineering college, the chief engineer of a construction administration, and a representative of the obkom.[17]

Commissions can be created for any question which might be discussed at the bureau of a Party organ or for any problem on which a complaint may be received. As a consequence, the number of commissions can become quite large. For example, during one two-month period the Omsk Oil Refinery was visited by five commissions of the local raikom and three of the gorkom. In 1959 the Lithuanian Central Committee received 7,592 letters, statements, and complaints. Fifty percent of them were investigated with "officials of the Central Committee participating" — phraseology usually suggesting the existence of commissions.[18]

The use of non-Party officials to assist the Party organs in conducting investigations was carried a step further in 1962 with the creation of the Committee of Party-State Control (*Kontrol*). The head of this committee at the oblast level was at the same time a secretary of the local Party organ and a deputy chairman of the executive committee of the local soviet, but the paid staff seems to have been quite small. Information about the size of the staff of the oblast committee is not available, but within the urban raion the committee chairman apparently had no full-time staff assistance.[19] At all levels most of the work was carried out by part-time (*vneshtatnye*) instructors and department heads.

If one were to read the legislation establishing the Committee of Party-State Control, one would assume that its officials had considerable independent power. They could "suspend" (*priostanavlivat*) illegal orders and activities of organizations, institutions, and officials; they could "fine officials" or "bring the guilty to responsibility [by] demoting them in position or removing them from their post." They had a general right "to give the appropriate leaders of the ministries, state committees, departments and other organizations, enterprises, construction sites, kolkhozy, and institutions instructions about the removal of deficiencies and violations in the fulfillment of decisions of the Party and the state." [20]

Whatever this language appears to suggest, the committees of Party-State Control did not in practice seem to be independent of the local Party organs. The republican, krai, and oblast committees were defined as organs of the local Party committee and soviet, and their chairman reported to the Party first secretary and the chairman of the executive committee of the soviet. Moreover, in all the cases on which information is available the chairman of the Control Committee was selected from among local officials — usually local Party officials — and he normally did not have the kind of experience or status to pose a serious challenge to the first secretary. At the city and raion level the chairmen were defined as the direct agents (*upolnomochennye*) of the oblast control committee, but they too seemed almost invariably to be from the local area.[21]

The main function of the Party-State Control Committee seemed to be to relieve the other secretaries of some of the burdensome task of investigation, particularly by providing a place for citizens to direct their complaints. As one official expressed it, "Now hundreds of people turn to the organs of Party-State Control concerning the most varied questions. Many of them speak about serious abuses at their enterprises, about cases of infringement of socialist legality." [22] Besides investigating individual complaints, the control committees conducted general investigations of conditions and of the extent to which a particular Party decision had been fulfilled. Even such a question as the amount of help given the enterprises by bank specialists could be the subject of a general investigation.[23]

The working relationships between the Party-State Control Committee and the local Party organs have not been discussed comprehensively in Soviet sources, but there is much evidence that the two usually worked closely together. The most typical working arrangement seems to have been that found in an Uzbekistan city: "The city Party-State Control Committee, together with the industrial department of the gorkom, decided to find out [what] prevented the Margilan Silk Combine from fulfilling the state plan." [24] In carrying out this work, both probably concentrated most of their attention on those matters of immediate interest to the first secretary and the bureau.

In 1965, the Party-State Control Committee was replaced by the Peoples' Control Committee. The chairman of the new committee is no longer a Party secretary, but his functions seem little different from those of his predecessor. The Committee of Peoples' Control is also staffed primarily by volunteer help, and Soviet spokesmen have emphasized its close connections with the local Party organs. The Committee's chairman (usually the same man who had been chairman of the Party-State Control Committee in the area) has normally been named to the Party bureau, and thus he is able to coordinate his work closely with the main concerns of the bureau and the first secretary.[25] As before, the investigations of the Committee of Peoples' Control are often conducted jointly with officials of the local Party organs:

"The organs of peoples' control [of Yaroslavl oblast] became interested in the reasons for the lag in a series of kolkhozy and sovkhozy and uncovered reserves which these farms possessed for increasing the production of grain, potatoes, vegetables, and other products. . . . This question was introduced to the [obkom] bureau by the oblast committee of peoples' control together with the agriculture department of the obkom. Close mutual ties have also been established between the other departments of the obkom, gorkomy, and raikomy and the corresponding organs of peoples' control. Joint investigations of the production capacity at the petroleum-chemistry enterprises, the conservation of water resources, and services in the rural areas have given positive results." [26]

Correcting Mistakes

Investigations by the local Party organs are to be undertaken not for their own sake but to provide the basis for corrective action. At a minimum, an investigation that discloses wrongdoing will be followed by a decision that obligates the director "to correct the mistake," but such very general decisions have often been censured by Party spokesmen. The Party officials are supposed "to help" the managers to find a correct solution to their problems, and throughout the post-Purge period the Soviet press has carried innumerable statements claiming that particular Party organs have done so. Bienstock, Schwarz, and Yugow quote the following passage from a 1940 article about the reaction of a raikom to a situation in which railway cars were standing idle instead of transporting peat to an electric power station: "It was, of course, possible to have the manager report [to the Party committee], to reprimand him, to make a decision to eliminate immediately the cause of such a situation. Such decisions are frequent in the practice of many town and district Party committees. But the Komsomolski district Party committee acted otherwise. In order to find causes, the district committee summoned a conference of dispatchers and engineers on duty. After having checked the situation in full detail, the district committee made a decision in which it pointed out to the power station management measures necessary for doing away with this defect. Very soon the idle cars were moved." [27]

In the mid-1950's the Soviet press was still carrying reports of concrete Party intervention to improve the situation in a lagging plant. The following example deals with one of the huge plants in the Ukraine: "The October Revolution Works in Voroshilovgrad did not fulfill its plan for tractor parts. The entire matter was held up by one shop. The gorkom bureau sent a group of Party officials into the shop. These comrades were given the job not of gathering material or writing reports, but instead of helping production. They consulted with the workers and engineers, they acquainted themselves with the particulars of the situation, and they were able to give a series of valuable suggestions to the economic leaders and Party organization." [28]

Suggestions such as these have usually been formalized in decisions of the bureau, and they can become quite demanding in tone. Even when the lowest of Party organs — the raikom — makes a decision on the most important of plants, it can be categorical in its phraseology: "In the decision of the plenum, as in the decision of the bureau of the raikom which preceded the plenum, the discussion chiefly concerned the economic leaders of the [Stalingrad Tractor Works]. In this decision the majority of points began with the words: (1) 'To direct the attention of the plant director . . .'; (2) 'To demand from the chief engineer and the chief designer . . .'; (3) 'To demand from the chief metallurgist . . .'; (4) 'To obligate the deputy chief engineer and the chief technologist . . .'; (5) 'To demand from the chief mechanic . . .'; (6) 'To demand from the deputy chief engineer of IDSA . . .' " [29]

There is a very thin line between Party intervention to correct a mistake and Party intervention that entails active and persistent involvement in the planning or even direction of the economic life of the enterprise. Because the plans are too complex to be completely fulfilled, an insistence on fulfillment of one plan indicator or completion of one item in an assortment plan may have a wide impact on other decisions. When, for example, the Cheliabinsk gorkom became concerned about "a serious lag in the output of chemical production and equipment for chemical industry construction" and ordered the industrial-transportation department of the gorkom and raikomy to take "the fulfillment of the organizational-technical measures [in this realm] under daily *kontrol*," [30] it was in effect telling the economic managers which items and which deliveries had the highest priority (assuming the decision was not a formalistic one).

Similarly, when a local Party organ corrects a managerial "mistake" with respect to some technical innovation, it can be determining the basic technical policy of the enterprise. The following example was chosen from the pre-sovnarkhoz period, and again it involves the interaction of an urban raikom and one of the most important enterprises in the country: "At times the [Ordzhonikidze] raikom in Zaporozhe has to concern itself directly with technical questions at the enterprises. In such cases the raikom secretary, Comrade Zakharov, boldly intervenes in the productive process, rendering help to the enterprise officials. . . . Sometimes the raikom has to break the resistance of conservative officials. For example, in the sheet-metal shop [of the Zaporozhe Steel Works] a metal worker, Comrade Udovenko, worked out a design for a machine to clean the sheet metal. The machine does the work of 150 workers. Comrade Pavlov, a brigadier of machine lubricators, also suggested eliminating one operation in the cold rolling of sheet metal by using palm-oil. These and other suggestions were not supported by the deputy head of the shop, Comrade Bogomaz. The raikom tried to persuade him to correct his mistake, but without success. Then the bureau [of the raikom] punished him, and it pointed out to the chief engineer that he had not been sufficiently strict in demanding that his subordinates introduce suggestions aimed at improving technology. The machine of Comrade Udovenko has been introduced, and it works successfully." [31]

Finally, it should be mentioned that at times the "correction of mistakes" can also lead the local Party organs into direct administrative work. Such behavior seems to have been particularly widespread in the coal industry prior to the creation of the sovnarkhoz. For example, the officials of the Party organs in Voroshilovgrad, worried about plan fulfillment in 1952, ordered the coal managers to conduct "days of high cyclical nature (*tsiklichnost*)": "On these days the plenipotentiaries of the [Kadievka] gorkom arrive at the mines. . . . On a "day of high cyclical nature" all leadership at the mine passes into the hands of the plenipotentiary of the city committee of the Party. He completely replaces the economic managers. The dispatchers report to him about the fulfillment of the plan by sections and by drifts, and it is to him that people turn when they want this or that kind of help. The leaders of the mines fulfill only his instructions." [32]

The officials of the Kadievka gorkom and the Voroshilovgrad obkom were severely criticized for their behavior, but two and a half years later the first secretaries of the two Party committees still retained their posts and *Pravda* carried an almost identical complaint about their work: "The Kadievka Party gorkom directly establishes the plan for coal extraction on the "storming days." . . . It gives orders about the number of coal-hewers to be sent to work. The leaders of the mines then report to the gorkom secretaries, comrades Shevchenko and Ermachenko, about the course of the fulfillment of the tasks. The decisions taken by the gorkom bureau are little distinguished from orders issued by the [coal] trust." [33]

Again, the *Pravda* correspondent seemed outraged by such behavior, but the reaction of the Party leadership was milder. The first secretary of the obkom (V. K. Klimenko) retained his post until 1961 when he was named chairman of the Ukrainian Trade Union Council. In 1956, the first secretary of the Kadievka gorkom (V. V. Shevchenko) was promoted to the position of obkom second secretary. In 1961 he became the first secretary of the obkom.[34]

In the last decade, no further reports of this type of Party participation in coal administration have been found, but there have been many reports of other detailed local Party involvement in detailed managerial questions. For example, when the new Sumgait Synthetic Rubber Plant was having very severe technical problems during the shakedown period in 1961, the first secretary of the gorkom went to the plant every morning at nine for an "operational session" (*operativka*) with management and had a key role in determining the day's work plan.[35] In the realm of construction, as will be seen in the next section, this type of involvement has been extremely frequent.

Although the removal of Khrushchev was accompanied by a criticism of excessive Party intervention in managerial details, the mandate of the local Party organs to "correct the mistakes" of the managerial personnel has not been revoked. The Party officials' influence on decisions taken within the plant can still be considerable. The following quotation is taken from a 1965 article written by the first secretary of the Dneprodzerzhinsk gorkom — one of only three gorkom first secretaries to be named to the All-Union Central Committee in the following spring:

"In the last two years the bureau of our gorkom . . . did not issue one reprimand to an economic leader. And not because we are kind-hearted or feeble. We simply think that it isn't necessary to wait until the director has to be "dragged" into the bureau. If it is necessary to talk over something with the leader of an enterprise, to warn him of a mistake, one of the secretaries goes to the plant near the end of the working day and has an explanatory conversation with him. . . . And the effect is usually such that a reprimand is not necessary. . . . We try not to tug at directors continually, but we also don't let them stew in their own juice (*varitsia v sobstvennom soku*)." [36]

Participation in Industrial Planning

In many of the examples cited in the last section, the local Party organs were obviously participating in the planning process. Frequently, however, the involvement of local Party officials in this process can become even more comprehensive and systematic. The local Party organs vigorously try to influence higher level investment decisions, and they also intervene forcefully in many planning decisions made within their locality. Their role has been particularly great in planning decisions on plants subordinate to the local soviets,[37] but they have not ignored ministerial (or sovnarkhoz) industrial enterprises.

During the pre-1957 period the impact of the local Party organs on the planning of the output of ministerial plants was limited by the frequent ability of the ministries to impose their will on these questions. However, even at that time, "the Party committees also examined the plans of the [individual] enterprises." [38] The context of the last quotation (taken from an article by an obkom first secretary) suggests that this examination was carried out systematically on an annual basis, and, in fact, the Soviet press cites cases in which a local Party organ did formally consider an enterprise's draft plan. For example, in 1955 the bureau of the Kemerovo obkom discussed the draft five-year plan of the Kuzbass Coal Combine.[39] Even if the annual plan of an enterprise was not always taken to a local Party organ, at a minimum the local Party organs had to become involved in the planning process any time that the plant director and the plant Party secretary disagreed about it.

Although the local Party organs had a general interest in preventing disabling imbalances in the development of local industry and services, there apparently was no systematic examination of the area-wide industrial plan by the local Party organs. Presumably the republican Party organs had an important role in the republican Council of Ministers' decisions about the development of industries administered by republican ministries, but prior to 1958 even the bureau of the republican central committee apparently did not examine the industrial plan as a whole.[40]

After the creation of the sovnarkhozy the local Party organs retained a keen interest in the planning of the output of individual plants. A most striking illustration of the extent of their participation in plant planning — and of the extent of their power — appeared in a *Pravda* article about the drafting of the plan at the Elgav Agricultural Machinebuilding Plant in Latvia. The plant had been ordered by the sovnarkhoz to produce air conditioners, and with difficulty its managers succeeded in setting up the necessary rigging. At this stage, however, "the officials of the Latvian Party Central Committee suggested that the production of air conditioners be discontinued." The article did not specify which officials were involved, but their "suggestion" was decisive. The plant management vigorously objected to the decision, and they were supported both by the sovnarkhoz and the Elgav gorkom. Indeed, the sovnarkhoz twice appealed the decision to the bureau of the Latvian Central Committee, but without success.[41]

Again and again the Soviet press of the sovnarkhoz period contains examples of detailed obkom decisions about the plans of individual enterprises. For example, at a plenary session of the Sverdlovsk obkom in April 1958, "the decision was taken to open the Volkhov mine and to put the first section of it into operation in 1962." In Briansk the director of the Bezhitsa Steel-Casting Works was told by the obkom bureau to reconstruct four of the works' shops during 1958 and 1959. Besides these seemingly independent decisions of the obkomy, the Soviet press repeatedly contained matter-of-fact references to joint obkom-sovnarkhoz decisions about individual plants. In discussing a conflict over the plan for the Vladimir Tractor Works, one article, for example, reported that "the Vladimir obkom and the sovnarkhoz approved the latter variant of the plan." [42]

The creation of the sovnarkhozy not only increased the effectiveness of obkom intervention in the planning process, but also changed its character. For the first time the plans of the individual enterprises were integrated into an oblast-wide plan, and the obkomy and republican central committees had their first real opportunity to engage in effective regional planning. G. Perov, the first deputy chairman of the USSR Gosplan, reported that the obkomy, in fact, utilized this opportunity: "[They] deeply and masterfully (*po-khoziaski*) examine the drafts of the plans for the development of the economy which are drawn up by the sovnarkhoz and the planning organs." At least in Rostov in 1957, the session of the bureau that undertook this task was not a formality, for it resulted in "the introduction of corrections" into the plan.[43]

To say that the obkom took decisions about economic planning is not necessarily to say that it participated intimately in industrial planning. As political scientists have come to recognize, taking official decisions may not be a sure sign of an institution's or official's real influence, for the final decision is usually but a formalization of decisions reached in earlier, informal discussions. If the officials with the final authority do not participate in the earlier discussions, if they do not hear the alternatives that are discarded at an early stage, they may well discover that they have little real choice when a policy question reaches them.

Nothing is more difficult to judge than the sources of informal influence on a decision, but the obkom officials had ample opportunity to participate in the early stages of decision-making if they so desired.

From 1957 to 1962, there were a number of mechanisms that helped to facilitate informal consultation between obkom and sovnarkhoz officials. Perhaps the simplest was the placing of the sovnarkhoz chairman on the bureau of the republican central committee or obkom. The sovnarkhoz chairman was thus permitted the opportunity to express his opinion on questions of concern to him and the sovnarkhoz, and he was also placed in a position where he might "often receive useful, businesslike advice" from Party officials.[44]

The Party officials themselves also could attend sessions of the council of the sovnarkhoz. In Kirov, for example, the secretary in charge of industry "frequently" attended these sessions, and this was probably a typical practice throughout the Soviet Union. Indeed, there are indications that Party officials may have been regular members of the sovnarkhoz council.[45]

Perhaps even more important was contact in between the sessions of the Party bureaus or the sovnarkhoz council. The Party officials could intervene at any stage when trouble threatened and could have the matter discussed in their presence. When, for example, the Cheliabinsk Metallurgy Plant failed to fulfill its plan in 1962, the obkom secretary called the plant director and a sovnarkhoz official into his office for a private conference.[46] In Kirov such conferences seem to have been a fairly regular occurrence: "Coming to the enterprise, the officials of the obkom most frequently conduct their business with the director and the chief engineer. . . . They fill their notebooks with the complaints of the economic managers, and having returned, they telephone the sovnarkhoz, summon its officials to the obkom, and conduct operational sessions with them." [47]

Obviously it was the republican central committee and the obkom whose role in industrial planning was increased the most by the creation of the sovnarkhozy. To the extent that the gorkomy and raikomy had access to the obkom they too shared in the increased opportunities for participation in planning, but there were many reports that they could be completely ignored by the sovnarkhoz.[48] At a minimum, however, their role with respect to the planning of the output of individual plants was no worse than it had been during the ministerial period. They continued to have the very important responsibility of resolving conflicts between the director and the plant Party secretary, and this alone guaranteed them some involvement in the planning process.

Since 1962 the position of the local Party organs (particularly the obkom) has been weaker than it was from 1957 to 1962, and their role in the planning process has obviously been affected. The announced purpose of the 1962 reorganization was to intensify the role of the local Party organs in the planning and supervision of the work of individual sectors of the economy or individual plants and, with more time to concentrate on the urban sector, the Party organs (particularly the obkomy) undoubtedly were able to intervene more frequently and persistently on these questions. However, with the amalgamation of the economic regions there apparently was no longer even a comprehensive oblast plan for the industrial obkom to examine, and obkom influence on sovnarkhoz decisions surely was curtailed. One would have expected the re-creation of the ministries to complete the re-establishment of the pre-1957 patterns of Party involvement in the planning process, and the language used in post-Khrushchev press discussions indicates that to a large extent this is the case. However, in two respects changes may have occurred.

First, the reorganization of 1962 seems to have reduced somewhat the time-span of the major planning decisions with which the local Party organs were primarily concerned. Although the Party organs continued to be interested in annual and long-range planning, their attention seems to have been focused far more on planning decisions that looked ahead several months, several weeks, or even several days in time. This involvement in short-range planning was particularly great in the field of construction. The industrial obkom had the duty to "examine and confirm measures for fulfilling the plans for construction work for each quarter of the year, each time providing for maximum concentration of resources on units which are near completion." In practice, this meant examining the list (*titulnyi spisok*) of planned construction projects, deciding which of these projects deserved priority in the quarter, and temporarily excluding from the list those "projects for which equipment, technical documentation, or a [sufficient] construction base had not been secured." [49]

The gorkomy and the raikomy often were concerned with planning decisions of even a shorter time-span. It was reported, for example, that at the bureau session of the Dzhambul gorkom there were established "not only the dates for putting houses into operation, but even the dates for digging their foundations, setting up panels, etc." Similarly, in the very large city of Cheliabinsk, "the bureaus of the city and raion Party committees often confirmed numerous schedules for putting houses, schools, and potato storehouses into operation; sometimes it was even indicated how many workers should work in specific shifts at this or that project." These two illustrations do not refer to large industrial projects, but other articles make it clear that the local Party organs were interested in their schedules as well.[50]

To provide more detailed direction to scheduling operations, the local Party organs frequently established staffs (*shtaby*), operational sessions (*operativki*), or planning sessions (*planerki*) to handle the most important construction projects. The staffs or operational sessions were headed by a local Party official (a secretary or, on lesser projects, a department head), and they included the top officials of different organizations involved in the construction projects. The role of the Party officials in these sessions could be quite decisive. In Kazan, for example, the raikom secretaries called themselves "the senior work superintendents" in the raion (the Russian term used — *prorab* — is most closely associated with construction administration). It was reported that "at the operational sessions [in Kazan] the gorkom and raikom secretaries distribute labor force, urge on the suppliers of materials, and establish [daily or weekly] work schedules." [51]

The scale of this work is perhaps best indicated in an article by the first secretary of the Cheliabinsk gorkom: "Until recently . . . it was fashionable for us (and obviously not only for us) to create all possible staffs — one for the construction of heating lines, one for the blast furnace, one for the rolling mill, one for the water line, etc. A responsible Party official — as a rule, a secretary of the Party committee, raikom, or gorkom — was appointed the head of each staff. And this head often led operational conferences, interfered in the decision of purely technical problems, shouldered the responsibility for many minor questions of materials supply, etc. The author of these lines had to appear more than once in the role of such a 'staffist' (*shtabist*)." [52]

The opening words of this quotation (as well as many other Soviet statements) suggest that Khrushchev's removal and the reunification of the Party apparatus ended this kind of detailed Party involvement in short-range planning. However, this suggestion is clearly incorrect, for reports on the creation of "staffs" have continued to appear in the post-

Khrushchev press. Thus, one 1965 article in discussing shortages in the water supply to the city of Lvov, asserts: "The Lvov gorkom manifested creative initiative. Together with the construction administration, it made technical calculations, made estimates, and established a plan and schedule for constructing the Zarudtsy-Lvov water line. It created a staff for the construction, headed by the gorkom secretary, Comrade Sviatotski." [53]

A 1967 article about one of the most important construction sites of the five-year plan, the Balashov Cotton Combine, reported a similar response there. "For the coordination of the activities of the different construction sub-divisions, a staff has been created for the construction site. Its influence is felt all the more noticeably." [54]

It is difficult to judge whether the number of staffs has been reduced in the post-Khrushchev period. Certainly the local Party organs had had a keen interest in construction prior to 1962 (even in Smolensk in the 1930's [55]), and the more frequent references to staffs in recent years may reflect a change in policy with respect to newspaper reporting more than a change in the behavior of the local Party officials. Because of the increased work load produced by the reunification of the Party apparatus, it does seem likely that the scale of the local Party participation in short-term planning of the construction industry is less today than it was from 1962 to 1964. If one is to judge by the frequency of newspaper reports, however, this participation may still be somewhat more systematic than it was prior to 1957.

A second reason to suspect a possible — or at least a potential — difference in the pre-1957 and post-1965 patterns of local Party involvement in industrial planning is the experiments which have been initiated in the relations between the ministry and the plant. Although these changes remain relatively minor, any major delegation of authority from the ministry to the plants on questions of investment, product mix, and so forth, could result in a major expansion in the role of the local Party organs. If there were to be increased reliance on market mechanisms and on profitability as a success indicator, the local Party organs too would have to be guided by market considerations. Yet, for those who manage an enterprise in a market economy, the essential problem is predicting what will be profitable at a time in the future when an investment program or a product development program will come to fruition, and this is not an easy task. If the Party officials continue to be judged partly on the basis of the economic performance of their enterprises, it is certain that they will want a role in the process by which these predictions are made.

Already there are many indications that the local Party organs continue to participate vigorously in plant planning decisions, particularly in the decisions made at plants which have been transferred to the new system of planning. Consider, for example, the following account of the relationship of the Kalinin Party officials to one of the first plants transferred to the new system, the Kalinin Excavator Works: "From the gorkom and the obkom most frequently come only instructions: master the production of such a product, prepare so many spare parts immediately, assign persons to such-and-such a place. Recently the local organs also turned their attention to the plant's funds. They ordered that 74,000 rubles (the whole fund of social-cultural measures) be used for city needs." [56]

Judging from 1967 interviews, the Party decision to transfer the entire social-cultural fund to city funds was probably a temporary phenomenon. During the first year of the program, the plants often received their funds after the plans of the construction trusts had been completed, and hence their possibility of utilizing the funds themselves was limited. However, there are no indications that other types of Party participation in planning are temporary. Instead, newspaper articles continue to declare that the decisions of the economic manager "should be guided first of all by the interests of the state" and that he must not pursue the goal of profit maximization to the point of sacrificing the interests of the state or the consumer. The heavy industry plants and ministries are not to reduce their production of consumers goods items even if this can be justified in terms of plant specialization; the managers must not concentrate their attention on the production of the most profitable items if these items are not, in fact, those most needed. The local Party organs clearly intervene — and are instructed to intervene — to correct this type of managerial "mistake" in planning. Indeed, they still intervene to correct problems which the reorganization was designed to overcome: "A detailed, useful conversation was held in the [Leningrad] obkom with those directors of enterprises on the new system who have hoarded economized metal and material and have not used them themselves nor returned them to the supply organizations." [57]

Although a reform in the pricing system would surely reduce the possibility that a decision based on the criterion of profitability would be contrary to the interests of the state, it would not eliminate the problem altogether. In no modern society are the industrial managers permitted to make their decisions on the basis of market-place criteria alone. In no modern society is it assumed that the "invisible hand" will be sufficient to protect the interests of society as the managers seek their own self-interest defined by profitability. When one speaks of zoning laws, of minimum wages, of licensing of doctors, of air pollution laws, of auto safety standards, or of wage-price guidelines, one is speaking of cases in which the "invisible hand" was deemed inadequate. Under market socialism, with prices established or influenced by central planning organs, the problem would be worse, if anything, for there would almost surely be some delay in adjusting prices to new supply-demand relationships.

For this reason, as long as the local Party organs are the major political organ in their region, as long as they are judged in part on the basis of the performance of nonindustrial sectors and the degree of local political stability, it is certain that they will want a role in determining those cases in which the interests of profitability are to be sacrificed for other interests. And as long as they are the prefects in the system, it is certain that the Party leadership will want them to have such a role.

IX. Impact on Production, Technical, and Planning Decisions

Nothing is easier to demonstrate than that the local Party organs frequently investigate conditions at the enterprises, engage in informal conversations with economic managers during early stages of decision-making, and make decisions on rather detailed technical and planning questions. The problem still remains: To what extent are the decisions of the local Party organs in this realm really meaningful? To what extent do the local Party organs take advantage of their informal access in order to influence decisions? What is the nature of their impact on decisions when they intervene?

In no set of circumstances are such questions easy to answer, for measuring influence (as opposed to locating formal authority) is one of the most difficult tasks in political science. The influences on a decision may be subtle indeed, and the participants themselves may not be aware of all of them. An outsider faces a particular problem, especially if he is denied the opportunity to observe the decision-making process in a systematic manner or to examine very full documentation of it.

The measurement of relative influence in the Soviet Union is further complicated by the existence of formalism both in Party work and in the treatment of Party work in the Soviet press. The Soviet press contains many accounts of Party decisions, but it also reports that many decisions are empty forms taken for the record. At the Twentieth Party Congress, Khrushchev directed some of his heaviest attacks at this type of formalistic approach by Party officials, and he demanded radical change. Six years later, however, another Presidium member, Andrei Kirilenko, could still state of Party work in industry, "This is done in large part in a formalistic manner." [1] One reads of a manager drafting a decision which supposedly provides policy guidance to him, of Party officials adopting a decision for form's sake and then not attempting to enforce it, even of Party officials totally forgetting a decision which they had adopted. [2] Consequently, when a scholar reads a newspaper report about a decision taken by a particular local Party organ, he must ask himself: is this an indication of Party impact on industrial decision-making or is this another of those formalistic Party actions?

Unfortunately, Soviet press stories on Party work cannot be discounted in a single direction, for there is as much — or more — formalism in the criticism of the local Party organs. "Criticism and self-criticism" has become a sacred ritual in the Soviet Union, and it is imperative that the performance of a Party official be criticized at every meeting both by himself and others. In these circumstances, nothing is easier (and more painless) than to repeat the old clichés: the Party official should have been more demanding, he should have forced the managers to uncover more of their reserves, he should not have permitted certain machinations, and so forth. If any plant has not fulfilled any part of its plan, then by definition the Party organs have not been sufficiently alert in enforcing plan discipline. There have even been cases when the Party organs were proven negligent by a statistic showing that about one half of the area's enterprises had an increase in labor productivity below the average increase in the area. Consequently, when a scholar reads reports of inadequate Party supervision of industry, he must ask himself: are the Party officials being judged against a standard of performance which is humanly obtainable?

Unduly harsh criticism is particularly probable in the wake of any decision to reorganize the Party or industrial structure or to launch a new campaign. At these times all possible defects are cited (and described in the blackest terms), and they are all associated with the organizational forms or practices now being abolished. Malenkov's 1941 report to the Eighteenth Party Conference provides a particularly revealing example of this phenomenon. Some of the passages in this speech seem quite categorical:

> The chief [defect in the work of the Party organizations in industry] is that the Party organizations do not help the peoples' commissariats and the enterprises of their oblast, city, and raion. The Party organizations have weakened their work both in industry and transportation, incorrectly assuming that they do not bear responsibility for the work of industry and transporta-

tion. . . . Many Party obkomy, occupying themselves with agriculture and the delivery of agricultural production, have neglected work in industry and transportation . . . and the Party gorkomy who are obligated to devote their chief attention to industry and transportation do not concern themselves with this matter and do not take measures to improve the work of lagging enterprises and railroads. The Party gorkomy and obkomy . . . do not control (*kontrolirovat*) the work of the enterprises, do not verify how the supervisory personnel at the factories, plants, and railroads are working, do not uncover deficiencies in their work, and thereby tolerate these deficiencies.[3]

Yet, other passages in Malenkov's speech clearly demonstrate that the Party organs of that period had known full well that they had responsibility for industry (including commissariat-supervised industry) and that, in fact, they had intervened on industrial questions. Malenkov indicates that the local Party organs had a secretary for industry, that they heard reports of enterprise managers at sessions of the bureau, that they were very concerned with enterprises which were not fulfilling their plan, and so forth.[4] Earlier articles furnished many examples of concrete Party work with industry. Indeed, one of the major criticisms presented in these articles was that the Party organs had been so busy helping the enterprises with supplies procurement that they did not have time for supervisory work.[5]

If one must rely on reports of Party decisions that may have been taken for form's sake and on criticisms of Party organs based on a standard of perfection that is totally unreasonable, a definitive judgment about the impact of the local Party organs on technical-planning decisions is impossible. Hence this chapter is limited to a discussion of the major factors shaping the Party's role in this kind of decision-making and to an examination of those patterns of Party impact which have become apparent.

Factors Limiting the Effectiveness of the Local Party Organs

Even if a gorkom has powers the use of which "can put any director in his place," [6] the position of the local Party organs is not nearly so strong as appears on the surface. There are many factors which reduce the likelihood that the local Party organs will have a decisive impact on the resolution of questions that pertain to the performance of one plant or of one branch of industry.

As many scholars have pointed out, the most basic factor interfering with the ability of the local Party organs to enforce strict managerial adherence to the law and the plan has been their responsibility for economic development. Although the local Party officials have a strong self-interest in preventing actions that will lead to plan nonfulfillment, they (like the managers they supervise) may also have a self-interest in illegal or quasi-legal actions that improve the economic performance of their area or create the appearance of better economic performance. The same factors that lead a manager to attempt an illegal action also tempt a Party secretary to ignore it. Indeed, to formally expose the machinations of a director may be particularly dangerous. If the Party officials report, for example, that a manager "fulfilled" this month's plan by including some of next month's production in it, this only leaves them open to the question: why was your leadership so defective that the plan was not fulfilled? If the Party officials report any law violations, they face the question: why did you let them develop?

The local Party organs are caught in a similar conflict of interest in their duty to force local managers to reveal all their "reserves" and to seek a higher plan. As Fainsod states, the Party officials are "under constant pressure from above . . . to goad factory directors into promising increases [in production]." [7] Yet, although the rewards for successful goading may be reasonably high, the penalties will likely be even higher if the resulting plan proves to be unfulfillable.

No doubt, the enthusiasm of Party officials for demanding higher plans must be dampened somewhat by memories of unhappy cases such as that of Iurii Sviadoshch, secretary for industry of the East Kazakhstan obkom in the mid-1950's. In September 1955, the Kazakh Ministry of Nonferrous Metallurgy established a goal for increase in labor productivity of the miners during the Sixth Five-Year Plan which, according to Sviadoshch, was "obviously too low." "The Party organizations of the mines, the Zyrianov and Leninogorsk gorkomy, and the East Kazakhstan obkom could not agree with such a 'plan' and placed this question before the ministry, which was required to reconsider and to increase the goal." [8]

However, although the obkom was able to get the plan raised, it could not, despite strenuous efforts, persuade the economic authorities to allocate additional capital investment for the development of the mines. During 1956, the first year of the Five-Year Plan, the ministry (which was located in East Kazakhstan oblast) failed to fulfill its plan, the basic problem being the nonfulfillment of the plan for ore extraction. At the next conference of the East Kazakhstan Party organization, Iurii Sviadoshch was removed from office, and subsequently he was named shop head in a local plant. Although the reason for his removal was not given, the difficulties in nonferrous metallurgy almost surely lay behind the action, for that is the major industry in the oblast.[9]

Another factor limiting the influence of the local Party organs in industrial decision-making has simply been a shortage of time in relation to their many responsibilities. In particular, the local Party officials have been greatly tempted to neglect industry in order to have more time to devote to agriculture. This might seem paradoxical in view of the lower priority given by the Soviet leadership to agriculture than heavy industry. However, the national concentration of investment resources on heavy industry has made agricultural plan fulfillment very difficult, and it has also caused a flow of the best managerial talent to industry. Given the leadership's need for a scapegoat for agricultural problems, the local Party organs have often had a self-interest in relying heavily on the trained industrial administrators for the supervision of industry and in spending their own time at the point where resources are scarcest and the danger is greatest.

There is much evidence that all levels of the Party apparatus have been much absorbed with agricultural questions. It was not accidental that the bifurcation of the Party was suggested at a Central Committee session dealing with the improvement of industrial administration, and that the examples of one-sided Party work almost all concerned Party organs too deeply involved in agriculture. According to one source, "The officials of the [Odessa] obkom gave all their attention and energy to agriculture. And it couldn't be otherwise. The situation demanded it." In Svetogorsk raion in Belorussia — the scene of major industrial development and construction — the raikom bureau discussed only twenty-two industrial and construction questions during 1962 (out of a total of 223 questions discussed).[10]

Soviet spokesmen have a tendency to use hyperbole during periods of reorganization, and it would be a mistake to accept uncritically Soviet statements made in the fall of 1962. Surely it is an exaggeration to say that the officials of the Odessa obkom devoted "all their attention and energy" to agriculture, particularly as the obkom first secretary had been a plant director before spending ten years as first secretary of the Kiev gorkom.[11] Similarly, when Khrushchev said that only five of over one hundred questions discussed by plenary sessions of the republican central committees during the previous year were of an industrial character, one should recall that important decisions are taken by the bureau and the secretariat rather than plenary sessions of the committee.[12] (It is perhaps even more important to recall that the spring plenary sessions usually discuss agriculture and that any summer plenary session to be devoted to industry was undoubtedly postponed so that it could discuss the decisions of the forthcoming session of the All-Union Central Committee.)

Despite the exaggerated nature of the 1962 comments, the local Party organs clearly have long had a tendency to give a disproportionate amount of time to the agricultural sector. This is a tendency already alluded to a number of times in this book. In 1941 Malenkov asserted that many obkomy were neglecting industry in favor of agriculture, and in 1947 Brezhnev explicitly referred to agricultural responsibilities in trying to justify the Zaporozhe obkom's relative neglect of the construction project at Zaporozhestal.[13] In 1956, it was reported that "the Central Committee of the Estonian Party organization is still little concerned with the work of industry. The Central Committee devotes its basic attention to agriculture." Even as late in 1959, as has been seen, Khrushchev could say to the obkom first secretary in industrialized Saratov: "You know how many calves and how many milkmaids there are in the oblast, but you do not have a good idea about the kind of machines produced in Saratov and the way in which they are produced."[14]

In the rural raion, concentration on agriculture must have been common, but even city organizations have often been drawn into these activities. The "milk and vegetable" districts surrounding the city have periodically been placed within the city limits, and the obkomy have always demanded that the city Party organs help the countryside. At times even the industrial departments of the gorkom and raikomy in a large city such as Cheliabinsk might virtually close down during the harvest period.[15]

The emphasis placed on agriculture by the local Party officials does more than reduce their time for supervision of the industrial sphere. It also increases their dependence on the industrial managers for the fulfillment of the area's industrial plan, and intensifies the pressures on the local Party organs to adopt a "servile attitude" toward managers who achieve plan fulfillment. The relative scarcity of top-flight ability makes it difficult for any superior in any country to override a subordinate who is producing results, but in the Soviet Union it is particularly true that an effective director is "a great asset for an ambitious local Party official" [16] and that he may be difficult to control.

In Vladimir Dudintsev's novel, *Not by Bread Alone,* one of the characters — Drozdov, the factory director — discusses this question in Marxist terms. In one scene Drozdov talks to his wife about the fact that the raikom secretary does not like him. The secretary thinks that Drozdov rules the plant with too firm a hand; as Drozdov expresses it, "Sometimes I don't follow the book, and that jars him." However, the attitude of the raikom secretary does not alarm the manager in the least, and he reassures his wife: "He is afraid to fight [me], for he would not be able to take me. His raion is a poor one. . . . All its economic base is in [my] hands." [17]

Two final factors limiting the role of the local Party organs are associated with the basic role of the area coordinator. The first of these is the subordination of local administrative officials to a specialized hierarchy as well as to the provincial organ. The second is the relative imbalance of knowledge between the coordinator and the men he supervises.

Even if an area coordinator wants to provide policy guidance to his specialized subordinates, the existence of the specialized hierarchy often effectively precludes this possibility. Sometimes in a situation of "dual subordination," the subordination of the local specialized official to the functional hierarchy can be fairly informal,[18] but in the Soviet Union the subordination of the plant to the industrial hierarchy has been quite explicit and formal — even more so than the subordination to the Party organs. In such a system of dual subordination, as James Fesler has pointed out,[19] the area coordinator inherently tends to be in a weaker position than the specialized hierachies.

If the local administrator receives an unpleasant order from the area coordinator — particularly one on a question of some substance — he can refer to a conflicting instruction from his functional hierarchy and can, if necessary, appeal to the hierarchy for support. In a showdown the area coordinator normally finds it quite difficult to prevail over the functional superior, for the latter has the advantage of national perspective, greater technical knowledge, and more intimate access to the central leaders.

In a conflict with a specialized hierarchy the local Party organs are further handicapped by the high degree of centralization in investment decision-making in the Soviet Union. If a local manager does not agree with a Party suggestion for technical innovation or product change, usually he is not even required to appeal the Party organ's decision to his industrial superior. Rather, because these innovations, if they are significant, will require capital appropriations or a change in the plan, it is the Party organ that will have to appeal for funds. In such a case the manager can support the request formally but can tell his superiors informally of any doubts he has about it.

Even if a local administrator's superiors do not become involved in making a decision, the area coordinator may not have sufficient knowledge to supervise his nominal subordinates effectively. This is one of the most prevalent problems in modern administration, for the administrator in any large organization often supervises men whose work is almost totally incomprehensible to him.[20] The area coordinator encounters this problem in particularly intensified form because of the multiplicity of specialties among the men within his jurisdiction.

The policy of selecting Party secretaries from among graduate engineers is an obvious attempt to combat this problem, but the industrial sector itself is very broad. Except for that branch of industry or even that plant with which he has a special familiarity, a Party official can never have the same detailed knowledge of a factory as does the man who is administering it directly. Consequently, he is always at somewhat of a disadvantage when the discussion turns to questions of the plant's reserves, desirable changes in production techniques and product design, and so forth, and his real influence with respect to these matters inevitably suffers.

The impact of the generalist administrator on specialized decisions is reduced not merely by his inability to intervene effectively, but also by his awareness of his own limitations. He frequently must have the suspicion that the record of plan fulfillment will be better if the more specialized decisions are left to experts. Of course, Bolshevism has always contained an anti-specialist strain — an assumption that organization and mobilization can conquer all and that any "objective" difficulties cited by experts can be overcome. However, one of the most important developments of the post-Stalin period has been a weakening of this strain, particularly with respect to the industrial sphere. Even the "subjective" Khrushchev declared, "The Party officials of the krai and oblast should manifest more understanding and, I would say, modesty, and they should not proclaim their opinion on all questions but listen to the voices of experienced people." [21]

In the post-Khrushchev period, as a Party raikom secretary has stated, "there surely are no more widespread words in our lexicon than 'science,' 'scientific approach,' 'scientific substantiation,' and so forth." [22] A 1968 summary article on Party work placed its greatest emphasis on the need for Party officials to adopt such an approach to decision-making: "The scientific approach in Party work is not a fashionable phrase. If the engineer and the agronomist all the more often act in accordance with the achievements of science and with advanced experience, then the Party official all the more cannot rely on his own intuition." [23]

The Impact on Intra-Plant and Intra-Sovnarkhoz Decisions

It is relatively easy to ascertain a number of factors that limit the effectiveness of the local Party organs in intra-plant decision-making; it is much more difficult to judge the extent to which the effectiveness of the Party organs is actually reduced. Precise and definitive conclusions are not possible because of the great variation in the influence of different local Party organs, particularly over time. However, one can differentiate between situations in which the influence of the local Party organs is fairly great and those in which it is minimal.

One key variable affecting the influence of the local Party organs has been the background and interests of their first secretaries. If a local Party official has a special interest in a particular project or type of activity, he can often ensure that it is given special attention. For example, since 1960, the first secretary of the Tatar obkom has been F. A. Tabeev, a candidate of economic science. His articles show a great interest in the use of economics in industrial decision-making, and it is not surprising that the Tatar ASSR has been the scene of much experimentation in this realm.[24] A Soviet sociologist has indicated in an interview that the Tatar experience is not an exception. He stated that empirical sociological and economic research is developed far more quickly in oblasti (for example, Leningrad, Gorki, Sverdlovsk, and Perm) in which the Party officials were committed to it, for in these oblasti the Party officials have been able to persuade the oblast's institutions to finance research projects and to permit scholars the necessary access.

The interests of a Party official are, of course, often closely associated with his previous education and work experience. Thus, in the late 1950's the chairman of the Perm sovnarkhoz (Soldatov) was a former defense industry official with "great will power and persistence," whereas the obkom first secretary (Sokolov) was "a prominent specialist and organizer of agricultural production" who had been named to his post in the wake of severe agricultural problems in the oblast.[25] In such circumstances the situation that developed might have been expected: the sovnarkhoz chairman "often took decisions which contradicted the directives of the leading [Party] organs," and the obkom officials looked on his independent acts "in a concilatory manner." [26]

In other cases the role of the local Party officials is surely quite different. In Chapter VIII it was mentioned that the first secretary of the Sumgait gorkom attended a daily operational session at the new synthetic rubber plant in an attempt to help work out technical problems during the shakedown period. This man had been the deputy chairman of the Azerbaidzhan sovnarkhoz in charge of the chemical industry, and his impact on decisions at the enterprise must have been overwhelming. Indeed, he probably was the real director of the enterprise during this period, and he had probably been selected gorkom first secretary instead of director simply so that he would have the authority to obtain immediate help for the plant from local construction trusts and suppliers.[27]

There are a number of other instances in which the background of a newly selected secretary suggests that the leadership has deliberately tried to create a situation similar to that in Sumgait. For example, when a strike occurred at the giant steel plant construction project at Temir-Tau, it was no accident that the new obkom first secretary came from Cheliabinsk where he had been sovnarkhoz chairman and thus responsible not only for the Magnitogorsk Metallurgy Combine but also for a number of other iron and steel plants.[28] Surely his influence on decisions with respect to the construction project was not meant to be negligible, and just as surely it was not negligible.

A second variable influencing the impact of the local Party officials on intra-plant decision-making is the type of industry with which they are dealing. An industry with complex and changing technology poses far greater problems for the Party organs than one in which the technology is more familiar and stable. The Party secretary's knowledge of a modernizing industry is much more likely to be obsolete, and the involvement of the central ministry and the planning organs in plant decison-making is usually more frequent and direct.

The role of the local Party organs has been particularly great in the extractive industries — for example, coal, timber, construction materials, and fishing. Not only do these industries usually have fairly uncomplicated technologies in the Soviet Union, but also they are administered by ministries which often have oblast-level administrations, combines, or trusts. Such administrations — whether they be subordinate to an All-Union ministry (for example, the Ministry of Coal prior to 1955), a republican ministry, or the oblast soviet — are under close obkom supervision, and their enterprises therefore are also particularly subject to Party influence.

Another variable affecting the role of the local Party organs is the aspect of industrial decision-making involved. At one extreme the impact of the Party officials on labor relations is quite direct and quite overwhelming. As the men with prime responsibility for political stability in the region, the Party officials seem to have the decisive voice in determining the degree of strain to which the workers can be subjected in such realms as norm-setting, working conditions, and so forth.

In practice, the local Party organs often need not take the initiative on labor relations; rather, they may serve as a court of appeal for disputes between the trade unions (or the Komsomol) and plant management or for grievances brought to them by individual citizens. Because the trade unions and Komsomol have little ability to enforce their demands on the industrial administrators, such appeals or the threat of them are frequently the only powerful weapon at their disposal. For the same reason, an individual worker may also appeal directly to the Party organs if he thinks he is being treated unfairly, and he may also take this step if the trade union does not support him to his satisfaction. There is certainly no guarantee that the trade union, the Komsomol, or the individual worker will be supported by the local Party organs, but in any case the decision of the Party officials usually does seem to be conclusive.

At times the prior approval of the local Party organs may be required before a manager is permitted to take a particular decision affecting the labor force. It has been reported, for example, that for a long period in a large Moscow raion the plant managers could not distribute apartments in their new apartment houses until the list of recipients was cleared with a raikom secretary. Although the practice is now said to have ended, it may have been a general one in the years when the scale of housing construction was not large. Similarly, in a large-scale experiment with the introduction of the eight-hour day in Ivanovo textile plants, the obkom bureau was required to give the final approval to the specific arrangements established at each plant, and one of its explicit obligations was to see that the interests and wishes of the workers were not ignored. (The question of changes in norms was, of course, a crucial one here.) It is also likely that a manager may seek the approval of the raikom before committing a major violation of labor legislation (such as cancelling the day off).[29]

At the other extreme the impact of the local Party organs on the formulation of a plant's technical policy is usually fairly minimal. It is in this realm that self-interest is most likely to reduce the will of the Party officials to place pressure on the managers, and that the imbalance of knowledge will limit their influence if they do desire to intervene. Moreover, significant innovations in technology or in product design are certain to require the approval and the appropriation of funds by the ministries, and powerful research institutes may also be active participants in these decisions. Even during the sovnarkhoz period there were a number of central (or republican) officials whose approval was required before major innovations could be undertaken.

It would be incorrect to suggest that the local Party organs have no role in technical decision-making. As has been indicated, a Party secretary may be quite influential if he has an especially relevant technical background as well as a special interest in a particular plant, construction project, or innovation. In addition, the presence of the local Party organs may mean that the managerial personnel themselves will more frequently make decisions that further innovation. The Party organs' responsibility for promoting the advance of technology is so emphasized by Soviet spokesmen that the Party officials are virtually compelled to report impressive quantitative indicators of success in this realm. And so they too inevitably demand that the plant managers be able to report that so many suggestions of "rationalizers" have been introduced, that so many rubles have been saved, and so forth. The Party officials may not be particularly interested in the nature of the suggestion or in its source (whether it be from a worker or from the chief engineer), but in their concern for gross statistics, they do keep the managers conscious of the impossibility of ignoring altogether the proposals made by those below them.

The local Party organs' practice of establishing commissions to investigate complaints and the reasons for plan nonfulfillment may also promote technical innovation by ensuring that useful information flows to key personnel who otherwise might not receive it. Even the chief designer of a very large machinebuilding plant acknowledged the usefulness of many of the suggestions made by members of these commissions — and apparently he found particularly helpful those suggestions coming from managers in other branches of industry.[30] Such assistance is probably especially helpful to the managers of smaller plants in lower-priority industries, and may constitute one of their most important types of exposure to information on advanced techniques.

When a lower Party or managerial official complains about the technical policy of his plant's director, the commissions may also furnish valuable information to the local Party organs themselves. By creating a commission of specialists from the outside, the local Party officials place themselves in a position to make a choice, if necessary, between the advice of two sets of independent specialists. If the outside specialists agree with the complaint and convince the Party officials of the correctness of their judgment, the local Party organ may well decide to intervene in a decisive manner. Even if (because of the necessity of appropriations from higher officials) the Party officials cannot compel the director to take action, they can inform higher officials of their doubts on the wisdom of the given decision.

Even in this aspect of their work the direct impact of the local Party organs is probably not as great as the indirect impact. The potential threat of a commission is likely to be more effective than the actual creation of one, and the commissions that are created surely have their greatest influence through persuading administrators to take action rather than through providing the basis for local Party compulsion. To the extent that the local Party organs play a significant role in this realm, it is not because they are forever intervening to impose their will but because they provide a local channel of communication which increases the probability that local technical decisions are made only after objections to them are given serious scrutiny.

In aspects of plant (and sovnarkhoz) decision-making other than labor relations and technical policy, the influence of the local Party organs has been more variable. For example, ensuring a taut plan and enforcing adherence to the law and the plan are treated in the Soviet press as two of the most central responsibilities of the local Party organs, and Western discussions of local Party involvement in plant decision-making have focused almost exclusively on their success (or lack of it) in fulfilling this role.

It is quite obvious that the local Party organs do not regard these activities as their primary function and that they do not make a serious effort to rigorously carry them out. The attitude of local Party officials toward strict enforcement of the law and plan appears most clearly in a 1960 article in *Sovetskaia Rossiia*. Five months earlier the newspaper had carried a strong attack on V. A. Maiorov, the head of the Kirov Shipyards in Astrakhan: "Infringements of staff discipline, illegal granting of premiums, a system of tolkachi [pushers], a squandering of funded materials, a widespread habit of filling orders from private people at prices which clearly are too low — this is far from being a complete list of the incorrect activities of Comrade Maiorov." [31] Despite this condemnation, the local Party organs failed to act against Maiorov. Undoubtedly they were influenced by the fact that under Maiorov the shipyards had gone from the ranks of the chronically unsuccessful to become one of the best enterprises in the city.

After a number of months the newspaper correspondents returned to Astrakhan to follow up their story, and they asked the Party secretaries why the director had not been punished. They received a sharp rebuff. The obkom second secretary answered their charges directly: "Maiorov is not a man who is lining his own pockets. If he permits violations, then it is only for the sake of production." The second secretary of the gorkom was even more blunt: "You try to lead such an enterprise. How can you possibly get along without law violations?" [32]

Yet, although the local Party officials find it difficult to rise above it, self-interest dictates a far more complex reaction toward plant planning and production decisions than toward technical innovation. Because the local Party organs are judged on the basis of the performance of the administrators in their area, they must intervene if important administrators are acting in such a way that the anger of the center will be aroused. They know that the Soviet leadership has adopted a fairly understanding attitude toward the "Berliner practices" and that much will be excused if the main plan indicators are fulfilled. However, they also know that the leadership may be far less tolerant if the plan and law violations are not kept within reasonable limits or if they are motivated by considerations of personal gain. There is in the statements of the Astrakhan Party officials the very clear implication that their actions would have been different if Maiorov had been "lining his own pockets," and it must be true that Party intervention is usually much more vigorous on this type of violation.

Even if the local Party organs do not insist on the fulfillment of regulations and plan indicators for their own sake, they frequently do intervene to ensure that a particular indicator is fulfilled, especially some item in the assortment plan. Indeed, as will be discussed in the next chapter, the Party officials need not wait until there are indications that the assortment plan will not be fulfilled. They often become a regular — and powerful — participant in the process by which day-to-day production priorities are decided.

In their concern for filling specific orders, the local Party organs also come to have an impact on the nature of the enterprise plan. Normally the plan has not been laid down in completed form at the beginning of the year; the summary indicators are established at that time, but much of the assortment plan is "built up" by pieces as the plant is given individual or group orders over a period of time.[33] Although the local Party officials have often not been eager to increase the overall plan of an enterprise, they have had a strong vested interest in the inclusion of individual orders that are needed badly by other enterprises or institutions in the area. Consequently, they may almost unwittingly tighten the work schedule by demanding that "just one more" order be included in it. And even during the year, as will be seen in Chapter XII, the local Party organs may put additional strain on a plant's resources by requiring it to furnish above-plan assistance to other institutions who are facing difficulties in fulfilling their responsibilities.

Conclusion

Considerable attention has been devoted here to the limitations on effective local Party intervention in purely industrial technical-planning matters. Statements about this role of the local Party organs are not, however, meant to indicate that the local Party organs play a minimal role in industrial decision-making; rather they are intended to serve as an introduction to a discussion of the important role which the local Party organs do, in fact, play.

If one focuses on the roles most emphasized in the official Soviet publications, the local Party organs do appear somewhat ineffective. Yet, if these deficiencies are considered from the point of view of any reasonable administrative theory, they seem far less serious. Traditionally it has been accepted that specialized decisions should be made by specialists, and even those who speak of "dual supervision" take for granted that the area superior should provide "administrative" supervision and leave technical supervision to the functional superior. The participation of a man with a broader perspective in decision-making may have beneficial consequences, but there are few administrative theorists who would suggest that the area supervisor should have a powerful role in technical decision-making.

Likewise, when one examines the control responsibilities of the local Party organs, there is little reason to assume that they should be fulfilled with the vigor that the leadership demands. It would be most dysfunctional for all parts of the plan and every legal regulation to be enforced rigidly. As will be discussed further in Chapter XIV, the network of laws and rules governing an administrative office with non-routinized activities is inevitably so complex that it would interfere with the performance of the office's duties if it were taken literally. As Granick has pointed out, "railroad and bus unions have not infrequently threatened to bring transport lines to a standstill solely by rigid obedience to the rules of the companies themselves." [34] In the Soviet Union it is apparent that many of the illegalities described by Berliner are necessary if the plant is to operate effectively under the existing administrative-planning system.

Although the local Party organs can never be expected to play the major role in decisions of a technical-planning nature, this does not mean their overall role in industrial decision-making is a minor one. The classic responsibility of an area coordinator is to intervene not in questions affecting only one office or one plant, but rather in questions involving the interests of more than one office or plant.

And, quite clearly, it is the broader responsibility which absorbs most of the attention of the local Party organs — the responsibility by which they make their greatest contribution to the functioning of the administrative hierarchy. It is when two institutions in the area come into conflict over the priority of their relative plans and regulations or over the priority of the delivery of their supplies that the local Party organs begin to play a crucial role in industrial decision-making. And, paradoxically, it is at this point that they also have their biggest impact on plant planning-technical decisions. As the next two chapters will show, it is their intervention on supply priorities that gives the Party organs a major role in influencing production priorities and the extent of fulfillment of the assortment plan. It is their efforts to maintain proportional regional development that produce the largest impact on the nature of the enterprise plans.

X. Supplies Procurement and Production Scheduling

One of the most frequently criticized activities of the local Party organs has been their persistent practice of "beating out of the suppliers the equipment, materials, etc., which the enterprises have been allocated." [1] This practice more than any other has been the target of the warnings against usurping the functions of the economic organs. Yet, despite all the condemnations of this "unfit method," the Party organs have continued to intervene when supply bottlenecks threaten plan fulfillment, "doing this with good intentions — to speed up matters." [2]

This chapter is devoted to a detailed examination of supplies procurement, and distinguishes among several different types of Party involvement in it. Because, as Walter Lippmann has pointed out, disreputable institutions and institutional practices are likely to be "a crude and largely unconscious answer to certain immediate needs," [3] the emphasis here is on those needs which drive the Party committees to concentrate seemingly excessive attention on supply and scheduling matters.

The Nature of the Supply Problem in the Soviet Union

It is well known that the procurement of supplies has long been one of the most pressing problems facing any Soviet factory director. If documentation is needed, one may quote from a 1955 complaint by the director of the Stalin Auto Works that "sometimes a director spends 90 percent of his working time on settling supply questions." This man was managing one of the model plants of the Soviet Union, a plant which in that same year had succeeded in securing a relatively large reserve of component parts and because of this was able to work without storming. [4]

There are two components of the supply problem. The first is obtaining authorization for supplies, a task that mainly involves negotiations with higher administrative and planning officials; the second is

214

obtaining the physical goods for which the chits have been allocated.

The participation of the local Party organs in the authorization process has been limited primarily to the support of local managers in their requests for larger allocations of supplies.[5] As one Soviet official describes the normal operating procedure, the plant director and Party officials might draft a joint letter to the higher economic organs, and then the letter would be sent in the name of the Party organ "for the sake of solidarity." Or else, the economic administrator might draft a telegram and take it to the Party official for his signature. When one obkom secretary asked such an administrator why he didn't sign the telegram himself, the administrator answered, "Well, don't you know, your signature has more authority." [6]

In supporting the economic administrators, the local Party organs are acting as supplicants to officials at a higher territorial level, and the significance of their role is determined (and limited) by the various factors to be discussed in Chapter XII. In fact, their recommendations on supply allocations surely carry less weight than in other cases, for the planners and higher administrative officials once held managerial posts at the plant level, and they know quite well how the game is played.

In this chapter the concern is only with those problems that a director faces as he tries to obtain the materials for which he already has authorization. Theoretically, this would be a very minor problem in a perfectly functioning planned society, but, in practice, this *realizatsiia fondov* has produced many headaches. The extremely rapid rate of expansion of the Soviet economy has strained resources to the utmost and has resulted in limited inventories of key supplies. Whenever there is an imperfection in the planning of a factory's supply (and these have been numerous),[7] or whenever a supplier-plant fails to fulfill its plan, serious shortages may ensue. Moreover, if, as frequently happens, a product scheduled for delivery in a certain month or quarter arrives in the last days of the period, the recipient plant may encounter major difficulties because of the low-inventory policy.[8]

The result of all these factors is well summarized by a Soviet official: "Very often there are moments in the life of an enterprise when the fate of the plan is decided by an insignificant number of kilograms of this or that material." Then he added, "Unfortunately, almost every day we face the problem that there is not enough of one small item, then of another." [9]

These problems have produced a series of responses on the part of Soviet plant directors that have further complicated Soviet supplies procurement. The ways in which Berliner found the managers to be protecting themselves against supply shortages have been noted: asking for more supplies than they need, specifying an earlier delivery date than necessary, hoarding any excess supplies, sending out quasi-legal expediters (*tolkachi*) to speed deliveries.[10] One might think that Berliner's conclusions are suspect because they are based on refugee testimony or on the experience of the 1930's, but they can be documented from almost any issue of *Ekonomicheskaia gazeta* of the early 1960's. At times the language used in this journal is even harsher than that given by Berliner: " 'Give [me]!' remains the basic principle of the economic administrators, regardless of their post. On a baby's lips this word sounds . . . touching and nice, but even then the parents try with all their strength to suggest to the little one that it is not a bit worse to give to others. Our economic administrators have left the diaper stage long ago, but you can bet your life that no one has yet chanced to meet a supply agent who would offer anything without asking something in return. And they do not say simply, 'Give,' but instead, 'Give as much as possible!' " [11] All the participants in the Liberman debates take for granted that the problems described by Berliner exist; the disagreements concern the wisdom of the various measures proposed to correct them.

This managerial behavior is quite understandable in terms of the self-interest of those who engage in it, but it complicates further the whole process of supplies procurement. In particular, it increases the difficulties that managers face in setting production and delivery priorities. If, as the eminent Soviet mathematician L. V. Kantorovich has noted, all orders tend to carry the priority of "very necessary," "absolutely indispensable," these words quickly become debased. In such conditions of "priority-inflation" how is the plant director to determine which orders are actually "absolutely indispensable" and which should be produced first within the planned month or quarter? [12]

The director has not been completely helpless in sorting out the priorities of his various orders.[13] He would naturally know that an order from a defense plant has much higher priority than one from light industry. A phone call or two from a very high Gosplan or ministerial official would also be quite illuminating. However, the planning and administrative organs have been unable to solve the problem of priority-inflation completely. In practice, the plant managers have found it necessary to turn for assistance to their nongovernmental supervisors — the local Party organs.

The Participation of the Local Party Organ in Supplies Procurement and Priority Setting

A student interested in the problems of using Soviet sources for a study of the Soviet administrative system can find no better subject with which to begin than the role of the local Party organs in supplies procurement. It is a classic example of the favorite technique of the Soviet press for handling a normal operating practice of Soviet administrators which is somewhat disreputable.

Rather than recognize such a practice as typical and be forced to discuss the reasons for it, Soviet spokesmen are far more likely to criticize it as being a "defect" in the work of "individual" officials. When a reorganization occurs, the defect is recognized as having been absolutely standard under the old organizational forms. It is condemned in excessively harsh terms, and the assertion is made that the practice has disappeared because the reasons for it have been removed by the recent brilliant reorganization. For a number of months nothing is heard of the practice, but then, except for the rare cases when the reorganization really has corrected a problem, one begins to read again of the "defects" of "individual" officials. And the cycle is repeated.

One interesting exercise is to differentiate between a case in which a defect of an "individual official" is indeed just that and one in which it represents standard operating procedure. A second exercise is to judge when a reorganization has actually changed standard operating procedure to some extent and when it has failed to do so. In the case of Party involvement in supplies procurement, the task is greatly eased by the fact that there have been a number of Party and governmental

217

reorganizations in the last twenty years. As a result, it is possible to compare Soviet statements about this involvement through a number of cycles of criticism.

I have not examined the Soviet press of the early and middle 1930's, but from the end of the Purge to the present, the Soviet press has contained perennial complaints about the participation of the local Party organs in supplies procurement. Thus, in February 1941 — *before* Malenkov called for an intensification of Party intervention in industrial decision-making at the Eighteenth Party Conference — the first secretary of the Gorki obkom asserted that the Party organs were already intervening too vigorously in one phase of industrial decision-making:

> In the work of the raikomy there often occur such cases: It is morning. The raikom secretary has just arrived at work.
>
> "Is this the raikom? Yes? The raikom secretary? This is the plant director talking. Your intervention is required. The plant is threatened with a shut down."
>
> There then begins the listing of the raw materials and parts which are in short supply. The secretary sympathizes, reassures, promises to help.
>
> Half a day is spent in petitioning, phone calls, and requests. Finally, the "emergency" situation is liquidated, and both the director and the raikom secretary are satisfied.[14]

All Soviet accounts agree that Party participation in detailed economic management was greatly intensified during World War II. "The Party organs were often compelled to take on themselves operational work in administering the economy," [15] and this "operational work" obviously included involvement in supplies procurement. When a Party organ like the Perm obkom had at least thirteen departments specializing in different branches of industry,[16] it obviously had a staff of sufficient size to make this involvement a major one.

After the war, however, the Party leadership declared that although such a major involvement "was correct in its time," it was impermissible in the postwar period. "The Central Committee of the Party demanded that the practice of replacing (*podmen*) the Soviet and economic organs be liquidated" — a demand that has invariably referred to participation in supplies procurement.[17]

During the late 1940's the Party press occasionally carried reports of "individual" party organs that persisted in their old habits, but one would not necessarily have concluded that this behavior was widespread. Then in 1950 and 1951 came a flood of articles, each concerning an individual Party organ, each indicating that the Party organ had been acting as a "special kind of expediter (*tolkach*)." [18] Some of these articles were extremely graphic, and they give a very concrete sense of this role of the Party organs:

> In the reception room of the deputy director of the Kuznetsk Metallurgy Combine for supply, we [the *Pravda* reporter] happened to meet Comrade Ivanov, an instructor of the heavy industry department of the Kemerovo obkom.
>
> "As usual, I'm pushing things through," explained Comrade Ivanov, as if justifying his presence here. . . . In his briefcase were a multitude of letters and telegrams addressed to the Party obkom from different departments. They were requests to "push through" or to "speed up" an order for beams, for steel sheet, for construction steel, etc. . . . The officials of the department of heavy industry, headed by Comrade Iurev, are concerned only with economic questions . . . with the securing of supplies for the plant. . . . When [the officials of the heavy industry department] are at the enterprise, they usually drop in on the director or the chief engineer, but they rarely call on the primary Party organization. . . . During the last fourteen months, Comrade Iurev [the head of the department] has phoned the director of the combine daily, but he has not called the Party committee even once.[19]

If the local Party organs received requests for help in supplies procurement, naturally they also sent them. A local Party organ that decided to support the requests of a local director might write to the ministry or glavk of the offending supplier, but it was more likely to by-pass the official chain of command and to correspond "along Party lines" with the Party committees in the area where the supplier-plant was located. In one typical example the secretary of the Stalingrad gorkom sent a telegram to the secretary of the Barnaul gorkom: "The Barnaul Boiler Works still has not shipped the thermostat for Boiler No. 8. Because of the absence of this thermostat, the deadline for putting the boiler into operation during the third quarter has not been met. I ask you to exert your influence." [20]

It is not known whether the Barnaul secretary did, in fact, exert his influence decisively, but at a minimum the officials of the local Party organs surely followed the practice of the Kemerovo officials and at least phoned the director or carried their bulging briefcase to the plant, "pushing things through." Although the telegrams may sometimes have been passed on to the directors in a formalistic manner, the directors surely would not have turned to the Party organs if their appeals had not met with some success.

The reports of the Party conferences held in 1951 contained pledges that such activity would be curtailed, but in the summer of 1955 a plenum of the Central Committee noted that the officials of the industrial-transportation departments of a "series" of local Party organs "occupy themselves with minor economic affairs." [21] The press again became filled with sorrowful confessions of errors by lower Party officials and with promises of improvement. The abolition of the ministries in 1957, however, produced additional evidence of the persistence of this activity. From the city of Riga, for example, came a description of Party work at the raion level: "The ringing of the telephone resounded through the office of Comrade Shchukin, the head of the industrial department of the Lenin raikom in Riga. The director of the ski factory was calling to ask for help in getting fifty cubic meters of plywood for the enterprise. Such calls are not a rarity here. Almost every day economic administrators turn to the industrial department. One needs fuel, another, one-half kilogram of nails. A third requests a speeding-up of the allocation of an area for construction." [22]

An article in *Partiinaia zhizn* went further and charged that such behavior had been inherent in the ministerial system: "Until now we have not had administrative organs in the economic regions. But such regions actually existed in practice, and the functions of the leading organ of the region came to be fulfilled, willingly or unwillingly, by the Party organs." [23]

The creation of the sovnarkhozy put industrial administrative bodies in the regions, and a number of Party officials declared that this did, indeed, change the role of the Party organs substantially. The first secretary of the Penza obkom, for example, stated that "now the officials of the Party obkom, gorkomy, and raikomy have been freed from a great many current business matters." The first secretary of the Ivanovo obkom, speaking of the obkom departments, declared that "the scale of their work and the character of the questions they examine have sharply changed." [24]

Yet, other articles soon indicated that the change had not been complete. In 1958, *Pravda* reported that the oil industry department of the Bashkiria obkom was "preserving the unattractive features of the old system" and in essence was functioning as "a dispatcher's point of the sovnarkhoz." *Pravda*'s description of the work of the departments differed little from its pre-1957 descriptions: "Its [the *otdel*'s] officials frequently appear in the role of managers of economic affairs. They spend a great part of their day in telephone conversations. They intercede for some plant directors. They plead with others, while they put pressure on still others. Much time is taken in answering telegrams and requests coming from other cities." [25] The head of the department acknowledged to the newspaper correspondents that "we spend 90 percent of our time in solving such questions."

In 1960 a similar situation was reported in the republic of Turkmenia:

> The circle of questions which concern the officials of the branch departments of the gorkomy, obkomy, and even of the Party Central Committee in Turkmenia is, as before, largely limited to minor economic matters. . . . The officials of the industrial-transportation department of the Turkmen Central Committee, as well as those of the obkomy and gorkomy . . . take on themselves the improper function of beating out of the suppliers the equipment, materials, etc., which the enterprises have been allocated. "Even now we have to send many letters and telegrams on purely economic matters," says the head of the industrial department of the Ashkhabad gorkom, Comrade Gorbeshko.
>
> After becoming acquainted with the bulky file-cabinet in

which copies of the letters and telegrams are kept, we [the *Pravda* correspondents], were convinced of this fact by our own eyes. The telegrams directed to Saratov, Berezniki, Chimkent, and Tambov contained requests to expedite the shipments of molasses, fine sand, and chlorinated lime. The Ashkhabad gorkom was also begging Kemerovo for a half-ton of ammonium chloride and Minsk for ninety cubic meters of sawed oak boards of not worse than the second quality.[26]

In 1962 the officials of the industrial-transportation department of the Grodno gorkom in Belorussia were engaged in much the same kind of work:

> Sometimes the office of the head of the industrial-transportation department of the Grodno gorkom, Viktor Iosifovich Piasetskii, reminds one of a dispatcher's office. It is as if the two phones are competing to see which can transmit the most conversations while the head is here and not at an enterprise. . . .
>
> "Viktor Iosifovich? This is the furniture factory speaking. We need sixty railroad cars, but they are not even giving us ten."
>
> "Comrade Piasetskii? This is Leather Works No. 4. As before, we are not receiving the necessary raw materials. This also threatens our neighbor — the shoe factory." . . .
>
> "Auto Spare Parts Works speaking. We cannot agree with the Minsk Tractor Works about the delivery of forgings." [27]

After the 1962 bifurcation of the Party apparatus, Soviet spokesmen asserted once again that Party involvement in supplies procurement had been a major one during the period 1957 to 1962. The familiar refrain was repeated: "Earlier the Party officials often were turned into a special kind of expediter (*tolkach*)." And once again it was stated that the new reorganization (the bifurcation of the Party) had corrected the situation: "Now we strive to achieve the main goal — the rise of the economy, the fulfillment of the national plan — by lively organizational and educational work directly in the production collective." [28]

Despite these assertions, there is every indication that the 1962 reorganization did not produce such a development. To be sure, the first secretary of the Cheliabinsk gorkom wrote not long after Khrushchev's removal that although the folder of letters and telegrams that he received daily on supply questions was still large, it was "much less than two to three years ago" (that is, prior to the bifurcation).[29] Yet, although the inter-city correspondence on supply problems may conceivably have been reduced after 1962, it is absolutely clear that Party intervention in local supply problems was only intensified by the reorganization. This is particularly true of the regulation of supply of materials to construction projects. In conducting the operational sessions (*operativki*) and meetings of the staff (*shtaby*) discussed in Chapter VIII, the local Party organs were, first of all, "urging on the suppliers of materials"[30] and indicating to them the relative priority of the different construction projects. It is for this reason that the head of the industrial-transportation department of the Shakhti gorkom could in 1967 look back on this period and state: "Officials of our department often used to be considered economic administrators (*khoziaistvenniki*). . . . In essence, [they were] tolkachi, a kind of regulator of relations between enterprises."[31]

After 1964, the Soviet press once more demanded that the Party organs reduce their excessive involvement in supplies procurement and concentrate more on major policy questions and organizational work. Most of the articles suggested that this excessive involvement had resulted from the establishment of separate industrial (or urban) Party committees and the excessive central emphasis on economic decision-making. The reuniting of the Party apparatus and the introduction of a more "objective" approach would, it was said, correct this problem.

Yet, after the reunification of the Party, the familiar articles have reappeared. One still reads of local Party organs that continue to function as a "dispatcher's point."[32] When a plant in one oblast (in this case the Zhdanov Metallurgy Works) fails to meet a deadline in deliveries to a plant in another oblast, one still reads that the injured party "had to/appeal to different authorities: to the State Committee for Material-Technical Supply, to Soiuzglavmetall [the All-Union Administration for Metal Distribution], and the Zhdanov Party gorkom."[33] The reports on gorkom and raikom participation in distribution of local goods and services have been numerous: "At times the head of the construction department of the [Nizhnii Tagil] gorkom . . . has to 'divide' construction materials in short supply, the instructors of the industrial department to distribute means of transportation. And how many phone calls come to the gorkom daily — you can't count them! And the majority of them are on economic matters." [34]

Indeed, at least one gorkom secretary seems to have despaired of the possibility of change in this aspect of Party work. "How much time is taken by the beating out of materials for inter-plant deliveries," he complained. But then he continued, "We understand that this is an incorrect practice . . . but, together with that, we cannot watch indifferently as the plan collapses." [35]

Faced with such statements, indeed faced simply with the long historical record, a person would have to be rash indeed to suggest that the post-Khrushchev appeals for less Party involvement in supplies procurement will have a major impact on Party behavior, at least if there is no major change in the political-administrative structure. Yet, one is still left with unanswered questions. In particular, has the Party organs' role in breaking supply bottlenecks really remained unchanging over three decades? To deal with this question, one must explore the reasons that the Party organs have participated so persistently in this "incorrect method of work."

The Factors Underlying Party Participation in Supplies Procurement

On the surface at least, large-scale Party participation in supplies procurement poses some very puzzling questions. Given the tendency for all Soviet authorities to denounce this activity as an improper supplanting of the economic organs, why has Party involvement in it not been a more minor one? To be sure, there have always been numerous delays in deliveries, and the establishment of delivery priorities has never been easy. But why have these problems not been handled exclusively through administrative channels — that is, by the ministries, the sovnarkhozy, or Gosplan?

One part of the answer is simply the Leninist image of the Party. The Party Rules obligate the Party member "to uncover deficiencies boldly and to secure their removal, . . . to speak out against any actions which harm the Party and the state, and to inform the Party organs, right up to the Central Committee, about them." The Party Rules also give the member the right "to address questions, statements and suggestions to any Party body, right up to the Central Committee, and to demand an answer to the essence of his appeal." [36]

The latter statute was introduced into the Party Rules long before the revolution, and it then, of course, had no relation to questions, statements, and suggestions about defects in the supply system. Yet, when the Party organs were assigned a key role in economic supervision, this rule inevitably resulted in a flood of minor economic problems being brought to the Party organs. Lenin himself complained about the difficulties that this rule created for the central Party organs (without, however, offering a solution),[37] and the difficulties have been no less in the provinces. After all, should not a late delivery that threatens plan fulfillment be considered an "action which harms the Party and the state"? If so, is not a plant director obligated by the Party Rules "to inform the Party organs, right up to the Central Committee, about them"? And can the Party organs consistently refuse to respond? They have been repeatedly warned that "it is impermissible when some signal or another about defects remains without effect because of an inattentive attitude toward it on the part of the Party apparatus." [38]

It is this set of rights and obligations which lies behind a plaintive defense made by an obkom first secretary of his deep involvement in supplies procurement: " 'Of course, we should not be occupied with this,' recognizes the first secretary of the Party obkom, Comrade Petukhov. 'And, understand, we do not want to . . . but we must. If these questions are not decided by the sovnarkhoz, people turn to us (narod k nam obrashchaetsia).' " [39]

This behavior would not be impossible to stop if the leadership felt that it were counter-productive, but the costs involved in removing these statutes from the Party Rules (or redefining them) would be high enough to provide some considerable resistance to change. To remove them altogether would mean abandoning one of the oldest traditions of the Party — one intimately connected with the concept of a party both democratic and centralistic; [40] to reinterpret them in such a way as to avoid complaints about supply shortages would require a drastic modification in the present concept of the Party as the directing force in Soviet society.

The reason that such a reinterpretation would require basic modification in the concept of the Party — and probably the most fundamental reason that the Party organs continue to "beat out deliveries" from the suppliers — is that (Soviet theorists notwithstanding) supplies procurement is not a "minor business detail" in a scarcity economy. The Soviet press may speak of the importance of long-range policy-planning — and, of course, it is right — but the first priority of the Party leadership has been the fulfillment of this year's plan. If the intervention of the local Party organs can ensure that critical bottlenecks threatening plan fulfillment are overcome, then the Party organs must almost inevitably be drawn into this activity. Like long-range planning groups in the West, the Party officials often discover that the current crisis is, in fact, the type of top-level question that must be their highest concern.

Considerable insight into the reasons for Party involvement in supplies procurement can be gained by an examination of American experience in this realm.[41] Normally, of course, the purchasing department of the American firm finds itself in a buyers' market, and, consequently, its problems are much less severe than those of a Soviet director. Yet, even under American conditions the purchasing department constantly is confronted with the late arrival of some necessary material, particularly in the case of orders that must be manufactured individually.

The American purchasing agent has a number of devices to employ when he is threatened with late delivery. First of all, he can and does resort to vitriol or cajolery. Because it is a buyers' market, he can often threaten to change suppliers if goods do not arrive on time. When these tactics fail, he may turn to some special friend in the industry who may be in a position to help in an emergency and who has been cultivated specifically for this purpose.

Usually these methods prove successful, but when they fail, the purchasing agent may go over the head of the scheduling department of the supplier firm. He explains the problem to a higher official in his own plant (often a vice president or even the president in a small or medium-sized firm). This executive, in turn, gets in touch with his counterpart in the supplier firm and emphasizes the urgency of the given order. The purchasing agent seeks help at higher levels partly because the officials there may have friendship ties with their counterparts in the supplier firm, but, more important, he does so because this is a most effective way of dramatizing the high priority of the particular item. If a purchasing agent says that a delivery is urgently needed, he may be ignored; if a vice president takes the time to repeat the point, then it becomes clear that the need is really great.

When there is a sellers' market, the practice of appealing to the executive levels of a supplier plant becomes very widespread. In the United States these markets have existed primarily during wartime, and it is no accident that at these times American supplies procurement has included many activities common in the Soviet Union.[42] During World War II and the Korean War vice presidents who had concentrated their attention on other matters came to spend great amounts of time phoning suppliers and administrative agencies in Washington who controlled certain scarce materials. As this practice became typical, much of the responsibility for assigning production priorities also gravitated to the "vice-presidential level," for the proliferation of requests forced the supplier-plants' executives to choose among them. During World War II supply-priority decisions within the government also had a similar tendency to rise to higher levels. Gradually the War and Navy Departments themselves were forced to undertake the assigning of the highest priorities.[43]

In the Soviet Union chronic shortages and the intensity of the pressure for plan fulfillment obviously create an overwhelming inclination toward priority-inflation. Because the local Party organs carry great authority (the authority not only of the regional boss, but also that of the ruling party), it is inevitable that lower officials will try to use them as a means of dramatizing the priority of a critical delivery. If the local Party organs agree that the need for the delivery of some order is, indeed, great, it is almost inevitable that they must lend their support to the appeal of a local plant. They can never forget that they too are judged on the basis of the economic performance of their area. As one gorkom secretary asked rhetorically, "What [else] can we do when things go poorly?" [44]

From this point of view it is worth noting that managers interviewed in the Soviet Union implicitly saw a relationship between the level of supervisor making the appeal and the dramatic nature of the appeal.

There seemed to be a clear conception of proper stages in the process. According to these managers, one would turn to the Party organs only when appeals "along the economic line" had failed. Moreover, in seeking a delivery from a different city, one would first seek the support of the gorkom and would turn to the obkom (or republican central committee in a small republic) only when the gorkom's intervention had been unsuccessful. Although the question about the steps to be taken if the obkom failed was not raised in interviews, it is clear that in truly desperate situations the director of an important plant can appeal even higher than the local Party organs. One reads, for example, that the Pervoural Tubing Works filled a number of planned orders for special tubing "only after the interference of the officials of the Central Committee of the KPSS." [45]

Although the two factors discussed — the appeal clause in the Party Rules and the pressure on the local Party organs to ensure current plan fulfillment — provide a satisfactory explanation of local Party involvement in supplies procurement under existing political-administrative conditions, they do not adequately explain the continued existence of the basic conditions. Often an institution may continue to perform a function either because of inertia or because of its own ability to defend its vested interest in the function, but in the case of the local Party organs and supplies procurement there is a deeper explanation involved. In many ways the local Party organs are quite well situated to perform these functions, and thus they serve fairly well as the "crude and largely unconscious answer to certain immediate needs" of which Lippmann wrote.

In understanding the reasons for the unique position of the local Party organs in meeting several needs of the economy, one first must be careful to distinguish between two essentially different situations in which the Party officials help managers to obtain allocated supplies. The first of these situations arises when a plant requires a delivery from a supplier outside the jurisdiction of the local Party organ. In these cases one reads not of the telephone ringing in the industrial-transportation department, but of a briefcase and a filing cabinet filled with a "multitude of letters and telegrams." The second type of situation arises when a plant requires a delivery from a plant or a warehouse located within the same raion or city. The examples in the previous section describing the work of the Riga raikom in 1957, the Grodno gorkom in 1962, and the Nizhnii Tagil gorkom in 1967 are almost exclusively of this type.

Of the two situations, it is the "extensive correspondence with the Party committees of many oblasty and republics," [46] that is the more difficult to explain in terms of the needs of the economy. Clearly there is a major need for an institutional channel through which information can flow indicating what orders are, in fact, "absolutely indispensable"; but on the surface, at least, it is not so clear why the Party apparatus should serve as this channel. It would seem that there is one serious danger in encouraging the local Party organs to participate in this activity. Because the local Party organs transmit to the plants orders from within the area as well as from outside it, they may find it difficult to judge dispassionately the relative urgency of the two types of orders. They may well have a tendency to favor the local order for reasons of self-interest, thus falling into an unpleasant and dysfunctional form of localism.

Yet, even if the local Party organs have difficulty in judging the relative priority of an order from within the oblast or city as compared with one from outside, the problem of localism would not be solved by prohibiting them from corresponding on supplies questions. On the contrary. As long as the local Party organs have the responsibility of enforcing plan fulfillment, it is virtually certain that they will be particularly sensitive about plan nonfulfillment which affects deliveries to local plants and that they will therefore be a powerful force for localism in any case. Paradoxically, the participation of the local Party organs in inter-oblast correspondence on supplies questions may actually help to reduce this localism. In corresponding on these questions, they inevitably learn about the consequences of their localism, and they no doubt come to understand that if they want to receive urgent deliveries from other areas, they too must be accommodating on appeals from these areas.

In other respects the local Party organs have been in an excellent position to serve as a channel for communicating high priority appeals. They have had sufficient stature to dramatize the appeals, and they have had the power to enforce a priority decision on a local plant. Moreover, they are near enough to the plants to check on the real conditions there, and even have at their disposal a somewhat independent source of information within the plants — the secretaries of the plant and shop Party organizations.

Most important, the local Party organs have had a sufficiently wide range of enterprises and institutions under their control to be able to back up their appeals to each other with the tacit promise of a return favor in the future. This ability is a very important one. Whenever an organization or official proves willing and able to provide help in securing supplies, it soon can become inundated with requests. If, however, one of the parties in a channel of priority communication incurs a "debt" in transmitting an appeal for help, it is unlikely to transmit every managerial request in an automatic manner. Purely from self-interest, it would be extremely foolhardy to incur a debt just to obtain supplies that were not really needed or to discharge one owed to it by some frivolous delivery.

Under the ministerial system, the local Party organs have been one of the few authoritative bodies that can easily engage in the trading of favors, for the ministries and the glavki are often too specialized for this activity. There is relatively little, for example, that the Ministry of Agricultural Machinebuilding can offer to the Ministry of Ferrous Metallurgy in return for a speed-up in the delivery of a few tons of a specialized steel product. Since 1965, the regional offices of the State Committee of Material-Technical Supply have had some ability to perform this function, but they do not always have the perspective to judge the relative priority of claims and probably do not have the real authority to enforce a priority decision on a plant.

During the sovnarkhoz period, this advantage of Party participation in supplies procurement was considerably reduced, for the sovnarkhozy themselves had the range of responsibilities, the perspective, and the authority to engage in effective trading of favors. Indeed, it is quite possible that the creation of the sovnarkhoz did reduce somewhat the burdens on the local Party organs in conducting inter-oblast correspondence. When this question was raised in interviews in 1962, several officials insisted that they turned less frequently to the Party organs on this kind of problem. For example, an official of a Kiev spinning factory, who freely admitted seeking Party help in the delivery of certain locally produced construction materials, stated flatly that the factory's problems with cotton supply from Central Asia were now referred exclusively to the Ukrainian sovnarkhoz, whereas earlier they had been handled through Party channels. Certainly the quotations from the last section demonstrate that this was not a universal phenomenon, but it would have been normal if a number of the comparatively less urgent appeals that earlier had been directed to the local Party organs were routed through the sovnarkhoz after 1957. Similarly, it is possible that the creation of the State Committee for Material-Technical Supply — particularly of its regional offices — has had similar consequences during the present period. In either case, however, the Party organs continued to be "the authority," and the natural pressures to draw them into supplies procurement continued to exist.

In the second type of Party intervention in supplies deliveries, the local Party organs play a rather different role and serve rather different needs of the economy. In this role the local Party organ is not simply responding to the urgent appeal of another Party committee, but rather it is deciding which of two local plants, which of two local projects, should receive priority from a local supplier. Here the context is not one of an appeal-bargaining situation. The local Party organ chooses to intervene not because it fears the ill-will of the Party officials either in the center or in the area where the supplier is located, but because it is the executive that is held responsible for both of the potential recipients and must decide the relative priority of their needs.

The local Party organs can intervene in any conceivable type of local supply dispute, but the examples cited in the Soviet press suggest that the local disputes that require the most attention are those concerning rather undifferentiated goods and services which are produced or distributed locally through some local agency. Nonspecialized building materials (such as bricks, lumber, and nails), electricity, water, fuel, railroad cars — these are what plant officials seem to seek most frequently from the local Party organs. As more items come to be distributed through the oblast warehouses of the State Committee of Material-Technical Supply, the list of goods often distributed by the local Party organs may become larger, particularly if the warehouses are unable to establish substantial inventory reserves.

Many of the goods on whose delivery the Party officials concentrate their attention have been produced by enterprises that have been subordinate to the local soviets, but this fact has not been the crucial variable in defining the local Party organs' role. Their role has not been strikingly different in the distribution of those undifferentiated goods and services provided by local enterprises subordinate to the republican or All-Union ministries (or the sovnarkhoz). In either case the bulk delivery of these products has usually been conducted according to plan, but the local Party organs have been the main instrument for determining day-to-day or week-to-week priorities.

In many ways this might seem like rather unglamorous work for the "leading organ in Soviet society" — and to Soviet spokesmen it certainly does seem so — but it is of crucial importance for the proper functioning of the Soviet economic system. These locally produced goods and services have often been in short supply — often in even shorter supply than more complex products — and a shortage in one of them can be as crippling to a plant or a construction site as a delayed shipment of a specialized part.

Yet, to cite a concrete example, how should the decision be made if both a local machinebuilding plant and a local food processing plant insist that their monthly shipment of bricks be delivered at the beginning of the month rather than at the end? If the city water supply runs low or the electricity limit is reached, who decides which institutions and enterprises will have their supply restricted?

Naturally the formal authority to make such decisions resides in the officials in charge of the supplier-plant or distributing office, but these men hardly have the perspective or often the ability to determine the relative priority of the various claims. Moreover, in many of these cases it is scarcely rational to refer the matter to the economic hierarchy for the determination of the relative priorities. Under the ministerial system the industrial superiors might be located thousands of miles away, and the question of today's priorities might have become quite academic by the time that they would be notified and would have negotiated among themselves. Further, the scale of the questions is so small and the number of them that must arise in the Soviet Union every day is so large that the possibility of ministerial officials becoming regularly involved in them seems quite precluded.

It might appear that the creation of the sovnarkhoz would have increased the ability of the economic hierarchy to handle this type of problem, but it had this effect only in a minor degree. Even when the dispute concerned the relative priority of deliveries to two plants subordinate to the sovnarkhoz, the sovnarkhoz was usually still too far away in organizational terms, if not geographically. Perhaps it would be reasonable to refer a dispute on a day-to-day priority to the sovnarkhoz if both plants were subordinate to the same administration (*upravlenie*) of the sovnarkhoz, but if they were subordinate to different administrations then only the chairman or first deputy chairman would be in a position to give an authoritative decision. Again the questions would arise: Should officials of this level be concerned with such relatively minor questions? Would they even have the detailed knowledge of the local situation needed for an intelligent decision?

In many conflicts over the disposition of locally produced goods, the sovnarkhoz did not even have jurisdiction over all the officials involved. When the problem concerned a strain on the water or electric supply, then one of the most basic questions was whether it would be the industrial or nonindustrial sector whose supply would be curtailed. Similarly, a conflict over delivery priority might well arise between officials in industry and those in other sectors. Even in conflicts within the industrial-construction field itself, the sovnarkhoz often did not have full jurisdiction or an unbiased point of view. Particularly in the early years of the sovnarkhoz period, a number of the local suppliers were subordinate to the soviets, and the sovnarkhoz had no authority over them. After 1962, the construction administration and much of the building materials industry were given to the newly created construction administrations, which likewise were independent of the sovnarkhozy.

For all these reasons the pressures on the local Party organs — particularly the raikomy and gorkomy — to serve as regional coordinators of the deliveries of goods produced locally for local use have always been almost irresistible. There has been an imperative need for the job to be done, and the local Party organs alone have had the necessary authority, the necessary perspective, the necessary sources of information to perform it satisfactorily.

Indeed, throughout the post-Purge period there has never been any real question (whatever *Pravda* articles might imply) as to whether the Party organs would serve as a regional coordinator of local supplies. The only real question — and the only real variation in our period — has been whether the Party officials should be more passive arbitrators or whether they should direct the distribution of local suppliers systematically. Judging from Soviet press reports, the Party organs normally perform the former role, taking on the more direct distribution of supplies only in times of very serious shortage. From 1962 to 1965, however, the deep involvement in short-term construction planning came very close to giving them systematic operational control over the distribution of many kinds of local supplies. In determining the day-to-day, week-to-week priority of construction work, the local Party organs were also, in practice, determining the delivery priorities for the various building material suppliers.

At the present time, Soviet sources are warning again of excessive Party involvement in supplies procurement and calling for a change. However, if they want the local Party officials to abandon — or even sharply curtail — their role in supplies procurement, major policy changes will be required. One way of easing the pressures for local Party intervention would be a reduction in the tempo of industrial development and an increase in the size of inventories permitted. Another way would be to increase the reliance on market mechanisms, the priority of deliveries being determined by the willingness to pay and the general market power of the claimants. Even in these circumstances, a complete cessation of local Party participation in supplies procurement would surely require the creation of authoritative local state organs to assume their functions (perhaps by giving the soviets responsibility for and authority over all economic enterprises in their area), and it probably would require the abandonment of the policy of judging Party officials in part on the basis of the economic performance of the region's enterprises.

XI. Regional Coordination

The establishment of priorities in conflicts over supply deliveries is but one aspect of the broader responsibility of the local Party organs to coordinate activities of all the organizations in the area. Although this general responsibility (like that of intervention in supplies procurement specifically) has often led to a style of work that seems most distasteful to the leadership, it is the responsibility of the local Party organs that has been most vital for the operation of the administrative system.

The word "coordination" is a rather broad one, and it can refer to a wide range of different activities. Even the attempt to create a common set of values is in one sense an attempt to ensure that officials coordinate their work toward the fulfillment of a common goal. The responsibility of speaking out for proportionate regional development also is a type of coordination, for it entails making judgments about the way in which sectors of the economy should fit together.

This chapter is limited to two specific types of coordinating activities: first, the efforts of the local Party organs to ensure that a small part of the resources of one enterprise or office are utilized to fill urgent needs of other enterprises or other sectors of the economy; and, second, the participation of the local Party organs in the resolution of departmental disputes which arise within the area.

"Patronage" and Inter-Institutional Assistance

Responsible for the fulfillment of the plans of all the administrators within the locality, the local Party organs frequently find that the balance of plan fulfillment most acceptable to the leadership is not being met. One enterprise or institution may be overfulfilling its plan by a considerable amount at the same time that others are failing to fulfill theirs. A low priority enterprise or sector of the economy may be performing more satisfactorily than one of higher priority. In these circumstances the local Party organs have the authority — and the duty — to correct the situation. They are in a position to alleviate crucial marginal shortages or defects in one enterprise, branch of the economy, or sphere of activity by calling on the officials of other enterprises· to render assistance, and, in fact, they often do intervene to force such assistance.

The most officially approved form of inter-institutional assistance involves one "collective" assuming "brotherly patronage" (*shefstvo*) over another. Because of the special role attributed to the proletariat by Party theory (and because of the great resources available in the factories), it has been the "collectives" of the industrial enterprises which most frequently are called on to give aid to the more unfortunate in the farms, the schools, the pioneer camps, and so forth. As a Central Committee official's 1954 statement about patronage over agriculture indicates, the assistance rendered can take many forms:

> Patronage is expressed chiefly in providing the kolkhozy and the machine-tractor stations with organizational-economic and technical assistance. . . . It is possible to cite many examples of plant collectives . . . which prepare spare parts for agricultural machines, which help actively to build MTS garages, sheds, barns and housing and kolkhoz livestock buildings, hot beds and greenhouses, and which help to mechanize hand work on the farms. Many plants send qualified workers to the MTS to repair the tractor park and to transmit progressive methods of industrial labor to the rural mechanizers. The employees of the industrial enterprises help the rural mechanizers to raise their productive qualifications and to improve the organization of labor. . . .
>
> The progressive plants and factories do not limit their patronage functions to economic aid to the kolkhozy: they lead cultural-educational work there; they send reporters, lecturers, and concert brigades; they help to organize amateur art activities; they select literature for kolkhoz libraries; they concern themselves with the installation of a rural radio network.[1]

In practice, much of the patronage is directed in an *ad hoc* manner to those farms "where there is a break-down," [2] but ideally a plant should be attached to a particular farm or farms so that it can furnish systematic help and advice over a long period of time. Indeed, long-term patronage can be assumed over an entire rural raion. In the past, it usually was an urban raion collectively which took responsibility for a rural counterpart, but at the present time giant plants such as the Cheliabinsk Tractor Works and the Volgograd Tractor Works may also be attached to an entire raion.[3]

Although there have been frequent complaints about nonfulfillment of patronage duties, the amount of assistance to agriculture can be very significant. One official complained in 1954 that "the kolkhozy and the MTS of Venev raion with the support of the Party raikom presented their patron — the Tula Combine Works — an application of fifteen pages in which they requested materials and work which cost several million rubles." During this same period the enterprises of Stalin raion in Moscow prepared ten million rubles worth of hot-beds and greenhouses alone. The amount of assistance rendered in this period immediately after the September 1953 Central Committee plenum was unusually high, but even during the two-year period of the bifurcation of the Party apparatus the industrial enterprises of Lugansk oblast build 230 fodder cooking houses and shops (*kormo-kukhon* and *kormotsekov*) for the oblast's farms.[4]

Besides material aid, the enterprises also send large numbers of workers to the countryside to help in the harvest. In 1955, for exam-ple, thousands of Tashkent workers were sent to the farms for this purpose, and it was said that during the summer the role of the indus-trial-transportation department of the Vyborg raikom (Leningrad oblast) was limited almost exclusively to the organization of this work. The number of workers taken from each plant can be quite substantial. As noted before, in 1962 the Kalinin Railroad Car Construction Works had to send twelve skilled workers and two engineers to help harvest hay and four to five hundred employees to harvest potatoes — all at the plant's expense.[5]

The rules about patronage are rather murky. In 1954, *Partiinaia zhizn* strongly implied that concrete patronage assistance merely in-volved the agreement of the plant to accept orders from a farm and that the farms should pay for the items given.[6] However, even this article indicated that the collective farms often did not pay their bills (and never intended to), and I have seen no mention of payment in any other reference to patronage. Indeed, in the Stalin period at least, the plant patronage would sometimes include a small gift of money to the farm (in one case, 3,000 rubles [7]). In discussions of the participation in the harvest, there are (as seen above) references to the plant's obligation to pay the workers, and Soviet sources are insistent that the workers' wages be equal to those they would have earned in the factory. One official who was asked about this question in a 1967 interview expressed surprise at the very thought that the kolkhozy would be required to pay for patronage.

Soviet spokesmen emphasize the voluntary nature of this patronage assistance, but they also assert that the Party organs have the responsibility "to ensure without fail that a worker's collective provides active patronage." The local Party organs can assign patronage obligations directly. For example, in 1962, the managers of the Kalinin Railroad Car Construction Works were bitter about having to send so many workers to help in the hay and potato harvest. Yet, they still had to send them. In the words of the plant's Party secretary, "That is the decision of the Party raikom, and we are obligated to fulfill it." Shortly before proposing the bifurcation of the Party in 1962, Khrushchev complained that the local Party organs exempted no enterprise from the responsibilities of patronage over agriculture, even though the aid given was often very costly to the economy. The Central Aviation Research Institute (TsAGI) built a cattle-yard for a collective farm out of duraluminum, and an obkom "forced" a factory producing apparatus for space flights to work out apparatus for the automation of cow-milking. Even more usual, no doubt, was the practice followed in Saratov oblast in early 1957: "At the instruction of the obkom, Saratov enterprises of different subordination prepared parts for thousands of silage-gathering combines and for thousands of complicated grain-cleaning machines." [8]

Thus far, only examples of industrial patronage over agriculture have been cited, and it is not accidental that the discussion of patronage has begun with them. Because agriculture poses such a danger to a Party secretary, because this sphere of the economy has received limited central investments, the Party officials have been particularly tempted to ensure that the farms receive outside assistance in times of special need. However, agriculture is not unique in receiving patronage from the industrial enterprises. A local Party organ can decide that the interests of any institution are sufficiently important at the moment to require help.

Because patronage is often portrayed as aid by the fortunate (usually the proletariat) to the unfortunate, the Soviet press has emphasized the need for patronage over the children's institutions — the schools, nursery schools, and pioneer camps. The reported cases frequently have involved rather minor assistance (providing some cloth for the pioneer camp, an apparatus on which children may climb in the school play-yard, and so forth), but at times the Party organs can become more demanding. As the beginning of the school year approaches, the completion of school construction and repairs takes on a high priority, and there are many reports of assistance during this period. The construction trusts may concentrate their efforts on the schools (sometimes doing "outside the plan" work as well as scheduled work), and the railroads will accept as their "patronage" obligation the speedy delivery of some urgently needed supplies for this task.[9] In addition to this material aid, the "collectives" of the enterprises may also furnish various types of advisory assistance to the children. In Moscow, at least, the brigades of Communist labor took patronage over teen-agers in the juvenile rooms of the police, presumably attempting to facilitate their rehabilitation.[10]

The emphasis placed on polytechnical education during the Khrushchev period required the Party organs to demand even more systematic help to the schools than had been provided earlier. A raikom instructor has described fully the nature of this type of patronage:

> Recently the question of polytechnical education has been discussed twice at sessions of the bureau of the [Elgav] gorkom. One of the preconditions of successful polytechnical education is assistance to the schools from the factories, plants, sovkhozy, and kolkhozy. Taking this into account, the gorkom bureau studied all sides of the question of aid to the schools from the enterprises of the city, and it confirmed a list of patrons (shefy) who should help the individual schools. Now each school has its own patron which renders [it] great help. It supplies instruments, ma-

chines, and raw materials to the school workshop, and if necessary, it assigns some of its engineers to the school as instructors.

However, not all enterprise leaders completely understood their responsibility for polytechnical education in the schools. Such leaders have been found in our city too, in particular at the leather works. This plant turned out to be a poor patron of its school, not helping it very much. It felt that the patronage was a burden. I had to concern myself with this question, to speak with the leaders of the plant and its Communists, and to remind them about the decision of the gorkom bureau. Now this enterprise fulfills its patronage obligations well.[11]

Another realm to which the industrial enterprises often are required to render assistance is the "social-cultural and communal construction" of the city. Funds for the improvement of municipal services are allocated through a number of independent departments and ministries, and no systematic attempt is made to ensure that the services are provided in a proportionate manner. Moreover, the pressures on resources caused by the rapid industrialization policy are felt most severely in the realm of municipal services (particularly in the construction of repair and service shops).[12] If difficulties arise, one or another of the agencies responsible for a project may delay its contribution, and even more disproportion may result.[13]

The city soviet — the single state institution with the responsibility for coordinated city planning — is one of the institutions with the fewest resources. In the mining city of Krivoi Rog, for example, "the gorispolkom has comparatively few funds and depends wholly on its 'rich uncles' — the leaders of the ore administration, trusts, and enterprises."[14] These officials apparently were willing to spend resources on the improvement of "their" workers' settlement, but not on the city as a whole.

The local Party organs do not always intervene "to make such leaders face the city." In Krivoi Rog, it was reported, "the Party gorkom is firm and decisive about the fulfillment of the production plan, but for some reason it is timid when questions of living conditions are discussed."[15] Although the attitude of the local Party organs inevitably reflects the high priority that the leadership places on economic plan fulfillment, there are many indications that frequently the Party officials do, in fact, put considerable pressure on the city's "rich uncles."

In one area the Party organs "categorically demanded" that local construction trusts build hospitals, stores, and other municipal objects "outside the plan," even though their demand was said to be illegal. In another raion the Party officials compelled the local machinery works to build five hundred meters of stone wall around the city park (at a cost of 100,000 rubles). When the plant director protested, the raikom secretary remained adamant: "We will force the leaders of the enterprises and the institutions to empty their pockets for the beautification of the city." [16]

At times a "staff" may be created to deal with urban improvement (blagoustroistvo), and directors of important enterprises may be included in it so their contributions to city construction can be coordinated. In 1966, the "staff" in Novocherkassy included not only the important directors, but also the city architect, representatives of the educational institutions, and officials of the gorkom. It decided architectural and landscaping questions and "agreed about the financing of the work." The gorispolkom had a role no larger than the "formal confirmation of the measures which had been worked out." [17]

All levels of local Party organs can require assistance from the local enterprises. However, when the sovnarkhozy were placed in the oblasti, the obkomy had a particularly great opportunity to ensure the diversion of industrial resources to other sectors of the economy. (This was especially true in the early period when the sovnarkhoz's autonomy on investment was still fairly substantial.) In August 1958, it was reported that in Karaganda oblast 24.6 million rubles had been diverted from heavy industry appropriations for the construction of a circus, a drama theater, a rest home, a sanatorium, "and other non-planned objects." "Besides that, the Karaganda sovnarkhoz arbitrarily included in the 1958 plan 12.5 million rubles for the construction of a miner's school, two swimming areas, and other cultural-service objects." Similar actions were taken in other oblasti. Although the Central Committee decision which described (and condemned) these actions was directed first of all against the sovnarkhoz chairmen in these regions, it made clear that the decisions were "in a series of cases the result of [the obkom's] compelling the economic leaders to fulfill non-planned work which was favorable to local interests." [18]

It is still too early to determine the significance of the post-Khrushchev economic reforms in this respect. In the case of at least one factory operating on the new principles of planning, the local Party organ was able to divert all of the plant's "social-cultural" fund to city needs, but this may have been an isolated incident. [19] However, the local Party organs surely will demand that part of these expanded funds be utilized for community projects. If the plant-level officials were to be permitted to decide the proportion of plant funds to be devoted to "social-cultural" work and to investment, the impact on the role of the local Party organs could be great indeed.

At the present time, the most frequent type of plant assistance to the community demanded by the local Party organs seems to be the supplementary production of badly needed consumers goods. The following report pertains to Gorki oblast: "The Party obkom, gorkomy and raikomy and the soviets have conducted a great deal of work in organizing the supplementary output of consumers goods. . . . The oblast committee of the Party took a decision about the supplementary output of goods, having in mind the maximum utilization of all reserves and local resources for this purpose. The raion committees of the KPSS and the primary Party organizations (with the officials of the enterprises, administrations, and trusts participating) examined the resources of each enterprise. In 1967, supplementary tasks were established for the production of consumers goods worth 41.6 million rubles in retail prices, including 5.7 million at enterprises of local industry (*mestnaia promyshlennost*)." [20]

Because the managers cannot themselves make major adjustments in the assortment of goods produced by their plants, the Party officials are in the strongest position when they demand the production of "the small items (*melochi*) which are very necessary to the population" and which can be made out of scrap. [21] However, as the second secretary of the Rostov obkom indicated, the local Party organs can appeal to the ministries in attempting to have more important items included in the plan: "At one of the most important plants in the country, the Rostov Agriculture Machinery Works (Rostselmash), consumers goods comprise only five percent of the total production.

Now they make coat-hangers and lawn-chairs but without harming their basic production, they could also produce side-cars for motorcycles, refrigerators, washing machines, and many other goods. . . . The Rostov Party obkom and the ispolkom of the oblast soviet more than once have turned to the ministries and departments with justified proposals about what kinds of consumers goods ought to be produced and how. We calculated that the fulfillment of these proposals would permit 28 to 30 million rubles of additional production in 1967. It is necessary to say that in many cases our opinion was taken into account." [22]

In all the examples cited thus far, it has been the industrial enterprise which has been required to sacrifice its specialized interests to aid other branches of the area's economy. The long record of industrial plan fulfillment and the obvious potential benefits from the fruits of industry make industrial assistance a natural phenomenon, but the local Party organs may also call on the nonindustrial sectors to contribute to the smooth functioning of industry.

The Soviet press reports innumerable examples of assistance provided to the plant at the initiative of the local Party organs. An additional — or perhaps simply a prompt — delivery of food for the plant dining hall may help a key plant acquire and retain the working force it needs. (It would be interesting to know whether factory patronage over collective farms entails some informal quid pro quo in this respect.[23]) The soviet may be induced to allot the enterprise additional housing, and a volunteer Sunday work detail may be organized to assist in a key construction project. Students of the local institutes may assume patronage over the workers' dorms, not only helping workers who are doing poorly in evening school, but also trying to improve dormitory living conditions. The local Party organ may also be able to intervene with a local scientific institute in an attempt to get it to do more work for local enterprises. And if keeping an important industrial administrator in the area can be accomplished only by the admission of his son to the local polytechnical institute, then the Party organs may even be able to be of assistance in this respect too.[24]

The local Party organs can also demand that one industrial plant or construction trust help another. Berliner cites the testimony of one

Soviet refugee who suggests that the plant management was actually hoodwinked into providing aid:

> If there is a sudden breakdown in some other firm in our district, it may take too long to repair it if it goes through regular administrative channels. Then the Party takes a hand. The director calls the Party secretary. The Party secretary goes to the secretary of the district Party organization (*raikom*), who calls the Party secretary of our plant to find out if we can do the repair. Our Party secretary does not go to our director at first, but goes directly to the Party secretary of the shop itself, to see if the job can be handled. This is called "operation tying up loose ends." If he finds that the job can be handled, then he calls the chief engineer. The chief engineer says, "This is impossible, the factory is already filled up with work." But the Party secretary says he has already been to the shop, and he knows it can be done as overfulfillment of the plan. The chief engineer calls the shop chief and asks why he gave the Party secretary this information. He says, "You made a fool out of me!" Sometimes a big scandal occurs because of this, but the Party secretary would do it anyhow because the secretary of the district Party organization is very hot about it.[25]

As one reads the continual complaint in the postwar period that officials of the local Party organs have very little contact with the secretaries of the primary Party organizations but instead conduct their conversations primarily with the plant directors and chief engineers, one doubts that the operating procedure described by this refugee is still prevalent. Yet, whatever the procedure, the plants are still called on to help other plants and construction trusts. Most frequently, inter-plant assistance simply involves early production or delivery of an item already in the enterprise's plan, but it also can entail acceptance of an "above-plan order." [26] As has been seen, the industrial plants can also be compelled to help each other by the temporary transfer of working force.

The Resolution of Interdepartmental Conflict

In attempting to promote proportional economic development in the region, the local Party organs can do far more than stimulate assistance from one institution to another.

First, as will be discussed in Chapter XII, they may attempt to see that investment decisions made by the specialized ministries do not create economic irrationalities or disproportions. In one region the railroad may decide to lay track in an area soon to be flooded by a dam, in another region the food industry administration of the soviet and the restaurant administration of the railroad may independently decide to build a bakery in the same small village.[27] The local Party organs themselves may not recognize the mistake in time (it is only then that one reads about the case in the press), but in many instances their intervention surely is in time. It must prevent many costly errors.

Frequently the conflicts among specialized hierarchies involve not investment decisions but regulations and directives that govern the actions of local administrators. As mentioned earlier, the directives and plans that come down the specialized lines of command ultimately derive from the same Party leadership, but, nevertheless, they still can never be totally consistent. Differences in emphasis among the different hierarchies, conflicts in their missions, the existence of departmental self-interest, inevitable misinterpretations — all combine to ensure that local officials will have plans and regulations that come into conflict with each other.

Unless these conflicts are resolved, the functioning of the system can be seriously impaired. One might consider with more care a case mentioned earlier — that involving a dispute between an energy shop and a construction trust in an outlying district: "They had finished building the boarding school. There was already frost in the air, but there was no heat in the building. The line [to the central heating system] had a section of several yards which was not insulated, and an argument raged: should the line be hooked on or not? The builders were in favor, but the 'bosses' of the heating system — the officials of the energy shop of the Aznakaev Oil Administration — were against. The specialists argued for five hours until they were hoarse.

While they talked on, the heating system of the boarding school began to freeze." [28]

How was the impasse to be overcome? It was not a dispute that could be solved in a "technocratic" manner, for both sets of officials were "right" within their own frame of reference. The officials of the energy shop knew that sending heat through an uninsulated section was not proper procedure, and undoubtedly there was a strict regulation against it. If the pipe burst, their initiative in breaking a rule was not likely to be rewarded. The construction officials, on the other hand, knew that the freezing of the school's heating system would lead to unfortunate and wasteful consequences.

It is difficult to exaggerate the number of disputes — or even the number of types of disputes — that arise between different Soviet agencies and are as difficult to resolve as the boarding school construction conflict. In this case (and in many others like it) it was a question of whether one agency would overlook its regulations in order to protect a large state investment in a project. In other cases the conflict may center on the extent to which a manager is justified in neglecting working conditions or even infringing labor regulations in order to fulfill the industrial plan. In others it may result from difficulties that the work methods of one institution create for another institution — as, for example, when the procedures used by a railroad in loading industrial goods cause inconvenience to the factory producing them.

The type of dispute that seems by far the most widespread is that over the relative priority given to the fulfillment of the plans of different enterprises and institutions. Consider the following examples, all of which have been discussed in the Soviet press or cited to the author by Soviet officials:

The housing department of the local soviet allots a certain number of square meters of housing to a construction trust for distribution to its workers; the trust management argues that unless this allotment is increased, the trust will not be able to retain enough workers to complete a key project on time. The housing department points out that other enterprises are making the same claim.

The city soviet, no doubt in response to legitimate demands and pressures, decides to concentrate this year's construction of stores and services in the center of the city. The plant managers in a suburb protest that unless more are located in their area they will be unable to curtail a serious problem of labor turnover.

The plan of a construction trust includes a store or apartment house to be subordinate to the local soviet and a project for a local plant subordinate to a central ministry. Both demand that their project be completed first.

During the Khrushchev period the local department of education had a plan for ensuring that a certain number of students be taught machine-practice at the local enterprises; the local sovnarkhoz or plant might state, however, that the teaching of such a large number of students would require so much of the available resources and personnel in its specific case that the fulfillment of its industrial plan would be threatened.

All of these cases represent rather serious problems for the state administrative machinery, particularly because they recur with great frequency. Often, no doubt, they can be resolved by the officials involved. One official might agree to bend a regulation or to yield in his demands for high priority, hoping to receive a favor in return at a later date. (The behavior and attitudes associated with the use of the *tolkach* may obviously be cited in this connection.) A compromise might also be worked out through informal bargaining. However, each official knows that he is judged on the basis of *his* plan fulfillment and *his* observance of state and Party discipline, and frequently the potential cost to him is simply too great to permit serious consideration of a voluntary sacrifice or compromise.

Disputes such as have been discussed arise in one form or another in any economy, and there are a number of mechanisms which can be used to settle them. One such mechanism — and a very important one in many societies — is the marketplace. Priority is given to the individual or the institution willing to pay the most or to the one whose threat to withdraw business is potentially the most painful; investment is channelled into areas where the return (and hopefully the need) is the greatest. A problem such as that of the boarding school construction can often be resolved by one side taking financial responsibility. The construction officials could say, "Send the heat through. We will pay for the damages, if any." In the Soviet Union,

247

however, this solution has not been a meaningful one because the financial indicators have been much less important to officials than those such as total amount of production and the dates of completion of projects.

Another "solution" to these disputes would be to do nothing and to let the official in the dominant position (that is, the official with the initiative) do what he wishes. In the boarding school controversy it was the heating shop that controlled the heat, and, left to itself, it was quite able to "resolve" the problem by refusing to turn on the heat. Yet, this is hardly likely to result in a sober balancing of the leadership's relative priorities. The plant manager is not best situated to judge how much industrial production should be sacrificed to the interests of in-factory education or better working conditions for the workers. An official of the housing department is not in the best position to determine which factory's or which construction trust's plan justifies it being given priority, nor is the head of a construction trust the best man to judge whether an apartment house or an industrial shop should be completed first.

Still another "solution" to these problems would be to refer the conflicts to the common governmental superior of the two officials. In the boarding school example the sovnarkhoz chairman or deputy chairman could have been phoned and asked whether the heat should be turned on. The relative priority of an apartment house or an industrial shop could be decided by the republican council of ministers. And so forth.

To some extent, at least, referral to a common superior has been the solution adopted. A number of disputes within an area may find their way to higher levels in the Soviet Union, and at times the leadership has even institutionalized the procedure. For example, a considerable proportion of housing has been placed under the direct administrative control of the industrial organs, and these organs are allocated funds with which to have their own apartment houses built. Thus, the conflicts between factories over housing priority can and must be decided within the industrial hierarchy.

Except in fairly exceptional cases, however, it is simply impracticable to have the multitude of minor departmental disputes referred to the common governmental superior. With important industry not subordinate to the local soviet, the common superior cannot be lower than the republican council of ministers whenever a significant plant is involved in a conflict, and in many such cases the lowest common superior is the USSR Council of Ministers. In these circumstances the superior is simply too far away to be familiar with the facts of the situation, and he has too many other responsibilities pressing on his time. If all such conflicts had to be settled through the normal governmental chain of command, the administrative system would almost literally break down. At a minimum, it would surely not have been able to function in such a way as to permit the achievement of the industrialization plan.

These, then, are the reasons that as early as the 1920's Lenin was driven to assert: "The absence of coordination (*soglasovanie*) of the work of the different departments in the provinces is one of the greatest evils hindering economic construction. We must devote immense attention to this question." [29]

The major answer given to the question was that traditionally adopted by a complex organization desiring deconcentration of authority — the establishment of an authoritative area coordinator to whom many of the departmental conflicts may be taken.[30] For reasons discussed earlier it was the local Party organs who were chosen to fulfill this function, to serve as a "Ministry of Coordination." [31]

As an area coordinator, the local Party organ has a broad set of responsibilities in resolving inter-departmental disputes. In many cases it may establish general rules that determine how a particular type of problem will be handled. When it hears, for example, that those engaged in excavation work are damaging underground communications, it can call in all the relevant people for a several-hour discussion at the bureau and can lay out rules on "who should coordinate their activities with whom."[32]

However, it seems far more usual for the local Party organ to play a more passive coordinating role — that of arbitrator of disputes or conflicts brought to it for resolution. In this role, "it is not the Party obkom which makes demands on the oblast organizations, but, on the contrary, the leaders of these organizations which present their endless demands to the obkom: do this, interfere in this, give such an instruction." [33]

In turning to the local Party officials, the managers seem to follow the principle of appealing to the lowest possible Party organ. If the officials of a factory come into conflict with officials of another factory or institution in the same raion (including an official of the raion soviet), the problem is taken to the local raikom. This was the course adopted in the case of the dispute on the boarding school construction. The matter was taken to the head of the industrial-transportation department of the local raikom. (He decided that it was possible to hook on the heat, and "nothing terrible happened.")

If the conflict arises between enterprises within different raiony of the same city or between an enterprise and an official of the city soviet, it is usually taken to the gorkom for resolution. If the conflict occurs between enterprises of different cities, between an enterprise and an oblast institution, or (from 1957 to 1962) between the oblast soviet and the sovnarkhoz, it is referred to the obkom. Of course, if the dispute is a major one and does not demand immediate solution, there is always the possibility that a decision of a lower Party organ may be appealed to a higher one.

All types of conflict can be taken to the Party organs, and their quantity seems limitless. It has been reported, for example, that in the city of Orsk (population: 176,000) "not one significant question which falls outside the framework of an [individual] enterprise is decided without the advice of the leaders of the gorkom and without receiving its support." [34]

Any institution in Soviet society can come into conflict with the plant in such a way as to demand Party intervention. Even educational officials have come into considerable contact with the factory, and the local Party organs have had a major role in regulating this relationship. The trade union and Komsomol officials also turn frequently to the Party organs as the only institution that can support them authoritatively in their disputes with plant managers.

The more usual type of dispute is that arising between the factory and those institutions with which it has continuous work relationships. The railroads are a typical example. The relationship to industry is critical; yet, they are supervised by an All-Union ministry and have no superior in common with an industrial manager short of the USSR Council of Ministers. Thus it is not surprising that even before

World War II one could read: "The mutual relations of the railroad organs and their clients have exceptionally great significance. The Party raikomy can do much to put them in order and to direct them into a normal channel." [35]

In the factory-railroad relationship it is the railroad which has the initiative in decisions about transporting the factory's supplies or products, and hence it is the factory that appeals to the Party organs for help. These appeals may concern the procedures used in loading railroad cars, or they may constitute an anguished cry for quicker service: "We need sixty railroad cars, but they are not even giving us ten." [36]

Probably the most important and time-consuming type of coordinating work for the local Party organs has been in the construction field. Both Chapters IX and XI have already discussed the frequent and detailed local Party involvement in the "staffs" and "operational sessions" which are established at many construction projects. These staffs, it should be understood, are not simply the result of a local Party desire to have an impact on technical construction questions; rather, they are the consequence of an administrative situation that requires authoritative local intervention. An earlier-cited quotation is worth repeating, for it summarizes succinctly a situation which in one form or another has plagued construction administration for nearly four decades: "In our city [Cherkassy] there are four construction trusts and over thirty subcontracting organizations. As a rule they are subordinate to different departments, but they work on one project. Since there is not an economic organization in the city which could coordinate their activity, the Party gorkom has to assume that role. The officials of the industrial-transportation department and the gorkom secretary who handles industrial questions continually coordinate (*soglasovaiut*), "settle" (*utriasaiut*), and call economic leaders to conferences." [37]

Even a Party secretary who considers continual intervention in construction to be improper work for the Party organs has despaired of the possibility of avoiding it: "I [the first secretary of the Nizhnii Tagil gorkom] remember how a *Pravda* article related that the secretary of the Solikamsk Party gorkom, comrade Diakov, conducted conferences on the enterprises every week, trying to adjust 'conflicts' between the builders and the customers. It was not from a desire for the good life that the secretary went to these *'operativki'!* I don't know how it is in other Party committees, but we in Nizhnii Tagil have to conduct them even up to the present day. Judge for yourselves. The leaders of the enterprises and the builders appeal: we have coordination difficulties with the designers, troubles with the financing and with supply. Help us look into it." [38]

The scale of the coordination effort in construction may be even greater than has already been indicated, for many of the press reports that seem to imply deep Party participation in industrial planning may, in fact, actually reflect their responsibilities in construction coordination. In one interview with a plant manager, I asked how one could speak of a centrally planned economy if a raikom is able to obligate the director of a huge plant like the Volgograd Tractor Works to expend very considerable funds in re-building four electric-smelting furnaces in the casting shop.[39] I was told that this kind of decision often does not entail intervention in technical decision-making, but may essentially be a replication of a decision already made at higher levels. The purpose of the replication, the manager declared, is to give the lower Party organs formal and specific authority to check on the progress of the construction project and, more important, to give it the specific authority to coordinate the activities of the various organizations contributing to the project. Of course, the lower Party organ already had this authority, and the real purpose of a replicated decision is probably to provide the excuse for preliminary discussions among the relevant local organizations before the project actually commences.

Conclusion

From the point of view of traditional administrative theory, much of the coordinating work of the local Party organs is of a rather peculiar nature. To be sure, one does find adjustments of personal and departmental conflicts taking place in an expected way. One also finds the Party organs making decisions on the relative priorities in a way that, although relatively unknown in the West, could be anticipated in a planned "command" economy such as exists in the Soviet Union.

Yet it is important to note that to a considerable extent the local Party organs carry out their coordinating responsibilities by compelling administrators to break the law or to violate some directive or plan indicator. Whatever Party sources may say about "patronage," it is against the law to divert industrial products or materials to an undesignated recipient or to pay the wages of men who work in other institutions. When the local Party officials demand that an institute admit the son of an important administrator, they cannot even excuse themselves by referring to the official sanction given patronage. Even when the local Party organ arbitrates between two institutions whose plans and directives conflict, the fact that it helps one institution fulfill its plan or directive does not change the fact that it is often authorizing or compelling the other to violate *its* plan or directive.

An understanding of this central fact about the work of the local Party organs is indispensable for an understanding of the role of the local Party organs in industrial decision-making. First, it helps to demonstrate to Westerners that the strict enforcement of legality is, despite the official images, one of the relatively minor functions of the local Party organs. Second, it helps to explain some of the ambiguity in Soviet discussions of the local Party organs and some of their unwillingness to fully discuss coordinating work. A thorough analysis of the coordinating role would be difficult to reconcile with the image of the Party as a tireless defender of the letter of the law and the plan.

That so much of the work of the local Party organs involves compelling or authorizing officials to violate the law also helps to explain the real authority position of the local Party organs in Soviet society. Their ability to compel illegal action is testimony to the extent of their authority, but the necessity for them to function in this manner also produces the major limitations on their power.

If a local Party official gives an administrator a categorical instruction — at least one that demands immediate execution and is within his physical power to fulfill — there are few circumstances in which the instruction would be disobeyed. Yet, this does not mean that the real authority of the local Party organs is unlimited. The Party officials realize that the accounts of their area's institutions will be audited and that the governmental superiors of local administrators will ask questions about deviations. They know that they may be required to defend their action if these superiors complain to higher Party organs. They also are certain that the higher Party officials will examine the performance records of the different institutions of the area and that these officials seldom excuse failure.

Consequently, although there are almost no direct restrictions on the authority of the local Party organs (at least with respect to decisions that do not require higher level investment or approval), the local Party officials know with virtual certainty the consequence of their compelling a heavy industry plant to send so many men to the farm and to city institutions that it fulfills its annual plan only by 50 percent. They need not be told that if they make demands in such a way that the communal construction plan is fulfilled 100 percent and the plan for a steel plant construction is fulfilled 80 percent, the results will not be pleasant. And if they require the local institute to admit only the sons of important administrators, the central reaction is scarcely likely to be less severe.

In short, the authority of the local Party organs becomes limited in practical terms to cases which, although very important in terms of the proper functioning of the area and the economy, are still more or less marginal in their scope. One would strongly suspect, for example, that the enterprises are usually called on to provide manpower to other institutions during the first ten days of the month when their own production load is at a low level awaiting the arrival of supplies. Only if there were an impending disaster in the harvest would the Party officials be likely to require an important plant to furnish significant aid during the last ten days of the month — its own "storming" period. On the contrary, it is during this period that the Party officials will be quite likely to overlook violations of labor regulations by the plant management — including the law that Sunday is not a workday — and will demand that the important plants be well supplied with different municipal and communal services. In emergencies the Party organs may judge that other goals are more important than industrial goals at the particular moment, however, and they have the authority to enforce that judgment.

If the conflict between two institutions in the area becomes major and persistent, it may well be beyond the ability of the local Party organ to resolve. Such a conflict is likely to be a reflection of a general conflict in mission between the two hierarchies involved, and in such a case the central leadership will be compelled to issue a general decision to settle the myriad of similar conflicts that will be occurring everywhere. Similarly, if the shortages in one sector become so chronically large that the local Party organ cannot achieve a level of performance in it without sacrificing other sectors to an extent that threatens the leadership's set of priorities, the problem may very likely be a general one that may compel the leadership to rethink the investment policy.

In this respect, the role of the local Party organs becomes more of an adjusting one. The responsibility of resolving conflicts between departmental plans and self-interests and of shifting resources within the area must always be fulfilled with the understanding that the Soviet system is a planned one and that the plans generally reflect the relative priorities of the leadership. The duty of the local Party organ is to see that these priorities are met in circumstances which, because of peculiar local conditions or because of the distortions caused by departmental self-interest, are somewhat different than the leadership could anticipate.

XII. Representation of the Locality

Previous chapters have focused on the different supervisory roles of the local Party organs, a treatment quite in accord with the official images of a centralized, "leading" party. Yet, studies of all levels of administrative personnel — whether they be foremen or cabinet officers [1] — have shown that organization charts can be misleading. Although the authority arrows on an organization chart of a bureaucracy all point downward, scholars have learned that pressures can flow up the chain of command as well and that the position of the middle-level and even higher-level administrator in any bureaucracy inevitably is ambivalent. The administrator often becomes as much a representative of the interests of his subordinates as of his superiors.

This familiar feature of modern bureaucratic life is clearly found in the work of the local Party organs. Their prime function is to ensure that the center's policies are carried out in the locality. However, being held responsible for the performance of their area, they, like the managers they supervise, have an interest in any action improving that performance. Because large appropriations of supplies or funds are vital for this goal, the local Party officials have been vigorous spokesmen for the needs and interests of their areas. Local administrative officials may often see the local Party organs as the stern enforcers of central priorities, but higher officials are likely to think of them as incorrigible representatives of localism.

The Local Party Organ as Advocate

The various administrative and Party reorganizations of the postwar period may have changed the influence of the local Party organs, but they have done little to change the behavior of the local Party organs toward administrators at higher territorial levels. As many American authorities have pointed out, the fact that the local Party officials are evaluated on the basis of the performance of their area has given them a powerful incentive to support any request by a local administrator that would help his plant to fulfill its plan. If a director has thought it useful to plead to his ministry for more funds or a larger allocation of supplies, then the local Party officials have almost always found it advantageous to support him.

While Western scholars have fully understood why managerial and Party officials have sought more funds or supplies to aid in current plan fulfillment, there has been less appreciation of the reasons that they would press for the initiation of new construction projects. Indeed, there has been a tendency to assume that the incentive system has tempted the local managerial officials to avoid all innovations. (If the manager undertakes to introduce new capacity or new products, these innovations are included in the current plan he is obligated to fulfill, and the almost inevitable difficulties in the introductory and shakedown periods endanger plan fulfillment with few compensating rewards.) In reality, however, a sharp distinction should be made between introduction of new capacity and introduction of new products, for it has been in the latter case that the reluctance to innovate has been most apparent.

To be sure, it might be pleasant for the manager to dream of a plan that remains at a low level over the years, but he can never forget what Berliner called the "ratchet principle" in planning.[2] (This principle was succinctly defined by a Soviet plant manager in 1965: "The plans everywhere are composed on a simple principle: base your calculations on the achieved indicators plus an obligatory supplement for next year." [3]) The manager knows that next year's plan will surely demand a higher level of gross output (or now, a higher level of gross sales) and that the plan for the year after will be still higher. Without new investment this increase will be extremely difficult to achieve. Hence, even though the introduction of new machinery or the construction of a new shop may complicate the life of local officials, they know that they must fight for such machinery and shops if they are to survive.

The local Party officials are caught in a similar network of self-interest. They too are eager that the local plants be able to expand so as to cope with the ratchet principle. They also have a number of reasons to desire the establishment of new plants in their area. A truly major project may give the first secretary an opportunity to establish a major reputation, and at a minimum it is likely to increase the size of the city sufficiently to permit the size of the gorkom staff (and presumably the salary of its top officials) to be increased. (As noted before,[4] each gorkom is placed in one of six categories, depending on the importance of its city, and the size of its staff is established by this category.) The construction of a smaller plant either to supply parts to one of the region's large plants or to produce goods for the local population may help to solve serious economic or political problems for the local Party officials.

Perhaps the best evidence of the pressure upon the local Party organs to support new construction projects (and of the deviousness of the support which results) is the persistence of the practice, despite repeated central denunciations, of the initiation of more construction projects in a period than can be finished in it. Believing that it will be easier to obtain appropriations to complete a project already begun (and that the obtaining of appropriations is vital), local officials have pushed an excess number of projects in an attempt to build up insurance for the future.[5]

Struggle by the local Party officials to obtain more appropriations for their region is not a new phenomenon in Soviet history. Even during the last decade of the Stalin period the local Party organs frequently expressed "to the ministries their ideas about the best way of using local reserves and resources."[6] The Soviet press of those years was filled with a continuous stream of their very concrete recommendations about improving the work both of regional industry as a whole and of individual factories.

The speeches made by the obkom first secretaries at the Nineteenth Party Congress in 1952 provide a good cross-section of the kind of recommendations and suggestions made by Party secretaries during this period. One type of suggestion that recurred frequently at this Congress was a simple request for more appropriations, more supplies, more attention, and the like. The secretary of the Ivanovo obkom asked the Ministry of Light Industry for more machinery for finishing cloth. The first secretary of the Molotov obkom complained that the construction of a planned brick plant had to be postponed because the Ministry of Building Materials had not completed the preliminary survey. The first secretary of the Cheliabinsk obkom noted with dissatisfaction that, although the planned production of the Cheliabinsk Tractor Plant already was several times larger than the originally projected capacity, Gosplan was still increasing the enterprise's spare parts plan.[7]

All the appeals mentioned thus far related fairly directly to the fulfillment of the current plan, but another type of request was less obviously self-serving. Many obkom secretaries proposed large-scale investment projects in their regions, even though this might mean more work and worry for them personally. The first secretary of the Khabarovsk kraikom, for example, stated that his territory needed timber-processing and chemical plants so that the large amounts of timber scrap there could be put to industrial use. The Rostov leader argued for the construction of a blast furnace at the Taganrog Steel Plant so that it could produce its own pig iron from local ore and would not have to import pig iron from distant enterprises. And from the Molotov obkom came an insistent appeal for the beginning of preparatory work for the construction of a hydroelectric station at Solikamsk on the Upper Kama River. Unless this was done, the Party leader warned, the new enterprises to be built in the oblasty in the next five-year plan would find themselves without sufficient electricity.[8]

A third type of recommendation called for eradicating some of the worst results of the departmental approach of the industrial ministries. The first secretary of the Leningrad obkom, for example, noted that "Leningrad receives 7,000 to 7,500 tons of nails [a year] from the South and the Urals, while there is a plant in Leningrad which produces 7,000 tons of nails and ships its entire output to points outside Leningrad."[9] He called for more rational planning in this matter. The first secretary of the Gorki obkom brought up the organization of timbering activities within his oblast. Deploring the multitude of ministries and departments engaged in this work in the oblast and citing the higher cost of lumber produced by the smaller organizations, he called for a large-scale consolidation of the timbering organizations.[10]

After the creation of the sovnarkhozy even the obkomy still had to appeal to the center and the republic if they were to have an impact on significant investment decisions, for the sovnarkhoz's powers in this realm were fairly restricted. Thus, one reads of a Party secretary appealing for an experimental spinning factory to be constructed in his oblast, and of another begging the RSFSR Gosplan for an additional nine thousand tons of steel to help complete the construction of a factory.[11] Frequently the obkom did not make an independent appeal to higher levels, but rather acted in conjunction with the sovnarkhoz. For example, in Kostroma the obkom and the sovnarkhoz became concerned about the depletion of the oblast's forests and the great waste of the scrap in the timber industry: "More than once they turned to the republican and All-Union organizations with proposals about the development of this branch of industry and about the integrated processing of the wood. Three bulky files of the correspondence are preserved in the sovnarkhoz." [12]

If the obkom appealed to the center for changes in the oblast plan, then the gorkomy and raikomy frequently turned to the sovnarkhoz and the obkom seeking their approval for local projects and needs. Consider, for example, the speeches by the gorkom first secretaries at a typical Party meeting — the 1963 Congress of the Moldavian Party organization (Moldavia is an oblast-less republic, and its sovnarkhoz was equivalent to an oblast sovnarkhoz in its powers and functions).

At this Congress a number of proposals were made about the proper investment policy to follow with respect to the development of the chemical industry in the republic. To be more precise, each gorkom first secretary demanded that the funds be invested in *his* city. The first secretary of the Beltsy gorkom suggested "that the structures prepared for the . . . gypsum works be used to create an enterprise to produce substitute construction materials out of chemicals." The first secretary of the Tiraspol gorkom requested that higher administrators "support the suggestion of the [Tiraspol] Chemical Works that the profile of the enterprise be changed to the output of plastic products." The first secretary of the Bendery gorkom thought it "expedient to decide [favorably] the question of constructing in Bendery a hydrolysis yeast works to process the waste products of the [plant] oil extraction works which will be completed in the next year." However, the gorkom first secretary in Kishinev (the republic's capital and largest city) objected to "the idea of creating several enterprises in Moldavia to produce plastic items, for this would lead again to cottage-style production." He thought that "the production of plastic items for industry and construction could be successfully organized in a centralized fashion at the [Kishinev] Artificial Leather and Technical Rubber Products Combine." [13]

Although one might think that the gorkomy limited their appeals to the local sovnarkhoz (and to the obkom or the central committee in a small republic), they could also carry their case to the central organs. For example, in the early 1960's the government approved the construction of a textile combine in Balashov, Saratov oblast, but no funds were allocated for the building of a construction base:

> Seriously disturbed by the unattractive prospects of the construction project, the Balashov gorkom sounded the alarm. During the last year this question was placed before the republican organizations several times.
>
> After a trip to Moscow by the gorkom secretary, comrade Konobeevskii, the RSFSR sovnarkhoz assigned 100,000 rubles for the construction of the base. However, the then-existing Saratov sovnarkhoz used half of these funds for other purposes.
>
> The gorkom again knocked on the door of the republican organizations. It suggested that part of the funds allocated for the construction of the combine be switched to the creation of a construction base, namely to the construction of a plant producing reinforced concrete items. The petition of the gorkom went to the USSR Gosplan . . . but no answer has been received.
>
> The first secretary of the Balashov gorkom, comrade Prazdikov, personally visited the RSFSR Gosplan and Sovnarkhoz. The officials in both organizations agreed to assign a half million rubles for building the reinforced concrete items plant, . . . but the gorkom secretary had hardly left Moscow when everything came to a standstill. Comrade Prazdnikov again had to go to the republican sovnarkhoz. [14]

The article from which this quotation is taken describes additional struggles required of the gorkom ("To the honor of the gorkom leaders, they did not retreat."), and its author complains that the battle still was not completely won.

Similar appeals continued to be made after the re-creation of the ministries. If one examines the speeches of the obkom first secretaries at the 23rd Party Congress in 1966, one finds almost precisely the same type of investment proposals that had been made by the first secretaries at the 19th Congress in 1952.[15] One such recommendation — that by the Gorki first secretary involving "the reconstruction of the auto works and its specialization" and "the development of associate-plants (*zavodov-smezhnikov*) in the automobile industry" — represented the continuation of a bureaucratic struggle which had already found expression in an article in *Sovetskaia Rossiia*. At that time the central leadership had decided to construct a new plant to produce small automobiles, and the officials of the Gorki obkom were eager that it be built in their oblast. In the article, the first secretary advocated that the new plant "be part of the Gorki [Auto Works] complex," and he cited arguments for this arrangement: favorable economic conditions, the help available from an experienced auto works, and the presence of an institute that specializes in the preparation of engineers for the auto industry. The Gorki leader also called for the construction of small specialized plants to produce parts for the Gorki Works. He suggested that these plants be located in small cities in Gorki oblast so that the main plant could furnish them assistance (and, no doubt, so that the obkom would have control over the major suppliers to one of the oblast's most important plants).[16]

In appealing for a project (or for supplies or for a favorable decision on some matter), the local Party organs have usually not been acting alone. Usually they have been supporting the position of local industrial managers or acting in conjunction with them. In many cases the alliance is not formally acknowledged in the article or speech available to us. (For example, nothing is said about the attitude of the director of the Gorki Auto Works toward the proposals of the obkom first secretary, but it is quite likely that he supported them enthusiastically or even helped to initiate them.) In other cases, as noted, the Party officials frankly state that they "support the suggestion of the [Tiraspol] Chemical Works that . . ." Similarly, the first secretary of the Dnepropdzerzhinsk gorkom explicitly asserted in 1965 that he had been vigorously supporting a local plant director in behind-the-scenes appropriations politics. The director (who managed the local steel plant, one of the largest in the country) had appealed to the sovnarkhoz, the Ukrainian Gosplan, and to Moscow for reconstruction of the plant. "Why new air heaters alone . . . would permit an increase in the production of pig iron from each furnace by 27,000 tons a year and would achieve an annual economy of 400,000 rubles." In complaining about the failure of higher officials to accept these proposals quickly, the gorkom first secretary wrote, "Of course, in such a situation the Party gorkom had to harness itself in one team with the [local] industrial administrators: to apply pressure, to push (*tolkat*), to solicit funds." [17]

The examples cited of alliances between local Party organs and local industrial institutions have involved appeals for capital investment, and, in fact, the struggle for appropriations has produced very frequent cooperation among local Party and industrial officials. However, the Party secretaries also may support their area's managers on other questions. For example, in 1959 the Kharkov obkom supported the local tractor plant and the Ukrainian Council of Ministers in a fight with the USSR Gosplan about the type of tractor to be produced at the plant; in the same year the Ukrainian Central Committee supported unnamed local construction agencies who were protesting against the high price set for semi-wire strand produced by the Khartsyz works. [18]

The Politics of the Appropriations Process

To understand the group structure of Soviet politics and the nature of the Party-state relationship, it is necessary to remember that the advocacy discussed in the last section does not take place in a vacuum. It is not a single Party organ which is seeking funds; instead, all the Party organs are engaged in this activity. Because, as in any bureaucratic situation, the center does not have sufficient funds to finance all projects suggested, seeking funds must always be a competitive process whether the applicants realize it or not.

In the Soviet Union the competition among the local Party organs can become quite open and direct. In 1957, for example, Nikolai Organov, then first secretary of the Krasnoiarsk kraikom, wrote an article for *Pravda* in which he extolled the virtues of the Krasnoiarsk Hydroelectric Station in comparison with others also under construction (such as the Bratsk Hydroelectric Station in nearby Irkutsk oblast). Organov advocated a rapid acceleration in the construction of the Krasnoiarsk Dam. Two weeks later Organov's article was answered by a secretary of the Irkutsk obkom (in conjunction with the chief engineer of the Bratsk project, the director of a Moscow design institute, and the head of the East Siberian filial of the Academy of Science). The authors of this article openly referred to Organov by name, and directly asserted that he was wrong. Pointing out that the construction of the Bratsk Hydroelectric Station was two years ahead of the Krasnoiarsk project, they objected to any transfer of funds from it to Krasnoiarsk. They recommended that the present rates of construction be continued.[19]

Such direct and explicit reference to a conflict within the Party apparatus is not a normal feature of the Soviet press. Usually a Party official will follow the example of the secretary of the Dneprodzerzhinsk gorkom and will simply point out that a certain appropriation would be extraordinarily advantageous for the economy. (Often he will also be damning higher officials — nay, "bureaucrats" — for failing to improve the economy in such an obvious way.) Yet, even in these isolated requests, the competition is scarcely hidden. In the discussion about chemical industry construction in Moldavia, for example, it is not at all difficult to reconstruct the behind-the-scene arguments that the various suggestions reflect.

Formally or informally the local officials are often asked to compete for funds at a middle stage of the appropriation process. In 1958 the first deputy chairman of the Odessa sovnarkhoz stated in an interview that a decision had already been made to produce automobiles in the Ukraine and that each oblast was — so to speak — to make a bid for it. Each was to indicate the reasons that some existing plant in its region could most economically be converted to automobile production, and the higher officials would then choose among the proposals. The deputy chairman stated that the competition was lively and that the Odessa obkom and sovnarkhoz were allied in advancing a candidate. The 1966 proposals of the first secretary of the Gorki obkom were obviously made within the same type of framework.

At least during the sovnarkhoz period the gorkomy and raikomy were involved in a similar two-stage appropriation process. Thus, in

1965, a decision had already been made to construct a spinning factory in Saratov oblast, and the dispute concerned the choice of a city within the oblast in which to locate it.[20] Given the growing controversy about the desirability of locating more industry outside the oblast centers, one would expect that even in the present ministerial period it may be normal for the location of many small and medium-sized plants to be decided in stages and for the gorkomy and raikomy to be asked to compete in the latter stages.

When one examines the role of the provincial officials in the appropriations process, the analogy that repeatedly comes to mind is the awarding of defense contracts in the United States. Just as the traditional American categories of "labor," "management," "Democrat," and "Republican" lose almost all real meaning in this process as the alliances center on certain key companies and the communities in which they are located, so the categories of "Party" and "state" have little relevance for understanding the way in which Soviet appropriations are made, at least once the basic investment level for the country has been decided. The conflicts arise between one group of industrial and Party officials who support one project and another group of industrial and Party officials who support another project.

In this alliance of community forces what, however, is the role of the local Party organs? Does the local Party organ endorse in a virtually automatic way every request made by a local industrial administrator and thus abandon any significant independent role in the appropriation process? Or, do the local Party organs make real choices in deciding which local projects to support and even in initiating investment proposals themselves? Have the local Party organs been doomed to be the representative of each individual interest in their locality or have they been able to represent either the interests of the Party or the overall interests of the locality as they themselves perceive their interests?

The answer to some of these questions is relatively simple. Certainly there is little evidence that the local Party organs have served as a nationally attuned control instrument, intervening to veto projects which are attractive from a localistic point of view but which are uneconomical from a national point of view. In fact, the Soviet press contains no indication that the local Party organs ever strive to reduce the requests made by the local plants to the ministries for more supplies or funds. As memory is imperfect, it is dangerous to make categorical negative statements, but I remember seeing not one article in which a local Party secretary boasted that his committee had accomplished such a feat. On the contrary, concrete Soviet discussions of this subject always describe the Party organs as supporting the managerial requests.

At the time of the 1957 industrial reorganization, for example, N. N. Smeliakov, the Minister of Machinebuilding, warned that localism in the seeking of funds was a universal phenomenon. In describing the communications he had received from the Party and economic organizations of the oblasti, cities, and plants, he made no distinction between Party and economic officials: "Analysis shows that they are chiefly demanding money for supplementary capital construction or are asking us to assign them materials and equipment. Until now the local officials have extremely rarely raised the quesiton of increasing the load of the plant — of taking on supplementary orders after finding reserves inside the enterprise or region. It is difficult to recall even one case of a refusal of capital construction because of a better utilization of the capacity of the enterprises." [21]

Perhaps as punishment for this rash statement, Smeliakov was soon sent into the provinces, first as chairman of the Gorki sovnarkhoz and then as first secretary of the Gorki obkom (the only industrial minister to receive such a post in the post-Purge period). However, Smeliakov apparently found localism easier to denounce from Moscow than to avoid in Gorki oblast. In the summer of 1958 his oblast was one of nine singled out for criticism in a Central Committee decision on sovnarkhoz localism, and he was one of the few obkom first secretaries in the postwar period to be removed before completing one year in office. [22]

The reasons for localism on the part of local Party officials go beyond the pressures of self-interest. Perhaps the most important of these reasons has been the absence of a rational price system and a set of success-indicators that would give local officials a reliable means of judging whether a proposal is indeed "localistic." [23] A major Soviet statement about the planning system has summarized the problem well: "We ought to note that localistic tendencies are not always the result of subjective motives [that is, self-interest] of local officials. In a series of cases they are the result of a one-sided approach to the local economy and of a lack of information about the national need for a particular product or about the material and financial resources at the disposal of the state." [24]

The most important information a local Party secretary lacks is that which would allow him to judge reliably whether appropriations needed for a local project might be more productively employed elsewhere. Consequently, when a secretary perceives an opportunity for increasing production or productivity — or is presented with such a proposal — he normally has little legitimate alternative other than to appeal for the necessary appropriations.

The more difficult question about the degree of local Party independence in the appropriations process concerns their ability to serve as a representative of overall regional interests rather than as a representative of each individual interest in the region. Here it is clear that the nature of the administrative situation places severe limitations on the real freedom of action of the local Party organs, but these limitations are not complete.

The central fact about the allocation of funds in the Soviet Union has been its branch-line character. At the center there undoubtedly has been fierce competition for funds between the steel industry and the chemical industry, the defense industry and the consumers' goods industry, and so forth, but once the decision is made at the central level, the competition between the branches for appropriation funds is usually not extended into the provinces. Except to a limited extent during the sovnarkhoz period, the oblast (let alone the city) has not been allocated a given amount of money or supplies and its officials then permitted to subdivide it among various industrial projects.[25] Instead, each ministry (or during the sovnarkhoz period, each branch department of Gosplan and then of the higher sovnarkhozy) has had the funds for its branch at its own disposal. Hence as each plant makes its requests to its own hierarchy, the local Party organs feel no discomfort in supporting the proposals for the expansion of the chemical plant *and* the steel plant, of the defense industry plant *and* of the textile combine. Indeed, the pressures which have been discussed lead them to want to support the expansion of each of the plants.

There are, however, circumstances in which the local Party organs do have some independent impact on the appropriations process. One such situation has arisen when more than one plant or sub-area within the region is competing for the same funds. When a number of enterprises in the region turn out precisely the same product (for example, in coal mining) and each seeks appropriations, the local Party officials may have the opportunity — or may be compelled — to choose among them. When higher officials ask the oblast to suggest a plant suitable for reconstruction into an automobile plant, there may be more than one candidate within the oblast and then the obkom will have to make a choice.

Similarly, when the location of a plant within the oblast is decided in two stages and the gorkomy are asked to compete for it, the opinion of the obkom officials will surely be solicited. In many cases the obkom may have a decisive role in determining the final location of the plant, but this is not an invariable rule. In the Saratov case mentioned earlier, the regional officials thought that the spinning factory should be built in a small town with an excess labor force. The RSFSR Gosplan insisted that it be built in the oblast center. The article cited was part of a late campaign to overcome the resistance of the Gosplan officials.

During the sovnarkhoz period there was a comprehensive oblast-wide plan for industry, and there were significant funds at the disposal of an oblast-wide institution. Consequently, the obkom was more frequently under pressure to make choices among various applicants within the oblast. To be sure, these decisions could be delegated largely to the sovnarkhoz if the obkom wished, but the possibilities of appeal within the Party hierarchy made obkom review almost inevitable. During the ministerial periods, the local Party organs have always been compelled to assume a similar role with respect to industrial investment by plants under the local soviets.

A second type of situation in which the local Party organs have an impact on the appropriations process is that created when they initiate investment suggestions themselves. Not all capital appropriations are allocated for the expansion of existing plants, and the competition for funds must also involve proposals for the development of untapped resources. Except during the sovnarkhoz period, no governmental institution has had the perspective and the self-interest to present the case for oblast development or city development in a persistent way. (The officials of the local soviets, who might be expected to perform this role, have not been responsible for industrial development, and hence even the oblast and city planning commissions, *oblplan* and *gorplan,* have only been concerned with a limited range of questions.)

The central planning organs, which have had the responsibility for ensuring coordinated industrial development, have been organized basically along branch-industry lines and have been primarily concerned with balancing the national output of different products.[26] As a Party official declared in 1952, Gosplan "essentially confines itself to industry-by-industry planning, to planning by ministries, and has lost contact with the localities." [27] Neither during the sovnarkhoz period nor during the post-sovnarkhoz period was there any fundamental change in the structure of Gosplan. In 1967 only 2 percent of the personnel of Gosplan worked in its territorial planning department, and their role is said to be minimal.[28] A similar complaint about an "underevaluation of the role of territorial planning" has been directed at the Russian Republic's Gosplan.[29] The planning commissions of the large economic regions have very limited authority, and, as the deputy director of the Institute of Economics complained dryly, their "functions are still defined with insufficient clarity." [30]

For these reasons the local Party organs have been forced to take the initiative in pushing for the construction of new factories in their particular area if they want to ensure that the area as area is fully taken into account. They may utilize the ideas of experts in local educational, scientific, and design institutes, but (except for the sovnarkhoz period) they have had to take the lead in organizing the presentation of the case. Indeed, even during the sovnarkhoz period there was no institution other than the gorkom and raikom that could speak out for the integrated development of the city and raion and could struggle for the appropriation of funds for it.

Probably the most important way in which the local Party organs are able to rise above the position of an adjunct to local managerial officials is through varying the intensity of their support. Although the local Party officials can usually be counted on to support the interests of the individual plants in their community when they compete with plants outside the community (the interests of the plants as perceived by the plant managers, it should be noted), the quality of the support can vary with the local Party officials' own perception of the overall interests of the region.

It is one thing to marshall a case and to see that it is presented forcefully to the proper Party and state officials at the higher levels; it is another to go to the official who has the authority to resolve conflicts between the functional hierarchy and the regional Party secretaries (that is, one of the top two or three secretaries of the Central Committee or on some lower questions the obkom first secretary) and to state emphatically, "We *must* have this project, this allocation of supplies, this technical decision. If we do not, the following disaster will occur." Such an appeal to the highest levels must surely be made with relative rarity, for the officials at that level are simply too busy to tolerate being bothered with great frequency. It must surely be made only when the lower Party officials are convinced that the performance of a major plant is being seriously jeopardized or that the pattern of investment decisions is threatening to create serious imbalances in the economic development of the region or city. But when it does occur, it may be very effective.

To use the term "filter" to describe this role would probably be misleading, for the local Party organs do not (except in the cases mentioned earlier) restrict the flow of proposals upward. Rather they are more of a watchdog of regional interests, ready to point out to the highest officials when the sum of departmental decisions will result in a situation within their area detrimental to the economy. But whatever term is used to describe this activity, it is one of the more useful services performed by the local Party organs for the economy. Although the presence of the local Party organs in the appropriations process may mean that at times "political factors" (such as the connections of an obkom first secretary with top figures in the factional struggles) will sway a decision about plant location,[31] this disadvantage is counterbalanced by the need for an institution that can speak out forcefully and authoritatively when proportionate regional development is threatened. The early sovnarkhoz period demonstrates the problems that would arise from allocating industrial investment funds primarily by regional institutions (at least given the present price and incentive systems), but the economic problems cited to justify the creation of the sovnarkhozy would be much worse if there did not exist a powerful institution applying pressure to have the regional point of view taken into account.

XIII. Evolution in the Role of the Local Party Organs and in the Nature of Soviet Society

In each of the chapters of this book there has been discussion of the changes that have occurred over time in the respective roles of the local Party organs in industrial decision-making. Yet, both the organization of the book and the use of the present tense may have given the reader a clearer impression of the continuities within the Party-state relationship from one period to another than of the discontinuities. And, indeed, if this has been the impression created, so much the better. Western political scientists have been prone to exaggerate the changes in the role of the local Party organs, particularly certain types of changes.

The type of change most exaggerated in the West is the change in the center's definition of the role and the scope of the responsibilities of the local Party organs. By choosing the analogy of the prefect, I have deliberately tried to indicate that the most basic functions of the local Party organs have remained fundamentally the same during the last forty years. The 1929 decree on edinonachalie, the Malenkov speech at the Eighteenth Party Conference in 1941, the reorganization of the Party secretariat in 1948 — all these events had a much lesser impact on the role of the local Party organs in industrial decision-making than has usually been suggested. Similarly, it is quite incorrect to assert that the local Party organs first acquired responsibility for large-scale industry in 1957 or that the creation of the sovnarkhozy changed the Party apparatus into the main instrument of control over Soviet industry. It is even more inaccurate to assert that the 1962 bifurcation of the Party apparatus legitimized Party intervention in technical and production decisions for the first time or that the reunification of the Party apparatus was accompanied by a denial of the legitimacy of such intervention.

A second type of change exaggerated by Western scholars has been that in the short-term variations in the influence of the local Party organs. To be sure, short-term variations have occurred, and, in fact, are built into any prefectoral system. The substantive decisions of any prefect must and do change to reflect the changing priorities of the center. When the leadership emphasizes agricultural development, the local Party organs surely are more insistent and wide-ranging in their demands for industrial "patronage" over the farms than when (as in early 1941) the leadership is preoccupied with the industrial preparations for an impending war. Party pressure for industrial patronage over education surely took on a different intensity with the 1958 decision to promote polytechnical education. More important, local Party instructions on priorities in construction and supplies deliveries must shift somewhat as the leadership changes the emphasis placed on economic sectors such as housing and the chemical industry.

Moreover, the basis for cyclical variation in the influence of the area officials is also created by the inevitable conflict between the area and the specialized officials in any system of dual subordination. The conflict requires resolution, and there are a variety of patterns into which this resolution may fall. At one extreme, the higher officials may habitually support the specialized officials, at the other extreme the area officials. More normally, their support falls into a wide range of intermediate patterns. However, it would be self-defeating to establish a system of dual subordination in which higher officials supported either the area officials or the specialized officials in any routinized manner, and normally there is considerable fluctuation in the pattern of support over time.

Certainly, if we examine the pattern of higher Party support in cases of conflict between the local Party organs and the industrial manager, we by no means find complete uniformity. The local Party organs quite probably received more support during the Khrushchev period than during the late Stalin period, and within the Khrushchev period they were more likely to be supported in 1957 and early 1958 than between 1960 and 1962. The official "campaigns" calling either for more or less detailed Party involvement in detailed decision-making may well have been associated with changes in the frequency with which the local Party organs have been supported in their conflicts with the managers. Of course, during the sovnarkhoz period, the obkomy and the republican central committees had less need for higher support on a number of questions (although not the most important ones), and their role was thereby increased.

Although these short-term changes in the role of the local Party organs must not be ignored, their range has, however, been quite restricted. The degree of higher support for the local Party organs clearly has varied far more from case to case within any one period than it has from one period to another. In fact, this variation has been so great that it has seemed more useful to organize the discussion around different categories of cases (for example, labor disputes versus decisions about new products) than to discuss the variations chronologically. The variations over time never have changed the disadvantageous nature of the position of the local Party officials vis-à-vis higher industrial officials on such crucial aspects of industrial decision-making as planning of investment, technical policy, and product innovation.

Yet, no administrative system remains completely static over a thirty-five year period. If we take a long-range perspective and compare the situation in the mid-1960's with that in the 1930's (and even more with that in the 1920's), we notice that a number of interesting changes have occurred. In this chapter the nature and scope of these changes will be examined; in the next two chapters the implications of the change and continuity in the Party-state relationship for administrative and development theory will be discussed.

Change in the Relationship of the Local Party Organs and the Industrial Administrators

From a thirty to forty year perspective, perhaps the most basic development in the Soviet administrative system has been the increasing specialization in administrative and Party structure and personnel. As Brezhnev recognized in 1965, "The objective tendency of the development of industry consists in the fact that the different branches are becoming all the more precisely differentiated and that they develop along their own specific paths." [1] In response to this growing differentiation, the organization charts within the industrial realm have become much "fuller" and more developed than they were in the twenties and the thirties. A similar development has taken place within the local Party organs. The experiments with the so-called functional form of organization have not been repeated since 1940; instead, every Party reorganization since that time has provided for specialized industrial departments and secretaries in each of the local Party organs. Indeed, the industrial-transportation department itself often is subdivided to take account of the structure of industry in particular areas.

The differentiation in the organization charts of the Party and industrial hierarchies has been accompanied by the specialization of the personnel staffing these hierarchies. Seldom do we find an industrial manager who (like the Red Directors of the 1920's) is a general organizer and is transferred from one specialized hierarchy to another.[2] Now the biographies of the managers usually are featured by the type of orderly promotion within a specialized hierarchy that would be expected in a Weberian bureaucracy.

Consider, for example, the biography of Nikolai Tikhonov.[3] He graduated from a metallurgical engineering institute and then spent fourteen years as head of a shift, head of a shop, and chief engineer in steel plants in Dnepropetrovsk and Pervouralsk. Then from 1947 to 1950 he was a director of a steel plant, from 1950 to 1954 the head of a glavk of the USSR Ministry of Ferrous Metallurgy, and from 1954 to 1957 a Deputy Minister of Ferrous Metallurgy. In 1957 he was appointed sovnarkhoz chairman in Dnepropetrovsk (a center of the iron ore and the iron and steel industries). Beginning in 1960 he became deputy chairman successively of the USSR State Economic Council, of the USSR Gosplan, and of the USSR Council of Ministers — in each case the deputy chairman with major responsibility for planning in the iron and steel industry. Such a biography has become quite typical in the Soviet Union; in fact, if one were to criticize the preparation of the important industrial administrator, one would be most apt to charge that it is overspecialized.

A similar specialization has occurred in the background of the officials of the Party apparatus. No longer does the apparatus contain a fairly uniform group of political workers — the so-called *apparatchiki* — but instead its officials have quite dissimilar and specialized career patterns. While the first secretaries often have had a more generalized background, even these men often have been selected from among the functional specialists, their specialty depending upon the predominant branch of the economy in their area.

A survey of the last thirty years also reveals that the differentiation in structure and personnel has produced many of the other changes predicted by those who have discussed the impact of industrialization upon society.

In the first place, the specialized, "orderly" career patterns for Party and state officials reflect an increasing tendency to choose and promote officials on the basis of performance. To be sure, membership in a political party is required for appointment to many significant administrative posts, and friendship ties with higher officials are said sometimes to play an important role in personnel selection. Yet, as we have seen earlier, these "political" factors tend to be far less serious in practice than appears on the surface. The requirement of Party membership for industrial managers has really changed the nature of Party membership far more than it has introduced a particularistic element into personnel selection. Moreover, Soviet complaints about friendship and nepotism almost always cite examples from rather low priority realms of the economy — realms in which there are relatively few qualified candidates for a post in any case.

In large-scale Soviet industry, personal acquaintance and friendship undoubtedly play the same sort of role in personnel selection and promotion that they do in the Western bureaucracies — a role that can be of some importance, particularly for the highest positions. We have examined the biography of Nikolai Tikhonov and have noticed a career pattern which strongly suggests professionalization. Yet, in 1960 there undoubtedly were many capable men who could have been named deputy chairman of the State Economic Council in charge of the iron and steel industry. It probably is not a total coincidence that Tikhonov had been the director of a major plant in Dnepropetrovsk oblast (Nikopol Southern Tubing Works) during a period when Leonid Brezhnev was obkom first secretary there — the same Brezhnev who was Central Committee secretary specializing in industry from 1957 to 1960. Nor is it likely to have been a coincidence that Tikhonov became deputy chairman of the Council of Ministers shortly after Brezhnev became First Secretary.

Personal acquaintance almost always must have a role in the selection of higher officials, if for no other reason than that it often is through personal contact that one man come to recognize the ability of another. But even if an official's choice of subordinates is somewhat restricted by the limits of his knowledge of lower personnel, a man who rises to become a high official has had contacts with many persons. Those whom he promotes may well be those among his acquaintances whose performance he evaluates most highly; indeed, it may well have been exceptional performance that led to the subordinate being noticed in the first place.

In all, the evidence still strongly suggests that the selection of personnel for important industrial posts is basically conducted on the basis of a proverb once cited by Khrushchev: "Friendship is friendship, but business is business." [4] The "intense career achievement orientation" which John Armstrong noted in the Soviet manager would not have been developed if there had not been a strong correlation between performance and promotion. [5]

A second change associated with the differentiation in personnel and structure — and a logical corollary of promotion on the basis of performance — has been the development of some informal and partial sense of tenure within the industrial service. The Soviet administrative system has been too strongly oriented towards performance norms for the concept of rigid seniority (or of a flat salary for a position) to be adopted, and an industrial administrator has no guarantee at all that he will never be demoted. However, except for the man who reaches the level of Deputy Chairman of the Council of Ministers, an industrial official seems rarely to be removed from the service (unless he is given a post in the Party apparatus or the like or is retired for reasons of health or age). It is even rare for him to be demoted more than one or two levels in the hierarchy unless he has committed a serious criminal act. And this was basically the case not only in the Khrushchev and post-Khrushchev period, but also to a very considerable extent in the last decade of the Stalin period. (An exception in the late Stalin period was the radical demotion of a number of Jewish directors around 1950, apparently for reasons that had little to do with rational-technical criteria.)

Just one sign of the development of the sense of tenure is the often-mentioned phenomenon of a man being removed from a post in Party nomenklatura and then almost always being given another post in Party nomenklatura (and expecting such treatment). And it is a phenomenon to be anticipated if promotion is predicated on competence. If those at a given level in a hierarchy have been promoted from among the most capable at the next lowest level, there usually is little reason to demote an administrator at that level more than one rung if his performance proves unsatisfactory.

A sense of tenure has been much slower to develop in the Party apparatus, but even here career patterns have become somewhat more stable. The difficulties in achieving fulfillment of the agricultural plan (and the manipulations in reporting to which this has led) have posed a major danger for the local Party officials, and the struggles for power among the Politburo members seem frequently to have involved them. Yet, since the purge of 1948–49 there has been a substantial tendency for those removed from local Party work to be given other fairly significant work. A fallen obkom first secretary may turn up as an ambassador, a lower official in the system of state or Party control, a chairman or deputy chairman of an oblispolkom, a director of a scientific institute, or a lower obkom secretary in another oblast.

A third change in the relationship of the local Party organs and the industrial managers has been in the spirit of Party work. One finds much less talk to the effect that "Bolshevik will" conquers all — that "objective conditions" cannot be used as an excuse for failure. Khrushchev himself warned Party secretaries to listen to the advice of specialists, and his successors have been much more insistent in their denunciation of "subjectivism" in decision-making. Even in ideological work, the agitator has undergone specialization, and the Stakhanov who produces an improbable number of tons of coal a day or the man who calls for impossibly high socialist obligations is no longer the hero that he was in the 1930's.

In all, there has been a movement, often halting, towards the establishment of a Party-state relationship that is basically orderly and "rational." In the organizational realm, as we have seen, there is not nearly so much disorder and confusion as might appear to a person looking at the organization chart from the outside. From below — that is, from the point of view of the lower officials — things seem much more well-ordered, and the spheres of jurisdiction do not appear so ill-defined. The Soviet administrator seems to know the relative authority of his various superiors, and he has a good sense of the type and importance of problems which each superior usually handles. Even when conflict is built into the system, there seem to exist fairly clear conceptions of the ways it is to be resolved if those with overlapping jurisdictions cannot reach agreement.

Despite all the talk about the "directing" role of the Party, the different Party officials have actually been granted quite varied authority, and this variation is easily explicable in terms of a desire for a system in which there is a reasonable relationship between function and legal authority and between legal authority and rational authority. If the specialized officials of the local Party organs and the secretaries of the primary Party organizations had the authority to obligate the economic administrators to take action, then, indeed, this would often result in the supplanting of one specialist by another (and often less qualified) one. It is only the bureau and the first secretary — that is, the only Party organ and the only official with the overall perspective to be a coordinating prefect — who have the authority to obligate the functional specialists. And, of course, even this authority is limited by the requirement that the Party organs work within the framework of the directives flowing down the chains of command in the functional hierarchies.

As a result, the ambiguity in authority and function between the Party officials and the industrial administrators has been most pronounced in the planning process — the realm in which the advantages of a freer flow of information and of a conflict in ideas make the overlap most functional. In those cases in which it is most vital that legal authority be unquestioned (for example, when an immediate decision or immediate execution is required), the responsible industrial or Party official usually has that authority.

Of course, the memory of some of the reorganizations of the late Khrushchev period is too fresh in mind to even think of suggesting that the movement towards an orderly administrative system has been an unswerving one. However, the fact cannot be ignored that Khrushchev's associates did feel compelled to take the unprecedented step of removing the First Secretary. To the extent that Khrushchev's "harebrained" administrative schemes were a factor in his removal, even the administrative disorder of the early 1960's, or at least its consequences, may be cited as evidence that there has been an overall trend towards orderliness in the system.

Evolution in the Soviet Society:
The Development of a Rational-Technical Society

As the opening pages of this book indicate, the question which provided the original stimulus for the study was: are there changes in the relationship of the Party officials and the economic managers that illuminate trends in the evolution of Soviet society? Although the focus of the book has been substantially changed in the course of the study, the original question still is relevant. In fact, what does the changing relationship of the local Party organs and the industrial administrators suggest about the evolution of Soviet society?

In order to focus the examination of this question and in order to prepare the ground for an analysis of several more general propositions about political development and administrative theory in the concluding two chapters, I will organize the discussion within the framework of the most successful model of Soviet society — Barrington Moore's model of rational-technical society. Specifically I will ask: Does the study indicate that "the technical-rational and formal legal features that exist in the Soviet system [have] come to predominate over the totalitarian ones"? [6] Has the Soviet Union moved far toward approximating the following type of society:

> The end result can be imagined as a technocracy — the rule of the technically competent. By definition, such a development would imply a heavy reduction of emphasis on the power of the dictator and its replacement by technical and rational criteria of behavior and organization. The share in power and prestige held by the instruments of violence and persuasion, the secret police and the Party, would decline. That of the industrial manager, the engineer, and the technical administrator would rise. The roles of the political and the technical administrators would be reversed,

in that the instruments of violence and persuasion would become the servants of the technocratic rulers, persuading "backward" elements of the population that industrialization really benefited them. . . .

Freed from continued political interference, administrative officials would be secure to enjoy the perquisites of office so long as they continued to perform their duties skillfully and accurately. Promotion in the bureaucratic hierarchy would be according to demonstrated merit. . . .

The mass of the population would receive a larger flow of goods and services than is now the case, but would not have a significantly larger share in the decisions determining their fate. . . . Though the power of the central authorities would remain very great, enforced conformity to a code of law would replace the present device of frequent shake-ups in the administrative apparatus as a means through which power and authority were exercised.[7]

In many ways the model of rational-technical society has stood the test of time rather well. Published in 1954, it was by far the most successful model of its time in predicting the major developments in the post-Stalin political system. In fact, it was even more successful than might seem on the surface, for Moore was careful to suggest that "probably the readily discernible movement in this direction will stop somewhere short of its logical culmination." [8]

The administrative changes discussed in the last section also correspond well to the predictions of the rational-technical model. The differentiation in structure and personnel was taken for granted by the model. The growing technical competence of the Party officials, the taking of personnel action on the basis of performance, the increasing frequency of the calls for "objective" decisions and for deference to technical advice, and the development of a basically orderly administrative system all are directly in line with its expectations.

Moore was not at all clear in specifying what would happen in rational-technical society when the specialists disagreed among themselves. However, the implicit answer of the model would seem to be that explicitly given by Almond and Powell in their analysis of a secular political culture. The conflicts in interest and perspectives presumably would be resolved through the "bargaining and accommodative political action [which] become a common feature of society." [9] If this assumption is correct, then one might also cite the general bargaining behavior and approach of the local Party secretaries in industrial decision-making as additional evidence of the movement of Soviet society towards the rational-technical model.

Moreover, if this book has been correct in explaining the evolving role of the local Party organs largely as a response to the needs of a well-functioning administrative system, it has lent support to the assertion that "industrialization exerts very strong pressures toward creating a society such as this." [10] Or, at least, it would support the assertion that the determination to promote rapid industrial growth results in the emergence of such pressures.

Yet, despite its evolution, the Soviet political system continues to deviate from the rational-technical model in many significant ways. This is not the place for a comprehensive discussion of the political system as a whole, but even in the relationship which we have been examining, there continue to be three major deviations from the model.

The first such deviation has been the persistence of administrative practices that are not adequately summarized in the phrase "enforced conformity to law." When Moore discussed "the rational-technical model of decision-making and problem-solving relationships," he pointed to the ship as "the epitome of the rational-technical model" — or at least the ship with the following administrative system: "On such a vessel, the captain has very wide authority, but there the resemblance to a dictatorship ceases. The subordinates of the captain, down to the lowliest member of the crew, have clearly defined spheres of competence. Each man has a job to do and a specified way in which he is supposed to do it. The chain of command, symbolized in uniforms and titles of rank, is clear to all concerned. Neither those in positions of authority nor those who carry out orders may violate the chain of command by skipping over one of its links." [11]

In his study of Soviet management in the 1930's, David Granick emphasized the absence in the Soviet administrative system of an atmosphere of predictability based on precise enforcement of precise rules.[12] In this respect at least the Soviet Union of the mid-1960's is not strikingly different. Instead of "clearly defined spheres of competence," one finds the overlapping Party-state relationship; instead of an "enforced conformity to the rule of law," one still finds that a manager cannot "get along without law violations." And there has been no lessening in the insistence that any citizen, any lower official may carry a complaint or suggestion "right up to the Central Committee" and that the Party officials have the duty of responding to these appeals, regardless of the number of levels in the chain of command that must be skipped.

A second deviation from the rational-technical model is the continuing vigor of the local Party organs' participation in industrial decision-making. To be sure, Moore focused his attention upon the criteria by which decisions are made (that is, whether power, rationality, or tradition is the dominant criterion) rather than upon the institutions making the decisions. However, the model did predict a decline in "the share in power and prestige held by the instruments of violence and persuasion, the secret police and the Party" and did suggest that the administrators would be "freed from continued political interference."

In reality, of course, the local Party organs remain much more than an "instrument of persuasion." Jeremy Azrael has analyzed the difficulties faced by the upper managerial elite in shaping even the policy followed with respect to industrial development,[13] and this study furnishes little evidence that the managers have emancipated themselves from political control at the provincial level. While the growing complexity of society has made effective Party supervision of the economy more difficult, this problem has been at least partially overcome by the rising level of technical competence within the Party apparatus. The Party officials have continued to have an impact even on specialized decisions, and their intervention, while usually rational in terms of other considerations, is often an arbitrary one in terms of the professional standards, the regulations, and the interests of the officials directly involved.

A third deviation — or at least partial deviation — from the rational-technical model is the political power function that continues to be served by the local Party organs. Although the decisions of the local Party organs have usually been guided by rational-technical considerations, these decisions sometimes must reflect the fact that they also are assigned responsibility for political stability. If the local Party officials normally apply rational-technical criteria in personnel selection, it is because the factor of loyalty seldom needs to be taken into account. If the first secretaries tend to neglect ideological work, it is because other means of socialization have become increasingly effective. But if an administrator needs to be reminded of some basic "truth" as the Party defines it, the Party secretaries have the possibility of reminding him. If he persistently ignores such reminders, the Party secretaries are in a position to apply nontechnical criteria in personnel selection.

Even when the Party secretaries do not consciously take "power" considerations into account in decision-making, they still undoubtedly serve to fortify the power position of the Party leadership. The more important the administrative or political position, the more the rational-technical criteria for selecting a man to occupy it become such vague concepts as "good judgment" and "wisdom." As C. Wright Mills has emphasized, bureaucratic superiors may find it quite difficult to credit good judgment to a man with politically suspect views, even if these superiors have no conscious desire to discriminate against him on account of his unorthodoxy.

Moreover, the mere presence of the local Party organs in the administrative process, combined with the requirement of Party membership for a successful managerial career, also contributes in indirect ways to the likelihood that the managers have a world view quite unlike that of, say, the American managerial elite — a world view in line with that desired by the political elite. In particular, the realization that the approval of the Party organs is required for appointment to the important posts surely affects the career choices of many of those who are politically disaffected, and it must restrain the speech and actions of the politically disaffected who do embark on a managerial career.

There has, therefore, been only a partial evolution of the Soviet political system in the direction of the rational-technical model. The crucial question is: what is the meaning of these deviations? Are they but an indication of the gradual nature of the impact of industrialization upon the political process and of the transitional character of the present stage of Soviet development? Or do they reflect more basic problems within the rational-technical model itself?

Certainly, it is within the realm of possibility that the Soviet Union will continue to evolve in the direction of the rational-technical model. Clearly the bargaining behavior that we have seen within the administrative system has already diffused to some extent through the policy-making process. In the Khrushchev period the Soviet leadership adopted a more pragmatic attitude in problem solving and was more willing to encourage competition and bargaining within the "monolithic" Party and bureaucracy. Increasingly, the representatives of the various interests have been permitted to seek support for their positions through appeals in the open press. At a minimum, Khrushchev's emphasis upon persuasion rather than compulsion implied some bargaining in policy-making, and some (not including this observer) would even assert that the Presidium decisions in the Khrushchev period were the product of a fairly free bargaining process. In the post-Khrushchev period, the Soviet leaders have placed even greater emphasis upon the need for "objective" decision-making, and the decisions that emerged in the first four years after Khrushchev's removal corresponded closely to those which might have been expected to result from bargaining among the major centers of power.

That the bargaining attitudes and behavior present in the administrative system should have diffused into the policy realms is not surprising. Most speculation on the agencies of change within the Soviet Union has focused on the industrial managers and the rationality supposedly inculcated by the industrial processes, but more attention should be given to the probable consequences of the assignment of the prefectoral role to the local Party organs. This role has virtually required the first secretaries in the republics, oblasti, and cities — even those of the Stalin period — to acquire a balancing, incremental perspective on many issues and to develop bargaining techniques. Or, at least, this role has meant that those without these perspectives surely have soon been selected out of these key positions. The fact that the republican and obkom first secretaries have been the major group from which the Soviet leadership has been chosen in the post-Stalin period (they constitute, for example, nine of the eleven voting members of the 1967 Politburo) may be quite important in explaining the political changes that have taken place. As these men moved into the central leadership posts, it would have been surprising if they had shed completely the habits and attitudes of a long career.

It is not difficult to imagine how this tendency might continue. The Party "line" may become even broader and more ill-defined. The conviction may grow that no major institutional center should "lose" completely in a policy conflict, and, as a result, these centers may acquire the characteristics of "veto groups." The political leaders may increasingly perceive of themselves as brokers rather than as guardians of the scientific truth, even as brokers who have the duty of seeing that "the armistice agreements signed by the negotiators fall within the high-ranking preferences of the greater number of citizens." [14] Even if no fundamental changes are made in the electoral system, the Soviet Union conceivably might develop the type of one-party democracy often seen as possible in Africa; [15] in fact, it should not be forgotten that the Soviet press has published proposals that the Party permit the nomination of several candidates in some elections.

Yet, although a development towards a pluralistic democracy of some type is possible, it is premature to predict its inevitability on the basis of the present evidence, particularly on the basis of the evidence of this study. On the contrary, there are a number of reasons to question the probability of such a development in the near or the intermediate future.

One of the most important facts about the evolution of the relationship of the local Party organs and the industrial administrators is the difference in conclusions that emerges from taking a fifteen-year perspective rather than a thirty- to forty-year perspective. Most of the changes discussed in this chapter had already taken place by the time of Stalin's death or were well on their way to doing so, and in the last fifteen years there actually has been only moderate movement towards the rational-technical model in the relationship we have been studying. The important political changes in the post-Stalin period have come in other realms. In essence, they have involved the spread of the bargaining, accommodative attitudes and the increasing professionalization already apparent in lower industrial administration to other parts of the administrative system and to some extent to the policy-making process.

Although the local Party organ-managerial relationship has evolved somewhat more closely to the rational-technical model in the last fifteen years (for example, the increase in the technical qualifications of the Party officials), there are very few signs that the three basic deviations from the model are tending to become less significant. If anything, Party involvement in the planning and investment spheres of industrial decision-making increased in the post-Stalin period, and the relative decline in the priority given heavy industry by the post-Stalin leaders surely affected the determination with which the local Party officials have insisted that nonindustrial criteria be taken into account in managerial decisions. If the Soviet leadership relies increasingly upon market mechanisms and delegates more autonomy in investment decision-making to the plant level, it is highly probable that the local Party organs will have an even larger impact upon basic investment, planning decisions.

The question is — why have the three deviations been so resistant to change in recent years? Is it simply that complete evolution in the prefectoral system is likely to come only in the last stages of an evolution towards a rational-technical society? Does it reflect the fact that political leaders beginning to reach policy decisions through a bargaining process would want to retain a prefect at first in order to ensure that the bargains struck in the center were actually reflected in the policy administered in the policies?

Or, does the failure of the role of the local Party organs to evolve more rapidly indicate the likely limits of its in-system evolution and thereby foretell limits in the likely evolution of the overall political process? Does it suggest that, even if the Party secretaries develop a bargaining perspective, they have little interest in strengthening the bargaining position of the mass of the population or the specialized hierarchies and that they retain the ability to defend the interests they consider most basic?

Ultimately, the answer to both of these sets of questions can be provided only by history, for both point to quite possible explanations. It certainly is true that one would expect abandonment of the prefectoral system to come late in any evolution towards a pluralistic one-party system, if indeed it came at all. It is also true, as we have seen, that the Party apparatus retains powerful weapons in its hands and that evolution towards a more pluralistic political system may move much, much more slowly as it approaches the point where the Party secretaries see it not simply as an aid to the more rational formulation of Party policy, but as a threat to the supremacy of the Party apparatus itself. A study limited to the local Party organs does not provide a very sound basis for judging which of these possibilities is the accurate one.

However, if the three deviations from the rational-technical model do not point with certainty to the future course of Soviet development, they do, I think, still have a broader significance. The particular nature of the deviations reflects the distinctive features of the Soviet political system, but the particular deviations are only manifestations of several basic problems with the rational-technical model — problems that inevitably mean that there will be analogous deviations in any society. In the first place, the administrative aspects of the model are based upon a model of bureaucracy that does not meet the test of rational-technical criteria: that of being "an effective way of getting results." In the second place, the model is based on a conception of rationality that neglects a number of important phenomena in the political process. If we understand these problems more fully, we are in much better position to trace possible courses of Soviet development.

XIV. The Monistic Model of Organization and Development Administration

Throughout this book we have examined an administrative system whose structure has differed significantly from that found in the model of rational-technical society. Yet, the local Party organs have been interpreted not as an intrusive element that interferes with the effective operation of the administrative system, but as an integral part of the system — one which, in fact, has played an important role in promoting its effective operation. To the extent that this analysis has been correct, it raises serious questions about the administrative system posited in the rational-technical model.

The Monistic Model of Organization and the Soviet Administrative System

The administrative system of rational-technical society corresponds very closely to that which American "conventional wisdom" has considered the optimal form of organizational structure. It is infused with what Victor Thompson has called the "monistic concept" of organization.[1] This concept — advanced by the administrative theorists of the first three decades of the twentieth century — has emphasized the importance of a strict line of command with a precise definition of the duties of each official in the hierarchy. In the words of the Hoover Commission Report, "the exercise of authority is impossible without a clear line of command from top to bottom, and a return line of responsibility and accountability from the bottom to the top."[2] Associated with this conception have been a series of assumptions about the need for a professional, politically neutral administrative staff with guaranteed tenure — assumptions that underlay the long struggle for a civil service uninfluenced by patronage considerations.

The administrative system of the rational-technical model also has much in common with the bureaucratic ideal-type developed by Weber:

(1) [The officials] are personally free and subject to authority only with respect to their impersonal official obligations.

(2) They are organized in a clearly defined hierarchy of offices.

(3) Each office has a clearly defined sphere of competence in the legal sense.

(4) The office is filled by a free contractual relationship. Thus, in principle, there is free selection.

(5) Candidates are selected on the basis of technical qualifications. In the most rational case, this is tested by examination or guaranteed by diplomas certifying technical training, or both. They are *appointed,* not elected.

(6) They are remunerated by fixed salaries in money, for the most part with a right to pensions. Only under certain circumstances does the employing authority, especially in private organizations, have a right to terminate the appointment, but the official is always free to resign. The salary scale is primarily graded according to rank in the hierarchy; but in addition to this criterion, the responsibility of the position and the requirements of the incumbent's social status may be taken into account.

(7) The office is treated as the sole, or at least the primary, occupation of the incumbent.

(8) It constitutes a career. There is a system of "promotion" according to seniority or to achievement or both. Promotion is dependent on the judgment of superiors.

(9) The official works entirely separated from ownership of the means of administration and without appropriation of his position.

(10) He is subject to strict and systematic discipline and control in the conduct of the office.[3]

Although Weber did not set for himself the task of advising "the prince," it is easy to draw the inference that the more closely an administrative structure approaches the ideal type, the more effectively it will be able to fulfill its mission.[4] In fact, despite his fears about bureaucracy, Weber himself was sometimes almost lyrical in his descriptions of its effectiveness: "Experience tends universally to show that the purely bureaucratic type of administrative organization — that is, the monocratic variety of bureaucracy — is, from a purely technical point of view, capable of attaining the highest degree of efficiency and is in this sense formally the most rational known means of carrying out imperative control over human beings. It is superior to any other form in precision, in stability, in the stringency of its discipline, and in its reliability. It thus makes possible a particularly high degree of calculability of results for the heads of the organization and for those acting in relation to it. . . . For the needs of mass administration today, it is completely indispensable." [5]

Scholars have long recognized that the monistic model does not reflect the real world accurately and that organizational behavior is shaped by many other values than those of efficiency and discipline. It has, of course, been the deviations of the Soviet administrative system from the model that have led many to speak of "what appears to the Westerner as rampart particularism and irrationality" in the Soviet system.

However, contemporary specialists on administrative theory and comparative government have tended to assume — consciously or unconsciously — that the monistic model does represent the kind of organization that — if feasible — would most efficiently fulfill the goals and directives of the men at the top of the organization. Hence the deviations from the monistic model have been interpreted as resulting not from the requirements of an effectively functioning organization, but from other factors. In the case of the Soviet Union, for example, the deviations have usually been treated as a reflection of a desire of the leadership to increase its political power and to maintain its political control of the administrative system. In the words of the foremost American scholar on the Soviet Union, "The leaders of the regime guard their power jealously. They are willing to forgo the advantages of a single, clearly defined administrative hierarchy, and they blur lines of authority by multiplying controls at every point of the government structure." [6]

If this book has been correct in insisting that the desire for political control is not the sole explanation for the deviations of the Soviet administrative system from the monistic model, then it is not enough to say that reality and the model often do not coincide. We must also recognize that in many circumstances the "single, clearly defined administrative hierarchy" has few, if any advantages as an administrative instrument. In many circumstances an organization based on the monistic model simply could not effectively carry out the mission assigned it by its leadership — even if other values could be completely ignored. Many of the Soviet deviations from the model constitute an answer to real problems of large-scale organizations — problems that must receive some analogous answers in any large organization if it is effectively to fulfill the tasks given it.

Effectiveness in Development Administration

When a model has a wide and prolonged popularity, it is axiomatic that the model illuminates the real world in many ways. Clearly it would be wrong to suggest that there is no relationship between the various features of the monistic model and the structure of an effectively functioning organization. Otherwise, Simon would not have had to complain about the difficulty of erasing what he called "the proverbs of administration" from our consciousness.[7]

Weber was certainly correct in insisting that many of the benefits of modern society have required the growth of large organizations with a detailed division of labor and with the staff selected on the basis of technical qualifications. Moreover, these organizations are based on a network of rules and commands that often do produce great predictability in the work of men many miles and many organizational levels removed from those at the top of the organization. The discretion of the lower social security official is often limited to the determination of the category to which a person should be. assigned, and hopefully a citizen would receive identical treatment in every office in the country. The clerk in the post office does, indeed, "follow the book" in making his decisions. In the industrial realm the worker on the assembly line is extremely restricted in the decisions he makes on the job. Even many professionals who have some independence from direct commands and precise rules may be effectively controlled by their professional training and standards.

In these cases (particularly the first ones mentioned), the responsibilities of the office can be routinized to a sufficient extent to permit the "constant use of categorization whereby individual problems and cases are classified on the basis of designated criteria and are treated accordingly." [8] And in these cases the Weberian ideal-type is a reasonable approximation of the type of organization that is required for executing the wishes of those at the top of the organization in an effective manner.

However, there are officials whose responsibilities are very difficult to routinize. These are the officials who must take a large number of variables into account in making decisions and who must be content with "satisficing." [9] These are the officials who must supervise a variety of subordinates with greater technical knowledge than themselves and who often must mediate among these subordinates. These are the officials whose own decisions in specific cases cannot always be programmed by guidelines established by their superiors. The position of such officials resembles that suggested in the bureaucratic ideal-type in a very rough way, but in their case precise administration on the basis of precise rules is either impossible or dysfunctional. If an attempt is made to establish a network of precise rules — or, rather, if an attempt is made to enforce strict adherence to such a network — the consequences may be disastrous.[10]

This is certainly not the place to develop an elaborate typology of bureaucracies, but for comparative purposes it is worth looking at a brief discussion of the routinization and categorization that can be involved in specialized administration: "Although an individual is to himself a total, complete person, in some ways unique, to the specialist he is a carrier of a class of data relevant to the practice of the specialty in question. He is a speeder, an income-tax evader, a disciplinary case, an applicant for a job, a coronary, etc." [11]

If one thinks of the men who deal with "a speeder, an income-tax evader, a disciplinary case, an applicant for a job, a coronary" — as well as of the lower social security official, the post office clerk, and the assembly line worker mentioned above — one notices several striking differences between them and the officials who have been the subject of this book. In the first place, the former are men who supervise few, if any, other men (except, perhaps, a few clerks or secretaries) — men who work at the very bottom level of their hierarchy. They may be associated with a very large organization, but in conventional American speech they normally would not be called "officials." In the second place, these men are not basically engaged in activities that would be classified as "development administration." They are not engaged in "carrying out planned change in the economy (in agriculture or industry, or the capital infrastructure supporting either of these) and, to a lesser extent, in the social services of the state (especially education and public health)." [12] In a few cases (for example, the assembly line worker) they may work for an organization that carries out development functions, but their own job is not to develop a program, to introduce change, and so forth.

Yet, there are many organizational levels in a large organization, and many of the most interesting problems in administrative theory concern the officials who do have substantial supervisory and developmental responsibilities. The head of a bureau, the head of a subsection, the manager of a plant of a large corporation or ministry, the director of a city office of a national or state department — each of these men often has duties that are very difficult to define in precise rules. He has the crucial task of selecting — in fact, often of recruiting — personnel for posts that are too nonroutinized to permit selection on the basis of examination or other precise criteria, and he must be ready to make the hard decision to replace a mediocre subordinate. He must develop the "art" (a revealing word) of maintaining high motivation and reasonable harmony among his subordinates. He often is assigned such general and vaguely defined tasks as "the development and introduction of new technology"; he may be expected to provide his superiors with policy advice and even with comprehensive plans for new projects. At a minimum he must represent his unit in appropriations struggles. In a democracy he may actually be delegated the real responsibility for resolving political conflicts that could not be fully resolved at higher levels.[13]

Of course, the middle-level official is subject to a variety of different types of rules and directives. There may well be rules that dictate what he should do in certain situations. (For example, the Soviet manager has precise instructions about the formal procedures to be followed in requesting supply chits and about the length of vacations to be awarded to workers with different lengths of service.) There also may be rules that prohibit him from taking some action or that establish limits beyond which he may not go. (An example of the former would be a law forbidding the hiring of persons under a certain age; an example of the latter might be the establishment of a general wage limit that the manager would not be permitted to exceed.) In production-like situations, it is also quite usual, Weber notwithstanding, for an official to receive specific directives or commands that tell him precisely what to do in a particular case. (The Soviet director may be told in categorical terms to produce or deliver a particular item immediately, while he himself may hold a morning "dispatching session" in which he outlines the day's priorities to his immediate subordinates, themselves middle-level officials.)

However, it still is hardly accurate to speak of the predictability of the actions of a middle-level official in the same way that one speaks of the predictability of the actions of a post office clerk. In practice, he may be given one major and general "rule" that summarizes the main mission of his job; he may be given very considerable autonomy in deciding how to fulfill this mission; and he then may be controlled primarily through an evaluation of the results he achieves. A classic example would be that found in American professional sports. The manager or the coach receives very few instructions about proper strategy from the owners or the general manager, but he knows that a low position in the final standings will seldom be tolerated, particularly on a year-by-year basis.

A less extreme and more typical example is that which we have been examining in this book. The Soviet manager receives direct commands and must work within the framework of positive and negative general rules, but his major "rule" always has remained "fulfill your gross output plan" (or, now, "fulfill your gross sales plan"). It is understood that other rules may at times be sacrificed in the interests of the major rule; for, as the Soviet press makes clear, usually "the winners are not judged" (*pobeditelei ne sudiat*). Indeed, the ideal towards which many Soviet economists have been striving is the creation of a system in which there is less need for direct commands, detailed rules, and detailed indicators and in which a single criterion (profitability) can be developed that will permit greater managerial discretion by providing a clear standard by which managers can guide their actions and can be judged.

Any attempt to develop a realistic model of an effective organization ("effective" being defined in terms of the organization's ability to fulfill the tasks assigned it by those at its head) must take into account the differences in administrative positions that we have discussed. Specifically, it must recognize that the more the office entails the performance of nonroutinized, developmental responsibilities, the more the requirements of effective administration deviate from the Weberian ideal-type and the conventional monistic model. The model of effective development administration must include a number of these deviations among its most basic features. [Here again we are using John Montgomery's definition of development administration: "Development administration is . . . defined as carrying out planned change in the economy (in agriculture or industry, or the capital infrastructure supporting either of these) and, to a lesser extent, in the social services of the state (especially education and public health)." [14]]

In the first place, a model of effective development administration must emphasize the need to judge officials more by their ability to fulfill the basic mission of their office rather than simply by the degree to which they adhere strictly to the rules. While the model must make provision for great predictability on a number of counts (particularly in the way lower employees are treated), it should place less weight upon the values of precision and predictability than upon those of creativity, initiative, and discretion.

Or, at a minimum, the model must recognize an inevitable and desirable tension between the need to permit maximum discretion to lower officials and the need to curb undesirable practices or unpredictabilities. The model should be infused with a spirit akin to what Dalton calls "the iron law of American bureaucratic practice": "There's always a way to get around the rule — look for it." [15] It should perhaps recognize the need for periodic campaigns in which the leaders emphasize the enforcement of certain rules that become too widely neglected. However, strict discipline should be emphasized only to the extent found in the Soviet concept of edinonachalie — that is, strict discipline when there is a direct command either to take some action or to adhere to a particular rule in a specific case.

In the second place, a model of development bureaucracy must include among the criteria for personnel selection not only technical qualifications, but also certain political and psychological values as well. Of course, this is not a complete departure from the Weberian ideal-type, for the ideal-type does not assume that administrators are value-free. Specifically, it assumes that the lower officials will have a strong conception of duty and a dedication to performance. While the ideal-type takes these values so much for granted that it does not include an incentive pay system or dismissal for mediocre performance, American advisers to Asian and African governments have long ago discovered that these values are not a universal aspect of human nature.

In development administration, however, it is important that administrators have other values than simply a sense of duty. Even the political values of the middle-level and many of the lower-level officials may be of crucial relevance for the effectiveness of the administrative system. It is fine to say that an administrator should serve any political master with "equal contempt," but in many situations this is a utopian ideal. If an administrator must try to achieve the substantive goals set by the men at the top without the aid of precise guidelines, then there are several reasons why he needs a deep understanding of, and general sympathy for, the program he is administering.

If the values of the administrators are strikingly different from those of the leadership, the most obvious danger is that the discretionary actions of these men often may not correspond to the expectations of those at higher levels. More important, however, the very probability of deviation is almost certain to produce a whole series of countermeasures that impair the effectiveness of development administration. In particular, if the leaders' confidence in their subordinates is undermined, the leaders will have a strong tendency to rely on very restrictive rules even in those circumstances in which it would normally be more functional to judge subordinates by results. They will find it very difficult to establish the atmosphere of permissible rule violation "for the sake of production" that is so vital to development administration.

For this reason the requirement that administrators share many of the political values of the leadership is far from unique to the Soviet system. As we have noted, loyalty oaths in the American government serve (in a less rigorous way) somewhat the same functions as Communist Party membership does in the Soviet Union. Of even greater significance is the tendency — emphasized by C. Wright Mills — for higher administrators unconsciously to take political attitudes into account as they evaluate whether a candidate for promotion has the "good judgment" that higher positions will require. Indeed, in the United States there often are fairly automatic mechanisms that produce a considerable degree of congruence between the values of the individual administrator and the values incorporated in the mission of the organization. Thus, it was normal for a Nixon to leave the WPA because of ideological uneasiness about its work and for liberals to leave the National Labor Relations Board after it become more pro-management with the passage of the Taft-Hartley Law in 1948.[16]

A model of effective development bureaucracy must emphasize not only the sympathy of administrators with the values incorporated in the program of their organization but also such psychological values as "drive" and dynamism. In a routinizable administrative situation, a sense of duty (and punishment for deriliction of it) may be sufficient to ensure adequate job performance. However, this is not enough for an official in a more nonroutinizable position, particularly one that entails the carrying out of a developmental program or substantial planning activities.

It may be vital that developmental officials have the sense of "calling" and the rationalizing drive that Weber saw arising from the Protestant Ethic in Western Europe. It is probably not a coincidence that rapid industrialization has been achieved thus far in only two countries outside Western Europe (and the areas in which European colonists became the predominant element in the population) — two countries, the Soviet Union and Japan, whose value systems have many important functional equivalents to the Protestant Ethic.[17]

A third feature of a model of development bureaucracy must be the use of incentive pay for positions in which there is a vagueness in the rule system and in which a significant part of the job is of a non-routinizable nature. Coupled with this must be a refusal to grant unconditional tenure, at least in a particular post. In any administrative system there will be no guarantee of tenure for a man who is guilty of "rank insubordination" and "willful disregard of regulations." Hence in a situation in which an official is expected to engage in a certain amount of rule violation, rule violation should not be the only way in which his performance can harm his career. As in the Soviet Union, the major danger to him should be the "violation" of the general rule incorporating the organization's mission. It is also highly desirable that significant material rewards flow from success in meeting this general rule, particularly if the "rule" calls for the exercise of creative initiative in the planning process.

It should be noted that the Soviet administrative system is not alone in following such a pay and tenure policy. In the American organizations that have spearheaded economic development, employees whose performance is not satisfactory have often been subject to dismissal. Supervisory personnel in particular have seldom had tenure in these organizations. Moreover, real annual salary (including bonuses and gains from stock options) have frequently been dependent upon performance, again particularly for supervisory personnel. The stock option has been an especially brilliant device, which rewards not only the achievement of current earnings but also the pursuit of policies that give promise of a growth of earnings in the future.[18]

A fourth feature of a model of development administration must be an organizational structure that incorporates the principle of "dual supervision" or at least sanctions behavior in accordance with that principle. A straight line-of-command implies a system relying either on direct commands or precise rules, indeed one in which the work is sufficiently routinized and simple that it is comprehensible to all the "line" officials. It becomes almost completely dysfunctional in large-scale organizations in which even some of an administrator's subordinates have jobs whose supervision requires an expertise that he does not have. For example, as Herbert Simon has noted, "If an accountant in a school department is subordinate to an educator, and if unity of command is observed, then the finance department cannot issue direct orders to him regarding the technical, accounting aspects of his work." [19] Even if the relationship between a lower technical specialist and his counterparts in the "staff" at the higher level does not include the issuing of direct orders, technical advice from above will — and should — carry real authority with it.

Dual supervision is required not only to facilitate supervision of lower-level specialists but also to promote a greater flow of information upwards. As indicated in Chapter IV, one of the major problems faced by the top officials in any large organization is that of receiving sufficient information about conditions in the field and a sufficient number of suggestions about needed changes in policies. The more monocratic an organization is, the greater the chance that one official in the chain of command will be able to block information and suggestions he considers harmful or irrelevant. By increasing the number of lines of communications upwards, a system of dual supervision increases the probability that information and suggestions will reach officials who require them.

Dual supervision is an inherent part of any organization, but it becomes especially important in an organization involved in development administration. There is a particular likelihood that such an organization will employ a number of different types of specialists to handle different aspects of its project — indeed, that it may have a variety of specialized units for this purpose — and that the line officials in the organization will be confronted with a difficult supervisory task. Moreover, such an organization almost invariably has large-scale planning responsibilities and therefore a special need for mechanisms to improve the flow of information upwards. It is not accidental that the concept of "dual supervision" was advanced in a study of the first American effort to establish an extremely large governmental organization with developmental responsibilities — the WPA.[20]

In a system of dual supervision, as we have seen, a number of relationships are possible between the different superiors. Within a single organization it is more usual for the subordination of the "staff" officials to their counterparts at a higher level to be less formalized than their subordination to the "line" official directly supervising them. Nevertheless, whatever the formal organization chart, when the line official's job becomes more one of supervising specialized officials and units than of supervising line officials who duplicate his responsibilities at a lower level, he often becomes something of a "prefect" within the organization, performing many of the same functions performed by the local Party organs and limited by many of the same factors that restrict their role.

Although the authority of the line official is much eroded when he is required to supervise men and units with greater technical expertise than his own, he still has a very important role to play because of the differences in perspectives, interests, and professional standards among those specialists and even in the directives they receive from above. On a day-to-day basis, conflicts among specialists are most often resolved by mutual give-and-take,[21] but there still must be a coordinating figure who has the perspective to represent the interests of the overall mission of the organization and who has the legal authority to impose a decision if necessary. This man need not be used with great frequency, but his presence is vital to maintain the possibility of an appeal to an authoritative common superior and to reduce the temptation for a specialist to insist too vigorously upon a position that is untenable in terms of the overall interests of the organization.

A fifth feature of a model of effective development administration is provision for a governmental mechanism on the regional level to regulate the relationships of the specialized development institutions with each other and with the community. Although governmental area coordination takes different forms in different societies, it remains a universal necessity in any modernized society. Even in a country like the United States where the marketplace is an important instrument of coordination, the "decisions" of the marketplace can be extremely painful to different groups and can lead to many consequences that the community considers unjust. Those who have stood to lose by these "decisions" and those offended by them have frequently turned to governmental agencies for assistance, and the resulting governmental action or inaction has been a major factor in defining the relationships among the interested parties. In addition, governmental units have come increasingly to promote integrated local development — or simply to promote economic development in general — either by initiating large-scale developmental projects themselves or by providing various types of inducements and support to attract private projects.

Although some governmental area coordination is necessary in all modernized societies, the mechanisms of such coordination can be structured in various ways. At one extreme, the mechanisms can be locally based, often pluralistic in nature. At the other extreme, the coordination can be provided by a man or institution responsible to the center, that is, coordination by a prefect.

The United States serves as a classic example both of pluralistic (one is tempted to say chaotic) governmental structure and pluralistic coordination. As Brian Crozier has emphasized, there are "multiple decision centers" at the city and county level in the United States. "Each of them has autonomous legal prerogatives and extremely confused and intricate duties: school boards, tax assessors, municipal councils, county officials, sheriffs, etc. — altogether, dozens of autonomous decision units, without even mentioning the local offices of state and federal authorities." [22] Indeed, when many local or state governmental units are created in response to federal grant-in-aid programs and when their officials are bound by federal guidelines, it is not always easy to make neat distinctions between federal, state, and local offices.

Certainly, the coordination of the activities of all these organizations has been far from perfect, but it has not been totally lacking. The most obvious figure performing this function has been the elected governor in the state and the mayor in the city. Even when the mayor does not have authority over many agencies (for example, the school board), he often is able to provide leadership in the bargaining among the interested parties and play a fairly decisive role in shaping its outcome. The mayor also is in a position to vary the intensity with which he fights for various federal grants, thereby influencing the balance that is struck so far as governmental development activity and services are concerned. At the state level the governor can influence the appropriations process in the same way.

Both in the city and state, however, there is not simply one coordinator. The legislature and the city council often are called upon to mediate the claims and demands of different governmental units. In fact, the basic rationale of the grant-in-aid program is that it permits state officials to determine important details of the federal program in order to bring it into closer correspondence with local priorities and values. Moreover, the U.S. Representative from an area or the U.S. Senator from a state often has a key role in determining the relative priority of projects in the area or in ensuring that important projects receive necessary support from related but autonomous federal agencies. Finally, various governmental officials may participate in extra-governmental groups or committees that formally or informally make key coordinating decisions. For example, a major developmental program such as the renovation of the downtown area in a city such as Pittsburgh or St. Louis seems to require a committee of governmental and nongovernmental civic leaders to gain the agreement of the different elements of the community and to focus community energies in a coordinated direction.

In a pluralistic system of local-based coordination, the relationship among the coordinators can be a very complex one, and it may vary considerably, depending upon the peculiarities of the local situation. In essense, however, the relationship is a bargaining one, with the values of the local population — or at least the politically active members of it — being the ultimate arbiter.

In the classic prefectoral system, on the other hand, there is but one coordinator, and his responsibility is to the center rather than to the local population. The responsibility of the prefect for law and order does require that he develop sensitivity to the type of unrest that might lead to political instability. However, fear of unrest is not likely to produce the same kind of responsiveness to popular demands that may be associated with fear about the possible outcome of the next election. Because the local Party organs really are a textbook example of the classic prefect in a modern setting,[23] it is not necessary to describe this form of coordination any further.

A third possible form of area coordination is the combination of prefectoral and locally based coordination that is found in France and in most of the democratic countries whose legal-administrative system ultimately derives from the French. In such a system, many specialized local administrators (particularly many of those in economic development and the services) have been removed from the legal jurisdiction of the prefect, often by the device of establishing administrative districts that do not correspond to that of a single prefect. Moreover, elected municipal officials and the local representative to the national legislature furnish locally based competition for the prefect on many questions.

Yet, despite the limitations upon his role, the prefect in a democratic society still retains a major role. Michel Crozier has described the contemporary situation in France: "A number of civil servants do not report to him, and many others report only in a formal way; but he has some degree of indirect control over them all, and the scope of his influence is still exceptionally wide. He exerts his influence through the numerous committees that have sprung up to handle the multiple decisions which may affect several different groups in the *département;* this is easy, since he is ex officio chairman of all those committees. He is the necessary co-ordinator of all co-operative activities and the natural arbiter of all conflicts. Moreover, the mayors and the municipal councils must operate under his guidance. This is stated officially and asserted in practice because of the very peculiar financial situation that makes towns and cities powerless, since they can raise only 10 to 20 percent of their expenditures through local taxes." [24]

Although the existence or nonexistence of a prefectoral system seems largely the result of historical accident,[25] some mixed pattern of area coordination is likely to prove optimal from the point of view of effective development administration. On the one hand, the difficulties the American government has encountered in development administration, particularly the difficulties in anti-poverty administration, suggest that some type of coordinating representative of the central government may become desirable and even necessary to supplement local coordinators as the complexity of development activities increase. On the other hand, the very real difficulties that led to the bifurcation of the Party apparatus in 1962 suggest that the scale of responsibilities of the prefect becomes too great in an advanced economy for him to handle area coordination exclusively. At a minimum, more of the coordinating activity may have to be "delegated" to market mechanisms.

In proposing that a model of effective development administration include these five features, I have meant neither to construct a comprehensive model nor to compile a list of operating instructions to cope with every organizational situation. Rather, the main purpose of this discussion has been to suggest to students of comparative politics that "non-Weberian" phenomena must be evaluated with great care. If one sees a particularly complex administrative structure which deviates from the Weberian ideal-type, if one sees "political criteria" being used in the selection and removal of administrative personnel, if one sees universalistic rules being violated, it may well be that efficiency is being sacrificed in order that other interests and values of particular individuals or groups will be better served. But one should not automatically jump to this conclusion. Perhaps those associated with the organization or administrative system have sensed that these practices are necessary in the given case in order to promote the system's effective operation. The scholar should also be aware of this possibility when he analyzes the complex of factors that shape a particular administrative situation.

XV. Rationality, Bargaining, and Political Development

If the basic analysis of this book is correct and if a model of effective development administration should have the features suggested in the last chapter, further questions need to be raised about the use of the criteria of rationality, power, and tradition as the basic means for distinguishing among political systems. Although Barrington Moore recognized that "no one of the three criteria . . . can ever become the sole basis for the organization of all decisions and behavior in any human society," [1] this book suggests that the overlap is considerably greater than Moore's analysis indicated. If the involvement of the local Party organs in industrial decision-making serves both the interests of political control and of administrative effectiveness, if an effective administrative system requires common political values (broadly defined), then it may not be enough to ask which criterion receives the greatest emphasis in decision-making and to assume that "an emphasis on one of the three criteria excludes emphasis on either of the other two." [2] Rather, it seems more useful to focus our efforts on trying to make "precise and meaningful statements about the extent to which [and the way in which] these elements can be successfully combined." [3]

Rationality and the Political Process

The most basic problems with the three-fold system of classification proposed by Barrington Moore arise with respect to the criterion of rationality. The model of rational-technical society suggests that there are rational-technical solutions to most of society's problems and that these solutions are fairly apparent to the man with the proper specialized preparation. Involved in the model is an image of society in which there can be very precise specialization of labor and a clear definition of the spheres of competence of the different specialists.

This book has evaluated the possibility of using rational-technical criteria in decision-making rather differently. Again and again, we have seen cases in which two or more specialized institutions were "right" within their own framework — that is, both were deciding on rational-technical criteria — but still arrived at different answers to a problem. Indeed, the point could have been pushed further. If the "specialist" is himself a line official (for example, a factory manager), he faces the same problem with respect to his own subordinates. He finds that there is what one Soviet manager called an "objective contradiction" between the points of view of such men as the chief economist and the chief engineer.[4]

Similarly, the analysis of the primary Party organization has implied that even specialists with very similar expertise may disagree profoundly as to the "technical requirements of the human and natural situation" and as to what measure is, in fact, "an effective way of getting results." If there were no such disagreements, there would be much less difficulty in ensuring that lower officials take decisions corresponding to the desires of the center, and there would be little reason for a "policy-making team" rather than a single manager.

In essence, this book is in agreement with Herbert Simon that administrative decisions, even by specialized officials, never can be completely rational:

> Actual [administrative] behavior falls short, in at least three ways, of objective rationality . . .
> (1) Rationality requires a complete knowledge and anticipation of the consequences that will follow on each choice. In fact, knowledge of consequences is always fragmentary.
> (2) Since these consequences lie in the future, imagination must supply the lack of experienced feeling in attaching value to them. But values can be only imperfectly anticipated.
> (3) Rationality requires a choice among all possible alternative behaviors. In actual behavior, only a very few of all these possible alternatives ever come to mind.[5]

This book has concentrated on differences in interests and perspectives that arise at middle and lower levels of a quite centralized hierarchy. However, this phenomenon manifests itself with even more severity in the "policy process" at higher levels. Let us assume that the Soviet leadership was determined to reach "objective" decisions based upon the expert knowledge of specialists. To whom would they defer?

Even on very specialized questions, the experts involved may be in substantial disagreement as to what policies should be followed. If, as frequently happens, there are generational differences in views, should policy reflect the more "modern" (but less experienced) perspectives of younger specialists or should it reflect the views of older specialists who have accumulated great experience in their rise to the top of their specialty or administrative hierarchy? What is to be the fate of the ideas of the innovator (or crackpot) who proposes radical changes that his fellow specialists do not seem ready to accept?

The difficulties in determining the rational-technical solution are even greater when two or more different types of specialists claim expert knowledge in a particular realm but still recommend sharply contradictory policies.

How is industrial planning and administration to be organized? Some, but by no means all, economists speak of the great benefits to be derived from relying more upon market mechanisms. A number of ministerial officials claim that such a policy would destroy the advantages of a planned system and would lead to a series of dysfunctional consequences.

What procedures should be used in dealing with those accused of crime? Many lawyers and jurists are pressing for added safeguards for the accused; the police in the Soviet Union as elsewhere have a rather different perspective on the requirements of law and order.

What restrictions, if any, should be placed upon the publication of literary works and upon the type of programs to be scheduled on the radio and television and in the movie houses and theaters? Many, but not all, writers demand that they be given freedom to pursue their craft as they see fit and that their works be freely presented to the public through the mass media. However, a wide range of groups (an American television writer could undoubtedly compile a suggestive list) object to a variety of types of presentations that they think undercut their own work. The military may worry about the creation of unpatriotic or defeatist attitudes; the police may be concerned about programs or films glorifying criminals or ending with crimes unsolved; certain psychologists may protest undue violence on television, asserting that it may have an unhealthy effect on part of the population. Many educators may insist that the mass media be used to show "quality" work that has an educational value, while the managers of the media may find that escapist fare increases their audience and makes plan fulfillment much easier.

What should be the policy in the realm of higher education and science? Professors and scientists may want to spend their time on research projects and specialized courses that have little discernible relationship to the solution of immediate, practical problems or to the needs of the students. Economic administrators have many immediate research questions to which they want answers, and they are eager that the college graduates seeking employment have a "solid," practical training. Even if it is decided as a general principle to permit great autonomy to the scientists and the professors, is large-scale financing of science to be left to institutions (for example, industrial corporations or ministries) whose self-interest in basic research is limited, or are large financial resources going to be placed at the disposal of committees of scientists who have a major interest in such research? If there is to be a combination of these methods of financing, what are the percentages of funds to be routed through each conduit?

In the appropriations process such conflicts occur incessantly because the successful realization of most specialized programs requires significant funds and the officials involved are not shy in advancing the claims of their specialty. The officials of the automobile industry advocate a mass expansion in the production of private cars and in the development of the highway system; the military see the need for more defense expenditures if their mission is to be carried out as their professional standards suggest necessary. The school officials, the hospital officials, the agricultural officials all point to the great benefits that would derive to society if they had the resources to perform their service as they think proper. The total amount perceived to be necessary always far outstrips the total funds available, and at a minimum the problem must be faced — how should limited resources be distributed to different claimants, all of whom can justify their demands on a rational-technical basis? In addition, however, one group of specialists may be vitally interested in the decisions made by another group (at least those that are very expensive), and it may be driven to challenge the other group's "rational-technical" judgment simply in order to protect its own position. (One such example is the attitude of many anti-poverty workers in the United States towards the judgment of the State and Defense Departments about the Vietnam war.)

Finally, of course, the question often arises — even if the specialists involved agree on a rational-technical answer, should this decision be overridden to protect other values more diffusely held by the population? A writer may feel that "literary values" or "literary honesty" demand that two of the characters in his play engage in sexual intercourse on stage, and the theater manager may believe that such a scene would not have an adverse effect upon attendance; others, however, may vehemently refer to "public indecency," "public immorality," "prevailing community standards," and so forth. Highway officials may choose a routing that is the most direct and the most economical to construct, but others may object if it turns out that this route requires the destruction of buildings of great historical significance. Industrial officials may discover — indeed, have discovered — that although it is most economic to build a paper plant on the shores of Lake Baikal or a steel plant in the Indiana Dunes, others can become quite incensed at these rational-technical decisions.

In all these examples, the conflict seldom can be settled by applying rational-technical standards. Basically, nearly all of them ultimately involve fundamental conflicts in values, professional standards, and interests, and they have no rational-technical answer at all. Even when factual disputes imbedded in them might be resolved by experimentation, the evidence is likely to take a long time to accumulate, and even then, it may well be ambiguous.

In essence, these problems are the epitome of "the political question" or "the political conflict." When we speak of the political process as entailing the authoritative allocation of values, we have in mind, first and foremost, cases in which specialists do not agree among themselves, in which men with different specialized knowledge, perspectives, and interests come into conflict, in which various groups in society seek redress from actions that specialized groups or organizations think are required by the "technical requirements of the human and natural situation," in which groups attempt to modify the way in which the fruits of society's labor are distributed. When we talk about differences in political systems, we are talking primarily about differences in the process by which conflicts are resolved.

Therefore, if we are concerned about the evolution of political systems, we cannot limit ourselves to asking whether there have been changes in the extent to which rational-technical criteria are used in decision-making, the extent to which they defer to experts or specialized institutions on specialized questions. Even more we must ask: Have there been changes in the way that questions with no rational-technical answer are decided?

Bargaining and Political Development

On questions for which there is no rational-technical answer, by what criteria are decisions to be reached in rational-technical society? As was discussed briefly in Chapter XIII, this question is not directly answered in the discussion of the rational-technical model. Clearly they are not to be resolved in any classic democratic manner, for "the mass of the population . . . would not have a significantly larger share in the decisions determining their fate." [6] Yet, although "the power of the central authorities would remain very great," [7] the basis which they would use for decision when the specialists disagree is not clear.

How should this gap in the model be filled? One answer has been provided by other contemporary social scientists who use the concept of rationality as a foundation stone in their discussions of "modern" society but who have faced the problem of conflict of values more directly. They have tended to focus not upon the nature of the resolution of these conflicts but upon the method by which the resolution is achieved. Some (for example, Talcott Parsons) have handled the problem by including democracy among the "universals" of modern society.[8] Others, not wanting to go that far, have merely insisted that the conflicts be resolved in a "rational" manner. "Rational" in this sense means that they are resolved through "bargaining and accommodative political action" [9] and that the existing political settlements of whatever origin be subject only to "gradual change whether in the direction favored by the left or the right." [10] In this view, rationality involves "incrementalism": "Patching up an old system is the most rational way to change it, for the patch constitutes about as big a change as one can comprehend at a time." [11]

In many ways this seems a reasonable solution to the question of how "political" conflicts are resolved in rational-technical society. Division of labor means that society as a whole is dependent upon each specialized group and in particular upon those groups whose training makes them difficult to replace. Specialized training might seem to give each group a basic bargaining position in defending its own interests and therefore to create the conditions which permit and necessitate decision-making through bargaining.

This line of analysis must, however, be advanced with the greatest of care, for the emotion-laden and ambiguous term "rationality" has served as a category into which many quite different conceptions and values have been fitted. One scholar may write as if there were a complete identity between rationality and incrementalism; another, the author of the rational-technical model, insists that "the comparative history of modernization [tells us that] the costs of moderation have been at least as atrocious as those of revolution, perhaps a great deal more." [12] One scholar may speak of democracy as one of "the universals" of modern society; another, again the author of the rational-technical model, asserts that "the rational-technical extreme imposes the single standard of technical efficiency on all decisions. Its spirit is opposed to the plurality of goals characteristic of democracy." [13]

This book too indicates that there are great dangers in using such concepts as bargaining, accommodative political action, and incremental style as general bases for a model of a "rational" political process. We have, after all, been examining what is usually cited as the classic example of a political system with an "ideological culture" and an "ideological style." Yet, the Party secretaries described in this book do not emerge as men whose decision-making "tends to be relatively rigid," as men with "an ideological form of political calculation and analysis" and a "rigid and closed . . . set of rules of conduct spelled out by the ideology." [14] Rather, they emerge (at least in the role we have been studying) as men "increasingly rational, analytical, and empirical in their political action," men with a "pragmatic, instrumental style" and "the open, bargaining attitudes associated with full secularization." [15] Although all discussions of bargaining recognize that some bargaining takes place "even in modern totalitarian societies," [16] we have not been examining a peripheral aspect of the political system. The men under discussion are full-time officials of the Party — the party that is supposed to give the political system its ideological nature, the party that sometimes is termed the totalitarian element in the system.

To be sure, the bargaining activity of the local Party officials takes place within a prescribed framework, and the results of the bargaining should correspond in a rough way with the relative priorities of the Soviet leadership. These relative priorities have reflected a number of factors, but among them certainly have been concern for the power position of the leadership and the beliefs about the prerequisites of the good society that have flowed from Marxism-Leninism. Although the desire of the local Party officials (and of the Party leadership) to maintain political stability has meant that the views of the population have entered into the bargaining equation, it is extremely unlikely that the central and local decisions would have been the same if the population had had the opportunity to bolster its position in the bargaining position by participation in meaningful elections.

Similarly, the instrumental style displayed by the local Party officials in many aspects of industrial decision-making has not necessarily characterized their behavior in other realms of decision-making. In the Stalin era many first secretaries apparently did attempt to emulate the style of the General Secretary in many of their relationships, and one gathers that many of them have continued to display a rather ideologically conditioned attitude towards (for example) deviant intellectuals.

However, it is precisely these limitations on the bargaining activity and the pragmatic, instrumental style of the local Party officials that are of crucial importance from a theoretical point of view. If such bargaining can take place within the framework of the highly centralized and highly "ideological" system represented by Stalin's Russia, if a man can be pragmatic and instrumental in one realm and ideological in another, then clearly bargaining is not the type of autonomous process whose widespread existence in a society ensures that group conflicts are inevitably resolved in an equitable, mutually advantageous manner.

While one might hypothesize that this combination of ideological and instrumental attitudes and behavior in the Soviet Union is associated with a transition from one type of political system to another, I think that this characteristic of the work of the local Party organs points to a more general feature of the political process. It is not only in the Soviet Union that one finds individuals who combine a flexible, instrumental approach on some questions with a rigid, closed approach on others. It is not only in the Soviet Union that bargaining takes place within the framework of a particular set of values and a particular set of power relationships.

Sidney Verba is but one of the most recent in a long line of analysts who have asserted that some type of combination of "rational" and "nonrational" thinking is an essential part of the political process. In particular, he focused attention upon what he called "primitive political beliefs" — essentially what Mosca called the "political formula," Pareto the "residue," and others "the fundamentals": "Primitive political beliefs are those so implicit and generally taken for granted that each individual holds them and believes all other individuals hold them. They are the fundamental and usually unstated assumptions or postulates about politics. In this sense they are unchallengeable, since no opportunity exists to call them into question." [17]

Verba was concerned primarily with the relationship of primitive political beliefs to political stability. He contended that "stability in 'modernized' systems may depend upon the maintenance of a residue of nonrationality — of the traditional, implicit, and unquestioned values discussed in the previous section — that keeps certain aspects of the political system out of the realm of the rational means-ends calculations." [18] One could make much the same assertion about bargaining, for, as Dahl and Lindblom have noted, "if leaders agreed . . . on nothing, they could not bargain." [19]

The framework of values and power relationships within which bargaining takes place naturally needs not be as hierarchically determined as that in the Soviet Union, but it usually is quite structured. Moreover, it may well have a major impact upon the results that emerge from the bargaining process. It is, of course, a cliché that the terms of bargaining agreements reflect the relative power of the various bargainers, but for a political scientist, relative power is not an autonomous variable. The relative power of the bargainers and therefore the outcome of the bargaining activity can be significantly shaped by the structure of the political-economic system. They also can be shaped by the nature of the primitive political beliefs, the nature of "the system of empirical beliefs, expressive symbols, and values which defines the situation in which the political action takes place" (Verba's definition of political culture).

For this reason it is not enough to assert that political conflicts in a rational-technical society or in a "modern" society are resolved in an instrumental manner or through bargaining and accommodative political action. Rather, in classifying political systems, we must ask a series of additional questions about the framework in which the bargaining and accommodative political action takes place. In essence, these questions center upon the way in which the factors of "tradition" and "power" shape the bargaining process in a particular political system.

We must not simply ask whether tradition has an impact on decision-making (for certainly it does), but rather we must inquire: What is traditionally taken for granted? How do particular elements of the primitive belief system condition the assumptions about the relative legitimacy and the relative priority to be accorded the claims of the different specialists and nonspecialists? Indeed, how do elements of the belief system shape the "rational-technical" answer that specialists give to different problems? (Surely the vast majority of engineers and agronomists in the Soviet Union have a different perception than their counterparts in the United States about the forms of economic organization that are optimal from a rational-technical point of view.)

Moreover, in emphasizing the importance of "ideas" in the political process, those of us who talk about "political culture" in one set of terms or the other must not fall into the same errors that Arthur Bentley and his followers have so devastatingly criticized. Barrington Moore's assertion that social continuity requires explanation is fully as relevant for a student of political culture as for a student of culture in general: "Culture, or tradition — to use a less technical term — is not something that exists outside of or independently of individual human beings living together in society. Cultural values do not descend from heaven to influence the course of history. . . . The assumption of inertia, that cultural and social continuity do not require explanation, obliterates the fact that both have to be created anew in each generation, often with great pain and suffering. . . . To speak of cultural inertia is to overlook the concrete interests and privileges that are served by indoctrination, education, and the entire complicated process of transmitting culture from one generation to the next." [20]

In analyzing political systems, we must ask, therefore, not simply what is traditionally taken for granted, but also what are "the concrete interests and privileges that are served" by the primitive political beliefs. To what extent do these beliefs legitimate the status and the power positions of groups in an uneven manner? To what extent are the groups that benefit most from the status quo able to ensure that the members of other groups and particularly the men rising into leadership positions accept the assumptions that fortify the essentials of the status quo? To what extent do mechanisms exist that increase the probability that there will be some questioning of the unquestionable and some thinking about the unthinkable and that this questioning and thinking has the opportunity to make a meaningful impact?

Similarly, we must ask not whether power is a criterion by which decisions are made (for surely it is in any society). Rather, we must ask: How does the political system structure the way in which political leaders acquire and maintain power? Are there mechanisms that give all the major groups the opportunity to defend their interests and viewpoints vigorously and that provide the political leaders with the self-interest to take these demands into account in a meaningful way? Does the political structure strengthen the bargaining position of particular groups by furnishing them — intentionally or unintentionally — with particularly strategic levers of power, indeed, even with veto points? If bargaining among the major groups does take place, are there mechanisms to ensure that "the armistice agreements signed by the negotiators fall within the high-ranking preferences of the greater number of citizens?" [21]

It is, of course, conceivable that industrialization is producing an "emerging world culture" in which the primitive political beliefs and basic political structures will be sufficiently similar in all industrialized countries to provide very similar frameworks for bargaining. Seymour Martin Lipset, for example, has foreseen "the emergence of a somewhat similar social and political culture, one which increasingly resembles the first advanced industrial society to function without institutions and values derivative from a feudal past, the United States." [22] If Professor Lipset is correct, we may well see fairly universal agreement on the nature of "rational-technical" solutions to basic questions and on the nature of the resolutions to some of the basic value and interest conflicts.

Yet, to say that this development is conceivable is not to say that it is certain or even likely. To assume that all political systems will evolve toward some common bargaining framework is to assume that there will not be powerful minorities who can establish or reinforce belief-systems and power relationships that are particularly beneficial to them. It is to deny the possibility that Talcott Parsons was correct in 1947 in speaking about the "precarious state of instability" of a system based on rational-legal authority and the vulnerability of such a system to a "large-scale charismatic movement in reaction against modern 'liberal' institutions." [23] (It is implicitly to deny the bases of these fears — namely that industrial society may produce not a sense of participation, but feelings of alienation, aloneness, and frustration among large segments of the population.) It is to deny the possible validity of Barrington Moore's contention about a conflict between technical efficiency and democracy.

What we ultimately may have to recognize is that there can be a variety of political systems with a large component of "rational" and "instrumental" behavior — including a number of political systems based upon values quite offensive to our own. We may have to abandon the language of "political development" with its inevitable images of lineal movement (whether forward or backward) or perhaps incorporate a more cyclical type of analysis into the theory of development. It may be that the type of "modern" but still quite authoritarian system into which the Soviet Union has evolved will prove quite durable and that it should serve as the basis for a model of one possible "modern" political system. [24] At a minimum, however, the ability of the local Party organs to reinforce an existing "ideological" belief-system and a particular nondemocratic set of power relationships while still serving in an instrumental way to fulfill the needs of the administrative system warns us about the dangers of simplistic approaches to the analysis of political change.

APPENDIXES, BIBLIOGRAPHY, NOTES, INDEX

Appendix A. The Party Committees and Bureaus

Soviet sources do not present comprehensive analyses of the membership of the Party committees and bureaus, and those statistics that are sometimes published are often marred by quirks in definition. (For example, "kolkhoznik" means any member of the kolkhoz, including the chairman.) However, at the time of Party congresses or conferences, a Soviet newspaper does print the list of members of the committee and bureau of the Party organ to which it is subordinated. If one carefully reads the newspaper in the months prior to and after the congress or conference, one usually can identify the position of all the members of the bureau and a high percentage of the members of the committee. This methodology does permit occasional error (for example, a change in position between the time of identification and the time of the conference or the confusing of two officials with identical initials), but the error is likely to be extremely marginal, particularly since the Soviet press has come to use full initials of officials more frequently in its articles of the last ten to fifteen years. (The member is considered identified only if initials are found; when initials are rarely mentioned in press articles, it is more difficult to identify the official within a short period from the conference.)

Table A.1 indicates the changing membership of the central committees in six republics. Three large republics (Belorussia, Ukraine, and Uzbekistan) and three small republics (Georgia, Latvia, and Moldavia) were chosen — the selection of particular republics being dictated by a desire to obtain geographical balance.

Perhaps a more concrete sense of the membership of the republican central committees can be gained by examining in detail the composition of two of them — the Ukrainian and the Georgian.

The 1966 Ukrainian Central Committee contained 127 full members, 124 of whom have been identified. (The unidentified are N. S. Kolomiets, V. I. Malov, and V. A. Stepanchenko.) Forty-two of these men (33 percent) were Party officials, 10 of them officials of the Cen-

Table A.1. Occupations of full members of six Republican Central Committees, 1956-1966.[a]

Occupational position	Belorussia			Georgia				Latvia				Moldavia				Ukraine			Uzbekistan		
	1956	1961	1966	1956	1956[a]	1961	1966	1956	1956[a]	1961	1966	1956	1956[a]	1961	1966	1956	1961	1966	1956	1961	1966
Party organs	57	50	52	36	59	43	47	28	45	35	37	46	58	42	43	40	40	42	63	55	59
Republican secretariat	15	15	13	12	13	14	15	11	17	8	14	14	17	13	15	7	9	10	10	10	12
Lower party organs including rural raikom	42	35	39	24	46	29	32	17	28	27	23	32	41	29	28	33	31	32	53	45	47
	28	13	14	10	24	18	21	10	15	16	11	28	36	25	23	5	3	6	20	19	16
State administration[b]	40	42	49	36	46	45	44	29	37	35	47	29	38	31	44	39	42	46	63	58	66
General republican	5	7	8	5	5	8	7	4	4	9	8	5	5	5	6	6	6	7	9	8	9
Republican industry–construction-transportation[c]	5	6	10	8	12	6	11	5	7	7	7	8	9	7	10	8	11	14	11	9	12
Republican agriculture[c]	5	5	4	2	3	5	5	4	5	4	5	3	4	3	8	3	4	3	7	5	6
Republican services[d]	7	7	9	6	6	9	6	4	5	3	9	4	5	2	11	5	5	3	8	6	8
Republican security and courts[e]	3	3	4	4	5	4	4	4	5	3	3	2	2	3	3	3	2	2	6	3	2
Local soviets	9	7	7	4	7	5	5	2	4	3	3	1	4	2	3	5	6	4	13	12	17
Industrial-construction managers	1	3	3	5	6	5	3	2	2	4	4	2	2	3	1	6	3	7	4	6	4
Kolkhoz-Sovkhoz Managers	5	4	4	2	2	3	3	4	5	2	8	4	7	6	2	5	5	6	5	9	8
Scientists	3	5	1	1	2	4	4	4	4	4	2	1	1	2	2	1	5	6	3	6	4
Educators	4	2	3	2	2	3	2	3	3	2	2	3	3	2	1	2	2	1	0	1	1
Writers and newspaper editors	5	4	6	3	4	3	3	3	4	4	5	4	4	2	4	3	4	3	2	6	2
Military officers[e]	8	8	7	3	4	2	3	6	8	7	4	2	5	2	2	7	7	6	5	3	3
Miscellaneous officials	2	2	2	2	3	2	3	3	4	4	4	2	5	2	3	3	3	2	3	3	3
Rank-and-file personnel[f]	3	5	4	1	3	7	13	4	5	7	13	1	3	9	7	11	11	18	4	20	16
Unknown	5	7	9	5	9	2	2	5	8	7	11	1	1	5	1	5	3	3	1	6	11
Total	127	125	133	89	132	111	121	85	118	105	125	89	118	97	107	110	117	127	144	157	165

[a] In 1956 the data for the three small republics include a column giving the distribution of the full and candidate members combined. In this way it was possible to obtain totals more comparable with later years.

[b] Deputy chairmen of the Council of Ministers and Gosplan are distributed according to their specialized sphere of responsibility.

[c] Rural construction is included under agriculture.

[d] Consumers coops, although "public" organizations, are treated as part of the state apparatus.

[e] Border guard officials are included among the military.

[f] Rank-and-file personnel are almost all workers, kolkhozniki, and sovkhozniki.

tral Committee. These 10 were the 6 secretaries of the Ukrainian Central Committee, the head of the agricultural department, the head of the Party-organizational work department, the head of the heavy industry department, and the head of the propaganda-agitation department. The other 32 Party officials included the first secretaries of 23 of the 25 obkomy in the republic, the second secretary of the Kiev obkom, the first secretaries of 2 gorkomy (Kiev and Krivoi Rog), and 6 secretaries of rural raikomy. (Actually, all 25 obkom first secretaries were named to the Central Committee, but 2 of them were immediately elected secretaries of the Central Committee and are included in that category.)

Among the 33 state administrators on the Central Committee were the chairman and deputy chairman of the Presidium of the Supreme Soviet, the chairman and 7 deputy chairmen of the Council of Ministers (including the chairman of Gosplan), the first deputy chairman of Gosplan, the chairman and first deputy chairman of the Committee of Peoples' Control, the chairman of the KGB, and 12 ministers (agriculture, chemical industry, coal industry, construction, ferrous metallurgy, finance, food industry, health, local industry, reclamation and irrigation, preservation of public order, and social security). The head of the Black Sea Steamship Line, the head of the Donetsk Railroad, and the head of the Southwest Railroad are also included among the republican, industrial, construction, and transportation officials. The four officials of local soviets were the chairmen of the Dnepropetrovsk, Donetsk, Kharkov, and Kiev oblispolkomy.

The industrial enterprise managers included the directors of Dneprodzerzhinsk Metallurgy Works, Kharkov Tractor Works, Kharkov Transportation Machinery Works, Makeevka Metallurgy Works, Southern Machinery Works in Dnepropetrovsk (a major defense plant), and another unspecified defense plant, and the head of the Artem Coal Trust. The six agricultural managers were all kolkhoz chairmen.

In the science category could be found the president and vice-president of the Ukrainian Academy of Sciences, the director of a research institute in the defense industry, an aviation designer (O. K. Antonov), the director of an agricultural selection station, and the director of the Institute of Party History. The educator was the rector of the Higher Party School, and the cultural figures included two writers (N. P. Bazhan and A. G. Korneichuk) and a poet (P. G. Tychina). No newspaper editors were named full members of the Ukrainian Central Committee — a phenomenon also found in the Ukraine in 1956 and 1961, but quite rare in other republics.

Three of the military officers held the posts of commander of the Kiev, Odessa, and Prikarpathian military districts respectively, one was head of the political administration of the Kiev military district, one was commander of the Black Sea Fleet, and one (A. I. Pokryshkin) was a top aviation commander. The two men included in the miscellaneous category were the chairman of the republican trade union council and the first secretary of the republican Komsomol organization.

The 11 workers and brigadiers came from a variety of industries — 3 from ferrous metallurgy plants, 2 from shipbuilding plants, 2 from coal mines, 1 from a transportation machinery works, 1 from construction, 1 from an oil refinery, and 1 from an unknown industry. The 7 rank-and-file agricultural personnel included 2 tractor brigadiers and the head of a sub-unit of a kolkhoz.

A typical central committee in a smaller republic is that selected in Georgia in 1966. Of the 121 full members, 119 have been identified. (The unidentified are R. Ch. Achba and L. R. Charaia.) Forty-seven of the full members (39 percent) were Party officials. The central Party officials included not only the 5 secretaries of the republican central committee, but also the chairman of the Party commission, and the heads of all 9 departments of the central committee. The 32 local Party officials included the obkom first secretaries in the two autonomous republics and the one autonomous oblast in Georgia, the 3 secretaries of the Tbilisi gorkom, the first secretaries of the Chiatury, Gori, Kutaisi, Rustavi, and Tkibulsk gorkomy, and 21 (of 66) first secretaries of rural raikomy. (In republics without oblasti, the percentage of first secretaries of rural raikomy named to the central committee is higher — for example, 23 of 26 in Moldavia; in some republics — for example, Latvia — the secretaries of the urban raikomy in the capital are central committee members.)

The 33 republican state administrators on the Georgian central committee were the chairman, first deputy chairman, and secretary of the Presidium of the Supreme Soviet, the chairman and the 6 deputy chairmen of the Council of Ministers, the chairman of the Peoples' Control Committee, the chairman of the KGB, the republican procurator, the chairman of the supreme court, 7 ministers (agriculture, construction, culture, finance, food industry, preservation of public order, social security), the chairman of Gosstroi, the chairman of the committee for vocational education, the chairman of the science commission, the chairman of Selkhoztekhnika (agricultural machinery supply), the chairman of the consumers' coops, the head of the highway administration, the head of the Transcaucasian Railroad, the head of the Transcaucasian Metallurgy Construction Trust, the head of a trust of the Ministry of the Food Industry, the head of the vegetable-milk sovkhoz trust, and the head of the Georgian Tea Trust. The five officials of local soviets were the chairmen of the councils of ministers of the Abkhaziia and Adzhariia autonomous republics, the chairman of the South Osetian oblispolkom, the chairman of the Tbilisi gorispolkom, and the chairman of a rural raiispolkom. (In Latvia and Moldavia, several heads of raion agriculture administrations are included in the "local soviet" category, although the administrations are not subordinated to the soviets.)

Among the enterprise directors on the Georgian Central Committee were the head of the Chiatury Manganese Trust, the director of the Kutaisi Auto Works, the director of the Rustavi Metallurgy Works, two kolkhoz chairmen, and the director of a sovkhoz. The four scientists included the President of the Academy of Sciences, the director of the Georgian Institute of Orchards and Vineyards, the director of the Institute of History of the Academy of Sciences, and the director of the Institute of Party History, while the two educators were the rector of Tbilisi University and the director of the Tbilisi Institute for Perfecting the Training of Doctors.

The three military officials named to the Central Committee were the head of the Transcaucasian border troops and the commander and head of the political administration of the Transcaucasian military district. The editor of the major Russian-language newspaper (*Zaria vostoka*) and the major Georgian-language newspaper (*Komunisti*) were given seats on the committee as was the chairman of the Union of Writers. The miscellaneous officials included the chairman of the republican trade union council, the first secretary of the republican Komsomol, and the chairman of the republican sports union. Finally, nine workers of diverse industries and four kolkhozniki and sovkhozniki have been identified among the central committee's full members.

The pattern of state administrators varies from republic to republic, but certain ministries and state committees are represented more frequently than others. The following list of administrative agencies indicates the proportion of the six republics in which each had a full member on the central committee: six republics — agriculture, gosplan, KGB, peoples' control, public order, and social security; five republics — auto transport, construction, culture, finance, and sel-khoztekhnika; four republics — consumers' coops, education, food industry, health, light industry, local industry, and municipal services; three republics — press committee, procuracy, and trade; two republics — communications, construction materials, energy-electrification, gosstroi, grain products, meat-milk industry, reclamation, radio, rural construction, and supreme court; one republic — statistical administration, higher and specialized secondary education, and vocational education. In addition, there were a number of specialized ministries (for example, cotton-ginning in Uzbekistan) which were represented on one of the six central committees.

As indicated in Table A.2, the obkomy of 1966 had a larger proportion of Party officials among their full members than did the republican central committees, but the general patterns of membership were not greatly dissimilar in the republics and the oblasti. The only criterion used in the selection of the obkomy analyzed in the table was that of availability of information. Each of the oblasts was on my 1967 itinerary in the Soviet Union, and it was possible to read the local oblast newspaper in the local library.

The Rostov obkom has a membership which is probably fairly typical for an oblast which is both an important industrial and agricultural center. One hundred and sixteen of its 130 full members have been identified, and 45 percent of these 116 are full-time Party officials. Twelve are officials of the obkom: the 5 obkom secretaries, the chairman of the oblast Party commission, and the heads of 6 departments — agriculture; industrial-transportation; light industry, food industry, and trade; organizational-Party work; propaganda and agi-

Table A.2. Occupations of the full members in five obkomy, 1966.

Occupational position	Krasnodar [a]	Rostov	Ulianovsk	Volgograd	Yaroslavl
Party organs	50	53	40	59	37
Obkom secretariat	13	12	13	18	15
Gorkomy and urban raikomy	14	18	7	13	10
Rural raikomy	22	22	18	26	9
Party secretaries, enterprises	1	1	2	2	3
State administration	32	31	33	42	24
General oblast administration	4	3	3	3	2
Regional and oblast industry–construction–transportation	6	9	3	8	4
Oblast agriculture	5	4	4	3	4
Oblast services	4	2	3	5	2
Oblast security and courts	3	3	3	3	3
Lower soviets	3	2	4	4	2
Raion agriculture administration	2	2	1	6	1
Industrial-construction managers	1	4	5	8	3
Kolkhoz-sovkhoz managers	4	2	7	2	3
Scientists	3	2	3	1	0
Educators	2	3	4	2	1
Writers and newspaper editors	1	3	1	1	1
Military officers	3	3	3	4	3
Miscellaneous officials	4	3	2	2	4
Rank-and-file personnel	15	18	11	4	5
Unknown	7	14	12	30	24
Total	117	130	109	145	99

[a] In the case of Krasnodar the officials listed as "oblast officials" are actually krai officials.

tation; and science and education. (The heads of the construction department and the coal industry department were candidate members of the obkom; the head of the administrative organs department and another unspecified department were members of the auditing commission.)

Sixteen of the cities in Rostov oblast had Party gorkomy, and thirteen of their first secretaries were named full members of the obkom. Also elected were the second secretary of the Rostov gorkom and 4 urban raikom secretaries, 2 in Rostov and 1 each in Taganrog and Shakhti. Of the 37 first secretaries of the oblast's rural raikomy, 22 were full members of the obkom. The remaining Party official identified was the secretary of the Party committee of the Rostov Agricultural Machinery Works, but it is probable that the worker and peasant members, in Rostov as elsewhere, included a number of part-time Party secretaries of shops and divisions.

The 31 governmental officials on the obkom included not only oblast-level administrators, but also a number of higher-level officials who work in Rostov — the head of the combine administration of the USSR Ministry of the Agricultural Machinery and Tractor Industry and the heads of the North Caucasian planning commission, the North Caucasian territorial supply administration, the North Caucasian civil aviation administration, the North Caucasian railroad, the North Caucasian construction trust, and the Volga-Don steamship line. The oblast-level officials were the chairman and 3 of the 5 deputy chairmen of the oblispolkom, the procurator, the chairmen of the peoples' control committee, the KGB, and the oblast selkhoztekhnika, and the heads of the agriculture, auto transportation, grain, and public order administrations of the oblast soviet, the head of the Rostov coal combine, and the head of the Rostov coal mine construction trust.

Among the lower state administrators named to the Rostov obkom were the chairmen of the Rostov gorispolkom and of a rural raiispolkom and the heads of 2 raion kolkhoz-sovkhoz agriculture administrations. The industrial directors managed 4 of the biggest plants in the oblast: the Novocherkassy Electric Locomotive Works, the Rostov Agriculture Machinery Works, the Taganrog Combine Works, and the Taganrog Metallurgy Works. One of the agricultural managers was the chairman of a kolkhoz, the other the director of a sovkhoz.

The two scientists selected as full members of the obkom were the director of the Don Agriculture Research Institute and the chief designer of a special design bureau, while the educators were the rectors of Rostov University, the Don Agriculture College, and the Novocherkassy Polytechnical Institute. The posts occupied by the military members of the committee were the oblast military commissar (*voenkom,* an official essentially concerned with the mobilization of draftees), the commander of the North Caucasian military district, and the deputy head of the political administration of the military district. (In similar situations elsewhere the head of the political administration is named to the Party committee — and usually the bureau — of another oblast within the military district.) The category "writers and newspaper editors" included 2 fiction writers (including the oblast's most famous writer, Mikhail Sholokhov) and the editor of the oblast newspaper. The men included in the miscellaneous category were the first secretary of the Komsomol obkom, an old Bolshevik, and the chief doctor (head) of a hospital. (The chairman of the oblast trade union council was to be replaced within a few months — and by a man already on the obkom, the first secretary of the Taganrog gorkom.) The inevitable worker and peasant members — at least those identified — were divided among 8 workers and 10 sovkhozniki and kolkhozniki.

The Rostov obkom also contained 69 candidate members, of whom 59 were identified. Twenty-two (37 percent) were Party officials: 3 obkom officials (the heads of the construction and coal departments and the deputy head of the propaganda-agitation department), 2 first secretaries of gorkomy, 6 first secretaries of urban raikomy, 10 first secretaries of rural raikomy, and the secretary of the Party committee of a sovkhoz.

Nine of the candidate members of the Rostov obkom were higher governmental officials: 2 deputy chairmen of the oblispolkom, the head of the Don wine trust, the heads of the culture, education, and radio administrations, the chairman of the consumers' coops, and the heads of 2 construction trusts. Six were enterprise directors — 5 of large industrial factories, 1 of a mine; 3 were kolkhoz chairmen.

Also included among the candidate members were the chairmen of the gorispolkomy of the second, third, and fourth largest cities, the heads of 2 agricultural administrations, the secretary of the oblast trade union council, the rector of the agriculture machinery educational institute, and a military officer. The 5 workers and 6 farmers were again widely distributed among the various occupations.

Very little information is available on the membership of the city committees of the Party. The only committee on which it was possible to collect fairly comprehensive data in recent years was the Ulianovsk gorkom named in 1966, and even here scarcely more than 75 percent of the 91 full members were identified. Using the categories utilized in analyzing the membership of the obkomy, we find the following distribution of the 70 members identified: 18 Party officials, 28 state administrators (including 11 plant managers and heads of construction trusts), 2 scientists, 1 newspaper man, 5 educators, 2 military officers, 4 miscellaneous officials, and 10 rank-and-file personnel.

Included among the Party officials named to the Ulianovsk gorkom were 2 officials of the obkom (the second secretary and the head of the organizational-Party work department), 7 gorkom officials, the first secretaries of the 4 raikomy in the city, the secretary and deputy secretary of the Party committee of the automobile works (the largest plant in the city — or at least the largest civilian plant), and the secretaries of the Party committees of 3 other industrial enterprises. (In addition, the 2 military officers were the Party secretaries of 2 officer training schools [*uchilishche*] in the city.)

Among the state administrators named to the Ulianovsk gorkom were not only city administrators, but also 6 oblast-level administrators who happened to work in the capital: the head of the oblast construction bank, the heads of automobile transportation and the movie distribution administrations of the oblast soviet, the oblast procurator, the deputy chairman of the oblast KGB, and the deputy head of the Ulianovsk railroad. The city-level officials were the chairman and two deputy chairmen of the gorispolkom, the chairman of the city peoples' control committee, the head of the municipal services administration of the city soviet, the head of the city administration for sale of fruits and vegetables, the head of the city communications center, and the head of the telecenter. The enterprise managers included 8 directors of industrial plants and 3 heads of construction trusts. Finally,

3 of the 4 chairmen of the city's raiispolkomy were named to the gorkom.

The educators on the Ulianovsk gorkom ranged from the rector of the pedagogical institute to the pro-rector of the agricultural institute to the director of a secondary school to a rank-and-file teacher. The men listed as scientists were the head of the civil design institute and a researcher at the Lenin Museum. The miscellaneous officials were the chairmen of the trade union obkom for state officials, the oblast sports society, and the union of artists, as well as the head of the oblast drama theater. Included in the rank-and-file personnel were not only the usual workers, but also a shop head and a junior design administrator. The 20 unknown included 13 women, and among them were probably represented a number of persons in normal "women's jobs" — doctors, trade personnel, light industry workers, and probably Party secretaries in enterprises in these realms.

If one has access to the appropriate newspapers, complete information on the positions of the members of the Party bureaus is much easier to obtain than that on the members of the Party committees. The following 3 tables summarize some of this material. Table A.3 presents aggregate data on the 14 republics with republican Party organs. (In 1954 and 1956 there was a fifteenth such republic — the Karelo-Finnish republic — but it is excluded in order to increase the comparability of the various years.) Table A.4 presents information on the members of all the 1966 obkom bureaus on which information was collected. Table A.5 presents such information on 7 gorkom bureaus in 1966, the gorkomy selected to give some sense of the range of possibilities found.

Table A.3. Membership of the Republican Party bureaus, 1954–1966.

Officials	1954 Member	1954 Candidate Member	1956 Member	1956 Candidate Member	1961 Member	1961 Candidate Member	1962–1964 Member	1962–1964 Candidate Member	1966 Member	1966 Candidate Member
FULL-TIME PARTY APPARATUS										
Republican secretaries	56	10	79	6	83	12	86	13	75	20
Rebublican department heads (usually Party organs department)	44	0	67	0	68	2	70	1	70	1
City and regional secretaries	7	4	3	3	3	7	0	3	0	5
Chairmen, Party-state control	5	5	9	3	12	3	3	8	5	14
Chairmen, Party control committee	0	1	–	–	–	–	13	1	–	0
REPUBLICAN STATE APPARATUS	62	4	55	6	56	8	33	11	48	15
Chairmen, Council of Ministers	14	0	14	0	14	1	14	0	14	0
Chairmen, Presidium Supreme Soviet	14	0	14	0	13	0	14	0	14	0
Deputy chairmen, Council of Ministers (agriculture)	5	1	8	2	4	1	1	4	5	2
Ministers (agriculture)	4	1	1	0	1	0	0	0	0	0
Deputy chairmen, Council of Ministers (industry)	9	0	6	2	9	0	1	2	6	2
Chairmen, sovnarkhozy	–	–	–	–	9	9	1	0	–	–
Ministers (industry)	1	1	0	0	0	0	0	0	0	0
Deputy chairmen, Council of Ministers (culture)	1	0	2	0	0	0	0	1	0	1
Ministers (culture)	1	0	0	1	1	0	2	4	1	3
Heads of police	11	1	9	0	5	0	2	4	8	6
Chairmen, state (peoples) control	1	0	0	1	0	2	–	–	–	–
Miscellaneous	1	0	1	1	0	0	0	0	0	1
OTHER										
Military	13	15	10	17	11	24	7	17	8	14
Republican Komsomol secretaries	5	2	6	1	5	3	5	2	6	1
Republican trade union chairmen	0	9	2	7	1	8	1	6	1	5
Newspaper editors	4	1	2	3	3	8	1	9	1	8
Miscellaneous	2	2	0	6	1	5	0	0	0	0
Unknown	1	0	0	0	1	0	0	0	0	0
TOTAL	131	29	144	29	150	44	126	41	131	49

Table A.4. Membership of seven obkom bureaus, 1966.[a]

Officials	Krasnodar[b]	Leningrad	Moscow	Rostov	Ulianovsk	Volgograd	Yaroslavl
Obkom secretaries	5	5	5	5	5	5	5
Head organizational-Party work department, obkom	–	1	C	1	1	–	C
First secretary, capital gorkom	1	1	–	1	1	1	1
First secretary, other gorkomy	1 [b]	–	1	–	–	1	1
Chairman oblispolkom	1	1	1	1	1	1	1
First deputy chairman, oblispolkom	1	–	–	–	1	1	C
Chairman peoples' control committee	1	1	1	C	C	1	1
Chairman KGB	C	1	1	1	1	C	1
Chairman trade union council	C	1	1	–	1	C	–
Editor oblast newspaper	1	C	–	1	C	1	C
Komsomol first secretary	C	–	–	C	C	1	C
Commander military district	–	1	–	1	–	–	–
Head regional construction administration	–	C	–	–	–	C	–
Head regional supply administration	–	–	1	–	–	–	1
Chairman, capital gorispolkom	–	1	–	–	–	–	–
Unknown	–	–	Two C's	–	–	–	–

[a] The number of each type of official who is a full member of a particular obkom bureau is indicated by numerals; the candidate members are indicated by C.

[b] The first secretary in this case is the first secretary of the Adygei obkom; the oblast officials in the Krasnodar case are actually krai officials.

Table A.5. Membership of seven gorkom bureaus, 1966.[a]

Officials	Ashkhabad	Kishinev	Krasnodar	Leningrad	Rostov	Tbilisi	Ulianovsk
Gorkom secretaries	3	3	3	5	3	3	3
Head organizational-Party work department, gorkom	—	1	—	C	1	1	1
First secretary, raikomy	2	1	3	1 + C	2	1	—
Chairman gorispolkom	1	1	1	1	1	1	1
First deputy chairman, gorispolkom	—	—	1	—	—	1	—
Chairman peoples' control committee	1	1	1	1	1	C	1
Factory manager	—	—	—	1	1	1	1
Party secretary, industrial plant	1	—	1	1	—	—	—
Army political officer	—	—	1	1	1	1	—
First secretary, Komsomol gorkom	—	1	1	—	C	C	C
Head oblast public order administration	—	—	—	1	—	—	—
Deputy head oblast KGB	—	—	—	—	—	—	C
Rector pedagogical institute	—	—	—	—	—	—	1
Secretary, oblast trade union council	—	—	—	—	C	—	—
Editor, city newpaper	—	—	—	—	1	—	—
Unknown	1	1	—	—	—	—	1

[a] The number of each type of official who is a full member of a particular gorkom bureau is indicated by numerals; the candidate members are indicated by C.

Appendix B. The Selection of the 170 Most Important Plants

Few tasks are more difficult in any country than ranking the importance of corporations and plants. If one utilizes the criteria of size of capital plant or number of workers, one faces the problem of differing labor intensity in different industries. Even if one uses the criterion of output value, one runs the risk of neglecting vital industries whose technology demands somewhat smaller production units. For the Soviet Union the general problems of ranking industrial enterprises are multiplied by a scarcity of information. Soviet sources almost never reveal the gross output or the size of the capital plant of individual enterprises and only rarely indicate their number of workers. For these reasons the compilation of the list of the 170 most important enterprises had to rest on judgment, judgment based on a variety of indicators.

There are many different types of information available which give some indication of the relative importance of Soviet plants. Occasionally a direct statement may be found. In 1967, for example, the Cherepovets Metallurgy Works was said to rank fourth in output among the Soviet steel plants, second in the RSFSR to the Magnitogorsk Combine. Several years earlier, an article asserted that the three largest plants in Gorki oblast were the Gorki Auto Works, the Krasnoe Sormovo Shipbuilding Works, and the Balakhna Cellulose-Paper Combine. Even more usual are references to a particular plant as *krupneishee* (one of the most important) in its industry, city, or republic. Infrequent indications of the number of employees or the number of Communists in a plant are also helpful.

The most important source of information about the relative size of plants, however, is the frequency with which they are mentioned in the press. When one examines the technical journals of the various industries, one quickly notices that certain enterprises are discussed very often and other enterprises infrequently. When one reads the Party press over time, one discovers that the managers of certain plants in a city or oblast are far more likely to speak at Party conferences and at meetings of the Party *aktiv* than the managers at other plants. Lists of important plants in either source tend to include the same plants from time to time, and their order often seems to represent relative importance. (In general, the frequency-of-mention indicator correlates very well with more precise comparative statements in the Soviet press.)

In order to alleviate the problem of comparing plants in industries of different labor intensity, I selected a number of industries which seemed quite important and which were sufficiently covered in the Soviet press to provide adequate data. For each industry, a round number of plants was selected, the number reflecting my best judgment about the general relative importance of the plants in the economy. In this way it was possible to include a number of machine tool plants which seem quite prominent but which probably do not rank in size with a number of steel plants and textile combines which do not seem so important.

In selecting the industries to be included, I excluded industries such as oil extraction and coal in which it was difficult to decide what constitutes the meaningful "enterprise." Industries such as building materials and the defense industry were excluded because of scarcity of information. In addition, certain industries (nonferrous metallurgy, oil refining, the food industry) were covered only in certain geographic areas because of sparse press coverage of their plants in other areas (particularly the region east of the Volga). It was exclusions of this type — motivated by the desire to avoid an unduly large "unknown" category and a fear that the scattered information available did not represent a reliable sample — which produced the decision to reduce the number of plants examined from 200 to 170.

Even if it were possible to make an unerring judgment about the 170 most important plants at a particular time, an attempt to analyze the tenure of plant managers involves the problem of change over time in the relative importance of enterprises. This problem is somewhat alleviated by the Soviet tendency to expand existing plants (each director being subjected to the ratchet principle), but rapid industrialization has also expressed itself in the construction of many new large plants. The list of plants appropriate for the discussion of the 1948–1953 period (Chapter III) is not the same list appropriate for the table on the tenure of 1967 directors found in Chapter III, note 87. However, the available information is not sufficiently precise to determine the relative changes in plant size over a reasonably short period of time.

For this reason the list of the 170 plants is based on my best judgment as to the situation in the late 1950's, midway between the 1948 and the 1967 analyses. Although this decision may have certain drawbacks, it does have the advantage of removing one possible source of bias. As the study progressed, as the conviction grew that managerial turnover had been low in the post-Stalin period, as analysis emerged to explain this fact, there may have been an unconscious tendency to select plants on the basis of the tenure of their directors. However, with 1962 and 1967 being chosen as the years for the construction of the tables, with the same list of plants being used in both years, the danger of being influenced by this factor was greatly reduced. The inclusion of a plant whose director was changed in 1963 might increase the percentage of 1962 plant directors with a tenure of over five years, but it simultaneously reduced the percentage of 1967 directors with such tenure.

The following are the industries and plants chosen for the most important 170. The final decision on inclusion is mine alone, but I would like to express my gratitude to Professor Leon Smolinski for unfailing help in the early stages of the construction of the list.

Iron and steel industry: Alchev Metallurgy Works (formerly the Voroshilovsk Works), Azovstal, Cheliabinsk Electrometallurgy Combine (formerly the Cheliabinsk Ferroalloy Works), Cheliabinsk Metallurgy Works, Cheliabinsk Tubing Works, Cherepovetsk Metallurgy Works, Dneprodzerzhinsk Metallurgy Works, Dnepropetrovsk Metallurgy Works named Karl Libknekht, Dnepropetrovsk Metallurgy Works named Lenin, Dnepropetrovsk Metallurgy Works named Petrovski, Dneprospetstal (Dnepro Special Steel Works, Zaporozhe), Donetsk (formerly Stalino) Metallurgy Works, Elektrostal (Moscow oblast), Enakiev Metallurgy Works, Krasnyi Oktiabr (Volgograd), Krivoi Rog Metallurgy Works, Kuznetsk Metallurgy Combine, Leningrad Steel Rolling Works, Magnitogorsk Metallurgy Combine, Makeevka Metallurgy Works, Nikopol Southern Tubing Works, Nizhnii Tagil Metallurgy Combine, Pervoural Tubing Works, Rustavi Metallurgy Works, Serov Metallurgy Works, Serp and Molot (Moscow), Taganrog Metallurgy Works, Zaporozhstal, Zhdanov (formerly Mariupol) Metallurgy Works, and Zlatousov Metallurgy Works.

Agriculture Machinery-Tractor-Automobile Industry: Altai Tractor Works, Cheliabinsk Road Machinery Works named Koliushchenko, Cheliabinsk Tractor Works, Gorki Auto Works, Kharkov Tractor Works, Kirovski Works (Leningrad), Krasnaia Zvezda (Kirovograd), Krasnoiarsk Combine Works, Krasnyi Aksai (Rostov), Krasnyi Ekskavator (Kiev), Lipetsk Tractor Works, Liubertsy Agriculture Machinery Works, Lvov Bus Works, Minsk Auto Works, Minsk Tractor Works, Moscow Auto Works, Moscow Small (*Malolitrazhnyi*) Car Works, Odessa Agriculture Machinery Works named October Revolution, Rostselmash (Rostov Agriculture Machinery Works), Serp and Molot (Kharkov), Sibselmash (Siberian Agriculture Machinery Works, Novosibirsk), Taganrog Combine Works, Tashselmash (Tashkent Agriculture Machinery Works), Tula Combine Works, Ulianovsk Auto Works, Ural Auto Works (Miass), Vladimir Tractor Works, Volgograd (formerly Stalingrad) Tractor Works, Yaroslavl Motor (formerly Auto) Works, and Zaporozhe Kommunar Works.

Transportation Machinery: Admiralty Ship Works (Leningrad), Baltii Ship Works (Leningrad), Izhorski Ship Works (Leningrad), Kalinin Railroad Car Works, Kharkov Transportation Machinery Works, Kolomna Locomotive Works, Krasnoe Sormovo (Gorki), Kriukov Railroad Car Works, Leninskaia Kuznitsa Ship Works (Kiev), Lugansk (formerly Voroshilovgrad) Locomotive Works, Lvov Auto-Carrier Works, Nikolaev Ship Works named Nosenko, Russkii Dizel (Leningrad), Sverdlovsk Transportation Works, and Uralvagon (Ural Railroad Car Works, Nizhnii Tagil).

Machine Tool and Miscellaneous Machinery Works: Alma-Ata Heavy Machinery Works, Borets (Moscow), Dnepropetrovsk Metallurgy Equipment Works, Elektrostal Heavy Machinery Works (formerly Novo-Kramatorsk Heavy Machinery Works in Moscow oblast), First Ballbearing Works (formerly Kaganovich Ballbearing Works, Moscow), Frezer (Moscow), Irkutsk Heavy Machinery Works, Ivanovo Textile Machinery Works, Iuzhuralmash (Southern Urals Machinery Works), Kalibr (Moscow), Kiev Automatic Machine Tool Works named Gorki, Kolomna Heavy Machine Tool Works, Krasnyi Proletariat (Moscow) Kuibyshev Fourth Ballbearing Works, Kuibyshev Ninth Ballbearing Works, Leningrad Textile Machinery Works named Karl Marx, Lt. Smith Machinery Works (Baku), Neva Machinery Works (Leningrad), Novo-Kramatorsk Heavy Machinery Works (Ukraine), Novosibirsk Heavy Hydro-press Machine Tool Works named Efremov, Odessa Crane Works named January Uprising, Sergo Ordzhonikidze Machine Tool Works (Moscow), Sibtiazhmash (Siberian Heavy Machinery Works, Krasnoiarsk), Srednevolga Machine Tool Works (Central Volga Machine Tool Works, Kuibyshev), Svet Shakhtera (Light of the Miner, Kharkov), Tashkent Textile Machinery Works, Tbilisi Machine Tool Works named Kirov, Tbilisi Machine Tool Works named Ordzhonikidze, Uralkhimmash (Ural Chemical Machinery Works, Sverdlovsk), and Uralmash (Ural Machinery Works, Sverdlovsk).

Electrotechnical Industry: Armenian Electric Machinery Works, Dinamo (Moscow), Elektrik (Leningrad), Elektrosila (Leningrad), Kharkov Electromechanical Works, Kharkov Heavy Electric Machinery Works, Kharkov Turbine Generator Works, Kiev Precision Electric Works, Metallist Works (Leningrad), Moscow Cable Works, Moscow Electric Works (earlier Moscow Auto-Tractor Electrical Equipment Works), Moscow Lamp Works, Novocherkassy Electric Locomotive Works, Sibelektromotor (Siberian Electric Works, earlier Tomsk Electromechanical Works), Sibelektrotiazh (Siberian Heavy Electric Machinery Works, Novosibirsk), Sverdlovsk Turbine Generator Works, Ukrkabel (Ukrainian Cable Works, Kiev), Uralelektrotiazhmash (Ural Heavy Electric Machinery Works, Sverdlovsk — formerly Uralelektroapparat), VEF (Riga), and Vladimir Ilich Works (Moscow).

Chemical Industry: Berezniki Nitrogen Fertilizer Works (later Berezniki Chemical Combine), Chernorechnyi Chemical Works (Dzerzhinsk), Chirchik Electrochemical Combine, Dorogomilov Chemical Works, Erevan Synthetic Rubber Works, Erevan Tire Works, Kauchuk (Moscow), Kiev Artificial Fiber Works, Kirovakan Chemical Combine, Lisichansk Chemical Combine, Moscow Tire

Works, Novomoskovsk Chemical Combine (formerly Stalinogorsk Chemical Combine), Rubezh Chemical Combine, Voskresensk Chemical Combine, and Yaroslavl Tire Works.

Miscellaneous Heavy Industry: Baku Oil Refinery named Karaev (formerly named Andreev), Baku Oil Refinery named XXII Party Congress (formerly named Stalin), Balakhna Cellulose-Paper Combine, Balkhash Mining-Metal Combine (earlier Balkhash Copper Works), Chimkent Lead Works, Dnepro Aluminum Works, Kama Cellulose-Paper Combine (formerly Krasnokama Cellulose-Paper Combine), Kolchugino Non-Ferrous Processing Plant, Krasnyi Vyborzhets (Leningrad), Leningrad Optics-Mechanics Works, Leninogorsk Polimetal Combine, Moscow Oil Refinery, Novo-Baku Oil Refinery, Solikamsk Cellulose-Paper Combine, and Ust-Kamenogorsk Lead-Zinc Combine.

Miscellaneous Light Industry: Bolshevik (Moscow), Bolshaia Ivanovo Manufaktura, Burevstnik (Moscow), Krasnodar Worsted Cloth Works, Krasnaia Roza (Moscow), Krasnyi Bogatyr (Moscow), Krasnyi Oktiabr (Moscow), Moscow Food Combine, Moscow Meat Combine, Moscow Silk Combine named Shcherbakov, Orekhovo-Zuevo Textile Combine, Parizhskaia Kommuna (Moscow), Skorokhod (Leningrad), Tashkent Textile Combine, and Trekhgornaia Manufaktura (Moscow).

Bibliography

Books and Articles

Books providing primary data on Soviet personnel are discussed in the next section.

Almond, Gabriel A., and G. Bingham Powell, Jr., *Comparative Politics: A Developmental Approach* (Boston: Little, Brown, and Company, 1966).

Armstrong, John A., "Sources of Administrative Behavior: Some Soviet and Western European Comparisons," *The American Political Science Review,* 59 (September 1965), 643–655.

—— *The Soviet Bureaucratic Elite* (New York: Frederick A. Praeger, 1959).

Avrich, Paul H., "The Bolshevik Revolution and Workers' Control in Russian Industry," *Slavic Review,* 22 (March 1963), 47–63.

Avtorkhanov, Abdurakhman, *The Communist Party Apparatus* (Chicago: Henry Regnery, 1966).

Azrael, Jeremy R., *Managerial Power and Soviet Politics* (Cambridge, Mass.: Harvard University Press, 1966).

Barnard, Chester I., *The Functions of the Executive* (Cambridge, Mass.: Harvard University Press, 1938).

—— *Organization and Management* (Cambridge, Mass.: Harvard University Press, 1948).

Berliner, Joseph, *Factory and Manager in the USSR* (Cambridge, Mass.: Harvard University Press, 1957).

—— "Managerial Incentives and Decision-Making: A Comparison of the United States and the Soviet Union," *Comparisons of the United States and Soviet Economies* (Washington, D.C.: US Government Printing Office, 1959), pt. 1, pp. 349–375.

Bienstock, Gregory, Solomon Schwartz, and Aaron Yugow, *Management in Russian Industry and Agriculture* (Ithaca: Cornell University Press, 1948).

341

Blau, Peter M., *The Dynamics of Bureaucracy* (Chicago: University of Chicago Press, 1955).

—— and W. Richard Scott, *Formal Organizations, A Comparative Approach* (San Francisco: Chandler Publishing Company, 1962).

Bridges, Peter S., "The Character of the Party Secretary in Postwar Soviet Literature," (Master's thesis, Columbia University, 1955).

Brzezinski, Zbigniew, and Samuel P. Huntington, *Political Power USA/ USSR* (New York: The Viking Press, 1963).

Bugaev, E. I., and B. M. Leibson, *Besedy ob ustave KPSS* (Conversations about the Rules of the CPSU; Moscow, 1962).

Carr, E. H., *The Bolshevik Revolution, 1917–1923* (New York: Macmillan, 1951–1953).

Chapman, Brian, *The Prefects and Provincial France* (London: G. Allen & Unwin, 1955).

—— *The Profession of Government* (London: G. Allen & Unwin, 1959).

Chernikov, K. V., ed., *KPSS i massovye organizatsii trudiashchikhsia* (The CPSU and Mass Organizations of the Toilers; Moscow, 1963).

Communist Party of the Soviet Union, Congresses. (See also Gruliow, ed., *Current Soviet Policies* for the Nineteenth Party Congress.)

  Vosmoi sezd RKP(B), Protokoly (Eighth Congress of the Russian Communist Party, Protocols [March 18–23, 1919]; Moscow, 1962.)

  Odinnadtsatyi sezd RKP(b), Stenograficheskii otchet (Eleventh Congress of the Russian Communist Party, Stenographic Report [March 27–April 2, 1922]; Moscow, 1961).

  XVIII sezd vsesoiuznoi kommunisticheskoi partii (b), Stenograficheskii otchet (Eighteenth Congress of the All-Union Communist Party, Stenographic Report [March 10–21, 1939]; Moscow, 1939).

  XXIII sezd kommunisticheskoi partii sovetskogo soiuza, Stenograficheskii otchet (Twenty-third Congress of the Communist Party of the Soviet Union [March 29–April 8, 1966]; Moscow, 1966).

Crozier, Michel, *The Bureaucratic Phenomenon* (Chicago: University of Chicago Press, 1964).

Dahl, Robert A., and Charles E. Lindblom, *Politics, Economics, and Welfare* (New York: Harper & Row, 1953).

Dalton, Melville, *Men Who Manage* (New York: John Wiley & Sons, 1959).

DeWitt, Nicholas, *Soviet Professional Manpower* (Washington, D.C.: US Government Printing Office, 1955).

Dodds, Harold W., *The Academic President — Educator or Caretaker?* (New York: McGraw-Hill, 1962).

Drucker, Peter, *Concept of the Corporation* (New York: John Day, 1946).

Dudintsev, Vladimir, *Ne khlebom edinym* (Not by Bread Alone; Munich: TsOPE Publishing House, 1957).

—— *Not by Bread Alone,* Edith Bone trans. (New York: E. P. Dutton, 1957).

Dunham, Vera S., *The Party Secretary in Postwar Soviet Literature* (Project on the Soviet Social System, Harvard University, 1953).

Edelman, Murray, *The Symbolic Uses of Politics* (Urbana: University of Illinois Press, 1964).

Efimov, A. N., *Perestroika upravlenii promyshlennostiu i stroitelstvom* (The Reorganization of the Administration of Industry and Construction; Moscow, 1957).

Ehrenburg, Ilia, *The Thaw,* Manya Harari trans. (Chicago: Henry Regnery Company, 1955).

Evdokimov, V. I., *Politicheskoe prosveshchenie — reshaiushchee zveno propagandistskoi raboty* (Political Education — The Decisive Link of Propaganda Work; Moscow, 1962).

Evenko, I. A., *Voprosy planirovaniia v SSSR na sovremennom etape* (Problems of Planning in the USSR at the Present Time; Moscow, 1959).

Fainsod, Merle, *How Russia Is Ruled* (rev. ed.; Cambridge, Mass.: Harvard University Press, 1963).

—— *Smolensk under Soviet Rule* (Cambridge, Mass.: Harvard University Press, 1958).

Fenno, Richard F., Jr., *The President's Cabinet* (Cambridge, Mass.: Harvard University Press, 1959).

Fesler, James K., *Area and Administration* (University, Alabama: University of Alabama Press, 1949).

—— "The Political Role of Field Administration," in Ferrell Heady and Sybil L. Stokes, eds., *Papers in Comparative Public Administration* (Ann Arbor: Institute of Public Administration, University of Michigan, 1962).

Fomin, I., *Podbor, rasstanovka, i vospitanie kadrov* (The Selection, Distribution, and Training of Personnel; Moscow, 1953).

Fried, Robert C., *The Italian Prefects* (New Haven: Yale University Press, 1963).

Granick, David, *Management of the Industrial Firm in the USSR* (New York: Columbia University Press, 1954).

Granick, David, *The Red Executive* (Garden City: Doubleday, 1960).

Groshev, I. I., ed., *Vospitanie kommunisticheskoi soznatelnosti* (The Training of Communist Consciousness; Moscow, 1964).

Gross, Bertram M., *The Managing of Organization* (New York: Free Press, 1964).

Gruliow, Leo, ed., *Current Soviet Policies* (New York: Frederick A. Praeger, 1953).

Herring, E. Pendleton, *Public Administration and the Public Interest* (New York: McGraw-Hill, 1936).

Hodnett, Grey, "The Obkom First Secretaries," *Slavic Review,* 24 (December 1965), 636–652.

The Hoover Commission Report (New York: McGraw-Hill, 1949).

Hough, Jerry F., "A Harebrained Scheme in Retrospect," *Problems of Communism,* 14 (July–August 1965), 26–32.

—— "The Party Apparatus," in F. Gordon Skilling and Franklyn Griffiths, *Interest Groups in Soviet Politics* (Princeton: Princeton University Press, forthcoming).

—— "The Soviet Concept of the Relationship between the Lower Party Organs and the State Administration," *Slavic Review,* 24 (June 1965), 215–240.

—— "The Soviet Elite: I. Groups and Individuals," *Problems of Communism,* 16 (January–February 1967), 28–35.

Inkeles, Alex, *Public Opinion in Soviet Russia* (Cambridge, Mass.: Harvard University Press, 1950).

Itogi vsesoiuznoi perepisi naseleniia 1959 goda RSFSR (The Results of the 1959 All-Union Census in the RSFSR; Moscow, 1963).

Kantorovich, L. V., *Ekonomicheskii raschet nailuchshego izpolzovaniia resurvov* (Economic Calculation of the Best Use of Reserves; Moscow, 1959).

Karpov, M., and G. Brovarski, *Partiinaia informatsiia* (Party Information; Moscow, 1962).

Khrushchev, Nikita S., *Stroitelstvo kommunizma v SSSR i razvitie selskogo khoziaistva* (The Building of Communism in the USSR and the Development of Agriculture; Moscow, 1962–1964).

Kochetov, Vsevolod, *Bratia Ershovy* (The Brothers Ershov; Moscow, 1959).

—— *Molodost s nami* (Youth With Us; Moscow, 1957).

—— *Sekretar obkoma* (The Secretary of the Regional Committee; Moscow, 1962).

Kolbenkov, N. F., *Sovershentsvovanie rukovodstva promyshlennostiu*

SSSR, 1956–60 (The Perfecting of the Leadership of Industry of the USSR, 1956–1960; Moscow, 1961).

Kozlov, G. A., and S. P. Pervushin, eds., *Kratkii ekonomicheskii slovar* (Short Economics Dictionary; Moscow, 1958).

Kukhalashvili, K. P., ed., *Partiinaia rabota v promyshlennosti* (Party Work in Industry; Kiev, 1959).

Kulev, I. A., *O dalneishom sovershenstvovanii planirovaniia i rukovodstva narodnym khoziaistvom* (About the Further Perfecting of the Planning and Leadership of the Economy; Moscow, 1957).

Landsberger, Henry A., "The Horizontal Dimension in Bureaucracy," *Administrative Science Quarterly,* 5 (December 1961), 299–332.

LaPalombara, Joseph, "Bureaucracy and Political Development: Notes, Queries, and Dilemmas," in Joseph LaPalombara, ed., *Bureaucracy and Political Development* (Princeton: Princeton University Press, 1963).

Leiserson, Avery, *Administrative Regulation: A Study in Representation of Interests* (Chicago: University of Chicago Press, 1942).

Lenin, V. I., *Sochineniia* (Works; 4th ed.; Moscow, 1941–1962).

Levine, Herbert S., "The Centralized Planning of Supply in Soviet Industry," Joint Economic Committee (86th Cong., 1st sess.), *Comparisons of the United States and Soviet Economies,* 1:151–176.

Lippmann, Walter, *A Preface to Politics* (New York: M. Kennerly, 1913).

Lipset, Seymour M., "The Changing Class Structure and Contemporary European Politics," *Daedalus,* Vol. 93, no. 1 (Winter 1964).

McClelland, David C., *The Achieving Society* (Princeton: Van Nostrand, 1961).

Macmahon, Arthur W., *Delegation and Autonomy* (Bombay: Asia Publishing House, 1961).

———, John D. Millet, and Gladys Ogden, *The Administration of Federal Work Relief* (Chicago: Public Administration Service, 1941).

Maddick, Henry, *Democracy, Decentralization, and Development* (London: Asia Publishing House, 1963).

Merton, Robert K., *Social Theory and Social Structure,* revised and enlarged edition (Glencoe: The Free Press, 1957).

Mickiewicz, Ellen Propper, *Soviet Political Schools* (New Haven: Yale University Press, 1967).

Montgomery, John D., "A Royal Invitation: Variations on Three Classical Themes," in John D. Montgomery and William J. Sifflin, eds., *Approaches to Development* (New York: McGraw-Hill, 1966).

Moore, Barrington, *Social Origins of Dictatorship and Democracy* (Boston: Beacon Press, 1967).

—— *Terror and Progress — USSR* (Cambridge, Mass.: Harvard University Press, 1954).

Morozov, P. D., *Leninskie printsipy podbora, rasstanovki, i vospitaniia kadrov* (Leninist Principles of the Selection, the Distribution, and Training of Personnel; Moscow, 1959).

Narodnoe khoziaistvo Belorusskoi SSR (The Economy of the Belorussian Soviet Socialist Republic; Moscow, 1957).

Nove, Alec, *Economic Rationality and Soviet Politics* (New York: Frederick A. Praeger, 1964).

—— "The Problem of 'Success Indicators' in Soviet Industry," *Economica,* New Series, 25 (February 1958), 1–13.

Novick, David, Melvin Anshen, and W. C. Truppner, *Wartime Production Controls* (New York: Columbia University Press, 1949).

Ovalov, Lev, *Partiinoe poruchenie* (Party Assignment; Moscow, 1964).

Ovechkin, Valentin, *Trudnaia vesna* (Difficult Spring; Moscow, 1956).

Pai, M. P. "The Emerging Role of the Collector," *The Indian Journal of Public Administration,* 8 (October–December, 1962), 478–488.

Panferov, Fedor, *Volga-Matushka reka* (Mother-Volga River; Moscow, 1954).

Panova, Vera, *Kruzhilikha* (Kruzhilikha; Moscow, 1948).

Parry, Albert, *The New Class Divided* (New York: Macmillan, 1966).

Parsons, Talcott, "Evolutionary Universals in Society," *American Sociological Review,* 29 (June 1964), 339–357.

Petrov, S. M., ed., *Uchenye zapiski kafedr istorii kommunisticheskoi partii Sovetskogo Soiuza vysshei partiinoi shkoly pri TsK KPSS i mestnykh vysshikh partiinykh shkol* (Learned Papers of the Department of the History of the Communist Party of the Soviet Union of the Higher Party School under the CC CPSU and of the Local Higher Party Schools; issue no. I, Moscow, 1959).

Plenum TsK KPSS, Stenograficheskii otchet (Plenum of the Central Committee [June 24–29, 1959], Stenographic Report; Moscow, 1959).

Pokrovskii, B. A., ed., *V tesnoi sviazi s zhizniu* (In Close Connection with Life; Moscow, 1958).

Promyshlennost SSSR — Statisticheskii sbornik (Industry of the USSR — A Statistical Handbook; Moscow, 1957).

Pye, Lucian, *Politics, Personality, and Nation Building* (New Haven, Yale University Press, 1962).

Riabtsev, I. G., *Sbornik statei po voprosam istorii KPSS* (A Collection of Articles on the History of the CPSU; Moscow, 1957).

Rigby, T. H., "Traditional, Market, and Organizational Societies and the USSR," *World Politics,* 16 (July 1964), 539–557.

——— "The Selection of Leading Personnel in the Soviet State and the Communist Party" (Doctoral dissertation, University of London, 1954).

Rokeach, Milton, *The Open and the Closed Mind* (New York: Basic Books, 1960).

Rush, Myron, *The Rise of Khrushchev* (Washington: Public Affairs Press, 1958).

Sbornik statei po voprosam istorii KPSS (A Collection of Articles on the History of the CPSU; 2nd ed.; Moscow, 1958).

Schachter, Ruth, "Single-Party Systems in West Africa," *American Political Science Review,* 55 (June 1961), 294–307.

Schapiro, Leonard, *The Communist Party of the Soviet Union* (New York: Random House, 1959).

Scott, Derek J. R., *Russian Political Institutions* (New York: Rinehart, 1957).

Selskoe khoziaistvo SSSR — Statisticheskii sbornik (Agriculture of the USSR — A Statistical Handbook; Moscow, 1960).

Shevtsov, N. S., and K. S. Vasilenko, eds., *Rabota partii po vospitaniiu kommunisticheskogo otnosheniia k trudu* (The Work of the Party in Inculcating a Communist Attitude towards Work; Moscow, 1965).

Shorina, E. V. *Kollegialnost i edinonachalie v sovetskom gosudarstvennom upravlenii* (Collegiality and One-Man Management in Soviet State Administration; Moscow, 1959).

Simon, Herbert A., *Administrative Behavior* (2nd ed., New York: Macmillan, 1961).

Slepov, Lazar, "Nezyblemye leninskie normy partiinoi zhizni i printsipy rukovodstva," (The Firm Leninist Norms of Party Life and the Principles of Leadership), in N. Barsukov, ed., *Borba partii za moshchii podem narodnogo khoziaistva, za zavershenie stroitelstva sotsializma, 1953–1958 godu* (The Struggle of the Party for the Powerful Rise of the Economy, for the Completion of the Building of Socialism, 1953–1958; Moscow, 1963).

——— *Vysshie i mestnye organy partii* (The Higher and Local Organs of the Party; Moscow, 1958).

Spravochnik partiinogo rabotnika (The Handbook of the Party Official; Moscow, 1957–1966).

SSSR: Administrativno-territorialnoe delenie soiuznykh respublik (The USSR: The Administrative-Territorial Division of the Union Republics; Moscow, 1960).

Stalin, J. V., *Works* (Moscow: Foreign Languages Publishing House, 1952–1955).

Suvorov, K. I., *Nekotorye voprosy organizatsionno-partiinoi raboty v sovremennykh usloviiakh* (Some Questions of Organizational-Party Work in Contemporary Conditions; Moscow, 1961).

Swearer, Howard, "Khrushchev's Revolution in Industrial Management," *World Politics,* 12 (October 1959), 45–61.

Tannenbaum, Robert, and Warren H. Schmidt, "How to Choose a Leadership Pattern," *Harvard Business Review,* 36 (March–April 1958), 95–101.

Thompson, Victor, *Modern Organization* (New York: Knopf, 1961).

Tolmadzhev, K., ed., *Na novom puti* (On a New Path; Riga, 1957).

Verba, Sidney, "Comparative Political Culture," in Lucian W. Pye and Sidney Verba, eds., *Political Culture and Political Development* (Princeton: Princeton University Press, 1965).

Vlasov, V. A., and S. S. Studenikin, *Sovetskoe administrativnoe pravo* (Soviet Administrative Law; Moscow, 1959).

Voprosy partiinogo stroitelstva (Questions of Party Structure; Leningrad, 1965).

Voprosy partiinoi raboty (Questions of Party Work; Moscow, 1955).

Voprosy partiinoi raboty (Questions of Party Work; 3rd ed., Moscow, 1959).

Vucinich, Alexander, *Soviet Economic Institutions* (Stanford: Stanford University Press, 1952).

Waldo, Dwight, *Perspectives on Administration* (University, Alabama: University of Alabama Press, 1956).

Walker, Charles R., Robert H. Guest, and Arthur N. Turner, *The Foreman on the Assembly Line* (Cambridge, Mass.: Harvard University Press, 1956).

Weber, Max, *The Theory of Social and Economic Organization,* trans. A. M. Henderson and Talcott Parsons (New York: Oxford University Press, 1947).

Primary Data on Soviet Personnel

In the two decades prior to 1958, very little biographical information was published on Party and governmental personnel in the Soviet Union, at least on personnel who were not in the Politburo. In the first years after the war, a number of the republican and local (for example, Moscow) newspapers did publish biographies of a number of the deputies elected to the soviets, but without complete access to the local newspapers in the Soviet libraries, the major source of biographical information in the 1938–1958 period has to be obituaries. Unfortunately, the relative youth of the middle-level Soviet officials during this period and the failure of the press to publish obituaries of men in disgrace reduce the usefulness of this source of information.

Since 1958, biographical information has been published on a more systematic basis. After the elections of 1958, 1962, and 1966, books were issued which contained pictures and short biographies of all the deputies to the USSR Supreme Soviet: *Deputaty Verkhovnogo Soveta SSSR* (Deputies of the Supreme Soviet of the USSR; Moscow, 1959, 1962, and 1966). Fortunately, photo-copies of this source are available through Micro Photo Division, Bell & Howell Company, Cleveland 12, Ohio. Since 1958 the *Bolshaia sovetskaia entsiklopediia* (The Large Soviet Encyclopedia; Moscow) has also become an important source of biographical information. Volume 51 of the encyclopedia (published in 1958) included biographies of the many new Presidium members and ministers. The 1958 yearbook (and all subsequent yearbooks) have a concluding section which provides biographies of certain categories of officials. The most notable categories for our purposes are the Lenin prizewinners (which include a number of plant managers) and the new members of the Council of Ministers. Most important, however, the 1962 and 1966 yearbooks contain a biographies of all the members and candidate members of the Central Committee and the members of the Auditing Commission selected at the XXIInd and XXIIIrd Party congresses respectively. These two volumes of the encyclopedia, in conjunction with the three volumes of the *Deputaty,* are indispensable for the student of local Party officials and top industrial administrators.

Frequently, however, the biographies published in the encyclopedia and the *Deputaty* are not complete, and the student must take care to compile a more comprehensive biography by utilizing all the available volumes. Information on an official's nationality and (in many cases) his social origin is available in the *Deputaty,* but not in the yearbooks of the encyclopedia. The *Deputaty* generally have more complete information on the early work experience of an official, but the yearbooks generally are more precise in specifying the jobs held by a man after entering Party work. The *Deputaty* based on the 1958 Supreme Soviet quite often simply stated that an official had been in "leading Party work" or "leading Party and soviet work" since, for example, 1939, and only indicate the precise post he held at the time of his election to the Supreme Soviet; subsequent *Deputaty* (particularly that of 1966) are much more likely to list previous positions that a man has held, but they often withhold dates of service and in many cases abbreviate the list. The yearbooks are also a better source on the education of Party officials, for they indicate the year of graduation and the nature of college training (whether as a full-time student, an evening student, or a correspondence student). In some cases the *Deputaty* imply a substantial college education, but the yearbook reveals that the man received his degree by correspondence while already a very high official. In these cases the degree may be somewhat akin to the American honorary degree.

Some of the problems in utilizing Soviet biographical data are suggested in two biographies of Semen Z. Borisov, the first secretary of the Yakutia obkom. In *Deputaty* (1958), we find "Born in 1911 of peasants, a Yakut, a Party member since 1932. Secondary education. From 1930 an elementary schoolteacher and the head of a raion department of education. In 1932–1943, an instructor of the executive committee [of Yakutia], chairman of a raiispolkom, instructor, head of the resettlement department of the Yakutia Council of Peoples' Commissars. From 1944, Peoples' Commissar of Agriculture, then Chairman of the Council of Ministers of Yakutia. Since 1951, first secretary of the Yakutia obkom." In the 1962 yearbook of the Encyclopedia, we find "Born 1911 . . . Party member since 1932. In 1939 graduated from the Higher Courses of Soviet Construction. From 1929 — in Soviet work. In 1941–1944, deputy chairman of the Council of Peoples' Commissars, Peoples' Commissar of Agriculture [of Yakutia], in 1946–1948 and 1950–1951 — Chairman of the Council of Ministers of Yakutia. Since 1951, first secretary of the Yakutia obkom."

Because of the omissions in the published biographies of many officials, serious study of elite Soviet officials is facilitated by the collection of information from the Soviet press on an individual basis. If in the course of reading the press one records references to particular men identified in particular posts, it is possible to compile a file of officials of various types and thereby to fill in gaps in the official biographies and to resolve many inconsistencies among them. This task is made easier by a series issued first by the Division of Biographical Information of the State Department, then by the Central Intelligence Agency, entitled *Directory of Soviet Officials*. The 1955 and 1957 editions have excellent data on the ministries (including deputy ministers and many heads of glavki) and on the obkom first secretaries, and the subsequent editions include the names of lower obkom secretaries and sovnarkhoz officials. For many types of officials, however, there is no alternative to the collection of individual references in the Soviet press to the occupants of posts. This procedure is unavoidable, for example, if one wants tenure data on plant managers or background information on the industrial secretaries of the gorkomy of the republican capitals.

A final Soviet source of biographical information should be emphasized once again — the obituaries, which are so indispensable in the pre-1958 period. They continued to be published after 1958, and they contain valuable information on a number of types of officials. They often contain supplementary data on men whose shorter biographies are available in the *Deputaty* or encyclopedia yearbooks, and they are the prime source of information on many lower-level types of officials. Moreover, obituaries are now published of many officials (notably obkom first secretaries) who fell into disgrace in the period before biographies were published systematically. Through this means it is becoming possible to increase substantially the size of the sample in tables on obkom first secretaries of the late Stalin period. Many of these obituaries are published in the *Current Digest of the Soviet Press* (Ann Arbor: The Joint Committee on Slavic Studies, 1949 to the present).

In addition to the Soviet sources of biographical information, there are several other English-language sources which should be mentioned. In particular, the Institute for the Study of the USSR in Munich has been instrumental in the production of three collections of biographies: *Biographic Directory of the USSR,* Wladimir S. Merzalow, ed. (New York: Scarecrow Press, 1958); *Who's Who in the USSR, 1960/1961,* Dr. Heinrich E. Schultz and Dr. Stephen S. Taylor, eds. (Montreal: Intercontinental Book and Publishing, 1962): *Who's Who in the USSR, 1965/1966,* Andrew I. Lebed, Dr. Heinrich E. Schulz, and Dr. Stephen S. Taylor, eds. (New York: Scarecrow Press, 1966). These volumes include full biographies from such sources as the *Deputaty* and the encyclopedia yearbooks, but also partial biographies of certain types of officials (most notably republican Party and state officials and in the 1958 volume also obkom first secretaries in the RSFSR and the Ukraine). Unfortunately, these volumes are marred by many errors in posts listed in the partial biographies and even in translation (for example, in the biography of Semen Borisov mentioned above the word *"sovnarkom"* — council of peoples' commissars — is translated "sovnarkhoz," a quite different institution). The two editions of the *Who's Who* are not as unreliable as the *Biographic Directory,* but a serious scholar of the Party apparatus should use all with great caution. The *Bulletin* of the Institute for the Study of the USSR also includes supplements listing the occupants of Soviet posts and has a particularly valuable monthly feature — "Changes and Appointments" — which helps to keep personnel data current.

Soviet Newspapers and Magazines

The primary sources of Soviet information on the role of the Party apparatus are not books and pamphlets, but newspapers and magazines. The most indispensable periodicals are the organs of the Central Committee itself — first and foremost, the newspapers *Pravda* (Truth) and *Sovetskaia Rossiia* (Soviet Russia) and the magazine *Partiinaia zhizn* (Party Life), earlier entitled *Partiinoe stroitelstvo* (Party Construction). No serious study of the lower Party apparatus can afford to neglect these three periodicals. Two other organs of the Central Committee — *Kommunist* (Communist), earlier entitled *Bolshevik* (Bolshevik), and *Ekonomicheskaia gazeta* (The Economic Newspaper) — are also of considerable usefulness for such a study. However, the articles on Party work in *Kommunist* and *Bolshevik* (at least prior to 1964) tend to be general summaries of aspects of Party work described more meaningfully in other sources. (There are several articles in recent years which suggest a change in this respect.) The articles on Party work in *Ekonomicheskaia gazeta* tend to focus more exclusively on ideological-mobilization work than do those of *Pravda* and *Sovetskaia Rossiia.* (However, *Ekonomicheskaia gazeta* is indispensable for understanding planning and incentive systems and the debate about them.) Two other Central Committee journals, *Politicheskoe samoobrazovanie* (Political Self-Education) and *Agitator* (Agitator), present information on their specialized subjects, but their usefulness is limited by the fact that they are directed more toward the agitator and the student than toward the middle-level ideological official.

A second type of newspaper of great use to the scholar of the Party apparatus is the republican and the local press. Each republic has at least one Russian-language newspaper and at least one in the native language, and these newspapers are similar to *Pravda* both in their format and their subordination to the Party organ of their area. The basic rule on the usefulness of the republican newspapers is: the larger the republic, the more insight to be gained from its newspaper. Thus, the major Ukrainian newspaper, *Pravda Ukrainy* (The Truth of the Ukraine), is nearly as vital to a scholar as *Pravda* and *Sovetskaia Rossiia*. (The second Russian-language newspaper, *Rabochaia gazeta* [The Workers' Newspaper] is of less use.) Similarly, the newspapers of Belorussia, Kazakhstan, and Uzbekistan — *Sovetskaia Belorussiia* (Soviet Belorussia), *Kazakhstanskaia pravda* (Kazakhstan Truth), and *Pravda vostoka* (The Truth of the East) — are also quite important sources of information. In the smaller republics, the newspapers which proved most useful over the years were *Sovetskaia Moldaviia* (Soviet Moldavia), *Sovetskaia Latviia* (Soviet Latvia), and *Kommunist Tadzhikistana* (The Communist of Tadzhikistan), but the other newspapers also provided considerable information: *Bakinskii rabochii* (The Baku Worker, Azerbaidzhan), *Kommunist* (Communist, Armenia), *Sovetskaia Estoniia* (Soviet Estonia), *Sovetskaia Kirgiziia* (Soviet Kirgizia), *Sovetskaia Litva* (Soviet Lithuania), *Turkmenskaia iskra* (The Turkmen Spark), and *Zaria vostoka* (The Dawn of the East, Georgia).

Each of the republics also has a magazine which is the equivalent of *Kommunist* or *Partiinaia zhizn* (usually one magazine which serves the function of both central magazines). However, each time one of these journals was examined, it proved of little use. The oblast papers read in 1967 in the Soviet Union also proved rather disappointing in their coverage of Party work in industry, but, of course, they are a vital source of personnel information on oblast officials in the RSFSR and might be quite useful for a study of a rural raikom.

Besides the organs of the Party organizations, there are many newspapers subordinate to trade union or state organizations. In general, these newspapers are not very revealing about the nature of local Party impact on specialized decisions in the particular branch they cover. In fact, they usually imply that the local Party organs have no such impact, and they have misled a number of Western scholars who work in specialized fields and who have not sufficiently studied *Pravda* or other Party newspapers. However, these "non-Party" newspapers do contain certain types of important information: considerable discussion of specialized ideological-mobilization work, information on the relevent "patronage" (*shefstvo*) demanded from or provided to the particular branch, and most important, an indication of the kind of conflicts which arise with other branches and which require Party intervention. (Unfortunately, the intervention itself is usually not discussed.)

For the subject-matter of this book, the most useful non-Party newspaper is *Izvestiia* (News) which contains excellent discussions of the consequences of subordination of industry to agencies independent of the local soviets. Also of great use on certain types of personnel questions is the organ of the trade union council, *Trud* (Labor). The specialized newspapers of most value for this book are *Gudok* (Whistle, the organ of the railroad industry), *Selskaia zhizn* (Rural Life), and *Stroitelnaia gazeta* (The Construction Newspaper). (*Selskaia zhizn* is actually an organ of the Party Central Committee and would be vital for an analysis of Party work in the countryside.) Other specialized newspapers consulted were *Lesnaia promyshlennost* (The Timber Industry), *Meditsinskii rabotnik* (The Medical Worker), *Sovetskaia torgovlia* (Soviet Trade), and *Uchitelskaia gazeta* (The Teachers' Newspaper). The journal *Sovetskoe gosudarstvo i pravo* (Soviet State and Law) contains discussion of industrial administration, but its articles are usually too legalistic to be of much use for a study such as this.

Notes

I. Introduction

1. Lazar Slepov, *Vysshie i mestnye organy partii* (The Higher and Lower Organs of the Party; Moscow, 1958), p. 11.

2. Joseph LaPalombara, "Bureaucracy and Political Development: Notes, Queries, and Dilemmas," in *Bureaucracy and Political Development* (Princeton, 1963). The quotes are from pp. 50 and 54.

3. Brian Chapman, *The Profession of Government* (London, 1959), p. 70.

4. Henry Maddick, *Democracy, Decentralization, and Development* (London, 1963), p. 52.

5. Brian Chapman, *The Prefects and Provincial France* (London, 1955), p. 17.

6. Arthur W. Macmahon, John D. Millet, and Gladys Ogden, *The Administration of Federal Work Relief* (Chicago, 1941), pp. 265–268. In 1961 Macmahon claimed authorship of the concept and discussed it briefly in terms of prefect-like officials in Asia. See Arthur W. Macmahon, *Delegation and Autonomy* (Bombay, 1961), pp. 28–31.

7. Chapman, *The Profession of Government*, p. 72.

8. *Ibid.*, p. 72.

9. T. H. Rigby, "The Selection of Leading Personnel in the Soviet State and the Communist Party" doctoral dissertation, University of London, 1954), p. 26. See also T. H. Rigby, "Traditional, Market, and Organizational Societies," *World Politics*, 16 (July 1964), pp. 550–553.

The danger of the phrase "Ministry of Coordination" is that it may suggest that the Party hierarchy is a unified "ministry," all of whose organs perform essentially coordinating functions. However, it would be quite misleading to interpret the functions of the primary Party organizations and most of the departments of the Central Committee in these terms. The image of the prefect avoids the danger of overgeneralization by restricting the focus to the provincial Party organs.

10. Victor Thompson, *Modern Organization* (New York, 1961), pp. 73–80.

11. Dwight Waldo, *Perspectives on Administration* (University, Ala., 1956), pp. 35–36.

II. The Organization of the Local Parties

1. A full discussion of some of these experiments in the organization of the secretariat can be found in Merle Fainsod, *How Russia Is Ruled* (rev. ed.; Cambridge, Mass., 1963), pp. 190–208.

2. Before 1948 the obkomy did have a special secretary for personnel and an organization-instruction department, but they also had a number of deputy secretaries for various branches of industry, for construction, and for transportation, each of whom also bore the title "head of department." In Perm oblast, for example, eight of these departments were created prior to World War II and at least another five were formed during the war. S. M. Petrov, ed., *Uchenye zapiski kafedr istorii kommunisticheskoi partii Sovetskogo Soiuza vysshei partiinoi shkoly pri TsK KPSS i mestnykh vysshikh partiinykh shkol* (Scholarly Notes of the Departments of the History of the Communist Party of the Soviet Union of the Higher Party School under the CC CPSU and of the Local Higher Party Schools; no. 1, Moscow, 1959), p. 160. Moreover, the organization-instruction and personnel departments were also subdivided on branch lines. See, for example, a list of medal winners published in *Pravda vostoka,* December 27, 1944, December 29, 1944, and January 1, 1945, for a comprehensive catalog of posts in the secretariat of the Uzbekistan Central Committee.

3. The one major exception to this generalization was the Party committee of the *kolkhoz-sovkhoz* administration, which is outside the scope of this study. See J. F. Hough, "A Harebrained Scheme in Retrospect," *Problems of Communism* 14 (July–August 1965), pp. 26–32.

4. Indeed, in the largest cities the city soviet is independent not only of any county soviet supervision, but also of that of the oblast soviet. The Leningrad city soviet and the city education administration are not, for example, supervised by the Leningrad oblast soviet and oblast education administration, but are supervised directly by the RSFSR Council of Ministers and the RSFSR Ministry of Education respectively. Prior to 1958 there were 18 such cities of "republican subordination" in the RSFSR (17 before the inclusion of the Karela-Finnish Republic into the Russian Federation), but in 1958 their number was reduced to two (Moscow and Leningrad). Compare the 1958 and 1959 RSFSR budgets for an indication of the difference. *Sovetskaia Rossiia,* January 29, 1958, p. 1, and December 27, 1958, p. 4. In addition, there are two cities in the Ukraine (Kiev and Sevastopol) which have also been subordinated directly to the republican level.

Fortunately for our purposes the city Party committee has almost always been subordinated to the local oblast Party committee, even in those cases where the city soviet is independent of the oblast soviet. The only exception has been Moscow and that only since 1954.

5. The names of the cities with urban raiony can be found in the annual *SSSR: Administrativno-territorialnoe delenie soiuznykh respublik* (The USSR:

The Administrative-Territorial Division of the Union Republics), published in Moscow by the Presidium of the Supreme Soviet. The population of the various cities can be found in the various republican reports of the 1959 census — e.g., *Itogi vsesoiuznoi perepisi naseleniia 1959 goda RSFSR* (The Results of the 1959 All-Union Census in the RSFSR; Moscow, 1963), pp. 30–38.

6. The towns with independent soviets are listed in *SSSR: Administrativno-territorialnoe delenie,* and their population can be found in the census reports. I know of no easy way to ascertain whether a city has an independent gorkom. The generalizations made here are based on press reports of the situation in individual cities. See, for example, *Sovetskaia Belorussiia,* December 1, 1962, p. 2, for a discussion of the change in the city of Baranovichi (population: 58,000).

7. In addition to these organs, Moscow also experimented with sub-raikomy (*pod-raikomy*) beginning in 1961. *Vecherniaia Moskva,* April 8, 1961, p. 1. See also *ibid.,* September 17, 1962, p. 2.

8. Prior to the 23rd Party Congress in 1966 only the Party congresses in the Ukraine, Belorussia, Kazakhstan, and Uzbekistan were held every 4 years. In the smaller republics the congresses were held every 2 years. Party Rules, Statutes 43 and 44.

The basic Party Rules can be found in *Pravda,* November 3, 1961. The 1966 changes in the Rules (with the corresponding 1961 version in a parallel column) can be found in *Partiinaia zhizn,* no. 9 (May 1966), pp. 8–13. The statute numbers cited in this book refer to the 1961 version.

9. Party Rules, Statute 44.

10. Fainsod, *How Russia Is Ruled,* p. 217.

11. Slepov, *Vysshie i mestnye organy,* p. 71.

12. Generalizations about the republican central committees are made on the basis of a study of the central committees named at the conclusion of the republican congresses held in late January 1956, late September and early October 1961, and February and March 1966.

13. This information is based on an examination of the oblast newspapers in each oblast. Krasnodar: *Sovetskaia Kuban,* February 27, 1966, p. 1; Rostov: *Molot,* February 26, 1966, p. 1; Ulianovsk: *Ulianovskaia pravda,* February 27, 1966, p. 1; Volgograd: *Volgogradskaia pravda,* February 27, 1966, p. 1; Yaroslavl: *Severnii rabochii,* January 30, 1966, p. 1.

14. Indeed, membership in the Party committee is a good indicator of the status of the officials and offices involved. An important official must be included if he is not to feel insulted. *Ekonomicheskaia gazeta,* January 5, 1963, p. 13.

15. For a comparison of the composition of the central committees in six republics in 1956, 1961, and 1966 and of the 5 oblast committees in 1966, see Appendix A, Tables 1 and 2.

16. Party Rules, Statute 46.

17. *Pravda,* November 20, 1962, p. 2.

18. *Voprosy partiinoi raboty* (Questions of Party Work; 3rd ed.; Moscow, 1959), p. 374.

19. Actually only 3 of the bureaus had a "typical" membership. See Appendix A, Table 3.

20. For a comparison of the republican bureaus in 1954, 1956, 1961, 1964, and 1966, see Appendix A, Table 3. In 1954 (but not during the late Stalin period) the Party officials usually held a minority position on the bureau and even in later years an occasional bureau did not contain a majority of Party officials. Except in 1954, however, no bureau could be found in which the Party officials fell more than one vote short of a majority, and in these cases at least one of the state officials had had a long career associated with the Party apparatus.

21. The seven oblasti are Krasnodar, Leningrad, Moscow, Rostov, Ulianovsk, Volgograd, and Yaroslavl. The data on Moscow and Leningrad can be found in the U.S. Government's revised 1966 *Directory of Soviet Officials,* pp. II-C1 and II-C7. The sources of information for the other oblasti are listed in note 13 above. See also Appendix A, Table 4.

T. H. Rigby found that in the early 1950's 55 percent of the obkom bureau members (including candidate members) were Party officials. Rigby, "The Selection of Leading Personnel," p. 313. See also John A. Armstrong, *The Soviet Bureaucratic Elite* (New York, 1959), pp. 13–14.

22. Leo Gruliow, ed., *Current Soviet Policies* (New York, 1953), p. 138.

23. The Party Rules stipulate only that a secretariat "can be created" (statute 45). In 1961 the Party leadership rejected suggestions that the creation of the secretariat be made obligatory.

24. This rule has sometimes (perhaps often) been violated during the harvest season. At that time the leading Party and state officials may each be assigned responsibility for agricultural deliveries in a specific rural raion and actually may be sent into these raiony as plenipotentiaries. This practice is officially condemned, but it has been suspiciously persistent. For a particularly detailed list of such assignments, see *Bakinskii rabochii,* November 1, 1958, p. 1.

25. Vsevolod Kochetov, *Sekretar obkoma* (The Secretary of the Regional Party Committee; Moscow, 1962), p. 164.

26. For a detailed description of the division of responsibility between the first and second secretaries in one obkom in 1929, see Merle Fainsod, *Smolensk under Soviet Rule* (Cambridge, Mass., 1958), p. 67.

27. The statements in this paragraph are based on extended reading of the various republican newspapers. A secretary's basic duties become readily apparent not only from direct references to them, but also from the subject matter of his speeches, his articles, and the conferences he attends.

28. The methodology here is the same as described in note 27. The uncertainty is much greater because of the more intermittent coverage of oblast officials in the central and republican press. The year 1959 was chosen for the survey because it was easy to determine the secretaries in charge of agriculture

from a list of medal winners published on December 30 of that year and because all the second secretaries had been listed in March when they were named to the republican supreme soviets.

29. *Voprosy partiinoi raboty* (1959), p. 373.

30. The change in name from Party organs department in organizational-Party work department was made between May 28, 1965, and July 1, 1965, as indicated by reports in the issues of *Pravda* of those dates. Prior to 1954 this department was called "the department for Party, trade union, and Komsomol organs." The shortening of the name in 1954 did not signify a loss of jurisdiction over the trade union or the Komsomol.

The construction department became a standard department in the early 1960's, the light industry and food industry department in the spring of 1967. For an indication of the universality of the construction department, see *Pravda*, May 29, 1965, p. 2. The obkomy in large oblasti had light industry and food industry departments prior to 1967, but in the spring of that year there apparently was a Central Committee decision to create such a department in all or nearly all oblasti. Thus, in 1967 the Ulianovsk oblast newspaper reported, "In accordance with the decision of the Central Committee, a department of light industry and food industry is formed in the obkom." *Ulianovskaia pravda*, May 30, 1967, p. 1.

31. On July 10, 1962, I was in the building of the Leningrad obkom (the obkom is located in Smolny) and discovered the indicated departments listed in the wall directory of room locations. The same departments, except for the defense industry department (which Soviet sources never publicly mention as existing in the local Party organs), were listed as part of the secretariat of the Leningrad obkom in 1965. *Voprosy partiinoi stroitelstva* (Questions of Party Construction; Leningrad, 1965), p. 184.

32. Donbass and Kuznetsk: *Rabochaia gazeta*, July 1, 1959, p. 2, and *Pravda*, February 26, 1967, p. 2; Arkhangel: *Sovetskaia Rossiia*, December 27, 1961, p. 3; Kharkov: *Pravda Ukrainy*, March 12, 1966, p. 2; Ivanovo: *Ekonomicheskaia gazeta*, no. 28 (July 1966), p. 30; Kuibyshev: *Pravda*, March 12, 1959, p. 2.

33. Party Rules, Statute 45.

34. See Myron Rush, *The Rise of Khrushchev* (Washington, 1958), pp. 74–76. Rush attributes the ambiguity to different conceptions of the proper role of the secretary held by different Party leaders. In part, this is no doubt so, but a large part of the ambiguity also derives from the embarrassing differences between practice and the democratically oriented theory.

35. *Voprosy partiinoi raboty* (1959), p. 373.

36. *Sovetskaia Moldaviia*, September 30, 1961, p. 3.

37. See, for example, *Zaria vostoka*, December 23, 1962, p. 2.

38. *Partiinaia zhizn*, no. 11 (June 1966), p. 18.

39. *Komsomolskaia pravda*, July 16, 1950, p. 2.

40. Between 1962 and 1964 the organization chart at this level was far more

complex. In the countryside, Party work was divided between the zonal indus-trial-production Party committee (in charge of rural industry and construc-tion) and the Party committee of the kolkhoz-sovkhoz administration (in charge not only of agriculture, but also of educational, cultural, and service in-stitutions serving the rural population). In many large oblast centers the gorkom was abolished, and the urban raikomy there were subordinated directly to the industrial obkom. In many smaller cities where the gorkom or raikom had re-sponsibility both for the city and the surrounding raion, an independent gorkom was now created. In all cities where a gorkom (or urban raikomy) existed, these Party organs were relieved of responsibility for food-processing plants and scientific and educational institutions related either to agriculture or the food industry, Party supervision of which was entrusted to the rural Party hierarchy. For a Central Committee decision on this subject, see *Spravochnik partiinogo rabotnika* (Handbook of the Party Official, 5th ed.; Moscow, 1964), p. 299.

41. Slepov, p. 71.

42. Baku: *Bakinskii rabochii,* December 8, 1957, p. 1; Ulianovsk: *Ulia-novskaia pravda,* January 30, 1966, p. 1. For more detail on the Ulianovsk gor-kom, see Appendix A.

43. N. F. Kolbenkov, *Sovershenstvovanie rukovodstva promyshlennostiu SSSR, 1956–1960* (The Perfecting of the Leadership of the Industry of the USSR, 1956–1960; Moscow, 1961), p. 138.

44. Statute 50 of the 1952 Party Rules (found in Gruliow, pp. 28–33) speci-fied that the raikom and gorkom bureau should contain from 7 to 9 members.

References to several of the larger bureaus can be found in *Bakinskii ra-bochii,* December 4, 1863, p. 1; *Sovetskaia Estoniia,* December 7, 1963, p. 3; *Vecherniaia Moskva,* March 5, 1966, p. 1. The 13-man bureau was formed in Riga in 1966. *Sovetskaia Latviia,* February 8, 1966, p. 1. See Appendix A, Table 5.

45. *Pravda vostoka,* May 13, 1966, p. 1. The only other larger secretariats that have been identified have resulted from the temporary naming of a fourth sec-retary to supervise an important construction site in a Lithuanian city, a fourth secretary to supervise agriculture in Baku during a brief period in the mid-1950's, and an additional part-time secretary in Dushambe (Tadzhikistan) dur-ing a campaign to attract the public into Party life. (The Dushambe experi-ment was very short-lived.)

46. *Zaria vostoka,* February 12, 1966, p. 1.

47. These percentages are similar to those T. H. Rigby found existing in the late 1940's and early 1950's. At that time 75 percent of the members of the gorkom bureaus were Party officials. Rigby, p. 313.

48. See, for example, *Vecherniaia Moskva,* March 5, 1966, p. 1; *Sovetskaia Latviia,* February 8, 1966, p. 1, and *Zaria vostoka,* February 12, 1966, p. 1. See also *Pravda vostoka,* July 27, 1966, p. 3.

49. In 1961 the gorkom and raikom bureaus of Saratov oblast contained

11 workers. *Partiinaia zhizn,* no. 15–16 (August 1961), p. 113. It has not been possible to identify a worker on the bureau of a gorkom in a republican capital, but one worker has been mentioned as a member of the bureau of the gorkom in Orekhovo-Zuevo (Moscow oblast) and another as a member of the bureau of the Belovo gorkom (Kemerovo oblast). *Ekonomicheskaia gazeta,* no. 7 (February 1966), p. 17, and *Pravda,* January 18, 1967, p. 2.

50. Vsevolod Kochetov, *Bratia Ershovy* (The Brothers Ershovy; Moscow, 1959), p. 33.

51. *Selskaia zhizn,* November 2, 1960, p. 4.

52. This generalization is based to a large extent on a long study of the secretaries of the gorkomy of the republican capitals. In 1958 the deputy head of the industrial-transportation department of a Moscow raikom told me that this was the usual arrangement in his area too. Even from 1962 to 1964, approximately one-half of the first secretaries of the gorkomy in the republican capitals handled organizational questions. During this latter period, however, a high percentage of the gorkom first secretaries in the medium-sized cities seem to have been chosen from the ranks of plant managers, and presumably they assumed special responsibility for industrial questions.

53. *Voprosy partiinogo stroitelstva,* p. 182.

54. Ivanovo (population: 350,000) was said to have a staff of 26 in 1965. *Partiinaia zhizn,* no. 19 (October 1965), p. 55. In Krasnodar, a city of almost identical size, the gorkom also had a 26-man staff at that time. *Pravda,* June 6, 1965, p. 2. The Leningrad figures are found in B. A. Pokrovski, ed., *V tesnoi sviazi s zhizniu* (In Close Connection with Life; Moscow, 1958), p. 53.

55. *Voprosy partiinogo stroitelstva,* p. 185.

56. Lenin raikom: Pokrovskii, *V tesnoi sviazi,* p. 52; Ivanovo: *Partiinaia zhizn,* no. 19 (October 1965), p. 52.

57. *Partiinaia zhizn,* no. 11 (June 1966), p. 18.

58. *Kommunist,* no. 9 (June 1967), p. 61.

59. At times Soviet sources suggest that the officials do little else. This side of Party work is discussed at length in Chapter X.

60. The concern of the instructor with negative facts (and the impact of this concern on the ability of the plant officials to accept him as a helpful comrade) has been a persistent theme in Party literature. See *Pravda,* August 22, 1952, p. 2; *Pravda vostoka,* November 16, 1957, p. 3; *Partiinaia zhizn,* no. 11 (June 1966), p. 18.

Indeed, because of a shortage in secretarial help, the instructor often has not only to write a report, but also to spend a good deal of time typing it and other documents and "sealing envelopes." In the oblast center of Cherkassy the gorkom has no stenographer, one secretary (in the American sense of the word), and one typist. Moreover, there have been complaints that these employees are not well qualified, for the gorkom has the lowest scale in the city for this category of employee. *Partiinaia zhizn,* no. 22 (November 1965), p. 35.

61. *Voprosy partiinoi raboty* (1959), p. 371.

62. *Pravda,* October 4, 1947, p. 2. Indeed, this statement refers to 25–30 organizations.

63. For a detailed description of the resulting structure of a gorkom secretariat in a city of 150,000 people (Chimkent), see *Kazakhstanskaia pravda,* May 18, 1957, p. 2.

64. E. I. Bugaev and B. M. Leibson, *Besedy ob ustave KPSS* (Conversations about the Rules of the CPSU; Moscow, 1962), p. 158, and *Voprosy partiinogo stroitelstva,* p. 37.

65. Bugaev and Leibson, p. 158.

66. *Voprosy partiinogo stroitelstva,* p. 37.

67. *Turkmenskaia iskra,* December 27, 1963, p. 6.

68. Questions have been raised in the Soviet Union about the limitations on the role of the instructor. See, for example, *Sovetskaia Rossiia,* December 22, 1961, p. 3, and January 19, 1962, p. 2.

69. Party Rules, Statute 19.

70. *Pravda,* October 29, 1961, p. 5.

71. Fedor Panferov, *Volga-matushka reka* (Mother-Volga River; Moscow, 1954), pp. 29–32, 164, 181, and 217.

72. N. S. Khrushchev, *Stroitelstvo kommunizma v SSSR i razvitie selskogo khoziaistva* (The Building of Communism in the USSR and the Development of Agriculture; Moscow, 1962), I, 204.

73. *Pravda,* July 2, 1959, p. 2. Just as the term "obkom" is applied not only to the oblast committee but also to its executive officers and staff, so the term "Central Committee" implies not the large committee, but rather the Presidium or the secretariat or both.

74. In *Pravda,* August 22, 1959, p. 1, the former first secretary, G. A. Denisov, is listed in his new post as head of the agriculture department of the Central Committee for the union republics.

75. Party Rules, Statute 49.

76. *Turkmenskaia iskra,* October 6, 1962, p. 2.

77. K. Tolmadzhev, ed., *Na novom puti* (On a New Path: Riga, 1957), pp. 15–16.

78. Panferov, p. 89.

79. Slepov, pp. 59–60.

80. *Pravda,* May 26, 1941, p. 2.

81. *Ibid.,* July 29, 1950, p. 2.

82. See Chapter VII.

83. Slepov, p. 88.

84. *Pravda,* August 25, 1947, p. 2.

85. *Ibid.,* May 28, 1955, p. 2. It is interesting that when the Stalingrad Tractor Plant failed to fulfill its plan in 1952, *Pravda* stated that this was "first of all' the fault of the local raikom and gorkom. *Ibid.,* September 10, 1952, p. 2.

86. *Partiinaia zhizn Kazakhstana,* no. 3 (March 1960), p. 14.

87. *Pravda,* July 29, 1950, p. 2. For other examples, see *ibid.,* August 24, 1956, p. 2 and *Partiinaia zhizn.* no. 11 (June 1966), p. 18.

88. Leonard Schapiro, *The Communist Party of the Soviet Union* (New York, 1959), p. 506.

89. Armstrong, p. 62. Armstrong's conclusion is strongly corroborated by Valentin Ovechkin's *Trudnaia vesna* (Difficult Spring; Moscow, 1956) — a novel hailed by Soviet critics for its realistic treatment of agricultural conditions prior to the death of Stalin. It is interesting that in the late Khrushchev period, the increase in the number of Communists in the countryside was accompanied by a reduction in the role of the raion level Party officials and a strengthening of the role of the administrative organs.

90. *Sovetskaia Rossiia,* April 29, 1960, p. 2.

91. *Kazakhstanskaia pravda,* November 26, 1958, p. 3. See also *Pravda,* February 6, 1967, p. 2: "In the activity of the gorkom, raikomy, and Party committees of enterprises there is much duplication. Often one and the same question is examined at two or three levels." For a complaint about local Party organs sending duplicatory investigating commissions to an enterprise, see *Pravda,* July 7, 1965, p. 2.

92. Slepov, p. 80.

III. The Party Secretary and the Industrial Manager

1. See, for example, Zbigniew Brzezinski and Samuel P. Huntington, *Political Power USA/USSR* (New York, 1963), p. 155, and Grey Hodnett, "The Obkom First Secretaries," *Slavic Review,* 24 (December 1965), pp. 636–652.

2. Armstrong, *The Soviet Bureaucratic Elite,* chaps. 4 and 7.

3. Semipalatinsk: M. P. Karpenko, *Deputaty Verkhovnogo Soveta SSSR, Sedmoi sozyv* (Deputies of the Supreme Soviet of the USSR, Seventh Convocation; Moscow, 1966), p. 199; Kemerovo: A. F. Eshtokin, *ibid.,* p. 158; Dnepropetrovsk: A. F. Vatchenko, *ibid.,* p. 83; Mogilev: G. A. Kriulin, *ibid.,* p. 239; Kalmyk ASSR: B. B. Gorodovikov, *ibid.,* p. 113; Vologa: A. S. Drygin, *ibid.,* p. 146.

4. Actually one of the oblasti is the Russianized Karaganda in Kazakhstan. The 25 are Moscow, Leningrad, Donetsk (formerly Stalino), Cheliabinsk, Sverdlovsk, Kemerovo, Kiev, Rostov, Gorki, Kuibyshev, Dnepropetrovsk, Kharkov, Novosibirsk, Perm (formerly Molotov), Odessa, Irkutsk, Saratov, Tatar Republic, Lugansk (formerly Voroshilovgrad), Volgograd (formerly Stalingrad), Yaroslavl, Krasnoiarsk, Zaporozhe, Ivanovo, and Karaganda.

Information on regional industrial output is spotty. The list was compiled in the following manner: because Soviet industry is over-concentrated in the larger cities, I took the 200 largest cities as of the 1959 census and grouped them by oblasti. I then assumed that the 25 oblasti with the most people concentrated in these cities were the most industrialized. The results corresponded fairly closely to my impressionistic evaluation of the comparative levels of industrial development, but as agriculture clearly overshadows industry in three of the regions near the bottom of the list (Altai, Bashkiria ASSR, and Omsk oblast, in each of which the rural population constitutes over 60 percent of the region's total population), I replaced them with three oblasti that just failed to make the top 25 but that clearly occupy an important role in the country's industrial life — Ivanovo, Karaganda, and Zaporozhe. The biographies of all these men can be found in *Deputaty* (1966).

5. Actually, these are not the 25 most important agricultural oblasti, but 25 of the most important such oblasti. The oblasti were chosen on the basis of the size of rural population in the 1959 census. However, since I wanted 25 oblasti whose first secretaries were presumably chosen because the Party leadership thought them best qualified to provide political leadership to the rural sector of the economy, I excluded oblasti already included in the 25 most industrialized oblasti as well as the autonomous republics where the problems of political control are complicated by the nationality question. The 25 oblasti are: Altai krai, Arkhangelsk, Belgorod, Briansk, Kalinin, Kirov, Krasnodar krai, Kurgan, Kursk, Lipetsk, Omsk, Orel, Orenburg, Penza, Pskov, Riazan, Smolensk, Stavropol krai, Tambov, Tiumen, Tula, Ulianovsk, Vladimir, Vologda, and Voronezh. In the 1941 table, Belgorod and Lipetsk oblasti, which did not exist at that time, are replaced by Kaluga and Kostroma.

6. For other information about these secretaries, see Table 12.

7. See Jeremy R. Azrael, *Managerial Power and Soviet Politics* (Cambridge, Mass., 1966), pp. 65–102.

8. Of 19 USSR Peoples' Commissars appointed in the industrial and construction realm in early 1939, 9 were removed and demoted by January 1942. However, this action had a different import than the earlier removals of the top industrial officials. A number of these men remained at the deputy commissar (or deputy minister) level for the next 15 years.

For the reference to the "men of 1938," see Armstrong, *The Soviet Bureaucratic Elite,* p. 26.

9. *Deputaty Verkhovnogo Soveta SSSR, Shestoi sozyv* (Deputies of the Supreme Soviet of the USSR, Sixth Convocation; Moscow, 1962), p. 256. *Bolshaia sovetskaia entsiklopediia,* 1962 yearbook, p. 603. *Tsvetnye metally,* no. 8, 1957, p. 8.

10. Full biographies have been found of the following first secretaries in the most industrailized oblasti (* denotes a man with engineering training): V. M. Andriianov*, A. A. Epishev*, A. I. Gaevoi, M. Ia. Kanunnikov*, N. S. Patolichev*, N. M. Pegov*, G. N. Pugovkin, M. I. Rodionov, Z. T. Serdiuk, A. S. Shcherbakov, V. G. Zhavoronkov*, and A. A. Zhdanov.

One obkom first secretary with an engineering background was Nikolai Patolichev, the USSR Minister of Foreign Trade after 1958. Born in 1908, Patolichev was one of the youngest obkom first secretaries, but in other respects his career was not atypical. He became a factory worker at the age of 17, and in 1928 (the year he joined the Party) he became secretary of the Komsomol organization at the plant. After serving as a raikom Komsomol secretary, he studied from 1931 to 1937 at the Moscow Technological Institute and at the Military-Chemical Academy. After his graduation he worked for a short time as assistant to the head of the chemical service of an army division. In 1938 he served successively as a responsible organizer of the leading Party organs department of the Central Committee, as Party organizer of the Central Committee at the Yaroslavl Tire Plant, and then as a raikom secretary in Yaroslavl. In early 1939 he was named first secretary of the Yaroslavl obkom. *Sovetskaia Belorussiia,* February 1, 1947, p. 2.

11. There is a striking passage (pp. 184–186) in Fedor Panferov's *Volga-Matushka Reka* that describes the education of one of the novel's leading characters, Semen Malinov, an obkom first secretary who had graduated from the Bauman Institute, probably the finest engineering school in the country. It probably has general applicability to the obkom first secretaries of 1941: "Even then Semen Malinov had one main gift — the ability to speak and to imitate. . . . Thanks to such oratorical gifts, Semen Malinov was 'loaded' and 'overloaded' with assignments: he was one of the Komsomol leaders in the institute, the chairman of the civil defense unit, of the Aid to the Revolutionaries Society, and even of the sports circle. . . . And science? Science remained somewhere at the side. He did not drag himself to the books, and he listened to lectures according to the proverb: 'In one ear and out the other.' But it was necessary to pass the exams, and Semen Malinov unwillingly had to resort to the method of 'dodging.' To some teachers he gave his honored word: 'I'll hand it in! I'll hand it in! Word of honor, I'll hand it in. Just give me a grade now. . . . I will get it in to you.' To others, who were a little sterner, he answered the questions with patter, impudently looking into their eyes. When he did not hit the point, he began to complain about being swamped with work. The 'stern' professor would yield, saying, 'Yes, yes. I know. I know. I've seen your picture in the Komsomol newspaper.' . . . And he wrote on the grade sheet, 'Passes.' . . . With such dodges [Malinov] left the institute, having received the diploma of an engineer but not the knowledge of one."

12. It is difficult to demonstrate this proposition in statistical terms. Phrases such as "medium machinery" and "general machinery" can refer to quite different products in different years, and the recurring amalgamation and subdivision of ministries often meant a different scope of activity for a man with the same title. However, although a minister might be shifted from the supervision of one type of machinery production to another (and this may occur less frequently than changes in title suggest), one finds no case in which a 1941 commissar was shifted to an entirely unrelated industry (except to some extent during World War II).

13. At least 5 of the 28 commissars had died by 1955, 4 of them (A. I. Efremov, S. G. Lukin, F. V. Sergeev, and V. V. Vakhrushev) while still min-

ister, one (P. V. Smirnov) while director of the main design institute for his industry.

Sixteen of the remaining 23 commissars remained at essentially the same level (or higher) in 1955. Twelve of these men were either minister or deputy chairman of the Council of Ministers for basically the same branch of industry that they had supervised earlier. These 12 were S. A. Akopov, A. A. Ishkov, N. S. Kazakov, A. N. Kosygin, P. F. Lomako, V. A. Malyshev, I. I. Nosenko, P. I. Parshin, M. G. Pervukhin, I. F. Tevosian, D. F. Ustinov, and V. P. Zotov. The Ministry of the Rubber Industry had been merged into the Ministry of the Chemical Industry, but the 1941 Minister of the Rubber Industry (T. B. Mitrokhin) occupied the post of First Deputy Minister of the Chemical Industry and continued to supervise the rubber industry. Two of the 1941 defense industry ministers (P. N. Goremykin and B. L. Vannikov) remained in very high but unspecified defense industry posts. Goremykin was actually named Minister of General Machinebuilding in April 1955, and Vannikov's position was of sufficient stature to warrant full membership in the All-Union Central Committee in 1956. The 16th commissar in this category (I. G. Kabanov) had been named Minister of Foreign Trade by 1955.

To be sure, not all of the 16 had remained continuously at the ministerial level during the 15-year period. There were periodic reorganizations in which one ministry might be merged with another, and at these times one of the ministers might become deputy minister while still supervising the same industry. For example, whenever the Ministry of Ferrous Metallurgy and the Ministry of Nonferrous Metallurgy were amalgamated, P. F. Lomako (the Minister of Nonferrous Metallurgy) invariably became First Deputy Minister of Metallurgy, but his basic responsibilities were unchanged. The only really significant demotions were those affecting the Ministers of the Automobile Industry (Akopov), of the Food Industry (Zotov), and of the Fish Industry (Ishkov) from 1950 to 1953.

An additional 4 of the 1941 commissars remained as deputy ministers in 1955: I. N. Akimov, S. Z. Ginzburg, A. I. Shakhurin, and L. A. Sosnin.

Only 3 of the commissars (N. N. Chebotarev, M. F. Denisov, and I. K. Sedin) could not be identified in the ministries in 1955, and one of them (Sedin) was still a director of a very large enterprise.

14. Immediately below each commissar, for example, there was an average of 5 deputy commissars in 1941, and their number tended to increase with the passage of time. Only 29 biographies of the 1941 deputy commissars — not quite 30 percent of the total — are available, and the sample is rather suspect because nearly all the men in it survived in high administrative posts until the 1950's. Yet, at a minimum it can be said that in 1941 there was a substantial bloc of deputy commissars who had a relatively common background and who (even more than their superiors) had been selected for reasons other than long involvement in Party work. Only 5 of these deputy commissars became Party members during the Civil War (at an average age of 20); the other 24 joined

the Party in 1931 on the average (at an average age of 26), and 5 of them did not join until 1938, 1939, or 1940. With four exceptions, they followed the familiar pattern of entering an industrial institute after a period of work in the 1920's (70 percent graduating in the 1928–1933 period) and then of being assigned to the industry in which they eventually became deputy commissars.

The deputy commissars in turn were also supported by an elaborate staff of trained personnel engaged in administrative and technical work. As Malenkov complained in 1941, there was a strong tendency for technical graduates to gravitate to these institutions. Of 214,000 specialists with higher education working at that time in the system of industrial commissariats, 95,000 were employed in the institutions of the commissariat system itself, 51,000 in the plant administration, and 68,000 directly in production. Of 164,000 such persons with specialized secondary education, 41,000 worked in the institutions of the commissariat system itself. *Pravda,* February 16, 1941, p. 3.

15. *Pravda,* March 14, 1939, p. 3.

16. David Granick, *Management of the Industrial Firm in the USSR* (New York, 1955), p. 55.

17. *Ibid.,* p. 37.

18. *Komsomolskaia pravda,* February 10, 1938, p. 2.

19. *Deputaty Verkhovnogo Soveta SSSR, Piatyi sozyv* (Deputies of the Supreme Soviet, Fifth Convocation; Moscow, 1960), p. 141. Henceforth, this volume will be cited as *Deputaty* (1958), the 1958 referring to the year in which the deputies were elected.

20. V. K. Pavliukov: *Moskovskii bolshevik,* January 30, 1947, p. 2; A. N. Isachenko: *ibid.,* January 4, 1949, p. 1; P. V. Abramov and Z. A. Gurina: *ibid.,* January 29, 1947, p. 2, and *Pravda,* January 14, 1951, p. 4; I. M. Kolotyrkin, S. I. Afanasev, and N. M. Surova: *Moskovskii bolshevik,* April 19, 1947, p. 3, *ibid.,* January 28, 1947, p. 3, and *Promyshlenno-ekonomicheskaia gazeta,* May 27, 1959, p. 4; S. V. Sazonov: *Sovetskaia Estoniia,* January 15, 1946, p. 2.

21. 1938: *Partiinoe stroitelstvo,* no. 13 (June 1938), p. 19; 1939: *ibid.,* no. 5 (March 1939), p. 27.

22. The only information available on the background of lower Party officials in this period comes from individual biographies. The task of making statistical summaries of this data is complicated not only by the difficulty in finding a reliable sample, but also by the failure of many later biographies to identify the precise Party post that a man held during these years. (It will simply be asserted that he was in "leading Party work.") However, again and again, one does find biographies of men with engineering and managerial backgrounds who held some Party post sometime in the period 1939 to 1945. I have, for example, been able to collect the biographies of 23 men who definitely were republican or obkom deputy secretaries for some branch of industry or for construction during this period. Nineteen of them had engineering-managerial experience before being transferred to Party work. At least 11 of them had held the post of director (or higher).

23. Gregory Bienstock, Solomon Schwartz, and Aaron Yugow, *Management in Russian Industry and Agriculture* (Ithaca, 1948), p. 117. The restlessness and the initiative of these young engineers also may have manifested itself in less attractive ways. Roman Belan, director of the Kuznetsk Metallurgy Combine from 1939 to 1953, had been elected a deputy to the Supreme Soviet in 1937 while still head of a shift at the Zaporozhe Steel Plant, and at that time *Komsomolskaia pravda* published a sketch about him: "Roman Belan is an energetic engineer who passionately loves his work and who is growing in it. . . . Belan tirelessly struggles with the enemies of the people (*vragi naroda*) and their protectors. He helped the Party organization to unmask people who had succeeded in working their way into the Party by fraudulent means. . . . Belan was one of the first to lead a struggle against the former shop head, who cultivated toadyism, suppressed self-criticism, and drove away young specialists. He exposed the inflated authority of the shop head, and daringly and decisively criticized him." *Komsomolskaia pravda*, December 17, 1937, p. 3. Whatever the role of "struggles with enemies of the people" among the criteria for promotion during this period, the pressure for plan fulfillment meant that a successful director would also have to be a man "who passionately loves his work and who is growing in it."

24. These figures refer to the industrial and construction ministries that have formed the basis of earlier tables. If a man became a deputy minister in the 1950's and was named a minister before 1957, he was not included in this group. The total number of men rising to the rank of deputy minister during this period is extremely difficult to estimate, but it is probably in the 125 to 150 range.

25. See Appendix B for a discussion of the methodology by which these plants were chosen.

26. This generalization is based on a sample of 114 of the 170 plants — the only plants on which I have enough information to determine whether or not the director had a tenure of this length. Since no announcement had been made of changes in plant directors in the post-Purge period, one learns of these changes only when a new man is casually mentioned as the director of a plant. The exact date of the change, and hence the exact tenure of a director cannot be determined. If a man can be identified both before January 1, 1948, and after January 1, 1953, then it can be determined that he has a tenure of at least five years; if two men can be identified in the directorship of a plant within the period, then obviously he had a lesser tenure. If the examination of the Soviet press focused primarily on the outer limits of the five-year period, the methodology would produce a sample which exaggerated the percentage with five years tenure; if it focused primarily on the period between the two dates, it would produce a sample with the opposite bias. I have tried to avoid this problem by a balanced program for collecting information.

Ideally, I would have liked to produce a table indicating the range of tenure for the directors of 1953, but the scarcity of information (particularly after the beginning of the Korean War) reduces the size of the sample as one seeks more and more specific information. On the basis of a sample smaller by twenty directors, however, the 68 percent of the directors with tenure under five years would be divided thus: 0–3 years: 57 percent; 3–5 years: 11 percent.

27. These sixteen men are V. G. Bereza, A. F. Borisov, O. A. Chukanov, V. N. Doenin, K. A. Eremin, A. A. Ezhevskii, L. A. Kostandov, A. M. Merkulov, N. N. Musakhanov, I. M. Prikhodko, N. N. Smeliakov, P. A. Soroka, A. M. Tarasov, S. Kh. Tevosian, N. A. Tikhonov, and V. T. Zabaluev. A few of these men were directors at smaller plants prior to 1947. The other five directors were N. I. Doktorov, I. S. Isaev, D. V. Ivaniukov, V. D. Maiboroda, and G. A. Vedeniapin. Most of the biographies of the twenty-one directors can be found in the various volumes of the *Deputaty Verkhovnogo Soveta*.

28. See Nicholas Dewitt, *Soviet Professional Manpower* (Washington, D.C., 1955), pp. 118–120 for a discussion of the changes in the quality of education during this period.

29. These sixteen directors are G. I. Ermolaev, A. A. Gromov, B. G. Guseinov, V. A. Ivanov, V. A. Kargopolov, A. I. Kritsyn, A. G. Krylov, Ia. P. Kulikov, I. M. Malkin, N. V. Matveenko, G. S. Osintsev, K. M. Simakov, N. A. Sobol, N. I. Strokin, A. M. Vartanian, and L. N. Vorozhein. The other two directors are A. P. Kriuchkov and F. D. Voronov. Again, the biographies of most of these men can be found in the various volumes of the *Deputaty Verkhovnogo Soveta*.

30. See Lucian Pye, *Politics, Personality, and Nation Building* (New Haven, 1962), esp. pp. 52–55.

31. *Pravda,* July 17, 1955, p. 6.

32. Leningrad: *ibid.,* July 28, 1955, p. 2, Voroshilovgrad: *Partiinaia zhizn,* no. 17 (September 1955), p. 24.

33. The following are the obkom first secretaries in the most industrialized oblasti in 1952: V. M. Andriianov, M. T. Efremov, A. I. Gaevoi, G. E. Grishko, I. D. Iakovlev, N. S. Khrushchev, A. I. Khvorostukhin, A. P. Kirilenko, N. V. Kiselev, V. K. Klimenko, N. V. Laptev, V. V. Lukianov, V. S. Markov, N. N. Organov, N. V. Podgorny, D. G. Smirnov, A. I. Struev, F. E. Titov, G. A. Borkov, I. T. Grishin, M. I. Gusev, S. Ia. Iakovlev, A. M. Kutyrev, Z. I. Muratov, F. M. Prass. Biographies have been found of the first eighteen listed, many in *Deputaty* (1958).

The following are the obkom first secretaries in the most industrialized oblasti in 1957: B. A. Barinov, G. A. Denisov, B. I. Deriugin, M. T. Efremov, A. I. Gaevoi, S. Ia. Iakovlev, N. G. Ignatov, I. V. Kapitonov, I. P. Kazanets, A. P. Kirilenko, N. V. Kiselev, V. K. Klimenko, B. N. Kobelev, F. R. Kozlov, N. V. Laptev, Z. I. Muratov, L. I. Naidek, N. N. Organov, S. M. Pilipets, V. V. Shcherbitskii, P. E. Shelest, A. I. Struev, F. E. Titov, V. N. Titov, and I. K. Zhegalin. With the exception of Deriugin, Iakovlev, and Muratov, all these men are included in *Deputaty* (1958).

34. The 1959 census is used for this purpose. The oblasti are Cheliabinsk,

Dnepropetrovsk, Irkutsk, Kemerovo, Kharkov, Kuibyshev, Leningrad, Lugansk (formerly Voroshilovgrad), Moscow, Stalino (later Donetsk), Sverdlovsk, and Tula.

35. See, for example, the biographies of O. I. Ivashchenko, G. I. Kadagidge, and I. T. Tazhiev in *Deputaty* (1958) and those of E. T. Astsatrian and I. A. Maniushis in *Deputaty* (1962).

36. See, for example, the biographies of K. I. Galanshin, V. K. Klimenko, P. E. Shelest, A. I. Shibaev, and M. S. Solomentsev in *Deputaty* (1966).

37. The biographies of F. R. Kozlov, I. V. Spiridonov, N. N. Rodionov, and G. I. Popov (one of the raikom secretaries) are contained in *Deputaty* (1962). That of S. P. Mitrofanov is printed in *Bolshaia sovetskaia entsiklopediia,* 1960 yearbook, p. 601. For the reference to I. K. Zamchevskii, see *Pravda,* January 1, 1941, p. 3. I learned of the background of the other two raikom secretaries (K. K. Berezin and A. A. Slepukhin) in an interview with Mr. Berezin in 1962, at that time chairman of the Leningrad Trade Union of the Machine Industry).

38. The biographies of two of these men, I. I. Diadyk and I. P. Kazanets, can be found in *Deputaty* (1958), and that of the third, A. P. Liashko, is located in *Deputaty* (1962).

39. *Partiinaia zhizn,* no. 3 (February 1957), p. 15.

40. The criticism of the levels of technical expertise within the sovnarkhozy was directed at the impossibility of assembling in each sovnarkhoz a technical staff large enough to handle the multitude of technical problems that might arise in a great variety of different industries. It was also directed at the fact that the major industrial research institutes were not supervised by the same organizations that administered industry. The qualifications of the higher sovnarkhoz officials were not questioned.

The relationship of Khrushchev (and Malenkov) to the industrial managers is a complex and somewhat obscure matter. The creation of the sovnarkhozy was surely motivated in part at least by Khrushchev's desire to strengthen the position of the obkom first secretaries (and to increase his support among them), but this does not necessarily mean that the First Secretary perceived the industrial ministries to be a hostile political force that had to be destroyed. Of course, Khrushchev's Presidium opponents were concentrated in the Council of Ministers, and he certainly was eager to destroy these men politically. However, the relationship of the industrial ministers and deputy ministers to the top officials of the Council of Ministers is not at all self-evident. Although the ministers (but not necessarily all the deputy ministers) had reason to oppose the creation of the sovnarkhozy, they may have felt quite uneasy at the prospect of Malenkov or Molotov becoming the Party leader. (Indeed, even Saburov and Pervukhin seem to have been ambivalent at best about this prospect.)

Moreover, Khrushchev himself clearly did not think that industrial managers were individuals whose specialized background had destroyed their *partiinost* (party spirit). From 1950 to 1964 he followed a consistent and vigorous policy of appointing managerial personnel to key posts in the Party apparatus, eventually including that of obkom first secretary. (In the postwar years the one period in which few industrial administrators were appointed directly to Party work was that between the death of Zhdanov and the transfer of Khrushchev to Moscow, when Malenkov was a dominant influence in the secretariat.) In addition, the stability among the top industrial administrators during the last seven years of Khrushchev's rule also raises grave doubts about the degree of hostility of this group to the First Secretary.

41. This figure does not include the Ministry of Construction of Electric Power Stations, the Ministry of Electric Power Stations, and the Ministry of Light Industry. The first two of these ministries were, in essence, merged, and the Ministry of Light Industry had had no minister since February 1957.

Of the eighteen industrial ministers whose ministries were abolished, five (A. A. Ishkov, G. S. Khlamov, E. S. Novoselov, N. I. Strokin, and V. P. Zotov) became high officials of the USSR Gosplan, six (A. I. Kostousov, P. F. Lomako, K. D. Petukhov, N. N. Smeliakov, S. A. Stepanov, and A. N. Zademidko) became sovnarkhoz chairmen, two (G. M. Orlov and F. D. Varaksin) were named RSFSR ministers (the RSFSR ministries for the timber industry and the paper-pulp industry were not abolished immediately), one (M. A. Lesechko) became a deputy chairman of the Ukrainian Gosplan, one (M. A. Evseenko) a deputy chairman of the RSFSR Gosplan, one (S. F. Antonov) a deputy chairman of the Moscow oblast sovnarkhoz, one (A. G. Sheremetev) the head of the Soviet steel plant construction in India, and the fate of one (P. N. Goremykin) is unknown. With the exception of Kaganovich, the construction ministers were given important operational posts associated with construction. A. K. Kortunov was named head of Glavgaz, N. A. Dygai was appointed Minister of Construction of the RSFSR, D. Ia. Raizer became Minister of Construction of Kazakhstan, I. K. Koziulia was named head of the Moscow oblast construction administration, and L. G. Melnikov became Chairman of the Kazakhstan Gosplan.

42. The names of these deputy ministers were found primarily in the 1957 State Department Directory of Soviet Officials. Those listed in this Directory but who could not be identified in their position in 1956 or 1957 were excluded. However, the 105 deputy ministers include several men not listed in the Directory, but identified in the Soviet press in 1956 or 1957.

43. *Pravda,* March 30, 1957, p. 3.

44. The names of the high officials of the USSR and RSFSR Gosplany were collected from the various Soviet newspapers of the time. The names of the officials of the Ukrainian Gosplan were published in *Pravda Ukrainy,* January 30, 1958, p. 4.

45. Formally, the State Economic Council (Gosekonsovet) was abolished, a USSR sovnarkhoz established, and Gosplan given responsibility for long-range planning instead of short-range planning. However, there was great continuity in personnel during the reorganization, and the men engaged in short-range planning became the core of the USSR sovnarkhoz instead of shifting their activity to long-range planning.

46. *Pravda,* March 14, 1963, p. 1.

47. The members of the Council of Ministers at this time were listed in *Bolshaia sovetskaia entsiklopediia,* 1963 yearbook, pp. 12–13.

48. The statistics on ministers appointed sovnarkhoz chairmen includes the head of Glavgaz. Actually, nine former ministers were appointed in June. However, one of the ministers (A. G. Sheremetev, the chairman of the Cheliabinsk sovnarkhoz) was sent almost immediately to the Russian steel plant construction project in India, and he was replaced by M. S. Solomentsev (the obkom secretary for industry and a former plant director). Solomentsev has been treated as the first real chairman of the sovnarkhoz.

These figures are based on the last known positions of these officials. In a few cases a man is known to have been removed from this position before 1957, and in a few other cases the last identification of a future sovnarkhoz chairman in the ministerial period was made over a year prior to the reorganization. (It is this fact which explains the difference between the number of former ministers among sovnarkhoz chairmen and the number of 1957 ministers who were listed as becoming sovnarkhoz chairmen in note 41.) However, the errors that were introduced in the statistics by this factor do not affect the basic conclusions presented. If any of the chairmen had been demoted in the period immediately prior to the creation of the sovnarkhozy, this would not lessen the experience they brought to their new position; if they had been promoted, the experience would be even more substantial than has been indicated.

49. The statistic on year of birth is based on a sample of 54, the statistic on Party admission on a sample of 52. Full biographies were found of the following 1957 sovnarkhoz chairmen (the majority of them in the volumes of the *Deputaty*): P. I. Abroskin, K. N. Beliak, V. G. Bereza, I. T. Borisov, B. F. Bratchenko, G. I. Chogovadze, A. V. Davydov, I. I. Diadyk, A. I. Eremeev, V. S. Fedorov, N. P. Gordeev, F. Kh. Khodzhaev, A. I. Kostousov, I. M. Kratenko, G. T. Kulik, A. S. Kuzmich, P. Ia. Lisniak, P. F. Lomako, M. N. Markelov, S. A. Movsesian, V. N. Novikov, D. G. Onika, S. A. Orudzhev, E. I. Ozarskis, K. D. Petukhov, M. Ia. Pludon, S. P. Polimbetov, I. S. Pribylski, K. Redzhebov, P. Seitov, N. A. Shchelokov, A. T. Shmarev, K. M. Simakov, I. F. Sinitsyn, S. A. Skachkov, N. N. Smeliakov, A. G. Soldatov, M. S. Solomentsev, S. A. Stepanov, N. A. Tikhonov, N. V. Timofeev, S. U. Utebaev, N. N. Vaniaev, A. T. Veimer, E. A. Veselovskii, K. V. Vorobev, V. T. Zabaluev, A. I. Zolov, and A. N. Zedemidko.

50. In the other republics, little more than a third of the sovnarkhoz chairmen of 1957 remained in this position in 1960. However, in a number of these cases, the sovnarkhoz chairman had been promoted to the position of first deputy chairman of the Council of Ministers and then supervised not only sovnarkhoz industry but a series of related ministries as well.

51. Biographies are available for the following men appointed sovnarkhoz chairmen in 1960 or after: V. K. Akulintsev, A. K. Antonov, E. T. Astsatrian, A. D. Biziaev, A. F. Borisov, N. N. Chepelenko, V. I. Degtiarev, V. N. Doenin,

A. M. Golovachev, L. E. Grafov, V. A. Ivanov, K. K. Kairis, V. A. Kargopolov, N. M. Khudosovtsev, S. L. Kniazev, K. K. Kostrov, V. V. Krotov, P. A. Kulvets, L. E. Lukich, N. A. Obolenskii, V. I. Smirnov, O. V. Soich, V. M. Sukhov, A. M. Vartanian, F. D. Voronov, V. F. Zhigalin, and G. V. Zubarev.

52. *Ekonomicheskaia gazeta,* January 5, 1963, p. 11.

53. *Promyshlennost SSSR — Statisticheskii sbornik* (Industry of the USSR — A Statistical Handbook; Moscow, 1957), p. 15.

54. A few of these directors received their degrees relatively late in their careers, at least in two cases after having become plant director. So far as can be judged, only four of the ninety-five directors correspond to this pattern, but they were at two of the most important plants in the country — the present directors of Uralmash and Rostselmash and their immediate predecessors. All four were men with long experience at lower levels in industrial administration.

55. A partial biography of Denisov can be found in *Bolshaia sovetskaia entsiklopediia,* 1962 yearbook, p. 593. He was listed as an obkom first secretary in *Pravda,* July 9, 1945, p. 3 and probably had held this post since 1943.

56. *Pravda,* July 2, 1959, p. 2.

57. *Pravda,* August 22, 1959, p. 1. The biography of the new first secretary (A. I. Shibaev) can be found in *Deputaty* (1962), p. 469.

58. Of the enterprise directors, five were plant managers (all at major heavy industry plants), one was the director of an electric station, and one was an important construction administrator — chief engineer of a trust and later first deputy chairman of the Leningrad gorispolkom.

The twenty-five first secretaries in 1962 were: G. G. Abramov, V. I. Drozdenko, L. N. Efremov, M. T. Efremov, K. I. Galanshin, F. S. Goriachev, I. V. Kapitonov, A. A. Kokarev, A. P. Liashko, F. I. Loshchenkov, L. I. Lubennikov, A. S. Murysev, K. K. Nikolaev, S. N. Shchetinin, V. V. Shevchenko, A. I. Shibaev, A. M. Shkolnikov, M. S. Sinitsa, V. V. Skriabin, N. A. Sobol, M. S. Solomentsev, F. A. Tabeev, A. A. Titarenko, V. S. Tolstikov, and N. P. Tolubeev. The biographies of all but Titarenko can be found in *Deputaty* (1962). Titarenko's biography can be found in *Deputaty* (1966). Nearly all the biographies are also printed (and in more complete form) in the 1962 yearbook of the *Bolshaia sovetskaia entsiklopediia.*

59. See, for example, the biographies of R. B. Baigaliev and P. E. Shelest in *Deputaty* (1962), and that of V. P. Lein in *Deputaty* (1966).

60. These men are A. F. Eshtokin, F. F. Kuziukov, and V. S. Oleinikov. Oleinikov's biography can be found in *Deputaty* (1958), p. 298, and Eshtokin's in *Bolshaia sovetskaia entsiklopediia,* 1966 yearbook, p. 587. For the earlier position of Kuziukov, see *Izvestiia,* April 27, 1957, p. 1.

61. The Karaganda secretary was N. V. Bannikov (*Bolshaia sovetskaia entsiklopediia,* 1966 yearbook, p. 577); the Kharkov secretary was G. I. Vashchenko (*ibid.,* p. 581). The first secretaries of these obkomy were respectively, M. S. Solomentsev and N. A. Sobol (*ibid.,* pp. 612–613).

62. *Pravda,* February 1, 1959, p. 5.

63. *Kommunist,* no. 8 (June 1959), p. 46; *Pravda,* February 18, 1959, p. 3.

64. *Kommunist,* no. 8 (June 1959), p. 46. The number of Kharkov raiony is found in *Bolshaia sovetskaia entsiklopediia,* XLVI, 79.

65. *Pravda,* February 18, 1959, p. 3. Actually 5 of these raiony are small towns (e.g., Pushkino) that lie in the countryside around the city proper. In most of these 5, as well as in several of the shopping raiony in the center of the city, there may be slight need for industrial specialists among the raikom secretaries. Evaluation of overall Leningrad statistics (including those given by Bulganin in 1955) should take this fact into account. SSSR: *Administrativnoe-territorialnoe delenie soiuznykh respublik* (USSR: Administrative-Territorial Divisions of the Union Republics; Moscow, 1960), p. 113.

66. K. P. Kukhalashvili, ed., *Partiinaia rabota v promyshlennosti* (Party Work in Industry; Kiev, 1959), p. 70.

67. Pokrovski, *V tesnoi sviazi,* pp. 52–53.

68. Their biographies can be found in *Deputaty* (1962), pp. 138 and 145.

69. RSFSR: *Kommunist,* no. 16 (November 1963), p. 4; Kemerovo: *Pravda,* March 1, 1963, p. 2.

70. In the months just prior to the reorganization a few of the new first secretaries may have been promoted to a higher post than that indicated. However, I have included only those men who can be identified in a position within a year prior to the reorganization. That a man was a second secretary is not necessarily indication of any lack of technical experience. Several of the second secretaries promoted in November 1962 are known to have been enterprise directors.

71. Included among the RSFSR and the Ukrainian first secretaries listed as directors is one high construction administration, one high railroad administrator, and a chairman and a deputy chairman of sovnarkhozy about whom no earlier data is available.

72. *Pravda,* December 1, 1964, p. 3.

73. *Ibid.,* September 24, 1966, p. 1.

74. The 1966 first secretaries of the most industrialized oblasti are N. V. Bannikov, V. I. Degtiarev, A. F. Eshtokin, K. I. Galanshin, F. P. Golovchenko, F. S. Goriachev, K. F. Katushev, A. A. Kokarev, V. I. Konotop, L. S. Kulichenko, F. I. Loshchenkov, K. K. Nikolaev, N. N. Rodionov, S. N. Shchetinin, V. V. Shevchenko, A. I. Shibaev, M. S. Sinitsa, A. N. Smirnov, M. S. Solomentsev, F. A. Tabeev, A. M. Tokarev, V. S. Tolstikov, G. I. Vashchenko, A. F. Vatchenko, and M. N. Vsevolozhski. Biographies of all these men can be found both in *Deputaty* (1966) and in the 1966 yearbook of the *Bolshaia sovetskaia entsiklopediia.*

The nine men listed as enterprise director include the electric station director and the construction administrator mentioned in note 58 as well as a man (A. N. Smirnov) who was promoted directly from enterprise chief engineer into the glavk and who served as head of the glavk of the cotton textile industry of Ivanovo oblast. N. N. Rodionov should conceivably be listed as a tenth director, for he was a lower-level industrial administrator who became sovnarkhoz deputy chairman after fifteen years work in the Party apparatus.

75. This paragraph describes the new first secretaries at the time of Table 11, that is, June 1966. By April 1, 1968, there had been four changes of first secretaries in the most industrialized oblasti. A. M. Tokarev, the first secretary of the Kuibyshev obkom and a man with years of Komsomol, soviet, and Party work in urban areas, had been replaced by V. P. Orlov, a man of very similar background. M. S. Solomentsev, the first secretary of the Rostov obkom and a former plant manager, has been replaced by I. A. Bondarenko, an agronomist whose career has been centered on agricultural supervision. S. N. Shchetinin, the first secretary of the Irkutsk obkom (a technicum graduate with almost no experience in industrial administration but thirty years of Party and soviet work in industrial areas), was replaced by N. V. Bannikov, the first secretary of the Karaganda obkom. Bannikov, a man with three decades of work in industrial administration and Party work in urban areas, was himself replaced by V. K. Akulintsev, an official with more impressive experience in administrative and Party supervision of industry (including stints as republican secretary for industry and republican sovnarkhoz chairman). Akulintsev's biography can be found in *Deputaty* (1962), those of Bannikov, Bondarenko, and Orlov are located in *Deputaty* (1966).

76. *Voprosy partiinogo stroitelstva*, p. 224.

77. These men are A. P. Botvin, N. G. Egorychev, G. V. Kolbin, P. S. Kolin, G. A. Martirosian, G. I. Popov, M. Z. Shakirov, M. G. Voropaev, A. P. Filatov, K. F. Kravchenko, S. N. Sabaneev, N. A. Seregin, A. I. Shitov, and I. E. Liaboga. The biographies of the first eight secretaries were found in *Deputaty* (1966) and the biographies of the next five men in the oblast press of February–March 1967 (located in Lenin Library). For information on Liaboga, see note 81.

78. These men are M. F. Deur, L. P. Garibdzhanian, A. M. Kadyrov, O. I. Lolashvili, K. Iu. Matsketvichius, L. P. Metlitski, F. I. Mochalin, S. Pulatov, S. R. Rasulov, M. K. Shabasanov, V. I. Vialis, and A. K. Zitmanis. Their biographies can be found in *Deputaty* (1966).

79. These men are A. I. Alizade, M. F. Deur, A. P. Filatov, L. P. Garibdzhanian, A. M. Kadyrov, R. Khodzhaev, P. S. Kolin, K. F. Kravchenko, I. E. Liaboga, O. I. Lolashvili, G. A. Martirosian, L. P. Metlitski, F. I. Mochalin, S. R. Rasulov, S. N. Sabaneev, M. K. Shabasanov, A. I. Shitov, G. M. Voskanian, and A. K. Zitmanis. The biographies of most of these men can be found in *Deputaty* (1966).

80. See, for example, *Pravda*, October 12, 1965, p. 2.

81. This man is I. E. Liaboga. *Pravda Ukrainy*, October 22, 1955; *Izvestiia*, July 29, 1965, p. 3.

82. The change of position for this man (I. D. Maslov) was observed during an examination of *Ulianovskaia pravda* of 1966 and 1967. The information about his engineering background was obtained in an interview in Ulianovsk.

83. The thirty-three ministers are: S. A. Afanasev, A. K. Antonov, S. F. Antonov, B. F. Bratchenko, K. I. Brekhov, B. E. Butoma, P. V. Dementev, V. N. Doenin, V. E. Dymshits, V. S. Fedorov, I. A. Grishmanov, F. B. Iakubosksii, A. A. Ishkov, V. D. Kalmykov, I. P. Kazanets, A. K. Kortunov, L. A. Kostandov, A. I. Kostousov, E. F. Kozhevnikov, P. F. Lomako, I. T. Novikov, E. S. Novoselov, K. N. Rudnev, V. D. Shashin, A. I. Shokin, I. F. Sinitsyn, E. P. Slavskii, A. M. Tarasov, N. N. Tarasov, N. V. Timofeev, V. F. Zhigalin, V. P. Zotov, and S. A. Zverev. The former obkom first secretary (I. P. Kazanets, the Minister of Ferrous Metallurgy), had worked for fifteen years at the Kuznetsk Combine and the Enakievo Metallurgy Works before entering Party work and becoming first secretary of the Stalino obkom in 1953; the former head of the construction department of the Central Committee (I. A. Grishmanov, the Minister of Building Materials) had nearly two decades of work in construction administration before assuming his Party post in 1955. The list of 1965 ministers can be found in *Pravda,* October 3, 1965, p. 2, the biographies of these men both in *Deputaty* (1966) and in the 1966 yearbook of the *Bolshaia sovetskaia entsiklopediia.*

84. The only ministerial positions considered higher than plant director for these purposes are head of glavk, deputy minister, and minister.

85. The "post-revolutionary professionals" are here defined as men born between 1905 and 1920 and admitted to the Party in 1938 or after. Without exception, the 1957 and 1965 ministers failing to correspond to this pattern were born before 1920 and were admitted to the Party before 1938. Data arranged as in Table 5 would show 16 ministers born in 1908 or earlier, 11 of them joining the Party at the age of 26 or before. Seventeen ministers were born in the period 1909–1918, 14 of them joining the Party after the age of 26.

As before, the ministers are supported by an apparatus whose size is unknown but which must be elaborate. Not enough information is available on the less experienced deputy ministers to justify confident generalizations about these officials. We can say that 30 percent of the 72 industrial deputy ministers identified had been deputy ministers by 1957. (The construction deputy ministers — fewer of whom had been deputy ministers in 1957 — are excluded from this statistic.) Most of the less experienced ministers whose background can be identified come from the same type of posts as their pre-1957 predecessors. However, there is one major exception to this pattern. Although Brezhnev called for the selection of very experienced Party officials to be secretaries of the Party committees of the ministries, those whose names have been found have not been prominent men. Nevertheless, in most ministries (perhaps in every ministry if more information were available) a high Party official has been named as one of the deputy ministers. For example, K. K. Cherednichenko (chemical industry), A. G. Dmitrin (timber, paper, and woodworking industry), F. S. Kolomiets (food industry), and F. F. Kuziukov (coal industry) had been obkom first secretaries; Ia. N. Zarobian (electrotechnical industry) had been a republican first secretary; and S. K. Grigorev (tractor and agricultural machinery industry), V. G. Khorkov (oil refinery and petroleum chemical industry), and P. I. Maksimov (light industry) had been high officials in the Central Committee apparatus. Though some of these men had been industrial administrators prior to being transferred to Party work and may have varied responsibilities in the new ministries, it is likely that their appointment represents a conscious policy and that they each perform similar functions. It is likely that each is the deputy minister for personnel.

86. This generalization is based on information available for 127 (74 percent) of the plants. A more specific breakdown of this statistic is given in the

Tenure of directors at a given plant of the 170 most important plants, January 1, 1967.

Type of Plant	Years at the plant				
	0–3	3–5	5–10	Over 10	Unknown
Iron and steel industry (N = 30)	6	7	4	10	3
Auto and agricultural machinery (N = 30)	7	4	11	2	6
Transportation machinery (N = 15)	4	1	2	3	5
Other machinery and machine tools (N = 30)	11	2	7	4	6
Electrotechnical industry (N = 20)	5	3	4	3	5
Chemical industry (N = 15)	4	4	1	2	4
Miscellaneous heavy industry (Nⱼ = 15)	2	5	1	3	4
Miscellaneous light industry (N = 15)	1	1	2	1	10
Total (N = 170)	40	27	32	28	43

table. The table is compiled on the same principles as Table 6. Six of the directors with at least five years tenure do not have continuous tenure. In 27 of the cases, it was possible only to determine whether the tenure was more or less than five years. In these cases, extrapolation was used to place the director in a more specific category. If it was possible to determine whether a director had a tenure of five years, the plant was placed in the "unknown" category.

87. The biographies of 26 of these men were found in the *Deputaty* (1966), the biographies of three of them in the oblast press at the time they were elected deputies to the RSFSR (and in one case the Ukrainian) Supreme Soviet in 1967, and the age of the others in lists of deputies elected to oblast soviets in March 1967. All directors for whom data was found in these sources are included, but a lack of time limited to 25 the number of oblasti whose newspapers were examined in the Lenin Library. No information was found on the deputies in the very largest oblasti (Moscow, Leningrad, Kiev, Kharkov, and Sverdlovsk), but twelve of the most industrialized oblasti and eight of the most important agricultural oblasti in the RSFSR were included among the twenty-five.

The 134 directors include men from all industries and from both large and small cities, and they probably are quite representative of the men named to the oblast soviets. It is, however, impossible to determine whether the deputies constitute a representative sample of all managers. It is conceivable that either the oldest or the youngest managers might be given preference in the composition of the lists of deputies. The biographical data available on directors of the 170 plants whose age is unknown suggests that the age distribution of these men is fairly similar to that found in the tables.

88. Since 1965, four construction ministries and two industrial ministries have been added to the original 33. Two of the new construction ministers (S. D. Khitrov and A. M. Tokarev) were obkom first secretaries; the other two (N. V. Goldin and G. A. Karavaev) were long-time construction administrators, aged 55 and 58 in 1968. One new industrial minister (P. V. Gusenkov, the Minister of the Medical Industry), had been deputy minister of health by 1955 — presumably the deputy minister in charge of the medical industry. The other new minister (V. V. Bakhirev, the Minister of Machinebuilding) is a typical "post revolutionary professional," born in 1916, admitted to the Party at the age of 35, a plant director (probably in the defense industry) in 1960. Khitrov's and Tokarev's biographies can be found in *Deputaty* (1966), Bakhirev's in *Deputaty* (1962), and Karavaev's in *Bolshaia sovetskaia entsiklopediia* (1962). For information on Goldin, see *Ekonomicheskaia gazeta,* no. 9 (March 1967), p. 2; *Pravda,* December 3, 1947, p. 1; *Trud,* April 17, 1954, p. 2; *Stroitelnaia gazeta,* January 29, 1960, p. 4.

IV. Soviet Administrative Theory: (1) Edinonachalie and the Primary Party Organization

1. *Kratkii ekonomicheskii slovar,* G. A. Kozlov and S. P. Pervushin, eds., (Short Economics Dictionary; Moscow, 1958), p. 75.

2. E. V. Shorina, *Kollegialnost i edinonachalie v sovetskom gosudarstvennom upravlenii* (Collegiality and One-Man Management in Soviet State Administration; Moscow, 1959), p. 11.

3. V. A. Vlasov and S. S. Studenikin, *Sovetskoe administrativnoe pravo* (Soviet Administrative Law; Moscow, 1959), p. 93.

4. *Ibid.,* p. 34.

5. *Ibid.,* p. 11.

6. Bugaev and Leibson, *Besedy ob ustave,* p. 166.

7. *Sovetskaia Moldaviia,* March 4, 1966, p. 3.

8. *Partiinaia zhizn,* no. 2 (January 1958), p. 29.

9. Bugaev and Leibson, p. 194.

10. This demand was formalized in the first systematic Party decision about the Party-state relationship — that taken at the Eighth Party Congress in 1919: "The Party should carry out its decision through the Soviet organs. . . . The Party tries to *lead* the activity of the Soviets, but not to replace them." *Vosmoi sezd RKP* (*b*), *Protokoly* (Eighth Congress of the Russian Communist Party, Protocols [March 18–23, 1919]; Moscow, 1959), p. 429.

11. Slepov, *Vysshie i mestnye organy,* p. 49.

12. Bugaev and Leibson, p. 144.

13. V. I. Lenin, *Sochineniia* (Works; 4th ed.; Moscow, 1950), XXVII, 238–239. The italics are Lenin's.

14. For a discussion of this period, see Paul H. Avrich, "The Bolshevik Revolution and Workers' Control in Russian Industry," *Slavic Review,* 22 (March 1963), pp. 47–63.

15. The debate on edinonachalie centered on two questions: should the administrative authority itself be single or multiple? what should be the role of the trade union (and the workers) in administration? See E. H. Carr, *The Bolshevik Revolution, 1917–1923* (New York, 1951–1953), II, 187–191.

16. *Trud,* March 7, 1963, p. 2.

17. *Pravda,* October 4, 1965, p. 3.

18. *Ibid.,* September 28, 1965, p. 4.

19. Bugaev and Leibson, p. 142.

20. *Pravda,* February 24, 1965, p. 2.

21. *Ibid.,* December 6, 1964, p. 4. In *ibid.,* February 1, 1958, p. 2, there is a similar criticism of the Novosibirsk obkom for "deciding many questions for the oblast and city soviets and for the sovnarkhoz. "Here again the criticism was based on the fact that this practice caused the obkom "to divert its attention from the solution of basic long-range problems."

The cases in which criticisms of Party intervention go beyond questions of detail invariably involve primary Party organizations (or their commissions) that try to obligate administrators in situations where they have the authority only to recommend. This matter will be discussed in the next section.

22. *Pravda*, March 28, 1951, p. 2. (This particular statement comes from an article by Frol Kozlov.) Similarly, the official Party handbook states: "The right of checking the activity of the administration is granted to the primary Party organizations of the production type in order to improve the administration of the economy and consequently in order to strengthen edinonachalie." *Voprosy partiinoi raboty* (1959), p. 237.

23. *Sovetskaia Belorussiia*, April 7, 1957, p. 2. The author of this article, a raikom secretary, complains that too often the activities of the primary organizations are evaluated simply on the basis of whether they " 'help' or 'don't help' in the work of the economic leaders."

24.. *Partiinaia zhizn*, no. 12 (June 1965), p. 28. See p. 30 of this article for a discussion of the way in which the various responsibilities of the primary Party organization are divided among bureau members of the organization in one enterprise.

25. *Voprosy partiinoi raboty* (1959) pp. 261–267.

26. *Pravda*, September 30, 1965, p. 2. However, see Chapter III, note 85.

27. *Voprosy partiinoi raboty* (1959), pp. 230–240.

28. Derek J. R. Scott has stated, "No clear distinction of meaning can be made between it [*kontrol*] and the word *revizija*. . . . *Kontrolj* is particularly associated with the checking on the fulfillment of instructions . . . and [is] synonymous with verification of performance." *Russian Political Institutions* (New York, 1957), p. 150, n. 2.

29. The second secretary of the Astrakhan gorkom once retorted to a critical Soviet correspondent: "You try to lead such a [large] enterprise. How can you possibly get along without law violations?" *Sovetskaia Rossiia*, April 8, 1960, p. 2.

30. Granick, *Management of the Industrial Firm*, pp. 262–268, 285.

31. *Sovetskaia Rossiia*, April 8, 1960, p. 2. The quotation is from the secretary of the Astrakhan obkom.

32. Kukhalashvili, *Partiinaia rabota v promyshlennosti*, p. 121.

33. *Voprosy partiinoi raboty* (1959), pp. 231, 237, 238.

34. *Partiinaia zhizn*, no. 9 (May 1965), p. 20.

35. *Voprosy partiinoi raboty* (1959), p. 237.

36. See *Pravda*, September 27, 1939, p. 3. The Party committees of the large Leningrad plants were said to serve as a "special kind (*svoeobraznaia*) of collegium for the director."

37. *XVIII sezd vsesoiuznoi kommunisticheskoi partii (b), Stenograficheskii otchet* (Eighteenth Congress of the All-Union Communist Party, Stenographic Report [March 10–21, 1939]; Moscow, 1939), p. 533. The italics are Zhdanov's.

38. Kolbenkov, *Sovershenstvovanie rukovodstva promyshlennostiu*, p. 143.

39. *Voprosy partiinoi raboty* (1959), p. 332.

40. *Voprosy partiinoi raboty* (1955), p. 48.

41. Bugaev and Leibson, p. 194.

42. *Partiinaia zhizn,* no. 9 (May 1965), p. 20, and no. 23 (December 1965), p. 34.

43. *Ibid.,* no. 23 (December 1963), p. 49.

44. *Leningradskaia pravda,* October 25, 1952, p. 2.

45. *Zaria vostoka,* September 22, 1965, p. 2.

46. *Kommunist,* no. 2 (January 1966), p. 19.

47. *Pravda,* December 12, 1966, p. 1.

48. In theory the secretary is merely the executive arm of the organization; in reality, particularly in the larger organizations, he is often a man selected by higher-level Party organs as their agent. In *Voprosy partiinoi raboty* (1959), pp. 356–358, there is a separate section entitled "The Role of the Raikom in the Selection of Secretaries [of the Primary Party Organization]."

49. *Partiinaia zhizn,* no. 23 (December 1965), p. 34.

50. *Ibid.,* no. 9 (May 1965), p. 20. The italics are in the original.

51. *Ekonomicheskaia gazeta,* January 19, 1963, p. 35; *Kommunist,* no. 2 (January 1966), p. 23.

52. See David Granick, *The Red Executive* (Garden City, 1960), pp. 38–39, and Joseph Berliner, *Factory and Manager in the USSR* (Cambridge, Mass., 1957), p. 267.

53. Any press report mentioning both the manager and the Party secretary always lists the manager first. Even within the Party the plant manager is more likely to receive the honor of election to, for example, the republican central committee than is the plant Party secretary. Armstrong, *The Soviet Bureaucratic Elite,* pp. 65–67. Armstrong's generalization holds true in other republics as well. In a detailed study of the 1966 central committees of six republics (Belorussia, Georgia, Latvia, Moldavia, Ukraine, and Uzbekistan), I found four plant Party secretaries among the central committee full members as compared with 19 plant directors.

The pay of the Party officials is discussed very infrequently, but in *Sovetskaia Belorussiia,* April 25, 1957, p. 2, the pay of the secretary of the primary Party organization is said to be considerably lower than that of the director.

54. This statement is true only for the precise positions named. Plant Party secretaries frequently are engineers with lower managerial experience (e.g., as shop head or even as high as chief engineer), and plant directors are often named secretaries of the local Party committees. Both of these career patterns, however, only confirm the general point made here.

55. *Partiinaia zhizn,* no. 12 (June 1963), p. 42. See also Party Rules, Statute 2.

56. "In 1959"; *Partiinaia zhizn,* no. 13 (July 1959), pp. 23–27; "Since 1962": *Pravda,* March 15, 1966, p. 4.

57. *Partiinaia zhizn,* no. 12 (June 1963), p. 40. The deputy secretary not only

supervises the groups of assistance but also coordinates their work with the other forms of "public *kontrol.*"

58. *Voprosy partiinogo stroitelstva,* p. 185.

59. See Chapter VIII, pp. 182–187.

60. See, for example, Peter M. Blau, *The Dynamics of Bureaucracy* (Chicago, 1955).

61. This theme has been widely discussed by Western economists. A useful general summary can be found in Alec Nove, "The Problem of 'Success Indicators' in Soviet Industry," *Economica,* new series, 25 (February 1958), pp. 1–13.

62. Discussions of this point can be found in Peter F. Drucker, *Concept of the Corporation* (New York, 1946), pp. 84–97; and Chester I. Barnard, *Organization and Management* (Cambridge, Mass., 1948), p. 88.

63. L. Slepov, *"Nezyblemye leninskie normy partiinoi zhizni i printsipy rukovodstva"* (The Firm Leninist Norms of Party Life and the Principles of Leadership) in N. Barsukov, compiler, *Borba partii za moshchnyi podem narodnogo khoziaistva, za zavershenie stroitelstva sotsializma (1953–1958 gody)* (The Struggle of the Party for the Powerful Rise of the Economy, for the Completion of the Building of Socialism, 1953–1958; Moscow, 1963), p. 29,

64. See, for example, *Pravda Ukrainy,* February 27, 1966, p. 2.

65. See, for example, Herbert A. Simon, *Administrative Behavior* (2nd ed.; New York, 1961), pp. xxiv–xxvii; and Harold W. Dodds, *The Academic President — Educator or Caretaker?* (New York, 1962), pp. 90–95.

66. J. V. Stalin, *Works* (Moscow, 1953), V, 264–265.

67. The immense literature on "communication with the masses" (*sviaz s massami*) is permeated with this theme.

68. *Sovetskaia Rossiia,* February 2, 1966, p. 2.

69. In *Kommunist Tadzhikistana,* June 9, 1956, p. 3, there is mention of a secretary with the philosophy: "There exists a [factory] administration; let it be concerned with production."

70. Even in recent years there have been published several complaints about Party organizations that have exceeded their authority by firing individual employees. *Partiinaia zhizn,* no. 24 (December 1963), pp. 41–42, and no. 1 (January 1964), pp. 49–50.

V. Soviet Administrative Theory: (2) The Local Party Organs

1. *Pravda,* May 12, 1946, p. 2.

2. This question will be discussed at length in Chapter XII.

3. *Pravda,* February 26, 1953, p. 1.

4. *Ibid.,* December 8, 1940, p. 1.

5. Party Rules, Statute 19.

6. *Ibid.,* Statute 42.

7. *Pravda,* December 23, 1964, p. 1, and July 17, 1960, p. 3.

8. Vlasov, *Sovetskoe administrativnoe pravo,* p. 68.

9. *Sovetskaia Rossiia,* November 30, 1957, p. 2.

10. For a biography of this man (S. A. Stepanov), see *Izvestiia,* March 16, 1962, p. 5.

11. See Chapter II, pp. 15, 21–22.

12. In one small town, for example, a dispute arose between a heating shop and a construction trust over whether to connect a heating line that was not yet properly insulated. (The builders insisted that it be done to prevent the freezing of a new building's heating system.) Unable to agree, they took the question to one of the lowest of Party officials, the head of the industrial-transportation department of the local raikom, and they accepted without question his decision to connect the line despite insulating regulations. *Sovetskaia Rossiia,* March 13, 1960, p. 2. For a further discussion of this case, see Chapter XI, pp. 245–250.

13. Of course, the real influence of a man in any decision-making situation is extremely difficult to determine, and there may be little correlation between a man's formal position and his real influence. Any attempt by an outsider to judge the relative influence of two officials always faces problems. Although there undoubtedly was variation in the relative influence of the sovnarkhoz chairman and the Party officials specializing in industry, there is much evidence to support the generalizations of this paragraph. Membership on the Party bureaus and committees is one such indicator; the order of officials who sign the obituary of an economic manager or Party official specializing in industry is another. Perhaps the best evidence is provided by a study of career patterns of officials on the rise.

14. *Sovetskaia Estoniia,* May 16, 1956, p. 2.

15. *Pravda,* February 16, 1941, p. 2. The italics are mine. Some have questioned whether prior to 1957 the local Party organs had responsibility for ministerial plants (particularly those with Party Organizers of the Central Committee as the secretary of their primary Party organization). In light of statements such as Malenkov's as well as the concrete examples cited throughout this book, it is not possible to sustain such a belief about the role of the local Party organs.

16. *Pravda,* April 19, 1947, p. 1. Indeed, as early as 1923 we find Stalin noting with the greatest approval and encouragement that "the guberniia [Party] committees . . . have got into their stride, they have taken up construction work in earnest, they have put the local budgets in order, they have taken control of local economic development, they have really managed to take the lead of the entire economic and political life of their guberniias." Stalin, *Works,* V, 219.

17. *Pravda Ukrainy,* March 12, 1947, p. 2.

18. Fainsod, *Smolensk,* p. 76. See the obkom first secretary's statement quoted in Chapter VI, p. 146.

19. *Deputaty* (1962), p. 469. The new first secretary was Aleksei I. Shibaev.

The man whom he replaced (Georgii A. Denisov) had been an obkom first secretary for at least 16 years and, on his removal, became head of the agricultural department of the Central Committee for the union republics. *Pravda* August 22, 1959, p. 1.

20. See Chapter III, p. 64.

21. The one exception to this generalization is the Party committee of the kolkhoz-sovkhoz administration from 1962 to 1964.

22. A fascinating outline of possible superior-subordinate relationships is presented in Robert Tannenbaum and Warren H. Schmidt, "How to Choose a Leadership Pattern," *Harvard Business Review,* 36 (March–April 1958), pp. 95–101.

23. Chapman, *The Prefects,* p. 17, and *The Profession of Government,* p. 70.

24. See, for example, M. P. Pai, "The Emerging Role of the Collector," *The Indian Journal of Public Administration,* 8 (October–December 1962), pp. 478–488.

25. Indeed, the local Party organs are usually described in language that identifies them with the Party. For an early such statement, see a speech made in March 1922 by Anastas Mikoyan, then secretary of the Nizhne-Novgorod guberniia Party committee. At the Eleventh Party Congress Mikoyan defended the involvement of the guberniia Party committees in economic work: "We, as the Party of the working class, . . . cannot not lead economic work. Of course, we should not interfere in administrative details, in trifles, but we should predetermine the policy of economic work. We graphically know how the New Economic Policy is to be put into practice." (The "we" referred to the guberniia committees.) *Odinnadtsatyi sezd RKP/b/, Stenograficheskii otchet* (Eleventh Congress of the Russian Communist Party [Bolsheviks], stenographical report [March 27–April 2, 1922]; Moscow, 1961), p. 431.

26. *Voprosy partiinoi raboty* (1959), p. 365.

27. *Pravda,* May 30, 1965, p. 2.

28. *VIII sezd,* p. 429.

29. A strike at a large construction site in Temir-Tau, Kazakhstan, in the fall of 1959 furnishes a most striking example of this policy. Not only were the Temir-Tau gorkom officials affected, but all 5 obkom secretaries were also removed. *Kazakhstanskaia pravda,* October 23, 1959, p. 2, and February 3, 1960, p. 2. The obkom first secretary (P. N. Isaev) was demoted to the post of head of shift (*smena*) in the Verkh-Iset Metallurgy Works in Sverdlovsk. *Deputaty* (1958), p. 168. Somewhat similar personnel changes followed the demonstration in Tbilisi in early 1956, an anti-Russian scandal in Latvia in the summer of 1959, and the demonstrations in Rostov oblast in the summer of 1962.

30. Party Rules, Statute 2.

31. *Ibid.,* Statute 41.

32. Bugaev and Leibson, *Besedy ob ustave,* p. 141.

33. *Pravda,* June 22, 1963, pp. 1–2.

34. *Ibid.*, July 14, 1955, p. 3.

35. Fainsod, *Smolensk*, p. 396.

36. Vera S. Dunham, *The Party Secretary in Postwar Soviet Literature* (Project on the Soviet Social System, Harvard University, 1953), p. 51.

37. Peter S. Bridges, "The Character of the Party Secretary in Postwar Soviet Literature" (Master's thesis, Columbia University, 1955).

38. *Voprosy partiinoi raboty* (1959), pp. 413–416.

39. *Ibid.*, p. 414, and *Partiinaia zhizn*, no. 1 (January 1964), p. 36.

40. *Pravda*, June 22, 1963, p. 2.

41. *Ibid.*, July 23, 1960, p. 1.

42. *Partiinaia zhizn*, no. 11 (June 1966), p. 14, and no. 12 (September 1954), p. 9.

43. See the Central Committee decision, "About the ideological-educational work with supervisory personnel in the Tashkent city Party organization," *ibid.*, no. 8 (April 1963), pp. 30–33. This decision speaks of the "ideological training of leaders of all echelons — from officials of the Party apparatus to the foremen" (p. 31).

44. Party Rules, Statute 42.

45. Slepov, *Vysshie i mestnye organy*, p. 18.

46. See *Voprosy partiinogo stroitelstva*, pp. 226–228. This matter is certain to be raised at any Party session dealing with personnel selection. See, for example, *Zaria vostoka*, June 27, 1962, p. 3, for a typical example of the way the question is discussed at a session of a republican central committee.

47. Bugaev and Leibson, p. 76.

48. *Partiinaia zhizn*, no. 3 (May 1954), pp. 50–53. It is interesting that even during the Stalin period "often . . . a Communist, having received the agreement of the raikom, has not waited for the permission of the obkom [before leaving]." In one raion in Stalinsk, Kemerovo oblast, 662 Communists moved in the period 1950–1953, and 427 left before the obkom acted (p. 51).

49. "Instruktsiia ob uchete chlenov i kandidatov v chleny KPSS" (Instructions about the Registration of Members and Candidate Members of the CPSU; Confirmed by the Central Committee CPSU), *Voprosy partiinoi raboty* (1959), p. 545.

50. *Partiinaia zhizn*, no. 22 (November 1965), p. 36. It is admitted, however, that this rule is often winked at.

51. *Voprosy partiinoi raboty* (1959), p. 549.

52. See, for example, Vlasov, p. 93. "The directors of the enterprises are appointed by the minister (leader of the department), by the chairman of the regional sovnarkhoz, by the head of the glavk, by the head of the trust, or by the executive committee of the local soviet, depending upon the established nomenklatura (*v zavisimosti ot utverzhdennoi nomenklatury*)."

53. P. D. Morozov, *Leninskie printsipy podbora, rasstanovki, i vospitaniia kadrov* (Leninist Principles of the Selection, the Distribution, and the Training of Personnel; Moscow, 1959), p. 38.

54. *Ibid.,* pp. 39–40.

55. In 1962 the heads of the territorial production (agricultural) administration, the Party organizers of the obkomy of these administrations, and the editors of the inter-raion newspapers were, according to G. I. Voronov, in the *uchetnaia nomenklatura* of the relevant Central Committee departments for the RSFSR. At the same time he clearly indicated that the obkomy had the major role in the "selection" of these officials, and it was obvious that these posts were in the regular nomenklatura of the various obkomy. *Pravda,* March 28, 1962, p. 1.

56. "Comrade Stalin indicates that 'leadership in general' is meaningless chatter." *Pravda,* September 20, 1950, p. 2. This theme was, of course, one of Khrushchev's most frequent.

57. I. Fomin, *Podbor, rasstanovka, i vospitanie kadrov* (The Selection, Distribution, and Training of Personnel; Moscow, 1953), p. 33.

58. M. Karpov and G. Brovarski, *Partiinaia informatsiia* (Party Information; Moscow, 1962), pp. 36–39.

59. Party Rules, Statute 2.

60. There are formal instructions governing the flow of information upward, but they have not been published. It has been stated, however, that the obkomy are required to send protocols of their bureau sessions to the Central Committee within 15 days of the meeting. Karpov and Brovarski, *Partiinaia informatsiia,* p. 38.

61. Morozov, pp. 50 and 52.

62. Bugaev and Leibson, p. 144.

63. *Pravda,* March 19, 1967, p. 2.

64. Slepov, *Vysshie i mestnye organy,* p. 50.

65. See, for example, Chapman, *The Profession of Government,* pp. 70–73.

66. *Partiinaia zhizn,* no. 23 (December 1964), p. 5. The quotation was actually in the past tense, referring with approval to the pre-1962 situation.

67. *Sovetskaia Latviia,* March 25, 1957, p. 2.

68. *Pravda,* March 22, 1941, p. 1. See also *ibid.,* August 30, 1946, p. 1.

69. *Ibid.,* December 16, 1967, p. 1.

70. *Promyshlenno-ekonomicheskaia gazeta,* February 24, 1960, p. 1.

71. *Partiinaia zhizn,* no. 21 (November 1956), p. 58.

72. *Ibid.,* no. 22 (November 1965), p. 36.

73. Kolbin's biography can be found in *Deputaty* (1966), p. 221.

74. *Pravda,* February 6, 1967, p. 2.

75. *Ibid.,* July 3, 1967, p. 2.

76. As is almost always the case with disagreements in the Politburo, it is difficult to document conclusively these hypotheses about the Malenkov, Zhdanov, and Khrushchev positions. Certainly, however, they seem more convincing than the conventional wisdom on this question. The usual interpretation of the Malenkov-Zhdanov struggle identifies Zhdanov as a man emphasizing Party organizational-ideological work and Malenkov as a man whose espousal of the

branch-department form of organization of the secretariat denoted a belief in the necessity of Party involvement in economic questions. According to the usual interpretation of the Malenkov-Khrushchev struggle, it was Khrushchev who believed in Party involvement in economic questions, Malenkov who stood for governmental freedom from Party intervention. Why Malenkov should have changed his position between 1948 and 1953 is not explained.

The interpretation offered here avoids the difficulty of explaining a highly improbable transformation in his viewpoint by suggesting a basic consistency in his position over time. Moreover, this interpretation also corresponds to the observed changes in the policy with respect to the selection of managerial personnel as Party officials in the 1940's and early 1950's, Khrushchev being far more closely associated with the selection of such personnel than Malenkov. Involvement in technical policy-making requires more technically-qualified Party secretaries than involvement in supplies procurement. (See Chapter III, note 40.) The interpretation is also consistent with Khrushchev's insufficient appreciation of the coordinating function served by the local Party organs — as seen in his 1962 bifurcation of the Party apparatus.

77. *Ekonomicheskaia gazeta,* November 18, 1964, p. 3.

78. *Partiinaia zhizn,* No. 23 (December 1964), p. 5.

79. *Pravda,* November 20, 1962, p. 2.

VI. Mobilizing the Population

1. *Spravochnik partiinogo rabotnika,* 4th ed., p. 119.

2. *Agitator,* no. 17 (September 1964), p. 32, and no. 11 (June 1965), p. 42.

3. For an editorial on this subject, see *Pravda,* August 27, 1965, p. 1.

4. *Sovetskaia Belorussiia,* November 21, 1962, p. 3.

5. The socialist competition movement began at the Krasnyi Vyborzhets Works in Leningrad in 1929. *Partiinaia zhizn,* no. 8 (July 1954), p. 11.

6. *Pravda,* April 29, 1949, p. 1; *Voprosy partiinogo stroitelstva,* p. 529.

7. *Izvestiia,* November 27, 1966, p. 2.

8. Mamai: *Pravda Ukrainy,* January 10, 1958, p. 2. For Gaganova's speech before the Central Committee in 1959, see *Pravda,* June 28, 1959, p. 4.

9. Granick, *Management of the Industrial Firm,* pp. 243–252.

10. *Ibid.,* p. 249.

11. *Pravda,* June 3, 1951, p. 2, and February 17, 1941, p. 2.

12. *Voprosy partiinogo stroitelstva,* pp. 348–351, 529–544.

13. *Agitator,* no. 9 (May 1963), p. 21.

14. *Ibid.,* no. 8 (April 1963), p. 11; 1965: *Voprosy partiinogo stroitelstva,* p. 348.

15. *Voprosy partiinoi raboty* (1959), p. 482.

16. A short summary description of visual agitation can be found in *Voprosy*

partiinogo stroitelstva, pp. 339–340. See also *Partiinaia zhizn,* no. 16 (August 1965), pp. 52–55.

17. *Voprosy partiinoi raboty* (1959), p. 482.

18. *Agitator,* no. 7 (April 1964), p. 31. These themes were chosen by local officials to guide work in their particular locality.

19. Alex Inkeles, *Public Opinion in Soviet Russia* (Cambridge, Mass., 1950), pp. 39–40.

20. *Pravda Ukrainy,* December 21, 1962, p. 2.

21. Dnepro: *Kommunist Ukrainy,* no. 8 (August 1957), p. 80; Odessa: *Agitator,* no. 5 (March 1963), p. 35.

22. *Sovetskaia Rossiia,* March 1, 1963, p. 2.

23. *Ibid.,* p. 2.

24. *Voprosy partiinogo stroitelstva,* pp. 335–338; *Zaria vostoka,* September 21, 1965, p. 2.

25. *XXIII sezd kommunisticheskoi partii sovetskogo soiuza, Stenograficheskii otchet* (23rd Congress of the Communist Party of the Soviet Union, Stenographic Report; Moscow, 1966), II, 316.

26. *Pravda,* December 25, 1967, p. 2.

27. *Ibid.,* March 17, 1967, p. 2.

28. *Ibid.,* December 25, 1967, p. 2.

29. See the discussion in Ellen Propper Mickiewicz, *Soviet Political Schools* (New Haven, 1967).

30. *Sovetskaia Rossiia,* September 17, 1965, p. 2. For suggested study plans, see *Partiinaia zhizn,* no. 16 (August 1965), pp. 48–52.

31. The pre-1964 statistics are found in V. I. Evdokimov, *Politicheskoe prosveshchenie — reshaiushchee zveno propagandistskoi raboty* (Political Education — The Decisive Link of Propaganda Work; Moscow, 1962), p. 20. The 1964/65 statistics were published in *Voprosy partiinogo stroitelstva,* p. 83 and p. 330.

32. *Voprosy partiinogo stroitelstva,* p. 330. Mickiewicz emphasizes this point in *Soviet Political Schools,* pp. 161–163.

33. 1965/66: Mickiewicz, p. 13; 1966/67: *Pravda,* September 4, 1967, p. 2.

34. *Pravda,* September 4, 1967, p. 3.

35. *Spravochnik partiinogo rabotnika* (The Handbook of the Party Official; Moscow, 1957), p. 347.

36. Fainsod, *How Russia Is Ruled,* p. 596.

37. Mickiewicz, p. 32.

38. Evdokimov, *Politicheskoe prosveshchenie,* p. 21.

39. *Leningradskaia pravda,* March 4, 1966, p. 2.

40. *Partiinaia zhizn,* no. 10 (May 1966), pp. 52–56.

41. *Pravda,* July 7, 1966, p. 2.

42. *Sovetskaia Rossiia,* December 5, 1962, p. 2.

43. *Zaria vostoka,* January 18, 1966, p. 3.

44. *Bolshevik,* no. 12 (June 1952), p. 60.

45. *Sovetskaia Rossiia,* December 5, 1962, p. 2.

46. *Kazakhstanskaia pravda,* September 11, 1965, p. 2.

47. *Leningradskaia pravda,* October 1, 1965, p. 2.

48. *Voprosy partiinogo stroitelstva,* pp. 391–400.

49. *Kommunist Tadzhikistana,* June 16, 1963, p. 2.

50. Mickiewicz, pp. 46–47.

51. *Spravochnik partiinogo rabotnika* (Handbook of the Party Official; 3rd ed., Moscow, 1961), pp. 456–457. For a description of this work, see *Agitator,* no. 3 (February 1963), pp. 35–38.

52. *Pravda Ukrainy,* September 20, 1958, p. 3.

53. I. I. Groshev, ed., *Vospitanie kommunisticheskoi soznatelnosti* (The Training of Communist Consciousness; Moscow, 1964), p. 75.

54. *Pravda,* October 25, 1949, p. 1.

55. See *Pravda Ukrainy,* April 25, 1958, p. 3, for a case in which the Dnepropetrovsk obkom called for socialist competition in the fulfillment of orders for the construction of several new blast furnaces.

56. See, for example, *Pravda Ukrainy,* November 27, 1956, p. 3.

57. *Pravda,* February 26, 1967, p. 2.

58. There is undoubtedly a considerable amount of informal contact among lower officials of the secretariat as well. The departments are small enough to permit the instructors to know each other fairly well, and the various instructors dealing with a plant surely exchange ideas and opinions about it.

59. *Partiinaia zhizn,* no. 3 (February 1955), p. 31.

60. *Sovetskaia Moldaviia,* November 27, 1963, p. 3. For an identical complaint from the Stalin period, see *Pravda,* June 3, 1951, p. 2.

61. *Ekonomicheskaia gazeta,* January 4, 1964, p. 6.

62. Fainsod, *Smolensk under Soviet Rule,* pp. 67–74; quote, p. 72.

63. *Pravda Ukrainy,* September 17, 1957, p. 2.

64. Fainsod, *Smolensk under Soviet Rule,* p. 76.

65. *Kommunist* no. 9 (June 1967), p. 63.

66. V. V. Shcherbitskii: *Deputaty* (1966), p. 505; A. I. Gaevoi: *Bolshaia sovetskaia entsiklopediia* (1962), p. 591; N. P. Tolubeev: *ibid.,* 618, and *Pravda Ukrainy,* July 6, 1963, p. 2; V. S. Oleinikov: *Deputaty* (1958), p. 298.

67. *Izvestiia,* January 9, 1962, p. 3.

68. Fainsod, *Smolensk under Soviet Rule,* p. 92.

VII. The Selection of Personnel

1. Slepov, *Vysshie i mestnye organy,* p. 18.

2. *Kommunist,* no. 1 (January 1966), p. 36.

3. K. I. Suvorov, ed., *Nekotorye voprosy organizatsionno-partiinoi raboty v sovremennykh usloviiakh* (Some Questions of Organization-Party Work in Contemporary Conditions; Moscow, 1961), pp. 299 and 310.

4. In the beginning of 1956, 22,000 officials were in the nomenklatury of the gorkom and raikomy in Moscow, as compared with 17,000 in 1958. *Ibid.,* pp. 298–299. In agriculture, the kolkhoz chairmanships were moved from the nomenklatury of the raikomy to those of the obkomy in 1953 and then later "many" of them were returned to the raikom nomenklatury. Morozov, *Leninskie printsipy,* pp. 34–35. See also *Pravda,* March 6, 1954, p. 4.

5. The major status difference — the one which seems to signify that a man has "arrived" — is that between a post in the nomenklatura of any Party organ and one that is not. See, for example, *Sovetskaia Litva,* February 25, 1962, p. 2. "Kalinkin [considered that] he was not a simple person, but a nomenklatured one."

6. 1930's: Fainsod, *Smolensk,* p. 64; later: Granick, *Management of the Industrial Firm,* pp. 218–220.

7. *Spravochnik partiinogo rabotnika* (1957), p. 429.

8. The first deputy chairman of the Belorussia sovnarkhoz gave these figures in an interview, and they are approximate. The percentage was obtained by dividing the figures by the number of Minsk's plants, a figure found in *Narodnoe khoziaistvo Belorusskoi SSR* (The Economy of the Belorussian Soviet Socialist Republic; Moscow, 1957), p. 13.

9. Morozov, p. 36.

10. These examples came from interviews with officials in the plants.

11. These percentages are based on the assumption that the statistics on distribution of plants by size in the Soviet Union are generally applicable to Minsk. Because Minsk has half a dozen giant plants, the percentage of workers in the top 10 plants may be even higher. *Promyshlennost SSSR,* p. 18.

12. This fact was elicited from the director of the plant. The first deputy chairman of the sovnarkhoz stated that there were about 5 plants in Minsk whose chief engineers were in the nomenklatura of the All-Union Central Committee.

13. The practice of including officials of the same institution in the nomenklatura of different Party organs is also followed in nonindustrial fields as well. Thus, a 1954 Central Committee decree ordered all collective farm chairmen to be placed in the nomenklatury of the obkomy, kraikomy, and republican central committees. The collective farm deputy chairmen, the brigadiers, and the heads of the livestock farms were to be in the nomenklatura of the raikomy. *Pravda,* March 6, 1954, p. 4.

14. *Voprosy partiinoi raboty* (1959), p. 356.

15. *Partiinaia zhizn,* no. 11 (June 1966), p. 19, and *Pravda,* November 30, 1967, p. 2.

16. *Sovetskaia Kirgiziia,* December 11, 1955, p. 2.

17. See p. 160 of this chapter.

18. Kolbenkov, *Sovershenstvovanie,* p. 64.

19. Morozov, p. 36.

20. *Vydvinul: Pravda,* July 23, 1957, p. 2; *otstranit:* Vsevolod Kochetov,

Molodost s nami (Youth with Us; Moscow, 1957), p. 49; *snialo: Promyshlenno-ekonomicheskaia gazeta,* March 4, 1960, p. 2; *osvobodilo ot raboty: Sovetskaia Rossiia,* September 19, 1967, p. 2.

21. *Partiinaia zhizn,* no. 1 (January 1964), p. 27.

22. *Ekonomicheskaia gazeta,* October 13, 1965, p. 6.

23. Slepov, *Vysshie i mestnye organy,* p. 62.

24. *Ekonomicheskaia gazeta,* June 30, 1960, p. 2.

25. Slepov, *Vysshie i mestnye organy,* p. 62.

26. *Partiinaia zhizn,* no. 22 (November 1965), p. 37, and no. 5 (March 1955), p. 58. In 1965 and 1966 there were many complaints about the lack of a governmental employment agency and steps have been taken to try to correct the situation. See *Ekonomicheskaia gazeta,* no. 32 (August 1967), p. 8.

27. *Zaria vostoka,* August 22, 1956, p. 2.

28. *Ibid.,* p. 2.

29. *Vecherniaia Moskva,* September 26, 1967, p. 1.

30. *Selskaia zhizn,* July 21, 1962, p. 2.

31. *Uchitelskaia gazeta,* July 13, 1967, p. 3.

32. *Pravda,* February 6, 1967, pp. 2–3.

33. *Trud,* April 8, 1965, p. 2.

34. *Pravda,* February 8, 1941, p. 3, and *Partiinaia zhizn,* no. 22 (November 1964), p. 23.

35. See, for example, *Pravda Ukrainy,* July 29, 1958 p. 2, and *Vecherniaia Moskva,* September 26, 1967, p. 1.

36. *Selskaia zhizn,* July 21, 1962, p. 2.

37. Party Rules, Statutes 67 and 68.

38. *Pravda Ukrainy,* November 18, 1955, p. 3.

39. *Ibid.*

40. *Voprosy partiinoi raboty* (1959), p. 357. An almost identical statement in 1966 referred to "the directing hand of the higher organs." *Partiinaia zhizn,* no. 11 (June 1966), p. 13.

41. *Voprosy partiinoi raboty* (1959), p. 358.

42. *Pravda Ukrainy,* May 26, 1959, p. 2.

43. "Instruktsiia o provedenii vyborov rukovodiashchikh partiinykh organov" (Instructions about Conducting Elections of the Leading Party Organs), *Spravochnik partiinogo rabotnika* (Handbook of the Party Official; 4th ed.; Moscow, 1963), p. 486. This instruction has been translated in Abdurakhman Avtorkhanov, *The Communist Party Apparatus* (Chicago, 1966), pp. 377–382.

44. *Spravochnik partiinogo rabotnika* (1963), p. 488.

45. *Pravda,* December 20, 1950, p. 2; May 10, 1951, p. 2; and September 5, 1951, p. 2.

46. *Ibid.,* September 27, 1956, p. 2.

47. *Kommunist Tadzhikistana,* September 22, 1961, p. 3.

48. See the discussion in *Partiinaia zhizn,* no. 1 (January 1966), p. 30.

49. Probably the most spectacular reported incident of this type occurred in

1954 when the Communists at the Sergo Ordzhonikidze Machine Tool Plant in Moscow (a very important plant) surprised the raikom by blackballing both the Party secretary and the director. The secretary was removed. *Ibid.,* no. 12 (September 1954), p. 8. This incident has sometimes been treated by Western observers as a sign (perhaps temporary) of renewed intra-Party democracy. Whether or not a general change of atmosphere did occur at this time, such incidents also occurred during the Stalin period. See, for example, the articles cited in note 45 of this chapter.

50. When Frol Kozlov discussed this matter at the Twenty-second Party Congress, he did so solely in terms of intra-Party democracy and the rights of the members. *Pravda,* October 29, 1961, p. 6.

51. Fainsod, *Smolensk under Soviet Rule,* p. 72.

52. Granick, *The Red Executive,* p. 36.

53. *Pravda,* February 6, 1967, p. 3.

54. See, for example, *Sovetskaia Rossiia,* September 29, 1960, p. 2; *Ekonomicheskaia gazeta,* January 26, 1963, p. 9.

55. *Pravda,* July 30, 1955, p. 2, and *Pravda Ukrainy,* December 10, 1957, p. 2.

56. *Kazakhstanskaia pravda,* December 19, 1957, p. 2 (elsewhere in the article it is stated that Morgunov was the secretary in charge of industry); *Partiinaia zhizn,* no. 17 (September 1965), p. 43.

57. *Sovetskaia Belorussiia,* January 5, 1958, p. 2.

58. Such a difference in evaluation may be one major factor in explaining the much-mentioned phenomenon of men "who have failed" being given another comparable job. In the eyes of one of his superiors, such a man may not be a failure.

59. *Ekonomicheskaia gazeta,* January 5, 1963, p. 12.

60. *Sovetskaia Moldaviia,* December 26, 1963, p. 5.

61. See p. 155 of this chapter.

62. *Partiinaia zhizn,* no. 3 (February 1955), pp. 57 and 58.

63. *Promyshlenno-ekonomicheskaia gazeta,* May 10, 1959, p. 2. After Khrushchev's removal, the leadership demanded that the primary Party organization also be asked for its evaluation of any of its members recommended for higher promotion.

64. *Kommunist,* no. 1 (January 1966), pp. 35–36.

65. *Partiinaia zhizn,* no. 9 (May 1959), p. 26.

66. See, for example, *Pravda vostoka,* September 29, 1961, p. 3, and *Zaria vostoka,* May 5, 1966, p. 2.

67. *Partiinaia zhizn,* no. 11 (June 1965), p. 39.

68. Lev Ovalov, *Partiinoe poruchenie* (Party Assignment; Moscow, 1964), pp. 3–8, 17, 29–34.

69. *Ibid.,* p. 8.

70. Fainsod, *How Russia Is Ruled,* p. 387.

71. Of the eight Komsomol officials elected as deputies to the Supreme So-

viet in 1966, two (S. P. Pavlov, the first secretary of the All-Union Komsomol, and S. Namatbaev, the first secretary of the Kirgizian Komsomol) joined the Party at the age of 25, and two (B. N. Pastukhov, the second secretary of the All-Union Komsomol, and G. N. Zhabitskii, the first secretary of the Belorussian Komsomol) became Party members at the age of 26. The ages of Party admission for the other Komsomol officials (all republican first secretaries) are: R. Kh. Abdullaeva (Uzbekistan), 20; L. L. Bartkevich (Latvia), 20; O. E. Cherkeziia (Georgia), 22; G. Bobosadykova (Tadzhikistan), 23. The biographies of all these officials can be found in *Deputaty* (1966).

In general, the pattern seen in the biographies of these eight officials is a general one for Komsomol officials who joined the Party after World War II. The officials in the Slavic republics tend to become Party members in their mid-twenties, the officials in the non-Slavic republics in their early twenties.

72. This generalization cannot be documented as such from Soviet sources. The biographical data certainly, however, confirms a relatively late age for Party admission. As seen in Chapter III, the average age of Party admission for various groups of industrial administrators in the 1950's and 1960's was usually 29, 30, or 31. Although the biographies themselves do not reveal the reason for the late admission age, a number of Soviet citizens explained to the author that a man would not be invited to join the Party until he had proven himself in his work and that this accounted for the later admission age.

73. Albert Parry, *The New Class Divided* (New York, 1966), p. 159.

74. *Kazakhstanskaia pravda*, January 26, 1958, p. 2.

75. Usually at least one from among the top 3 — director, plant secretary, and chief engineer — is a non-Russian. In the few cases when all 3 seem to be Russians, almost invariably the trade union chairman and several lesser officials (e.g., the chief mechanic, chief technologist, and/or shop heads) will be non-Russians. The "almost invariably" is required by a few exceptions in Kazakhstan, but even there Kazakhs could be found among the shop heads. These generalizations are based on my card file of factory personnel in the period 1955–1961. Impressionistically, it seems that the percentage of non-Russians among the top officials of these plants is increasing in the 1960's. Indeed, in republics like Georgia one finds many plants in which none of the top 3 is a Russian.

76. Ilia Ehrenburg, *The Thaw* (Chicago, 1955), pp. 142–154, 181–192.

77. Khrushchev, *Stroitelstvo kommunizma*, IV, 83.

VIII. Types of Intervention in Production, Technical and Planning Decisions

1. *Kommunist*, no. 1 (January 1958), pp. 60–61.
2. Pokrovskii, *V tesnoi sviazi*, p. 4.
3. *Pravda*, April 5, 1966, p. 5.
4. *Kommunist*, no. 1 (January 1958), p. 61.

5. *Spravochnik partiinogo rabotnika* (2nd ed.; 1959), p. 598.

6. The only printed references found to this network have been in two Soviet novels. Ovalov, *Partiinoe poruchenie,* p. 308, and Kochetov, *Sekretar obkoma,* p. 10. A Soviet plant manager, asked about this network in 1967, pointed to one of the phones on his desk. He stated that a manager can use it to call not just the obkom, but anyone on the network. He said that it was an extremely useful device for high priority calls, for it often gave access when a busy signal would be encountered on the regular phone.

7. *Pravda,* September 10, 1956, p. 2.

8. *Ibid.,* February 6, 1967, p. 2.

9. *Ibid.,* June 6, 1965, p. 2.

10. This practice has been explained by the fact that the official accountant's reports are not ready for 10 to 15 days after the end of the report period. "At times it is too late to remove the deficiencies about which the accounting has given signals." *Partiinaia zhizn,* no. 12 (June 1963), p. 25.

11. *Pravda,* June 6, 1965, p. 2.

12. See, for example, *Partiinaia zhizn,* no. 12 (June 1963), pp. 23–28.

13. See, for example, *Pravda,* March 9, 1967, p. 2. A 1968 summary article on the proper style of work of the Party officials placed great emphasis on sociological investigation. *Ibid.,* February 15, 1968, pp. 2–3.

14. *Bakinskii rabochii,* January 5, 1966, p. 2.

15. *Pravda,* September 17, 1952, p. 2.

16. Lvov: *Pravda Ukrainy,* March 27, 1956, p. 3; Kharkov: *Partiinaia rabota v Ukrainy,* p. 58.

17. *Sovetskaia Rossiia,* September 15, 1962, p. 2.

18. Omsk: *Pravda,* July 7, 1965, p. 2; Lithuania: *Sovetskaia Litva,* March 3, 1960, p. 1.

19. *Voprosy partiinogo stroitelstva,* p. 185.

20. *Partiinaia zhizn,* no. 2 (January 1963), pp. 10–11.

21. *Spravochnik partiinogo rabotnika* (5th ed.), pp. 305 and 306.

22. *Kommunist Tadzhikistana,* December 3, 1963, p. 2. It was reported that during the last 9 months of 1963 the Turkmen organs of Party-state control received 2,465 letters, statements, and suggestions, and they were visited personally by 3,528 citizens. *Turkmenskaia iskra,* December 29, 1963, p. 3.

23. See, for example, *Partiinaia zhizn,* no. 7 (April 1963), p. 36; *Ekonomicheskaia gazeta,* June 27, 1964, p. 29.

24. *Ekonomicheskaia gazeta,* June 23, 1965, p. 3.

25. In 8 of the republics, the chairman of the peoples' control committee was named a full member of the bureau in 1966, and in 6 of the republics he was named a candidate member. In the 7 oblasti on which information is available, 5 of the chairmen were full members of the obkom bureau, and 2 were candidate members. In 7 large cities (see Appendix A), 6 of the 7 chairmen of peoples' control committee were full members of the gorkom bureau, and

one was a candidate member. For an indication that this pattern was typical in the smaller cities and the raiony, see *Pravda vostoka,* July 27, 1966, p. 3.

26. *Pravda,* June 30, 1967, p. 3.

27. *Partiinoe stroitelstvo,* nos. 23–24 (1940), pp. 20–21. Quoted in Bienstock, Schwarz, and Yugow, *Management in Russian Industry,* pp. 23–24.

28. *Partiinaia zhizn,* no. 3 (February 1955), pp. 30–31.

29. *Sbornik statei po voprosam istorii KPSS* (A Collection of Articles on the History of the CPSU; 2nd ed.; Moscow, 1958), p. 152.

30. *Partiinaia zhizn,* no. 13 (July 1965), p. 16.

31. *Ibid.,* no. 2 (January 1956), p. 10.

32. *Pravda,* January 25, 1953, p. 2.

33. *Ibid.,* September 9, 1955, p. 2. It should not be thought that this style of work is peculiar to the two men involved. For an earlier description of similar work by the Kadievka gorkom, see *Pravda Ukrainy,* April 7, 1950, p. 2.

34. The biographies of Klimenko and Shevchenko can be found in *Deputaty* (1962), pp. 206 and 466. I might be noted that Shevchenko's biography illustrates one of the difficulties in using Soviet biographical data. The biography published in *Deputaty* (1962) states simply that Shevchenko graduated from the Lugansk pedagogical institute. As his subsequent career featured work in a raion soviet, a Komsomol organization, the partisans, and then the Party organs, one might be tempted to conclude that his work experience was primarily of a mobilization nature. The two quotations cited here demonstrate the error that would be involved in that assumption. The 1962 yearbook of the *Bolshaia sovetskaia entsiklopediia* indicates that Shevchenko graduated from the correspondence division (*zaochno*) of the pedagogical institute only in 1955 and that the significance of his degree is minimal. 1962 yearbook, p. 622.

35. *Bakinskii rabochii,* March 22, 1961, p. 3.

36. *Pravda Ukrainy,* October 28, 1965, p. 2.

37. See Fainsod, *Smolensk,* p. 72.

38. *Kommunist,* no. 1 (January 1958), p. 60.

39. *Pravda,* October 16, 1955, p. 2.

40. *Sovetskaia Moldaviia,* February 1, 1958, p. 1.

41. *Pravda,* August 18, 1959, p. 2.

42. Sverdlovsk: *Promyshlenno-ekonomicheskaia gazeta,* July 2, 1958, p. 2; Briansk: *ibid.,* October 15, 1958, p. 1; Vladimir: *Promyshlenno-ekonomicheskaia gazeta,* March 27, 1959, p. 2.

43. *Partiinaia zhizn,* no. 14 (July 1958), p. 15; *Pravda,* November 20, 1957, p. 2.

44. *Sovetskaia Rossiia,* February 10, 1960, p. 3.

45. *Ibid.,* September 26, 1961, p. 3, and *Kommunist,* no. 17 (November 1963), p. 27.

46. *Ekonomicheskaia gazeta,* September 15, 1962, p. 12.

47. *Sovetskaia Rossiia,* September 26, 1961, p. 2.

48. *Pravda Ukrainy,* February 12, 1958, p. 2; *Pravda,* January 17, 1958, p. 2.

49. *Ekonomicheskaia gazeta,* January 4, 1964, p. 6; *Pravda,* March 1, 1963, p. 2.

50. Dzhambul: *Pravda,* February 24, 1965, p. 2; Cheliabinsk: *Partiinaia zhizn,* no. 13 (July 1965), p. 18.

51. *Pravda,* January 16, 1965, p. 2.

52. *Partiinaia zhizn,* no. 13 (July 1965), p. 18.

53. *Rabochaia gazeta,* September 12, 1965, p. 3.

54. *Sovetskaia Rossiia,* July 6, 1967, p. 1.

55. Fainsod, *Smolensk,* p. 72.

56. *Pravda,* July 18, 1966, p. 2.

57. *Ibid.,* September 4, 1967, p. 2.

IX. Impact on Production, Technical, and Planning Decisions

1. *Pravda,* July 31, 1962, p. 2.

2. *Sovetskaia Rossiia,* September 26, 1961, p. 3.

3. *Pravda,* February 16, 1941, p. 2.

4. *Ibid.,* pp. 2 and 4.

5. See Chapter X.

6. *Partiinaia zhizn,* no. 2 (January 1958), p. 29.

7. Fainsod, *How Russia Is Ruled,* p. 517.

8. *Kazakhstanskaia pravda,* March 16, 1957, p. 3.

9. *Ibid.,* November 17, 1956, p. 2; April 9, 1957, p. 2; January 10, 1958, p. 2; July 4, 1959, p. 1. Sviadoshch's career illustrates the fact that a demotion need not be final. In 1962 he was still head of shop. By 1965, however, he had been named director of the Irtysh Polimetal Combine, and by 1966 had become a deputy minister of the Kazakhstan Ministry of Non-ferrous Metallurgy. *Ibid.,* November 2, 1962, p. 2, and September 11, 1965, p. 2. *Pravda,* July 4, 1966, p. 2.

10. Odessa: *Pravda Ukrainy,* January 12, 1963, p. 1; Svetogorsk: *Sovetskaia Belorussiia,* December 21, 1962, p. 1.

11. This man is M. S. Sinitsa. *Deputaty* (1962), p. 385.

12. *Pravda,* November 20, 1962, p. 2. He also noted that in the 25 most industrial oblasti in the RSFSR, only 14 of 215 questions examined by the obkom plenums concerned industrial matters.

13. See Chapter V, p. 107, and Chapter IX, p. 199.

14. Estonia: *Sovetskaia Estoniia,* January 19, 1956, p. 2; Saratov: *Pravda,* July 2, 1959, p. 2. See Chapter III, p. 64.

15. *Partiinaia zhizn,* no. 3 (February 1956), p. 13.

16. Berliner, *Factory and Manager,* p. 268.

17. V. Dudintsev, *Ne khlebom edinym* (Not by Bread Alone; Munich, 1957), p. 27. For a slightly different translation of this passage, see Vladimir Dudintsev,

Not by Bread Alone, trans. Dr. Edith Bone (New York, 1957), p. 51.

18. See the discussion in Macmahon, *Administration of Federal Work Relief,* pp. 230–235, 265–268.

19. James W. Fesler, *Area and Administration* (University, Ala., 1949), chap. 4, esp. pp. 81–84.

20. See, for example, Thompson, *Modern Organization,* pp. 6, 46–47.

21. Khrushchev, *Stroitelstvo kommunizma,* VII, 153.

22. *Pravda,* April 28, 1967, p. 2.

23. *Ibid.,* February 15, 1968, p. 2.

24. For biographical information on Tabeev, see *Deputaty* (1962), p. 410; on Tatar ASSR, see, for example, *Izvestiia,* January 20, 1962, p. 3.

25: A. G. Soldatov: *Sovetskaia Rossiia,* February 10, 1960, p. 3, and for a biography, see *Deputaty* (1958), p. 373. T. I. Sokolov: *Kazakhstanskaia pravda,* January 22, 1960, p. 1, and for a biography, see *Bolshaia sovetskaia entsiklopediia,* 1962 yearbook, p. 615. For a 1956 decree on agriculture difficulties in the oblast, see *Spravochnik partiinogo rabotnika* (1957), pp. 210–216. In the following year the situation does not seem to have improved. A perusal of *Pravda* for 1957 fails to turn up any indication that the Perm oblast fulfilled its delivery plan for any major project. (Such fulfillment would have been heralded on the front page.)

26. *Sovetskaia Rossiia,* February 20, 1960, p. 2.

27. See *Bakinskii rabochii,* May 9, 1959, p. 2, December 26, 1959, p. 2, March 22, 1961, p. 3.

28. For the biography of this man (M. S. Solomentsev), see *Deputaty* (1962), p. 396.

29. Apartments: K. V. Chernikov, ed., *KPSS i massovye organizatsii trudiashchikhsia* (The CPSU and Mass Organizations of the Toilers; Moscow, 1963), p. 80; 8-hour day: *Ekonomicheskaia gazeta,* no. 17 (April 1966), p. 29.

30. *Sovetskaia Rossiia,* August 4, 1965, p. 2.

31. *Ibid.,* November 11, 1959, p. 2.

32. *Ibid.,* April 8, 1960, p. 2.

33. *Ibid.,* February 20, 1968, p. 2; *Ekonomicheskaia gazeta,* November 22, 1960, p. 3.

34. Granick, *Management of the Industrial Firm,* p. 121. See also Bertram M. Gross, *The Managing of Organization* (New York, 1964), II, 719–745. The 1968 slowdown by U.S. air controllers embodied precisely such a tactic.

X. Supplies Procurement and Production Scheduling

1. *Pravda,* June 20, 1960, p. 2

2. *Partiinaia zhizn,* no. 6 (March 1957), p. 62, and no. 1 (January 1959), p. 11.

3. Walter Lippmann, *A Preface to Politics* (New York, 1913), p. 45.

4. *Pravda,* May 18, 1955, p. 1; *Partiinaia zhizn,* no. 3 (February 1956), p. 44.

5. See the statement of the Minister of Machinebuilding quoted in Chapter XII, p. 266.

6. *Pravda vostoka,* July 12, 1956, p. 3; *Kazakhstanskaia pravda,* March 24, 1956, p. 2.

7. See Herbert S. Levine, "The Centralized Planning of Supply in Soviet Industry," Joint Economic Committee (86th Cong., 1st sess.), *Comparisons of the United States and Soviet Economies* (Washington, 1959), pt. I, pp. 167–170. This problem has been discussed incessantly in the Soviet press since the Liberman proposals have received great attention. For example, see *Ekonomicheskaia gazeta,* January 27, 1965, pp. 3–4.

8. "For some reason the chits (*fondy*) for metal are allocated for the same quarter that the metal is to be turned into a manufactured product. Since the metal allocated by quarter is delivered primarily at the end of the quarter, the plants regularly have stoppages in supply, particularly in the first month of the quarter." *Pravda Ukrainy,* June 9, 1955, p. 3.

9. *Sovetskaia Latviia,* November 15, 1957, p. 2.

10. Such behavior is not peculiar to a totalitarian system. When the American economy experienced similar pressures on supplies during World War II, similar phenomena were experienced. See Joseph Berliner, "Managerial Incentives and Decision-Making: A Comparison of the United States and the Soviet Union," *Comparisons of the United States and Soviet Economies,* pt. I, pp. 349–376.

11. *Ekonomicheskaia gazeta,* June 10, 1960, p. 3.

12. L. V. Kantorovich, *Ekonomicheskii raschet nailuchshego izpolzovaniia resursov* (Economic Calculation of the Best Use of Resources; Moscow, 1959), p. 21.

13. See Berliner, *Factory and Manager in the USSR,* pp. 196–206.

14. *Pravda,* February 3, 1941, p. 2. At the same time the first secretary of the Rostov obkom noted, "Over one-half of the time allotted by us local Party leaders to industrial questions" is devoted to supplies procurement. *Pravda,* February 20, 1941, p. 4.

15. M. N. Poletava, "Borba kommunistichskoi partii sovetskogo soiuza za povyshenie proizvoditelnosti truda v tiazheloi promyshlennosti v period chetvertoi piatiletki (1946–1950)" (The Struggle of the Communist Party of the Soviet Union for a Rise in Labor Productivity in Heavy Industry in the Period of the Fourth Five-Year Plan, 1946–1950), I. G. Riabtsev, ed., *Sbornik statei po voprosam istorii KPSS* (A Collection of Articles on the History of the CPSU; Moscow, 1957), p. 31.

16. See Chapter II, note 2.

17. Poletaeva, p. 31.

18. *Pravda,* April 12, 1951, p. 2.

19. *Ibid.,* July 29, 1950, p. 2.

20. *Ibid.,* December 19, 1950, p. 2.

21. *Ibid.,* July 14, 1955, p. 3; July 17, 1955, p. 6.

22. *Sovetskaia Latviia,* March 25, 1957, p. 2.

23. *Partiinaia zhizn,* no. 6 (March 1957), p. 62.

24. Penza: *Sovetskaia Rossiia,* February 8, 1959, p. 3; Ivanovo: *Kommunist,* no. 1 (January 1958), p. 66.

25. *Pravda,* July 27, 1958, p. 2.

26. *Ibid.,* June 20, 1960, p. 2.

27. *Sovetskaia Belorussiia,* September 18, 1962, p. 2.

28. *Ekonomicheskaia gazeta,* February 1, 1964, p. 12.

29. *Partiinaia zhizn,* no. 13 (July 1965), p. 15.

30. *Pravda,* January 16, 1965, p. 2.

31. *Molot* (Rostov), March 16, 1967, p. 2.

32. *Sovetskaia Latviia,* December 4, 1965, p. 2.

33. *Ekonomicheskaia gazeta,* no. 37 (September 1966), p. 27.

34. *Pravda,* February 6, 1967, p. 3.

35. *Partiinaia zhizn,* no. 22 (November 1965), pp. 36–37.

36. Party Rules, Statutes 2 and 3.

37. In 1922 when Lenin complained about the number of problems that reached the level of the Politburo, he placed his finger directly on the right of complaint as the primary cause. Yet, Lenin shied away from taking concrete steps to end this right, for such an action would strike too deeply at the official image of the Party and the individual Party member. "We cannot revoke the right to complain to the Central Committee," Lenin said, "because our Party is the sole ruling Party." Lenin, *Sochineniia,* XXXIII, 274–275.

38. Slepov, *Vysshie i mestnye organy,* p. 126.

39. *Sovetskaia Rossiia,* September 26, 1961, p. 2.

40. It should be noted that when Lenin prepared his famous draft of the Party Rules in 1903 — the one which eventually led to the split between the Bolsheviki and the Mensheviki — he included this point (differing only in a minor degree in phraseology) as one of his 12 proposed clauses. Lenin, *Sochineniia,* VI, 433.

41. I owe many of these points about American practices to the former head of a purchasing department of a medium-sized plant, who prefers to remain anonymous.

42. See Berliner, "Managerial Incentives and Decision-Making," pp. 349–376.

43. David Novick, Melvin Anshen, and W. C. Truppner, *Wartime Production Controls* (New York, 1949), p. 275.

44. *Partiinaia zhizn,* no. 6 (March 1957), p. 62.

45. *Izvestiia,* July 7, 1962, p. 3.

46. *Pravda,* December 19, 1950, p. 2.

XI. Regional Coordination

1. *Partiinaia zhizn,* no. 3 (May 1954), pp. 17–18.
2. *Sovetskaia Rossiia,* December 21, 1965, p. 2.
3. *Pravda,* April 16, 1948, p. 2; *Sovetskaia Rossiia,* November 2, 1967, p. 2. The information about the Volgograd Tractor Works came from a 1967 interview.
4. Venev: *Partiinaia zhizn,* no. 3 (May 1954), p. 20; Stalin: *Moskovskaia pravda,* October 6, 1953, p. 2; Lugansk: *Trud,* March 30, 1965, p. 2.
5. *Selskaia zhizn,* July 21, 1962, p. 2; *Pravda vostoka,* September 22, 1955, p. 3.
6. *Partiinaia zhizn,* no. 3 (May 1954), p. 20.
7. *Pravda,* June 20, 1951, p. 2.
8. *Lesnaia promyshlennost,* March 15, 1962, p. 1; *Selskaia zhizn,* July 21, 1962, p. 2; Khrushchev, *Stroitelstvo kommunizma,* VII, 151 and 133; *Trud,* April 4, 1957, p. 2.
9. *Gudok,* June 17, 1955, p. 2.
10. *Agitator,* no. 12 (June 1963), p. 30.
11. Tolmadzhev, *Na novoi puti,* pp. 80–81.
12. *Izvestiia,* April 3, 1962, p. 3.
13. For example, in the first Supreme Soviet session after Khrushchev's removal, the first secretary of the Kiev obkom repeated a familiar complaint: "Apartments are built on the established schedule, but cultural and communal services are not built for a series of years." *Pravda,* December 11, 1964, p. 3.
14. *Pravda Ukrainy,* July 15, 1960, p. 2.
15. *Ibid.*
16. *Stroitelnaia gazeta,* April 27, 1960, p. 4, and *Partiinaia zhizn,* no. 8 (April 1960), p. 56.
17. *Pravda,* May 20, 1966, p. 3.
18. *Spravochnik partiinogo rabotnika* (2nd ed.), pp. 596 and 598.
19. *Pravda,* July 18, 1966, p. 2. Chapter VIII, p. 195.
20. *Ekonomicheskaia gazeta,* no. 26 (June 1967), p. 27.
21. *Ibid.*
22. *Izvestiia,* July 27, 1967, p. 2.
23. In an apparently realistic novel about factory life, the director had his quasi-legal sources of information about available food in the countryside. The mechanisms of obtaining this information are not made clear, but it is quite possible that patronage assistance (or assistance in the guise of patronage) is useful in this respect. Vera Panova, *Kruzhilikha* (Kruzhilikha; Moscow, 1948), p. 13.
24. *Pravda,* September 14, 1949, p. 2; *Trud,* April 25, 1952, p. 2. Of this assistance, the one most frequently discussed in the Soviet press is that required from the local scientific institutes. See, for example, *Pravda,* June 13, 1960, p. 2.

For a case dealing with college admission, see *Sovetskaia Rossia,* May 20, 1959, p. 2.

25. Berliner, *Factory and Manager,* p. 270.

26. *Sovetskaia Rossiia,* February 19, 1965, p. 1; March 11, 1965, p. 1; April 27, 1965, p. 1.

27. *Pravda,* December 28, 1940, p. 3; *Izvestiia,* June 7, 1960, p. 3.

28. *Sovetskaia Rossiia,* March 13, 1960, p. 2.

29. Lenin, *Sochineniia,* XXVII, 238–239.

30. David Truman, *Administrative Decentralization* (Chicago, 1940), pp. 56–57.

31. See note 9, Chapter I.

32. *Pravda,* January 16, 1965, p. 2.

33. *Partiinaia zhizn,* no. 4 (February 1958), p. 5.

34. *Sovetskaia Rossiia,* April 29, 1960, p. 2.

35. *Pravda,* December 28, 1940, p. 3.

36. *Sovetskaia Belorussiia,* March 6, 1958, p. 3; *ibid.,* September 18, 1962, p. 2.

37. *Partiinaia zhizn,* no. 22 (November 1965) p. 36. See also *Pravda,* March 19, 1967, p. 2.

38. *Pravda,* February 6, 1967, p. 2.

39. In this interview, I based my questions on the incident mentioned in Chapter II, p. 30.

XII. Representation of the Locality

1. See, for example, Richard F. Fenno, Jr., *The President's Cabinet* (Cambridge, Mass., 1959), and Charles R. Walker, Robert H. Guest, and Arthur N. Turner, *The Foreman on the Assembly Line* (Cambridge, Mass., 1956).

2. Berliner, *Factory and Manager,* pp. 78–79.

3. *Sovetskaia Rossiia,* January 5, 1965, p. 1.

4. See Chapter II, p. 23.

5. In 1965 the chairman of the Central-Ural sovnarkhoz complained that the Tiumen oblast organizations even were deliberating exaggerating the oil reserves found in the oblast by the geological administration. Their purpose was to generate enough enthusiasm in the sovnarkhoz so that the development of these reserves would be begun. *Trud,* February 17, 1965, p. 2.

6. *Kommunist,* no. 1 (January 1958), p. 61.

7. Ivanovo: Gruliow, *Current Soviet Policies,* p. 145; Molotov: *ibid.,* p. 174; Cheliabinsk: *ibid.,* p. 179.

8. Khabarovsk: *ibid.,* p. 152; Rostov: *ibid.,* p. 167; Molotov: ibid., p. 173.

9. *Ibid.,* p. 156. This situation was caused by the subordination of the nail factories to different ministries, each of which wanted to be supplied by its own factory rather than to be forced to trust another ministry for prompt delivery. In 1957 Khrushchev used a similar Leningrad example: 110,000 tons

of iron and steel castings were exported from the city, and 40,000 tons were imported. *Pravda,* March 30, 1957, p. 2.

10. Gruliow, p. 198. For a virtually identical complaint by the Gorki obkom first secretary in 1941, see *Pravda,* April 21, 1941, p. 1.

11. *Plenum TsK KPSS, stenograficheskii otchet* (Plenum of the Central Committee [June 24–29, 1959], Stenographic Report; Moscow, 1959), p. 559, and *Stroitelnaia gazeta,* June 25, 1958, p. 2.

12. *Sovetskaia Rossiia,* August 23, 1962, p. 2.

13. *Sovetskaia Moldaviia,* December 27, 1963, pp. 2–4.

14. *Stroitelnaia gazeta,* July 5, 1963, p. 2.

15. For a discussion of these proposals at the 23rd Congress, see J. F. Hough, "The Party Apparatus," in F. Gordon Skilling and Franklyn Griffiths, eds., *Interest Groups in Soviet Politics* (Princeton, forthcoming). This article also discusses at length the role of the local Party organs in seeking appropriations in nonindustrial realms and the relationships which arise among the specialized secretaries of the local Party organs in this process.

16. *XXIII sezd,* I, 198–199. *Sovetskaia Rossiia,* March 15, 1966, p. 2.

17. *Pravda Ukrainy,* October 28, 1965, p. 2.

18. *Ibid.,* January 17, 1959, p. 6, and *Plenum TsK KPSS,* June 24–29, 1959, p. 534.

19. *Pravda,* April 18, 1957 p. 4, and May 4, 1957, p. 3.

20. *Sovetskaia Rossiia,* April 15, 1965, p. 2.

21. *Pravda,* April 3, 1957, p. 4.

22. *Deputaty* (1958), p. 367. *Spravochnik partiinogo rabotnika* (2nd ed.), pp. 595–599.

23. Alec Nove, *Economic Rationality and Soviet Politics* (New York, 1964), pp. 57, 86–87, 96, 132–133.

24. I. A. Evenko, *Voprosy planirovaniia v SSSR na sovremennom etape* (Problems of Planning in the USSR at the Present Time; Moscow, 1959), p. 16.

25. This generalization applies only to large-scale industry. In those realms of the economy supervised by the soviets (including local industry), the funds for each branch are often subdivided in large part by area rather than by project or plant. This means that the role of the local Party organs in these realms can be substantially different from that with respect to large-scale industry.

26. A. N. Efimov, *Perestroika upravlenii promyshlennostiu i stroitelstvom* (The Reorganization of the Administration of Industry and Construction; Moscow, 1957), p. 78.

27. Gruliow, p. 201.

28. *Ekonomicheskaia gazeta,* no. 29 (July 1967), p. 11.

29. *Sovetskaia Rossiia,* April 15, 1965, p. 2.

30. *Ekonomicheskaia gazeta,* no. 29 (July 1967), p. 11.

31. Only one Soviet statement has been found which would suggest that localistic considerations have affected decisions made in the center. (Of course,

there were many complaints about localistic decisions of the sovnarkhozy.) In 1957 a deputy chairman of the State Economic Commission wrote: "A serious and critical consideration of the question of locating new enterprises has been needed, for in this realm there have been serious mistakes which have cost the economy very dearly. Thus, for example, two new metallurgy works — the Cherepovetsk in Vologda oblast and the Rustavi in Georgia — were built in the last five-year plan . . . These two plants alone will present losses of almost 370 million rubles a year to the state. It may be asked, why has this occurred? . . . The main reason can be found in definite errors made by the design organizations in selecting the place of construction. . . . It is also necessary to note that the selection of the place of construction of the plants was influenced by the 'localistic' approach of the pertinent organizations, which wanted to have 'their own' metallurgy at any cost." I. A. Kulev, *O dalneishom sovershenstvovanii planirovaniia i rukovodstva narodym khoziaistvom* (About the Further Perfecting of the Planning and Leadership of the Economy; Moscow, 1957), p. 12. In the Stalin era it is not difficult to identify one of the "localistic" influences in the case of the Georgian plant, but few "pertinent organizations" come to mind in the Cherepovetsk case other than the local Party organs — presumably not only the Vologda officials, but also those from other oblasti of the Northwest (including Leningrad) who saw advantages in a nearby metal supplier.

In recent years there has been some discussion of the difficulties created by the failure of oblast boundaries to coincide in many cases with natural economic regions. "Let's take the Western-Siberian lowlands. This region is a united whole from the natural-economic point of view. A single economic complex should be created here. Any attempt to cut it by oblast borders can only harm the general cause. But such attempts are sometimes taken. The forcing of work on the fields of Tiumen oblast already to a certain degree retards the development of oil and gas production in Tomsk oblast, although the resources here have some advantages over those in Tiumen." *Ekonomicheskaia gazeta*, no. 29 (July 1967), p. 11.

XIII. Evolution in the Role of the Local Party Organs and in the Nature of Soviet Society

1. *Pravda*, September 30, 1965, p. 1.

2. See Azrael, *Managerial Power and Soviet Politics*, pp. 65–102. V. V. Vakhrushev, a Red Director who survived the Purge, serves as an interesting example of the extent to which these men could be shifted from one branch of industry to another. Born in 1902, he joined the Party in 1919 and soon entered political work. From 1926 to 1937 he was successively director of the Kosogor Metallurgy Works, the Kalinin Railroad Car Works, the Kadir Electric Station, and the Moscow Energy Administration. In 1937 he became

RSFSR Peoples' Commissar of the Local Industry, and in 1939 he was named USSR Peoples' Commissar of the Coal Industry. *Pravda,* January 14, 1947, p. 3.

3. *Deputaty* (1966), p. 441.

4. This point is discussed in the last section of Chapter VII.

5. John A. Armstrong, "Sources of Administrative Behavior: Some Soviet and Western European Comparisons," *The American Political Science Review,* 59 (September 1965), pp. 651–653.

6. Barrington Moore, *Terror and Progress USSR* (Cambridge, Mass., 1954), p. 223.

7. *Ibid.,* pp. 189 and 224.

8. *Ibid.,* p. 224.

9. Gabriel A. Almond and G. Bingham Powell, Jr., *Comparative Politics: A Developmental Approach* (Boston, 1966), p. 60.

10. Moore, *Terror and Progress,* p. 225.

11. *Ibid.,* p. 187.

12. Granick, *Management of the Industrial Firm,* pp. 262–271.

13. Azrael, *Managerial Power and Soviet Politics,* especially pp. 90–102, 122–137, 173–177.

14. Robert A. Dahl and Charles E. Lindblom, *Politics, Economics, and Welfare* (New York, 1953), p. 504.

15. See, for example, Ruth Schachter, "Single-Party Systems in West Africa," *American Political Science Review,* 55 (June 1961), pp. 294–307.

XIV. The Monistic Model of Organization and Development Administration

1. Thompson, *Modern Organization,* pp. 73–80. By "conventional wisdom" or "conventional images," I have in mind the set of concepts usually referred to in the literature as "traditional administrative theory." I am using the word "conventional" in order to restrict the use of the word "traditional" to its Weberian meaning.

2. *The Hoover Commission Report* (New York, 1949), p. 3.

3. Max Weber, *The Theory of Social and Economic Organization,* trans. A. M. Henderson and Talcott Parsons (New York, 1947), pp. 333–334.

4. As Blau and Scott point out, "A careful reading of Weber indicates that he tends to view elements as 'bureaucratic' to the extent that they contribute to administrative efficiency. . . . Again and again, he addresses himself to the problem of how a given element contributes to the strength and effective functioning of the organization." Peter M. Blau and W. Richard Scott, *Formal Organizations* (San Francisco, 1962), p. 34.

5. Weber, *The Theory of Social and Economic Organization,* p. 337.

6. Fainsod, *How Russia Is Ruled,* p. 245.

7. Simon, *Administrative Behavior,* pp. xxxiii–xxxiv.

8. Robert K. Merton, *Social Theory and Social Structure,* revised and enlarged edition (Glencoe, 1957), p. 196.

9. Simon, *Administrative Behavior,* pp. xxiv–xxvii.

10. See Chapter IX, pp. 212–213.

11. Thompson, *Modern Organization,* p. 17.

12. John D. Montgomery, "A Royal Invitation: Variations on Three Classical Themes," in John D. Montgomery and William J. Sifflin, eds., *Approaches to Development* (New York, 1966), p. 259.

13. E. Pendleton Herring, *Public Administration and the Public Interest* (New York, 1936), and Avery Leiserson, *Administrative Regulation: A Study in Representation of Interests* (Chicago, 1942).

14. Montgomery, "A Royal Invitation," p. 259.

15. Melville Dalton, *Men Who Manage* (New York, 1959), p. 265.

16. Murray Edelman, *The Symbolic Uses of Politics* (Urbana, 1964), p. 53.

17. For a recent discussion of the Weberian thesis and for an attempt to generalize from it, see McClelland's discussion of the "achievement motive" (*n achievement*). David C. McClelland, *The Achieving Society* (Princeton, 1961).

18. The price of a stock is, of course, determined by the marketplace, and it only partially reflects the present earnings. In 1966 three corporations in the business machine field had very similar earnings per share: Addressograph-Multigraph earned $3.33; Burrough earned $3.82; Xerox earned $3.73. As of March 3, 1967, a share of Addressograph sold for $54, a share of Burroughs sold for $103, and a share of Xerox sold for $243. The price differential reflected the judgment of the investment community about the different growth potential of the three companies over the next few years. The reward for Xerox officials who were granted options at lower prices were great indeed. (At the beginning of 1961 a share sold for around $16, at the beginning of 1964, around $80.) The Xerox officials also face a large potential loss if Xerox loses its growth image. The 1966 earnings for Addressograph-Multigraph ($3.33) were actually higher than those in 1960 ($1.94), but the price of the stock dropped from around $100 at the beginning of 1961 to the $54 of March 1967 — a painful reflection of the investment community's opinion about the ability of the company's management to maintain dynamic earnings growth. *The Value Line Investment Survey,* March 3, 1967, pp. 780, 782, 791.

19. Simon, *Administrative Behavior,* pp. 23–24.

20. Macmahon, *The Administration of Federal Work Relief,* pp. 265–268.

21. See Henry A. Landsberger, "The Horizontal Dimension in Bureaucracy," *Administrative Science Quarterly,* 3 (December 1961), pp. 299–332.

22. Michel Crozier, *The Bureaucratic Phenomenon* (Chicago, 1964), pp. 235–236.

23. Actually, in the truly classical prefectoral system of the nineteenth and early twentieth century, all communications between the functional departments in the capital and those in the field were routed through the prefect.

405

Robert C. Fried, *The Italian Prefects* (New Haven, 1963), pp. 306–307. However, such a practice is clearly impossible when the scale of information expands to that found in development administration of any size. Consequently, there is little point in retaining the truly classical prefectoral model in attempting to illuminate administrative systems which conduct developmental activities.

24. Crozier, *The Bureaucratic Phenomenon,* p. 235.

25. James Fesler has suggested that "the nature and seriousness of threats to stability are a key variable in determination of the character of field organization," and he associated a prefectoral system with a society in which "consensus is absent or weak." James W. Fesler, "The Political Role of Field Administration," in Ferrell Heady and Sybil L. Stokes, eds., *Papers in Comparative Public Administration* (Ann Arbor, 1962), pp. 120 and 129. However, many countries are not easily reconcilable with this line of analysis. For example, Denmark, Norway, and Sweden have prefectoral systems but have not been notably plagued by a lack of consensus. The United States does not have a prefectoral system, but the difference in values between the North and the South has been great indeed. Although the degree of consensus in society seems to affect the type of prefectoral system that has evolved in a particular country, the most obvious explanation for the existence or nonexistence of a prefectoral system in a country in the 1960's is a historical one. Countries populated predominantly by Anglo-Saxons have adopted a system of local government in which, as in Great Britain, there is no prefect; countries whose legal systems have been heavily influenced by the French system (and this includes most of the world) have normally adopted some variant of the French prefect. Prefectoral organs also are normally found in former British colonies in which the Anglo-Saxons were a small minority and relied heavily upon a district officer (or the equivalent) as an instrument of rule over the native population.

XV. Rationality, Bargaining, and Political Development

1. Moore, *Terror and Progress,* p. 222.
2. *Ibid.*
3. *Ibid.*
4. *Ekonomicheskaia gazeta,* no. 31 (August 1967), p. 10.
5. Simon, *Administrative Behavior,* p. 81.
6. Moore, *Terror and Progress,* p. 189.
7. *Ibid.,* p. 224.
8. Talcott Parsons, "Evolutionary Universals in Society," *American Sociological Review,* 29 (June 1964), pp. 339–357.
9. Almond and Powell, *Comparative Politics,* p. 60.

10. Seymour M. Lipset, "The Changing Class Structure and Contemporary European Politics," *Daedalus*, 93 (Winter 1964), p. 296.

11. Dahl and Lindblom, *Politics, Economics, and Welfare*, p. 86.

12. Barrington Moore, Jr., *Social Origins of Dictatorship and Democracy* (Boston, 1966), p. 505.

13. Moore, *Terror and Progress*, p. 193.

14. Almond and Powell, *Comparative Politics*, pp. 61 and 312.

15. *Ibid.*, pp. 24, 61, and 87.

16. Dahl and Lindblom, *Politics, Economics, and Welfare*, p. 324.

17. Sidney Verba, "Comparative Political Culture," in Lucian W. Pye and Sidney Verba, eds., *Political Culture and Political Development* (Princeton, 1965), pp. 518–519. The term is borrowed in part from Milton Rokeach's *The Open and the Closed Mind* (New York, 1960). See Verba's discussion of this derivation. *Ibid.*, p. 519, note 5.

18. *Ibid.*, p. 546.

19. Dahl and Lindblom, *Politics, Economics, and Welfare*, p. 326. Almond and Powell follow the lead of Dahl and Lindblom: "It may be that only underlying nonrational agreement on some values and goals makes it possible to bargain and manipulate pragmatically in other areas." *Comparative Politics*, p. 63. See also Verba, "Comparative Political Culture," pp. 544–550. However, what one misses in all these analyses is some exploration of the implications of this point.

20. Moore, *Social Origins of Dictatorship and Democracy*, p. 486.

21. Dahl and Lindblom, *Politics, Economics, and Welfare*, p. 504.

22. Lipset, "The Changing Class Structure," p. 287. Lipset justifies this assertion with a basically Marxian line of analysis: "The most developed industrial society should also have the most developed set of political and class relationships. Since the United States is the most advanced society technologically, its superstructure should be more likely to correspond to the social structure of a modern industrial society than the 'less' developed economies of Europe. In addition, one might argue that the absence of a traditional feudal past should mean that the United States has been most likely to develop the pure institutions of a capitalist industrial society." *Ibid.*, p. 272.

23. Talcott Parsons, "Introduction," in Weber, *The Theory of Social and Economic Organization*, pp. 84–85.

24. In a new book, George Fischer presents such a model (termed the "monist model"), derived in part from the model of rational-technical society. *The Soviet System and Modern Society* (New York, 1968), pp. 1–18, 135–153.

Index

Committee; Coordinating responsibilities; Criteria used in Party decision-making; Dual supervision; Enforcement of the law; Gorkom; Ideological work; Investigating work; Obkom; Personnel Section; Raikom; Representation of region; Secretariat

Lomako, P. F., 40

Lugansk (Voroshilovgrad) Locomotive Works, 162

Lvov Auto-Carriers Works, 181

Magnitogorsk, 146

Magnitogorsk Metallurgy Combine, 42

Maiorov, V. A., 210–211

Malenkov, G. M., 107, 198–199; on role of local Party organs, 123, 386–387n76; relation to industrial managers, 370–371n40

Mamai, Nikolai, 129

Manager, *see* Director

Margilan Silk Combine, 183

Marketplace: limits on coordinating role, 196, 301; coordinating role, 247

Mary (Turkmenia), 27

Material-Technical Supply Committee, 223, 230, 231

"Men of *1938*," 38–47, 48, 50

Mikoian, A. I., on role of local Party organs, 384n25

Mills, C. Wright, 284, 298

Ministers: of *1941* (commissars), 39–40, 41–42, 47, 365–366n13; of *1940's* and *1950's*, 47–48, 55–58, 371n41; of *1965*, 75, 76, 77

Ministers, Deputy: of *1941* (commissar), 366–367n14; of *1950's* 48; of *1965*, 376–377n85

Ministries: local Party relations with, 101–102, 165–168, 203–204, 208–209. *See also* Dual supervision

"Ministry of Coordination," 5, 249, 355n9

Minsk, 73, 119, 121, 152, 153

Minsk Ballbearing Works, 153, 164

Mitrofanov, S. P., 54

Mogilev (Belorussia), 37

Moldavia, 18, 167, 260–261, 264, 321, 322

Molotov, 258, 259

Monist model of society, 407n24

Monistic concept of administration, 6–7, 289–292

Montgomery, John, 296

Moore, Barrington, 7, 280, 306, 312, 317. *See also* Rational-Technical Society

Moscow, 141, 237, 239, 333, 356n4; size of Party apparatus, 20, 357n7; Party officials in, 44, 67; managers in, 60; number of officials in Party nomenklatura, 151, 390n4

Moscow Electric Works, 43

Murmansk, 59

New Karaganda Machinebuilding Works, 31

Nizhnii Tagil, 122, 123, 157, 180, 224, 251

Nizhnii Tagil Metallurgy Combine, 180

Nomenklatura (list of positions): rules with respect to, 29–30, 115–116, 150, 155; number and nature of posts in, 151–154, 390n4; informal Party role with respect to, *see* Personnel selection

Nosov, G. I., 42

Novgorod, 27

Novocherkassy, 241

Obkom (regional committee of the Party), 10, 12, 29, 30; relations with sovnarkhoz, 104, 108, 155, 189–192, 206, 241–242, 260–261; role in personnel selection, 115, 168–169; role in planning-technical decision-making, 181, 186–187, 189, 190–192, 195, 243, 263; coordinating role, 192, 249, 250, 251, 252; role in labor relations, 208; role in supplies procurement, 219, 221, 398n14. *See also* Bureau; Committee; Secretariat

Oblast (region), 9, 10, 123; twenty-five most industrialized, 37–38, 363–364n4; twenty-five most important agriculture, 37–38, 364n5

Oblispolkom (executive committee of oblast soviet), 10, 243, 250. *See also* Soviets

Odessa, 201, 202, 264

Odessa "Kinap" Works, 160

Odessa Steel Rolling Works, 133

Oleinikov, V. S., 147

Omsk Oil Refinery, 182

One-man-management, *see* Edinonachalie

Orekhovo-Zuevo Cotton Combine, 93

Organov, N. N., 263–264

RUSSIAN RESEARCH CENTER STUDIES

* Out of print.
† Publications of the Harvard Project on the Soviet Social System.
‡ Published jointly with the Center for International Affairs, Harvard University.